ADVERTISING MEDIA PLANNING

JACK Z. SISSORS

Professor of Advertising
Northwestern University

E. REYNOLD PETRAY

Director of Media and Research Services
Tatham-Laird & Kudner, Chicago

Crain Books
A Division of Crain Communications, Inc.
740 Rush Street/Chicago 60611

Copyright © 1976 by Crain Books

All rights reserved. This book may not
be reproduced in whole or in part in any
form or by any means without written
permission from the publisher.

Library of Congress Catalogue Card Number: 75-21742
ISBN 0-87251-017-4

Third printing

Printed in the United States of America

preface

This book is an introduction to the subject of making decisions about advertising media and covers a broad spectrum of decisions that must be made about selecting and using media to fulfill marketing objectives and strategies. It includes descriptions of media practices in planning media as well as selected analytical methods on which decisions may be based. In a sense then, the book is both theoretical and practical.

The book was written to meet the special needs of those who have little or no knowledge about planning media. This would include college seniors or graduate students majoring in advertising; beginners in the media departments of advertising agencies, account executives or others in agencies whose training has not been in media, and anyone in marketing who would like an overview of making decisions about media.

In presenting the material, the authors divide the book into two non-labeled general segments. The first segment, from Chapters One through Nine, deal with concepts and practices in planning, while Chapters Ten through Fifteen deal with special problems that affect planning.

In the first nine chapters, the authors tried to present the material in a way that tends somewhat to parallel media planning procedures in large agencies. For example, Chapters Two and Three deal with marketing analysis that must be done before media strategy decisions can be made. Chapter Five covers concepts and explains measurements on which following chapters will be based. Chapters Six and Seven deal with special problems in selecting broadcast and print media. Finally in Chapters Eight and Nine, all of the material that pertains to media strategy concepts and planning are discussed.

The last six chapters deal with problem areas that also affect media planning, but in a less direct way. For example, Chapter Ten covers Intermedia Comparisons, and Chapter Fourteen covers Testing and Experimentation in Planning. Both are important in planning, but not on a day-by-day basis.

The authors would like to call the reader's attention to some special problems they faced in writing the book. One problem is that not all media professionals agree on the explanations of concepts used in this book. Media planning is far from being a science, where there are indisputable principles or practices. One only has to read the trade press or advertising journals to know that many controversies exist about concepts, techniques, measurements and practices within the media planning field. Rather than avoid these issues entirely, the authors have attempted to present consensus or prevailing opinions. However, space does not permit an exhaustive discussion of the merits or limitations of every media planning concept.

Secondly, methods of planning media have been changed more within the last

15 years than have methods in almost any other era of advertising. Presumably this degree of change will continue. New research methods may become available and new ways of analyzing media may replace existing ways. Even new media vehicles may enter the marketplace with accompanying new kinds of problems so that at any one time, the world of media planning may be changing. Yet in no way should the value of this book be limited by the changing nature of the business. The prevailing concepts, practices and subject matter covered in this book should all be valuable despite the fact that some techniques are no longer in vogue after a period of time has passed.

Finally, the authors want the reader to know that this book cannot be all things to all people. For example, it deals exclusively with planning media and says very little about media buying. The basis for limiting the scope to planning is that planning is an executive function that precedes and affects media buying. While both functions are important, planning ranks first.

Furthermore, the book covers only consumer product advertising rather than industrial or retail advertising media planning. This in no way deprecates these latter two important media planning functions. But the authors felt that if the concepts and practices used in planning consumer product media are understood, they can be translated to industrial and retail media planning with a minimum of further education.

The last point to be made is that the book covers only the major measured media such as newspapers, magazines, television, radio and outdoor. Again the authors do not deprecate the value of other media, but simply feel that the scope of the book should be limited to those media where the greatest expenditures and problems exist.

In conclusion then, this is a book that should help the inexperienced understand "why" some media were selected and others rejected, or "how" media are best used. Perhaps any adult can select media for advertising, but it is indeed a difficult task to explain why one media alternative is better than any others that could be selected.

J.Z.S.
E.R.P

contents

chapter 1

An Introduction to
Media Planning Activities

What is media planning? Media planning involves thinking and solving problems ahead of time rather than at the spur of the moment. It consists of finding optimal solutions to two broad media problems: which media to select to deliver messages, and how to best use the media selected? Considerable thought is given to finding the most effective way of delivering advertisements to people in the market. These decisions eventually are organized into a media plan that consists of recommendations and details to the client for the use of media. After approval by the client, the media plan is given to buyers (in larger advertising agencies) for implementation. In smaller agencies the planner and buyer may be the same person.

Media planning, however, does not exist in isolation from marketing. In fact, media decisions are closely related to the objectives of a marketing plan, and should attain, or help attain, some marketing goal. Since there are many ways of attaining these objectives, strategies have to be devised. Strategy selection is an important kind of media planning. It is concerned with finding the most effective action, from among alternative courses of actions, that could be used to attain a marketing objective.

While media planning includes decisions of many kinds, it is strategy decision-making that is most significant. When one talks about media planning, he most likely is referring to the problems and practices of deciding which strategies to choose.

The importance of media planning in agencies today. Media planning has become one of the most important tasks to be performed in advertising agencies, ranking in importance with marketing and creative planning. This is quite a change from the early days when persons employed in the media departments of advertising agencies performed simple clerical tasks in the selection and use of media. Planning today has become an executive function which, although seemingly involved in the same tasks of selecting and using media, is much more difficult than it was in the early days. Today, the planner must know more, not only about media, but about marketing, research and advertising than his counterpart of years ago. Most significant is the fact that media planners are held

1

more accountable for their decisions than they were previously. The planner is called upon not only to make decisions, but to defend them as the best ones which could be made from among many alternatives.

What brought about this change? Foremost was the rise of new marketing concepts, where media planning is not an isolated activity, but is more closely related to marketing planning than before. In fact, one way in which a media plan may be judged is by the degree of effectiveness with which it helps attain marketing objectives. But another cause of the change was the development of new and more definitive media audience research. As a result, the planner has more research tools available to help him make decisions from among a myriad of alternatives. Finally, the change was due to the increase in advertising expenditures by companies which had smaller profit ratios to selling expenses. Now the managements of such companies want better proof that their money is well spent, and the media planner has the responsibility of providing more detailed and valid explanations of his decisions than ever before.

In effect then, media planning is not so much a matter of being able to decide in which medium to place advertisements, or how many advertisements should be run each week, as it is in proving that optimal decisions were made under a given set of marketing circumstances. Advertisers exercise the right to demand such explanations, and media planners must have the abilities to make them. So today's media planners must have breadth of knowledge, marketing understanding, research familiarity, creative planning awareness, and media acumen to do the job competently. It is within this framework that media planning now takes place.

How Planners Look at Media

Media are vehicles. Planners look at each medium as a carrier or vehicle for delivering advertisements to a desired group of individuals. Mass media, such as newspapers, magazines, radio and television programs are especially well-suited for delivering to the public, advertisements as well as news, entertainment and educational material. Planners find the mass media valuable because: (1) such media may be able to deliver large-sized audiences at relatively low costs; (2) the delivery of advertisements may be directed to special kinds of audiences because of the medium's editorial or programming appeals; (3) audiences may be reached with different degrees of repetition because they tend to develop strong loyalties and return to their favorite medium with a high degree of regularity. If a planner wants to reach a special kind of audience, repeatedly within a time period, he will find some media better suited for this purpose than others. Recent research suggests that certain types of broadcast programs also provide higher degrees of viewer interest than other program types, thus offering better environments for commercials.

Planners, however, also know that there are limitations in using mass media. The most serious limitation is that audiences of mass media do not buy, see, hear or read a medium simply because they want to see advertisements. In fact, media classes vary in their abilities to get both editorial and advertising material exposed. A newspaper has excellent readership of both, serving as a buying guide for readers who are looking for many different kinds of products. Housewives, for example, may check newspaper ads in their communities immediately before their regular food shopping day to find the best grocery bargains. In a sense then, newspapers have a catalog, news and entertainment value for their audiences. For high turnover products, where prices are prominently displayed, newspapers can be very effective in selling. Magazines, on the other hand, are somewhat different in their abilities to get ads exposed or read. Although some persons buy magazines because they are looking for a specific product such as a car or a piece of furniture, most magazine readers are looking for interesting editorial material rather than products.

The use of specialized editorial magazines, however, related to specific reader interests such as skiing, money management, photography or antiques, provides a greater editorial compatability with advertising related to such special interests. Therefore, these magazines often attract readers who not only purchased the magazine because of the editorial material, but also for its product types found in advertisements.

Broadcast media, such as radio and television, are least sought out for their advertisements. However, broadcast commercials have an intrusive character, breaking into the play or action of a program, thus compelling some attention to the sales message. Whether any given viewer will or will not watch the commercials is affected more by the ingenuity and value of the message than by the fact that commercials appear on an interesting program.

Some specialized media simply deliver advertisements. Some media, very specialized in nature, exist exclusively for the purpose of delivering advertising messages. They carry no editorial material, and are not requested by readers to the same extent as mass media. Such media are direct mail, outdoor billboards, car cards that appear on buses or the outside of trucks, and handbills. Another special medium is the catalog. Catalogs, however, are often requested by consumers, but consumers do not read them with the same degree of frequency that they read mass media. Therefore, their value is somewhat limited. On the other hand, telephone books carry advertising, and the medium may be considered to also carry editorial matter: telephone numbers. Telephone books serve both as a catalog and as an editorial medium to meet special needs of consumers. A plumber might correctly use telephone book advertising exclusively because he isn't needed until emergencies arise. On such occasions, the consumer may search ads in telephone books to find a plumber.

Industrial, business and professional media serve very specialized needs. A large category of media exist to meet the exclusive needs of industrial manufacturers, service companies, wholesalers, retailers and professional workers such as physicians, attorneys and teachers. These media may take the form of publications which contain editorial matter pertaining to the specialized market, as well as advertising. However other unique forms of media exist to meet such needs. Moving picture films, trade shows, exhibits at conventions and phonograph records are some examples of unique media. But for most mass consumed products, planners tend to use the mass media most often because they are effective and economical in reaching large audiences.

Exposure: a basic media measurement unit. One of the most significant measurements used for comparing and selecting media is *exposure*. Exposure means "open eyes facing the medium." While it may be convenient to use such terms as "readers," "viewers," or "listeners," to describe a medium's audience, such terms may be misleading. For example, how many pages of a magazine must an individual read before he can be counted as a reader? Or, how long does an individual have to watch a television program in order to be counted as a viewer? There is no agreement among advertising experts about these questions. If there is no consensus, then how will it be possible to determine the size of a medium's audience so that it can be compared with some other medium?

Media planners would prefer to have measurements of how many individuals either read, viewed or listened to every advertisement within a given medium. Using such measurements, planners could compare alternative media choices on the basis of the largest number of prospects reached. But such measurements are not available. Since they are not, planners would settle for measurements of the number of individuals who were, at least, exposed to most of the advertisements within each medium. But even that kind of measurement is not available on a continuing basis.

As a result, most media planners have agreed to use exposure to a medium as the basic measuring unit for determining the size of a medium's audience. Exposure data, then, is the minimum measureable relationship between an individual and a given medium. There is a great difference between being exposed and not being exposed. To be exposed gives the reader the *opportunity* to see the advertisements; so the number of individuals who are exposed to a medium within a given measuring period constitutes its audience. Exposure measurements pertain mostly to print media such as newspapers and magazines. In broadcast media a slightly different basic measuring unit is used: the number of homes or individuals who have tuned in to a program for at least five or six minutes out of a fifteen minute segment. There is an implied assumption that those who tune in are exposed in such measurements.

Exposure measurements are necessarily crude; but they are relatively inexpensive to make. A discussion of better media audience measurements will be found in Chapter 11.

Qualitative evaluations help planners go beyond exposure. Is an advertising medium a passive carrier of ads? If so, much of the planner's work may be concluded when he finds the vehicles that account for the largest number of exposures. Most planners, however, believe that media are not passive, but active carriers of ads, and vary in their abilities to get audiences to also perceive ads within the vehicles. As a result, it has been proposed that the perception of ads in vehicles be substituted for exposure measurements, since audiences who are exposed to a vehicle may not necessarily see the ads. But another method of going beyond exposure involves making a qualitative evaluation of vehicles. Such evaluation combines both exposure and perception.

Dr. Seymour Banks, Vice President in charge of media and program analysis at the Leo Burnett Company, Chicago, summarized consensus opinion about exposure versus perception when he wrote:

> "I believe . . . exposure, perception and response to individual advertisements are very much affected by the advertising vehicle through its entire pattern of exposure, but also the mood, and expectations created in their minds by combined mixture of editorial and advertising content which has been observed on previous experience with the vehicle or medium."[1]

In essence then, Banks felt that media differ in their ability to get advertisements exposed *and* perceived. He pointed out, however, that at present there isn't a satisfactory method of measuring a medium's perceptual effects.

If media affects the audience's perception of advertisements, then the planner must evaluate the quality of each alternative medium in order to decide which is best. Quality of a medium represents the value of the editorial environment in getting audiences to perceive advertisements. Perception is more desirable than exposure because it is a preliminary step to response. Advertisers want to select those media which not only get most of their advertisements exposed, but those which get the advertisements perceived. Most decisions about qualitative media value are made on a rather subjective basis. There is some research available to help the planner, but it is not enough.

Media must reach selective audiences. Planners do not choose media in order to reach every member of an audience, but they do seek those media which reach a large number of prospects at an affordable cost. In other words, planners want "selective" audiences who usually are found within the total audience of any given medium. Some media deliver more prospects than others. Since the editorial matter of one medium differs somewhat from that of another medium, it is likely that their audiences differ too. One magazine may appeal to upper income readers who have college degrees and are employed in professional or managerial occupations. Another medium may appeal to an entirely different audience, composed primarily of persons who only have graduated from high school and who tend to work in skilled and semi-skilled occupations. Meanwhile other media have specialized appeals mostly to women, or teenagers, or sports enthusiasts. Media which reach selective audiences are available to the planner and enable him to direct his advertising to the best prospects. In such cases, one medium may do a better job for one advertiser than it does for another. Planners then look for differentiation of audiences based on different editorial or programming appeals.

General Procedures in Media Planning

Pre-planning procedures. Media planning should not start with answers to

---

[1] Banks, Seymour, "Media Performance vs. Copy Platform," *Medialscope*. August, 1961, p. 55

media problems such as: "Which magazine shall we select?" or "Shall we use newspapers or radio?" Planning grows out of a marketing problem which needs to be solved. To start without knowing or understanding the underlying marketing problem is illogical, because media is primarily a tool for implementing the marketing strategy. So the starting place which leads to a media plan should be an analysis of a marketing situation. This analysis is made in order that both marketing and media planners can get a bird's-eye view of how a company has been operating against its competitors in the total market. The analysis serves as a means of learning the details of the problem, where possibilities lie for its solution, and where the company could possibly gain an advantage over its competitors in the marketplace.

After the marketing situation has been analyzed, a strategy is devised in which objectives are stated and actions which accomplish the objectives are spelled out. These objectives are the basis on which action will be taken to solve the problem. A market strategy plan, then, is the basis for action in solving the problem. When advertising is required in the market strategy plan, it is usually to communicate some information to consumers that affects the attainment of a marketing objective. Media, then, becomes the vehicle whereby advertisements are delivered to the market.

Once a market strategy has been devised, then a creative strategy must also be determined. This kind of strategy consists of decisions about the nature of the communication and what it is supposed to accomplish. A statement of advertising copy themes, and how copy is to be used to communicate the selling message are also part of the strategy. Media decisions are affected by creative strategy because some strategies are better suited to one medium than others. Examples: if a product is to be demonstrated, then television might be required, or if an ad must be shown in high fidelity color, then magazines or newspaper supplements might be required.

Finally, the planner is ready to study the best media alternative which will eventually play a role in achieving some marketing objective. Up to this point, persons other than the media planner have been making decisions which will ultimately affect the media plan. The marketing or marketing research persons were responsible for the situation analysis and market strategy plan, though media planners are, at times, involved at the inception of the marketing plan. Copywriters and art directors are most responsible for the creative strategy. Or a market strategy plan may be either a memorandum from a marketing vice-president to the media planner, or even an idea in an advertising executive's mind. In such informal situations, media planning may begin almost immediately with little or no market research preceding it.

After the market and creative strategy plans have been written, the planner may begin by analyzing the best media alternatives and eliminating from consideration those media which obviously could not achieve the marketing objectives. He may be aided in his decision-making by studying and analyzing media research data provided by syndicated media research services. After the best alternatives seem to have been chosen, the planner may temper his decisions by his own judgment, based on logic and experience. While the research analysis may lead to fairly clear alternatives, the planner's judgment may modify these alternatives in some way. For that reason many advertisers, all selling the same kind of product, use widely differing media to advertise their brands. What is the correct decision for one brand of product may be incorrect for another competing brand. A dramatic example of this occurred when Shell Oil Company, some years ago, selected newspapers, exclusively, to deliver their ads, while all other major oil companies used a combination of television, radio, magazines, billboards and newspapers. The tempering process depends to a great extent on the amount of creativity in which the planner can fashion his decisions. An example of this creativity applied to a media-marketing problem has been provided by Leonard Matthews, then Vice President of Marketing Services of Leo Burnett Company, Inc., Chicago when he wrote:

> "A couple of years ago we introduced a new product on a regional basis, achieving national distribution in about an 18 month period.
>
> " . . . our problem was to advertise in 10 or 12 key market areas and to put extra advertising weight against a very selective local audience in these areas—for example, the factory worker in Columbus, Ohio. All local media are mass in their approach. There are no local magazines beamed at the blue collar worker.
>
> "The media planner on this account came up with what I believe was a creative solution to a fairly knotty problem. He isolated the major factory locations on a map of each market involved. He did some research on where these people lived in relation to where they worked. He worked out an outdoor poster showing which was tailored to the traffic pattern of the factory workers going to and from work. In some cases, he caused boards to be erected opposite plant gates or in plant parking lots."[2]
>
> ". . . An obvious idea? A simple idea? Sure. But the outdoor plants, the National Association of Outdoor Advertising, and the client all thought it one of the most creative uses of local media planning they had ever seen."[3]

So the decision-making process for media involves not only the use of research as an aid, but judgment and creativity to make the decisions effective. Matthews summed up this combination of talents as follows:

> "Judgment, then, is the catalyst, the homogenizer which creates a media strategy out of an everglade of facts and opinion. Good judgment is the prime requisite for a good problem-solver, and a good problem solver is a good media planner."[4]

[2,3,4] Matthews, Leonard S., "The Role of Judgment in Media Planning," in *How to Put Media Research Into Proper Perspective in Media Planning*, American Association of Advertising Agencies, Papers from the 1960 Regional Conventions, 1960, pp. 32-33

As better media measurement techniques and data become available, they will still require good judgment on the part of a decision-maker.

Kinds of decisions involved in media planning. When making media plans, the executive proceeds from selection decisions to media-use decisions. Selection decisions involve answers to such questions as: In which broad media classes shall the advertisements appear: newspapers, magazines, radio, television, or others? It also involves the practice of comparing each of these media classes on the basis of their ability to reach (or be seen by) the potential consumer, called *inter*-media comparisons. Once the broad classes have been selected then it is necessary to select media within those classes based on what is called *intra*-media comparisons. For example, if magazines were selected in the first step, then decisions must be made to determine in which magazine the advertisements should appear, e.g., *McCalls, TV Guide, Readers' Digest*, or others. If television was selected originally, the decisions must be made whether to use network or spot announcements in which to place commercials. If network television was selected, then the decision must be made to determine in which programs to place commercials. On the other hand, if spot television was selected, then the cities in which the spots are to appear and approximate times of day in which the commercials are to appear must be selected. So the selection process consists of a chain of decisions, each of which is based on a preceding decision.

Media-use, as the second major area involved in planning covers a multitude of decisions such as: (a) the number of times the advertisement is to be exposed to the same audience, (b) whether the advertisements are to be exposed to different or the same audiences every time they appear; (c) the scheduling of advertisement or commercials, indicating the day and month in which each advertisement is to appear; (d) the placement of advertisements within media (e.g., front or back of magazines); (e) the allocation of the advertising budget to the various media; (f) determination of cost efficiency standards whereby the media plan may be judged to be worth the total cost. Figure 1 shows in simplified graphic form the kinds of decisions involved in media planning and the approximate order in which they should be made. Later discussions will consider in detail the factors and problems involved in making such decisions.

General principles for selecting media vehicles. Of all the media decisions made, perhaps the most important is selecting individual vehicles. Planners tend to use the following principles for selecting vehicles: the goal is to select one or more that effectively reaches an optimum number of prospects (a) with an optimum amount of frequency (or repetition), (b) at the lowest cost-per-thousand prospects reached (called cost-efficiency), (c) with a minimum of waste (or non-prospects), (d) within a specified budget.

These principles apply mostly when selecting vehicles for mass-produced and consumed products such as food, clothing or automobiles. They may not be appropriate for highly selective markets such as non-commercial airplanes or yachts. The reason is that such selective prospects are distributed unevenly

Figure 1

The Scope of Media Planning Activities

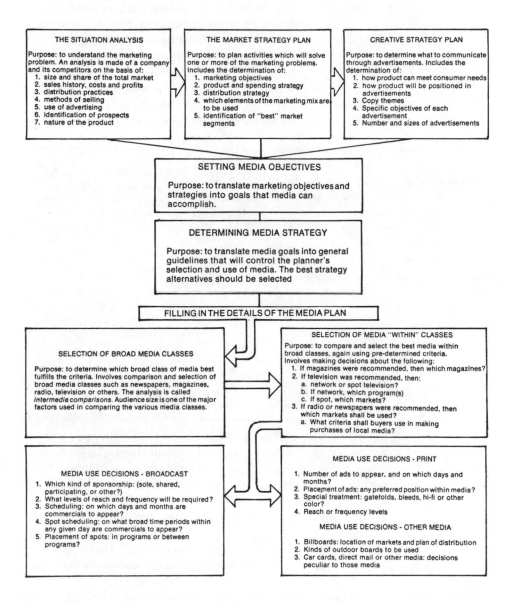

THE SITUATION ANALYSIS

Purpose: to understand the marketing problem. An analysis is made of a company and its competitors on the basis of:
1. size and share of the total market
2. sales history, costs and profits
3. distribution practices
4. methods of selling
5. use of advertising
6. identification of prospects
7. nature of the product

THE MARKET STRATEGY PLAN

Purpose: to plan activities which will solve one or more of the marketing problems. Includes the determination of:
1. marketing objectives
2. product and spending strategy
3. distribution strategy
4. which elements of the marketing mix are to be used
5. identification of "best" market segments

CREATIVE STRATEGY PLAN

Purpose: to determine what to communicate through advertisements. Includes the determination of:
1. how product can meet consumer needs
2. how product will be positioned in advertisements
3. Copy themes
4. Specific objectives of each advertisement
5. Number and sizes of advertisements

SETTING MEDIA OBJECTIVES

Purpose: to translate marketing objectives and strategies into goals that media can accomplish.

DETERMINING MEDIA STRATEGY

Purpose: to translate media goals into general guidelines that will control the planner's selection and use of media. The best strategy alternatives should be selected

FILLING IN THE DETAILS OF THE MEDIA PLAN

SELECTION OF BROAD MEDIA CLASSES

Purpose: to determine which broad class of media best fulfills the criteria. Involves comparison and selection of broad media classes such as newspapers, magazines, radio, television or others. The analysis is called *intermedia comparisons*. Audience size is one of the major factors used in comparing the various media classes.

SELECTION OF MEDIA "WITHIN" CLASSES

Purpose: to compare and select the best media within broad classes, again using pre-determined criteria. Involves making decisions about the following:
1. If magazines were recommended, then which magazines?
2. If television was recommended, then:
   a. network or spot television?
   b. If network, which program(s)
   c. If spot, which markets?
3. If radio or newspapers were recommended, then which markets shall be used?
   a. What criteria shall buyers use in making purchases of local media?

MEDIA USE DECISIONS - BROADCAST

1. Which kind of sponsorship: (sole, shared, participating, or other?)
2. What levels of reach and frequency will be required?
3. Scheduling: on which days and months are commercials to appear?
4. Spot scheduling: on what broad time periods within any given day are commercials to appear?
5. Placement of spots: in programs or between programs?

MEDIA USE DECISIONS - PRINT

1. Number of ads to appear, and on which days and months?
2. Placement of ads: any preferred position within media?
3. Special treatment: gatefolds, bleeds, hi-fi or other color?
4. Reach or frequency levels

MEDIA USE DECISIONS - OTHER MEDIA

1. Billboards: location of markets and plan of distribution
2. Kinds of outdoor boards to be used
3. Car cards, direct mail or other media: decisions peculiar to those media

9

throughout the population. Therefore, it may be less cost-efficient to reach those prospects than it would be to reach prospects for mass-consumed products, who are easier to reach. Also, planners may have to select media that contains large amounts of waste to reach such selective markets. There are other times when the principles may have to be discarded. For example, if a creative strategy calls for certain kinds of media such as those that produce ads in high-fidelity color, then cost or waste may have to be disregarded in favor of meeting creative goals. Most often, however, these principles are followed consistently in planning.

Media delivery: a goal of planning. When a planner applies media selection principles, he will use media delivery statistics as evidence of having achieved his goals. Delivery simply means the number of audience members who are prospects, reached (exposed) by a medium or a combination of media.

So with this goal in mind, the planner starts by looking among the many alternatives for media that will reach prospects. He does this through the use of media audience research data for individual media. The data are in the form of numbers classified by audience types, and the numbers listed for each medium may be used as proof of audience delivery. In other words, the planner may use statistical evidence to prove that he has found the best medium for reaching his prospects. Obviously there are other considerations in making this decision. Costs of media, for example, may be so large, per prospect reached, that the planner may have to reject his first choice in favor of other media that reach smaller numbers of prospects, but at lower costs.

Once audience delivery numbers have been found, they are related to the total number of prospects in the market. If a market consisted of 35,000,000 women in the United States who purchased a given kind of product within the last month, then the size of the market is 35,000,000. The planner may select a certain magazine that reaches 17,752,000 purchasing women, or 50.2% of the market. Is 50.2% enough? It depends on the marketing objectives he is trying to attain. If it isn't enough, he may select one or more other media to increase his percentage reached. Since the marketplace does not operate in a vacuum, he must also take into consideration the creative, promotional and executional goals at the same time, while evaluating media's ability to deliver prospects.

Is there a best media strategy? The underlying force of a media plan is the thinking that shaped the decisions. This thinking is called the strategy of a plan, and it consists of the sum of all decisions aimed at attaining media and marketing objectives. In planning, there are many alternate strategies that could have been chosen, and the ones that a planner finally selects should represent the best of all alternatives for the available budget.

One may ask whether there is a best media strategy that applies to most marketing-media situations? The answer is no. Each company sees the marketplace somewhat differently, and it is expected that each one would have different goals and strategies. So, what is good for one company may not be good for another.

Even for companies selling virtually the same kind of product or service, there may be widely differing media strategies, and each may be appropriate for the

Table 1
Media Selections for Four Major Airlines*

	Percent of Airlines Total Budget Spent in Major Media			
Media selected	TWA	American	United	Eastern
Magazines	11.2 %	11.5%	4.3%	11.4%
Supplements	.05	—	.1	—
Newspapers	35.1	37.7	52.0	38.3
Network Television	24.2	2.4	—	18.6
Spot Television	13.7	26.8	24.9	10.7
Spot Radio	15.0	17.7	17.4	17.1
Outdoor	.7	3.9	1.4	4.6
Totals	99.95%	100.0%	100.0%	100.0%
Total expenditures in 000's	$21,420	$19,818	$19,699	$14,765

*Source: Media Decisions, "Top Brands in 75 Major Categories," Dec. 1974, p. 139

company in question. Table 1 shows the media selection strategy for four major airlines.

Table 1 shows that although each company is selling the same service, each approaches its market somewhat differently. While each uses spot radio and television heavily, there are differences in the use of magazines, network television, outdoor and supplements.

Media plans are custom-tailored. A media plan is designed expressly to meet the needs of an advertiser at a given point in time for very specific marketing purposes. Today's media plan is usually not a copy of last year's plan, nor is it simply a blank form with spaces that can be filled in quickly with selected dates or times for running ads. Each media plan should be different from others that have been done in the past.

Why, then, are plans custom-tailored? The answer is that the marketplace is a dynamic center of activity that is rarely the same from year to year. Change is the cause of the dynamic character of markets. Competitors may be changing their messages, changing their marketing expenditures, introducing new brands or discontinuing distribution of old brands. Competitors rarely stand still in their marketing activities. Consumers, too, may be changing—moving to different geographical areas, getting new jobs, retiring, getting married, adopting different leisure-time activities, or buying new kinds of products.

As a result, the marketing situation of an advertiser represents new opportunities as well as new problems. The result is a need for a tailor-made media plan to fit a specific marketing situation.

The implications are that media planning activities are not a science with hard and fast rules that can be easily implemented. Since marketing situations change, new approaches to planning are constantly needed to keep up with, or ahead of, competitors. Furthermore, the study of media planning is also affected, as new kinds of research or analysis is needed to keep abreast of a changing business world. Media planning requires a great sensitivity to change.

Problems in Media Planning

While the function of making media decisions has become very important within advertising agency operations, it is not performed as efficiently as one might suppose. The reason is that the planner is faced with many different kinds of problems which make his task difficult. Although the media planner of today is more sophisticated than his counterpart was years ago, these problems stand in the way of the planner making all decisions in an objective manner.

Problems dealing with information.   Media planners almost always require more data about markets and media than is available. Some data never will be available either because audiences cannot be measured, or they are too expensive. For example, there is no continuing research service which measures the audience exposure to outdoor advertising, or to AM or FM radio listening in every market in the United States, or to portable television viewing. Why? Because such services are too costly to provide, and because there is no adequate way of measuring them. Both outdoor exposure and local radio listening have been measured—but not on a continuing basis in all cities so that the planner may have comprehensive and up-to-date information. There is also little research data showing the amount of money which competitors spend yearly for outdoor advertising or for local radio advertising.

In television planning, measurements of the audience size to commercial messages are not available. Most television rating services measure only the audience size of individuals or homes tuned in to programs. This kind of measurement does not constitute exposure measurements because there is no assurance that those who keep diaries are actually watching what they claim to have watched. In those homes measured by an audimeter, it is possible for viewers to turn on their sets and then leave the room. Meanwhile the audimeter will continue to record that the set was tuned in to the program. Even if it can be shown that there is an audience in front of the television sets watching a given program, there is no guarantee that they will watch the commercial. How, then, can the media planner know with any degree of certainty how many persons will view or hear a commercial on any given program?

Furthermore, there are many kinds of data which are needed, but there is little possibility that it ever can be obtained. While it may be possible *to estimate* the size of the audience to a given commercial, there is little likelihood that it will be possible to measure the degree of attention which audiences pay to that commercial. As the Audience Concepts Committee of the Advertising Research Foundation pointed out in their report titled *Toward Better Media Comparisons*:

> "Television presents . . . difficult problems . . . Exposure to television, unlike exposure to billboards, is not public and cannot be publicly measured. It is not conceivable that we shall be able to obtain any objective measure of the number of people whose eyes are confronted by a television commercial.

> "Television . . . raises another problem. It may be that someone is exposed . . . for only a few minutes. Are we to classify him as exposed to the

advertising vehicle or as *not* exposed to it? Clearly we need some criterion for a minimum exposure."[5]

If such data were available, it would enable the planner to make decisions about television with a greater degree of confidence than is now possible.

Another problem concerns the necessity for basing decisions on the future performances of television programs on data which represent past performance. If the future is radically different from the past, then the data on which a decision is based may be worthless. William E. Matthews, former Director of Media Relations and Planning at the Young & Rubicam agency explained the problem as follows:

"Take spot broadcast ratings. The ratings assigned to a station-break spot is an artificial quantity, a sort of average of preceding and succeeding program ratings, which become applicable the moment adjacencies change. Suppose you are buying spots in August for late September scheduling. You have no record for the fall because that is in the future, programming is not fully set, new shows are involved, and you are dealing with a radically different group of factors from those on which you have measurements."[6]

As a result, when a decision is made on the basis of past data it is no more than a rough estimate of what the planner hopes to achieve in the future.

The problem of obtaining sufficient information is especially acute for small advertisers, many of whom cannot afford to buy research data. These companies often do not know how large their own sales are in retail stores because they sell only to distributors or wholesalers. The media planner, then, must guess at his client's sales position nationally or locally in any given market.

Lack of information about how people read newspapers and magazines are another problem. How much of any given magazine or newspaper is read? How many advertisements are read? How well are they read? What is the value of placing an advertisement in one medium versus another? How does each medium affect the perception of an advertisement in that periodical? Answers to these and many other questions are not available on a continuing basis, so the media planner must make decisions without knowing all the pertinent facts.

Pressure-of-time problems. A problem which affects media planning in an entirely different way is that of time pressure required in making decisions. When the agency and advertiser are ready to start their advertising program, the planner often is faced with a lack of sufficient time to solve his problems thoroughly. For example, in many cases, the planner would require competitive media expenditure analysis showing how much each competitor spends in major markets throughout the country. This is a time-consuming task on the part of media analysts and often the planner simply bypasses the problem and makes decisions without having such information.

---

[5]Audience Concepts Committee Report, "Towards Better Media Comparisons," Advertising Research Foundation, N.Y., 1961, p. 18

[6]Matthews, Wm. E., "There's Always Another Set Of Numbers You Don't Have," in *Hidden Media Values, or Going Beyond the Number,* American Assn. of Advertising Agencies, N.Y., 1961 (Papers from the Regional Conventions) p. 39

Another related problem is the fact that there are usually a limited number of broadcast times and programs available at any one time to be purchased by advertisers. The agency may want to start running ads in media, but the client may not have yet approved the budget. Therefore, if the client does not approve a budget quickly enough, the best commercial availabilities (the most desirable broadcast time periods and/or programs) may be exhausted before the advertiser enters the marketplace with his ads.

In other situations, new research data is so plentiful that there is neither enough personnel, nor time, to make the best use of it as an aid in decision-making. This is especially true in the large amount of data received from computer reports of media audiences and brand usage. The computer is able to produce masses of cross tabulations at lightning speeds; but often such data may go unused because there is insufficient time to analyze it.

Problems of Terminology. Still another problem deals with inconsistent use of words, phrases and measurements throughout the advertising industry. Variations in terminology affect understanding and communication. For example, the term "coverage" means something different when applied to network television than it does to newspapers. Furthermore the terms "reach, cumes, cumulated audiences, audience accumulation" as well as "coverage" are used indiscriminately in place of each other. Yet "coverage" and the other terms do not mean the same thing except in magazines. So confusion must reign until the industry standardizes terminology. Different agencies use different terms to apply to the same ideas, and this practice often makes it difficult for the unsuspecting to know which meanings are involved.

The term "market," for example, can be: (a) a geographical place such as the St. Louis market; (b) a group of persons of a certain sex (the male market), age, (the 18-24 market), income, (the upper income market), occupation, education; (c) a special age group such as the "teenage market," or the "over-45-market"; (d) a product, such as the "television set market"; (e) a brand such as the "Kellogg market." Yet it is doubtful whether anyone ever takes the time to explain just what a person means when he says "this is our market."

And standards of measurement often differ too. Two magazines may produce data showing income classes which differ as follows:

Income of Audience Members

Magazine A	*Magazine B*
Under $5,000	Under $3,000
$5,000 to $7,499	$3,000 to $7,499
$7,500 to $9,999	$7,500 to $9,999
$10,000 to $14,999	$10,000 to $13,999
$15,000 to $24,999	$14,000 to $19,999
Over $25,000	Over $20,000

So the media decision-maker may find it difficult to make comparisons of audiences of the two magazines because the breakdown differs.

Problems of objectivity in decision-making. One of the continuing problems of media decision-making is that of lack of objectivity. For example, the misuse or over-dependence on numbers in decision-making affects objectivity. Often there is a feeling among media executives that when a decision is substantiated by numbers, such as television ratings, the decision must be valid because the numbers prove it so. It is often difficult to argue with decisions proved by numbers; yet the numbers, indeed, can be wrong. The methods of measurement may be imprecise; the sample size may be too small; the technique of measurement may be biased or too insensitive to really measure what it is supposed to, or there may be a set of numbers of major significance which the media planner did not have, all of which may affect the objectivity of the decision-maker. Uncritical acceptance of numbers can be a dangerous practice. Sometimes the numbers may lead to decisions which common sense indicates are wrong. But the planner may fall back on the numbers and feel more secure in his decisions than he might be on some other basis.

On the other hand, another problem of objectivity, occurs when a planner makes decisions entirely on the basis of experience, to the total neglect of any kind but the most elementary data. Clients must be certain to challenge the basis upon which media decisions are made.

Still another problem of objectivity occurs when a planner accepts relative data as absolutes. For example, the size of television audiences reported through ratings are not absolute measurements. When a television rating service shows that 15,000,000 homes tuned-in to a given television program, this does not mean, necessarily, that precisely 15,000,000 homes actually tuned-in to the program. Since the sample of homes measured was only about 1200, projections from 1200 to 65,000,000 homes means that the margin of error may be quite large. It may be plus or minus a million homes. Such data is to be used for relative purposes only, and the data merely shows that program A has a larger audience size than program B.

Problems of measuring advertising effectiveness. Since there is no valid way of measuring advertising effectiveness, it is often difficult to prove that media decisions were effective. Consequently, decision-making cannot advance enough to the point where there is always substantive proof that one medium is that much better than another. Often a media planner has biased preferences in favor of one class of media over others and he will favor such media regardless of what statistics or other objective evidence might indicate.

So, there are problems in making decisions which affect the status of the art. Notwithstanding these problems, however, decision-making is improving and will undoubtedly improve as long as those who are in charge realize there are problems which need solutions, and make attempts at improving the situation. The Advertising Research Foundation (ARF), and the Association of National Advertisers (ANA), have attacked some of the more pressing problems of research data and methodology. Furthermore, new and more highly qualified personnel within both the agency and the client organizations have shown a dissatisfaction with traditional methods of decision-making and have demanded new and better evidence for decisions. They are critical of the misuse of statistics, and have a broad enough background in research, marketing, advertising and media to set high standards of performance. Under the watchful eyes of such persons, plus efforts of organizations such as the ARF and the ANA, progress will be made. The era of accountability, in which many large companies now operate, also will act to improve the decision-making function by demanding better research data and the removal of major obstacles which stand in the way.

QUESTIONS FOR DISCUSSION

1. Why is exposure a relatively crude measurement that can be used to compare alternative media vehicles?
2. What kind of media vehicle measurements would be better than exposure? Why?
3. Why do most large advertisers prefer to use mass, rather than specialized media, to deliver their messages to their markets?
4. Explain why the media vehicle that reaches the largest number of people is not necessarily the best medium for every advertiser.
5. What is meant by the concept of "waste" in media planning?
6. At times a media planner may have to disregard waste in planning. Under what conditions might this happen?
7. Why does media planning require good judgment if the research data on media audiences is considered valid and accurate?
8. What conditions brought about the need to custom-tailor each media plan for each advertiser?
9. The consensus of experts is that media are active rather than passive carriers of ads. In what ways are media active?
10. What is meant by the term accountability as it pertains to media planning and marketing?

SELECTED READINGS

Conley, J. C. S., "Five Basic Steps to Effective Media Selection," in *Industrial Marketing*, Sept., 1973, pp. 70+

Deckinger, E. L., "Media Strategy and Accountability," in *Perspectives in Advertising Management*, Association of National Advertisers, 1969, pp. 159-172

Deckinger, E. L. "The Magnitude of the Media Problem and What to do About It." in *Papers from the American Association of Advertising Agencies 1960 Region Convention*, 1960, pp. 1-14

Gudrian, H. D., "How to Evaluate and Select Business Media for More Effective Advertising," in *Industrial Marketing*, Nov., 1972, pp. 119-120

Jones, Richard P., "Quiet Revolution in Media Planning," in *Media Decisions*, Sept., 1967, pp. 36-40+

Keshin, Mort, "The Illusion of Numbers," in *Media/scope*, Mar. 1966, p. 12+

Kemp, Frank B., Rush, Holton C., and Wright, Thomas A. Jr., *Some Important Things I Believe a Young Account Representative Should Know About Media*, Committee on Client Service, American Association of Advertising Agencies, Dec., 1963

Liddel, Robert, "Advertising Doesn't Work Overnight," in *Papers from the American Association of Advertising Agencies Region Conventions*, pp. 29-36

Maneloveg, Herbert, "How Media Men Buy Media—Six Factors for a Good Plan," in *The New World of Advertising, Advertising Age*, Nov. 21, 1973, pp. 62+

Matthews, Leonard, "The Role of Judgment in Media Planning," in *Papers from the American Association of Advertising Agencies 1960 Region Conventions*, pp. 23-33

Matthews, William E., "There's Always Another Set of Numbers You Don't Have," in *Hidden Media Values, Or Going Beyond the Numbers*, American Assn. of Advertising Agencies, 1961, pp. 37-42

Sales Management, "Systematize the Logic of Media Planning," in *Sales Management*, Dec. 1, 1970, pp. 42-43

Vlàdamir, A., "No Magic Formula for Media Mix," *Stores*, June, 1973, pp. 28-29

Zeltner, Herbert, "Assumptions, Logic and Media Planning," in *Media/scope*, Aug., 1963, pp. 8-10

chapter 2

Marketing Analysis Needed
for Media Planning

There are many ways in which one could start the media planning process, but there is no question that the most logical place to start is by analyzing the situation in which a brand and its competitors stand in the marketplace. Market problems usually arise out of the dynamics of a company competing with others. In order to gain or keep an advantage over competitors, one must know as much as possible about their marketing activities. A situation analysis consists of market research data used for analyzing facts about an industry and for uncovering relationships between a company's marketing activities and those of its competitors. The analysis may either show clearly or provide clues about where weaknesses or opportunities lie in the solutions to marketing problems.

Without such an analysis, one is faced with a number of marketing questions which will have to be answered, somehow, in order to plan media intelligently. In the latter case, it is possible to substitute assumptions for facts about how a brand fares in the marketplace. But the more assumptions that are made, the more likely that judgmental errors will occur in the media planning process. The situation analysis, therefore, serves somewhat the same purpose as military intelligence to a general. It aids by directing media selection toward the best prospects in an efficient manner.

Situation analyses, however, may take many forms, from a detailed and thorough analysis of a brand in a market, to a very simple examination of marketing-media usage of products to learn who are the best prospects. Both kinds of analyses require an understanding of how to look at and use marketing research data.

How marketing-media data are classified.   Marketing and media planners require that people in markets be classified on the basis of demographic groupings as a means of learning where the best opportunities for sales are located. Research data may either be in the form of sales, or users broken down into demographic classifications. There are also two broad demographic categories that are used by the planner for market analysis and media planning: geographic classifications and personal classifications. Furthermore, data may be analyzed on the basis of households or individuals, or both by geographic and personal demographics.

Geographic classification usually includes an analysis of markets on the basis of regions of the United States and county sizes (divided into A, B, C and D segments) See Figure 2. Personal classifications are usually divided by age, sex, income, occupation, education, family size, plus other categories that may be valuable to some planners and not to others.

A sub-committee on Media Research of the American Association of Advertising Agencies has prepared a classification system for reporting media audience data. Because companies like Simmons and Axiom report both user and exposure data, these classifications are used for marketing and media analysis in planning.

Figure 2

AAAA's RECOMMENDED STANDARD BREAKDOWNS FOR DEMOGRAPHIC CHARACTERISTICS IN SURVEYS OF CONSUMER MEDIA AUDIENCES*

I. DATA FOR HOUSEHOLDS:	Minimum Basic Data	Additional Data Highly Desired
A. County Size:	A County Size B County Size C County Size D County Size	

B. Geographic Area:
 	
(As defined by
Bureau of Census)
	Inside Standard Metro-
	politan Statistical Area
	Outside Standard Metro-
	politan Statistical Area
	Urban
	Rural
		Central City/Other
		
		Urban:
		  Urbanized Areas
		    Central Cities
		    Urban fringe
		Other Urban:
		  Places of 10,000 or more
		  Places of 2,500 to 10,000
		Standard Metropolitan
		Statistical Area:
		  4,000,000 or over
		  1,000,000 to 3,999,999
		    500,000 to 999,999
		    250,000 to 499,999
		    100,000 to 249,999
		     50,000 to 99,999

C. Geographic Region: (As defined by Bureau of Census)	North East North Central South West	New England Consol. Metro N.Y.* Mid Atlantic East Central Consol. Metro Chicago* West Central South East South West Pacific Metro L.A.*

*Note: If consideration is given to reporting metro or individual local market data, the unduplicated TV coverage areas are acceptable alternatives.

Figure 2 (Cont'd)

	Minimum Basic Data	Additional Data Highly Desired
D. Ages of Children:	No Child under 18 Youngest Child 6-17 Youngest Child Under 6	Youngest Child 12-17 Youngest Child 6-11 Youngest Child 2-5 Youngest Child Under 2
E. Household Size:	1 or 2 members 3 or 4 members 5 or more members	
F. Number of Children Under 18:	None One More than One	Number of children by household size
G. Household Income:	Under $5,000 $ 5,000 to 7,999 $ 8,000 to 9,999 $10,000 to 14,999 $15,000 to 19,999 $20,000 & Over	$12,000 to 14,999 $25,000 & Over *Household Income By Quintile (See Example at end of recommendations)
H. Home Ownership:	Own home Rent home	Residence in past Five Years Prior to Survey Date 　Lived in same house 　Lived in different house 　　In same county 　　In different county
I. Dwelling Characteristic:	A. House (unattached) B. Attached home C. Apartment D. Mobile home or trailer	Own home Rent home

II. DATA FOR INDIVIDUALS:

	Minimum Basic Data	Additional Data Highly Desired
A. Age:	Under 6 6 - 11 12 - 17 18 - 24 25 - 34 35 - 44 45 - 54 54 - 64 65 & Over	6 - 8 12 - 14 18 - 21 35 - 49
B. Sex:	Male Female	

C. Education:	Grade School or less
	  (Grades 1-8)
	Some high school
	Graduated high school
	  (Grades 9-12)
	Some College
	Graduated College
		Some Post Graduate
		College work

D. Marital Status:	Married Widowed Divorced or Separated Single (Never Married)	
E. Occupation:	Employed Professional and technical	

Figure 2 (Cont'd)

Managers, officials and
   proprietors, except farm
Craftsmen, Foremen
Operative; Non Farm Laborers;
   Service workers; and
   private household workers
Farmers, farm managers;
   Farm laborers and Foremen
Armed Services
Retired
Students
Housewives (not employed
   outside home)
Unemployed - looking for work
Other

F. Color: White/Non-White

G. Principal Language
   Spoken at Home: English
                        Spanish
                        Other

III. DATA FOR HOUSEHOLD HEADS:

A. Sex:	Male	Both Male & Female
	Female	Male Only
		Female Only
B. Age:	24 and younger	35 - 49
	25 - 34	
	35 - 44	
	45 - 54	
	55 - 64	
	65 & Older	
C. Education:	Grade school or less	
	(Grade 1-8)	
	Some high school	
	Graduated high school	
	Some College	
	Graduated College	Some Post Graduate
		College work
D. Occupation:	Employed	Employed
	Professional and technical	Full time 30 hours
(As defined by	Manager, officials and	or more per week
Bureau of Census)	proprietors, except farm	Part time Less than
	Clerical; Sales	30 hours per week
	Craftsmen, Foremen	
	Operative; Non Farm Laborers;	
	Service workers; and	
	Private Household workers	
	Farmers, farm managers;	
	Farm laborers and Foremen	
	Armed Services	
	Retired	
	Unemployed - looking for work	
	Other	
E. Color:	White/Non-White	
F. Principal Language		
Spoken at Home:	English	

Figure 2 (Cont'd)

	Spanish	
	Other	
G. Individual Employment Income:	(See I.-G. for definition)	

IV. DATA FOR HOUSEWIVES:

A. Age:	24 and younger	35 - 49
	25 - 34	
	35 - 44	
	45 - 54	
	55 - 64	
	65 & Older	

B. Education:	Grade school or less	
	Grades 1-8)	
	Some high school	
	Graduated high school	
	(Grades 9-12	
	Some College	
	Graduated College	Some Post Graduate College work

C. Employment: (As defined by Bureau of Census)	Employed outside the home	No. of hours of working
	Employed Full Time (30 hours or more per week)	Before 6 P.M.
	Employed Part Time (Less than 30 hours per week)	After 6 P.M.
	Not employed outside the home	
	Unemployed - looking for work	
	Other	

D. Color:	White/Non-White

E. Principal Language Spoken at Home:	English
	Spanish
	Other

*HOUSEHOLD INCOME BY QUINTILE

Quintile	% Adults	Income Interval Low	High	Median Income
1	20	—	$ 5,000	$ 4,300
2	20	$ 5,001	$ 8,300	$ 7,900
3	20	$ 8,301	$12,800	$10,300
4	20	$12,801	$19,000	$17,500
5	20	$19,001	–	$23,500

*Reprinted by permission of the American Association of Advertising Agencies.

Classification of geographical areas. In studying marketing and media research data, the analyst will find a number of different methods used to divide the country geographically. The Census Bureau divides the country into four regions and nine divisions. The Media Audience Research Committee of the American Association of Advertising Agencies recommends that the country be divided into four areas. The A. C. Nielsen Company, however, uses a division consisting of 10 geographical territories, although it will divide the country in almost any way most suitable for a specific client. A comparison of these divisions are shown below:

21

4-A's Media Audience Research Committee Divisions	Nielsen's Basic 10 Territories	Census Bureau's Nine Divisions	Census Bureau's Four Regions
1. North East	1. New England	1. New England	1. North East
2. North Central	2. Middle Atlantic	2. Middle Atlantic	2. North Central
3. South	3. Metro New York	3. South Stlantic	3. South
4. Pacific	4. East Central	4. East N. Central	4. Pacific
	5. Metro Chicago	5. West N. Central	
	6. West Central	6. East S. Central	
	7. South East	7. West S. Central	
	8. Metro Los Angeles	8. Mountain	
	9. South West	9. Pacific	
	10. Remaining Pacific		

Figure 3 is a map that shows the states in Nielsen's ten territories.

What is a local market to a media planner?   A market is a group of people who are likely to buy a given product or brand. But that definition is unsatisfactory for planners when it comes to determining the nature of a local market because there are many definitions, depending on the research company providing the data. It is ironic that different research companies define markets differently, but they do it because it tends to meet the needs of their users. A local retailer who advertises exclusively in newspapers in a given city may prefer to think of his market as the *retail trading zone* which includes the central city and surrounding suburbs. But a national advertiser who uses all media may prefer his market defined in terms of the entire metropolitan area, so he would use the *Standard Metropolitan Statistical Area* definition. Another manufacturer who uses television almost exclusively, however, may prefer to use the *area of dominant influence.* Each of these local market definitions are somewhat different.

As a result, it becomes important to know the various definitions of a local market when planning media. Which is most suitable? There has been some agitation from a group of media planners to standardize definitions, but without much success. Perhaps, standardization will become acceptable in the future. In the meantime, however, the differences should be clearly understood. Following is a list with explanations of the most often-used definitions:

Area of Dominant Influence (ADI): All counties in which the home-market stations receive a preponderance of total viewing hours. This definition was conceived by Arbitron.

"The ground rules for the ADI allocations are relatively simple. Once the estimated total viewing hours for a county and the percentage of such estimated total for each station are known, Arbitron sums the station percentages by market of origin. The market of origin having the largest total percentage is deemed by Arbitron to be the "dominant influence" in the county under consideration, and thus the county is allocated for ADI purposes to that market of origin."[7]

Figure 3
Nielsen Territories*

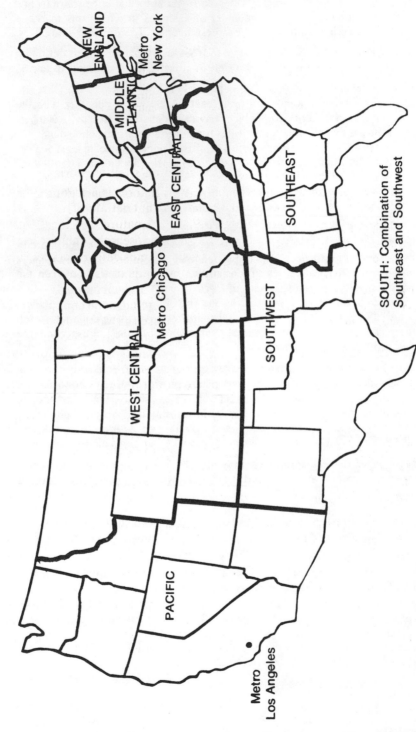

SOUTH: Combination of Southeast and Southwest

*Reprinted by permission of the A. C. Nielsen Company

23

Designated Market Area. This definition includes (a) counties in the Metro Area of a market provided that at least one station in that metro area is estimated to have the largest average quarter hour audience share from 9 a.m. to midnight, plus (b) remainder of counties in which this market's station are estimated to have the largest average quarter hour share.[8]

Standard Metropolitan Statistical Area (SMSA) or Metro area. This definition is provided by the Bureau of the Census. Each SMSA contains at least:

(a) One central city with 50,000 population or more, or:

(b) a city having a population of at least 25,000 which together with the population of contiguous places having a density of at least 1,000 persons per square mile, constitutes for general economic and social purposes a single community with a combined population of at least 50,000; provided, that the county (or counties) in which a city and contiguous places are located has a total population of 75,000.

(c) in New England, the cities and towns qualifying for inclusions in an SMSA must have a combined population of at least 75,000[9]

City Zone and Retail Trading Zone. These terms used by newspapers in defining their markets. A city zone represents either the corporate city limits, or in the case of heavily populated areas adjoining a city, newspapers sold within this wider area as designated by an agreement between the publisher and the Audit Bureau of Circulation.

A retail trading zone is an area beyond the city zone from which retailers draw sufficient customers to warrant spending advertising dollars to reach them. This area is also determined by agreement of the publisher and the Audit Bureau of Circulation.

Primary Market Area. This is another newspaper classification, and covers the geographical area in which the newspaper provides primary editorial and advertising services. Decisions about which areas are to be included and the boundary lines are made by the ABC in consultation with the publisher. Publishers who report their circulations by Primary Marketing Areas usually eliminate the city and retail trading zone designations circulation data.

Newspaper market definitions may also be made by counties in which coverage percents are computed. Data is shown where newspapers have at least 50% coverage, or 20% coverage, etc.

To illustrate how market definitions vary, even within one geographical market, a map of the city of Chicago and outlying areas is shown; Figure 4. Outlines have been drawn to indicate the ADI (with 20 counties in Illinois, Wisconsin, Indiana and Wisconsin); and the Retail Trading Zone of one of the Chicago Newspapers (with 7 counties in Illinois and Indiana).

Bases for analyzing data.   Data for sales may be reported in dollars per time period, pounds, units, or people. Media planners should be able to use all kinds of data for their analysis although, eventually, their most important kind of data

---

[8]Nielsen, A.C., *Viewers in Profile, Chicago,* Feb-Mar., 1974, p.2

Figure 4

ADI, SMSA, and Retail Trading Zones of Chicago (by counties)

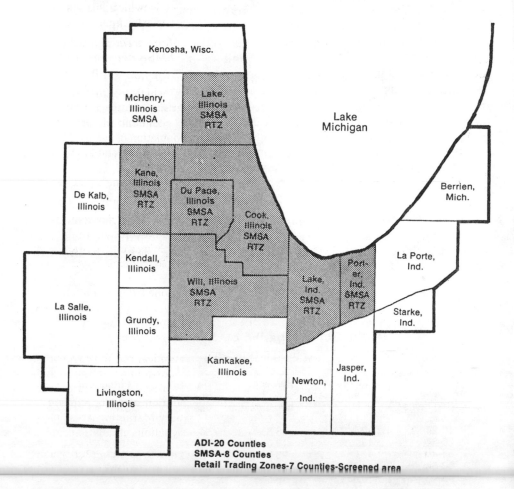

Kenosha, Wisc.

McHenry, Illinois SMSA

Lake, Illinois SMSA RTZ

Lake Michigan

Kane, Illinois SMSA RTZ

De Kalb, Illinois

Du Page, Illinois SMSA RTZ

Cook, Illinois SMSA RTZ

Berrien, Mich.

Kendall, Illinois

La Porte, Ind.

Will, Illinois SMSA RTZ

Lake, Ind. SMSA RTZ

Porter, Ind. SMSA RTZ

La Salle, Illinois

Grundy, Illinois

Starke, Ind.

Kankakee, Illinois

Jasper, Ind.

Newton, Ind.

Livingston, Illinois

ADI-20 Counties
SMSA-8 Counties
Retail Trading Zones-7 Counties-Screened area

will be in numbers of people in markets, classified demographically or psychographically.

In making comparisons of demographic data, there are three commonly used bases: raw numbers, percentages and index numbers. Raw numbers are used least because they are so large, and because it is difficult to compare sales or usage of one brand with another brand since each may have radically different bases. Percentages are a means of equalizing the bases of numbers from two or more companies and are preferred to raw numbers most of the time when making comparisons. But for ease and quickness of seeing the relationship between many numbers, index numbers are preferred over the other two.

Use of Index Numbers for Analyzing Markets

An index number as used most often in marketing and media analysis is a number that shows a relationship between two percents or between two numbers. Generally index numbers are expressed as whole numbers though they can be expressed as percents. The concept behind an index number is that it relates population demographics to sales or product usage for many different demographic segments, enabling one to have a common method for comparison. If the population segment is considered to be "average," then an index number tells how much above average sales are, in absolute terms. An example of how index numbers may be used is shown as follows:

Which demographic segments should be selected as target markets for media to reach? The usual answer is: select those demographic segments with the largest volume of sales, or the largest number of users. In other words: advertise where the brand has a history of success. According to the traditional point of view then, three age segments of homemakers, from Table 2 below, would be the prime targets in the age category. Obviously, income, occupation, education and other demographic categories would also have to be checked before a final decision could be made.

Table 2
Use of Soft Margarine by Age Segments*
(000's omitted)

Age Segments	No. of homemakers in U.S.	Percent of U.S. homemakers	No. of homemaker users	Percent of homemaker users
18-24	8,949	13.5%	4,421	17.3%
25-34	13,070	19.8	5,777	22.6
35-49	17,567	26.6	6,812	26.6
50-64	15,682	23.7	5,426	21.2
65+	10,834	16.4	3,142	12.3
Total	66,102	100.0%	25,578	100.0%

*Source: Target Group Index, *Sample Product and Brand Tables*, 1973, p. 10

An analysis of Table 2 shows that three demographic segments represent the best potential targets of media vehicles. The 25 to 64 age segments had the largest number of users in it. This finding is shown in both the raw numbers and in percentages. The assumption is that if these three groups represented the largest number of users in the past, they will continue to have the largest number of users in the future, or until any evidence becomes available to change this assumption.

However, there is another way to look at the data in Table 2, and that is by comparing the percent of usage in each segment, with the percent of population in the same segment. One could compare the raw numbers of usage and population distribution in each segment, but such comparisons are more difficult than those made by using percentages.

When the percent of usage is compared with the percent of population distribution in each segment, an index number may be calculated making the comparisons easier to analyze. The formula for calculating such numbers is as follows:

$$\text{Index number} = \frac{\%\text{ of users in a demographic segment}}{\%\text{ of population in the same segment}} \times 100$$

Using the formula to calculate index numbers for the data in Table 3, the following was found:

Table 3
Calculating Index Numbers

Age segment	Method	Index numbers
18-24	17.3 ÷ 13.5	128
25-34	22.6 ÷ 19.8	114
35-49	26.6 ÷ 26.6	100
50-64	21.2 ÷ 23.7	89
65+	12.3 ÷ 16.4	75

These index numbers then, show how well the product is being used, compared to the potential (or population proportion) for use in each segment. In the 35-49 segment, the index was 100, or average. But in the 18-24 and 25-34 segments, both were above average. Now one can see that the potential for usage has shifted a bit to younger aged segments. In a sense then, index numbers indicate potential for usage or sales. One cannot easily see this kind of relationship, however, without first calculating the index numbers.

It may be helpful to think of the meaning of index numbers as measures of central tendency, which *averages* or *means* are in the statistical world. An average does not describe any one person in a group, only the group as a whole.

So when an index number is over 100, it means that the usage of the product is *proportionately* greater in that segment than one that is average (100) or below average (any number below 100). Note that segments with index numbers over 100 do not necessarily have more users in them than there are people in that segment. They may only have *proportionately* more. Theoretically, the segment with the largest index numbers represents the best potential for usage. So, in analyzing marketing data, one should calculate index numbers for all demographic groups such as age, sex, income, occupation education, etc.

A note of caution about using index numbers. One may be easily misled by believing that the demographic segment with the largest index number always represents the best potential. This is not true. Aside from the fact that there may be some other qualification that one segment has that is of great marketing value there is the possibility that a segment with a high index number also has low product usage or sales. If so, then this segment with the highest index number may not represent the best potential for continued usage. To illustrate, marketing data for a fictitious brand is shown in Table 4:

Table 4
An Example of Misleading Index Numbers

Age segment	Percent of population in each segment	Percent of product usage in each segment	Index numbers
18-24	11.1%	15.0%	134
25-34	19.3	17.8	92
35-49	30.2	29.2	97
50+	39.4	38.0	96
Totals	100.0%	100.0%	

Table 4 shows that, although the 18-24 segment has a relatively large index number (134), it also has the lowest percent of product usage. It would not be very meaningful therefore, to limit the media selection to the 18-24 segment and ignore the other segments, especially since 85% of the usage is in the others.

Therefore, one should first examine the volume of usage or sales in each demographic segment and determine whether the volume warrants inclusion as a media target. Afterwards, index numbers may help locate good potential segments.

Another method of calculating index numbers. Although the technique of calculating index numbers, as shown in Table 3, can be used, there is a more simple way of computing the numbers that is preferred more often by agencies and other marketing planners. This latter method is based on the same concept. Briefly stated, the method starts with the computation of the total number of users in a market. A percent of the universe is then computed. This percent then indicates that of the total potential in the population, X percent are users. Then, the number of users is compared to the number of individuals in each population segment and percentages are calculated. Finally, each of these segment percentages is divided by the total percent of users. See Table 5.

Note that the index numbers obtained by this method are identical to those obtained in Table 3.

Table 5
Another Method of Calculating Index Numbers

Step one: Find total number of users compared to total population in the market as follows:
a. Total number of users in all segments: 25,578,000
b. Total number of housewives in the United States: 66,102,000
c.. Percent of total housewives that are users: 38.7%

Step two: Find the percent of usage in each demographic segment:
a. (From Table 2): 18-24   4,421 ÷ 8,949 = 49.4%
                 25-34   5,777 ÷ 13,070 = 44.2
                 35-49   6,812 ÷ 17,567 = 38.8
                 50-64   5,426 ÷ 15,682 = 34.6
                 65+   3,142 ÷ 10,834 = 29.0

Step three: Divide each of the percents in step two by the percent in step one:
                 18-24   49.4 ÷ 38.7 = 128 index
                 25-34   44.2 ÷ 38.7 = 114 index
                 35-49   38.8 ÷ 38.7 = 100 index
                 50-64   34.6 ÷ 38.7 =   89 index
                 65+   29.0 ÷ 38.7 =   75 index

Questions That May Be Answered Through
Marketing Analysis

Early in the decision-making process a number of questions arise which can be answered through use of marketing research of a situation analysis. One question deals with the problem of deciding where, geographically, advertising should be placed? Another concerns identifying the persons to whom advertising messages should be directed, and still another with the size of a market (in terms of the number of individuals who are considered the best prospects for purchasing a brand). All other media decisions will be influenced by these answers. For example, once it is known where, geographically, the best sales potential areas are for a brand, then it becomes a matter of selecting media which best reaches those areas. But even then, not all persons are equally valuable as potential purchasers. It is necessary, then, to examine sales figures to see which kinds of purchasers have the best history of purchasing the brand. These may then become the targets for further advertising. Finally it is important to determine how many such persons there are throughout the country, or in any geographic area so that a sufficient number of messages and media may be used to maximize the communication value of the advertising.

The following discussion deals with the various kinds of market research data and how it is used to answer the questions raised above, plus others which are important at the beginning stages of media planning.

Where to advertise? Distribution analysis. It seems obvious that advertising should be placed wherever the product is distributed. So media selection could be affected by the ability of media to reach geographic areas of distribution with little or no waste. If a medium is selected which goes into an area where the product is not distributed, this may be considered wasted effort. After all, consumers who read or see an advertisement cannot buy the product if it is not available for purchase. Research data, therefore, should show where the product is distributed and the volume of distribution in each geographical area.

Distribution, however, is much less valuable than sales as a factor in deciding where to place advertising. If there is a choice of using the most suitable data in learning where to advertise, then sales volume by geographical regions is much more important. There are many manufacturers whose products are distributed in just about every community in the country, but sales may be concentrated in only a small number of cities. In the latter case, then, media might be used only in the high-volume sales markets.

In some marketing situations, a manufacturer may sell his product through food brokers or other middlemen. In such cases, the sales volumes of these persons become the key factors in determining where to advertise. If sales volume in a certain geographic area is high, those regions will be allocated considerably more money than low-volume areas. But the sales are not evaluated on a retail basis. They are evaluated on the basis of broker-potential and actual sales. The following table shows sales potentials by brokers' markets.

Table 6
Analysis of Markets by Food Broker Territories*

Broker Territory	% of Total U.S. Population	% of Total Sales of Product Category	% of Total Sales Brand "A" by Brokers	Category Development Index	Brand Development Index
Seattle	1.23%	2.71%	3.09%	221	252
Portland	1.02	2.17	2.48	212	242
Los Angeles	5.54	10.41	6.74	188	122
Boston	2.18	3.85	3.49	177	160
San Francisco	3.66	6.41	7.22	175	198
Toledo	.79	.81	.97	102	123
Albuquerque	.79	.81	1.13	102	143
Baltimore	2.67	3.00	3.12	113	117

*Source: Data provided by a major advertiser

The data in Table 6 shows percentages and index numbers that can be used to determine where to advertise. The category development index simply indicates the potential for an unnamed product category for each geographic market. The brand development index shows the same thing for Brand A. From the data, Seattle and Portland, each with index numbers over 200, represent the best sales potential of markets listed. But one should not ignore the fact that both Los Angeles and San Francisco show larger percents of sales than Seattle and Portland, and therefore merit consideration as excellent potential sales areas despite the fact that each of their index numbers is less than Seattle's or Portland's. So it is possible to learn which geographical areas are best in which to advertise by examining either distribution data or sales data to the middleman. However, the best method of determining where to advertise will come from examining retail sales to consumers in each market.

Where to advertise? Sales Analysis. If sales volume information about a brand and its competitors are available, then it is possible to start making decisions about where to advertise. One alternative of deciding where to advertise is to select geographic markets on the basis of sales or market share each has produced in the past. In these situations, the volume of sales rather than the index of potential sales is used as a deciding factor. Without a doubt, the volume of sales produced by a geographic market in the past has to be the first consideration in making the selection decision. The question of whether to go to high index markets depends to some extent on whether sales have been optimized in the high volume markets. Perhaps an increase in advertising will result in an equivalent incremental increase in sales.

The following table shows the sales of a company and its competitors reported on the basis of seven regions plus three large metropolitan areas, New York, Chicago and Los Angeles:

Table 7
Sales of Brand X and Competitors — by Regions*

Region of the U.S.	Total industry sales Sales % of U.S.** H.Hlds.	Sales percent	Index	Brand X Sales Percent	Index	Brand Y Sales Percent	Index	Brand Z Sales Percent	Index
New England	5.8%	3.4%	59	3.5%	103	3.5%	103	2.4%	71
New York	8.4	5.0	60	4.6	92	4.5	90	6.5	130
Middle Atlantic	11.4	10.8	94	11.0	102	10.1	94	12.9	119
East Central	15.8	17.6	111	19.5	111	16.8	95	18.3	104
West Central	14.0	16.0	115	17.5	109	16.2	101	16.4	103
Chicago	3.7	5.4	144	7.1	131	5.4	98	5.3	98
South East	15.7	13.3	85	13.1	98	12.1	91	14.0	105
South West	9.9	8.8	89	9.4	104	9.2	105	7.5	85
Los Angeles	5.1	7.0	138	4.7	67	9.1	130	5.8	83
Remaining Pacific	10.2	12.7	124	9.6	76	13.2	104	10.9	86
	100.0%	100.0%		100.0%		100.0%		100.0%	

**Base of 64,850,000 U.S. Households
* Source: Data provided by a major advertiser

In Table 7, the population base for computation of index numbers was the sales percent of U.S. households. Sales percentages for each brand and the total industry were compared to sales by households per region. Does Table 7 tell the planner precisely where to advertise? No, but it tells where his brand is doing well compared with competitors: in New England states, East Central, West Central, Chicago and the South West. This kind of information is necessary before proceeding to more specific information that will help him pinpoint markets in which to advertise.

Sales analysis by regions usually is followed by a county-size analysis which provides another dimension for the media planner in selecting media to reach markets.

In order to deal with county sizes conveniently, an A, B, C, D classification system is used, as follows:

A counties — All counties belonging to the 25 largest metropolitan areas
B counties — All counties not under A, and that are over 150,000
C counties — All counties not in A and B that are over 35,000 population, or in metro areas over 35,000 population
D counties — all remaining counties

Table 8
Sales of Total Market and Segments — by County Size*

County Size	Population Distribution	Total Market Sales Percent	Total Market Sales Index	Powdered Market Segment Sales Percent	Powdered Market Segment Sales Index	Liquid Market Segment Sales Percent	Liquid Market Segment Sales Index
A	41.4%	42.3%	102	39.1%	94	45.4%	110
B	27.2	26.9	99	27.6	101	26.2	96
C	16.3	19.2	117	20.6	126	17.9	109
D	15.1	11.6	76	12.7	84	10.5	70
	100.0%	100.0%		100.0%		100.0%	

*Source: Data supplied by a major advertiser

In which county size are sales best? For the total market county sizes A and C have the best potential. The same pattern is true for the liquid market segment of the unnamed product. But it is not true for the powdered segment market where B and C counties have the best potential. Once again, attention is called to the

Table 9
Heavy Users of Selected Products*

	Heavy User Percent of Population Group	Heavy User Percent of Total Usage
Car rentals in past year	3.6	89.6
Liquid dietary products	4.1	98.0
Air trips in past yr., men	7.8	87.3
Automatic dishwasher detergents	9.0	100.0
Hair coloring rinse or tint for women	11.3	88.1
Scotch whiskey	12.6	98.6
Cigar smoking, men	17.1	98.6
Rye or blended whiskey	18.4	98.5
Bourbon	18.8	98.7
Canned dog food	19.3	99.2
Dry dog food	20.7	99.2
Canned ham	22.8	83.0

*Source: Garfinkle, Norton, "The Marketing Value of Media Audiences—How to Pinpoint Your Prime Prospects," Speech presented at the Assn. Of National Advertisers Workshop, July 19, 1965, p. 17.

potential for sales shown by index numbers and the actual sales volume shown by percentages in A and B counties for the total and market segments. However, sales volume for the powdered segment is fairly high in C markets. Both volume and potential will have to be weighed before a decision is made.

Heavy-user data analyzed on the basis of geographics. While the preceding geographic analysis may be enough to start answering the question of where to advertise, some additional insight may be found through an examination of heavy-user data. Such data is based on the fact that, often, a small percentage of heavy users account for the largest percentage of usage. This is true for many product categories but not for all. Table 9 shows a list of some product categories where heavy users account for substantial proportions of total usage.

Table 10
Heavy and Light Users of Dish-Washing Liquids*

	All Users Index	Heavy User Index	Light User Index	Non User Index
SMSA Central city	98	98	101	109
SMSA Suburban	100	96	107	101
Non-SMSA	102	107	90	89

*Source: *Target Group Index,* Liquid dishwashing detergents Vol. 13, p. 13001A, 1974

Using the concept of heavy users, then, it is possible to find a different dimension of where the market is located. If the marketing strategy calls for heavy users, then their whereabouts becomes important.

Table 10 shows that the best geographical area for reaching heavy users of liquid-dish-washing detergents is in non-SMSA areas, whereas the best areas for reaching light users is primarily within the SMSA.

Market by market sales analysis. While regional and county sales analyses are useful in learning how a brand is selling in broad geographical categories, the data is often too general to meet the needs of a media planner. He knows that even within any one of the categories, there could be great variation between individual markets that do not show up in data. To find the answer of the value of each individual market, specialized and detailed data is necessary. A number of advertising agencies have devised a market-by-market analysis technique whereby the information may be found. While each agency's technique may differ somewhat, they are similar in certain kinds of basic information.

Leo Burnett Company has what is known as an MCA analysis (Market Coverage Analysis) used to help evaluate each individual market in terms of sales and potential. The data and calculations needed are shown below:

Data from Figure 5
For Harrisburg, Lebanon, Lancaster, York, Pa.
(000's omitted)

a. Total homes: 226.9, and percent of U.S.: .392
b. Television homes: 217.7 and percent of U.S.: .399
c. Sales of an unnamed brand: 1,003 and percent of U.S.: .620

d. S/M TLH (means sales per 1000 total homes) 1,003 ÷ 226.9 = 4.42

e. Index: Sales to Total Homes: .620 ÷ .392 = 158

f. Industry sales: 15,675, and percent of U.S.: .574h.

g. S/M TLH: 15,675 ÷ 226.9 = 69.08

h. Index: Industry sales to total homes: .574 ÷ .392 = 146

i. Share is a percentage showing the relationship between industry and brand sales: 1,003 ÷ 15,675 = 6.3987.

One of the most important uses of this kind of analysis is to rank markets in terms of potential. The sales per thousand homes index is a means of ranking the markets. In the example shown, Harrisburg was ranked 24, Charleston S.C., 25, etc. Later, when spot television or other local media, or even national media are being selected, additional weights can be given to these markets on the basis of the data therein, or the list may be used to determine which markets should be selected. Cut-off points may be determined more easily when such a list has been prepared.

Figure 5 shows a page from a computer printout of a market-by-market analysis for an unnamed client:

The data for each market therefore, represents a combination of brand and market potential for a television coverage area. The use of coverage areas is assumed to be related to a client's frequent use of television as a basic medium in most of his strategies. Decisions about where to advertise are made considerably easier with this kind of analysis.

A very important use of market by market analysis is shown in Chapter 13 where methods of allocating budgets to individual markets are explained.

Use of buying power indices. There are times when an advertiser does not know his sales volume in each geographical market. This might occur because the advertiser sells through distributors and wholesalers. While many manufacturers in the food, drug and appliance fields know, from their own records, how large their sales are to wholesalers or distributors, they often do not know how well sales are going at the retail level. The factory is separated from the consumer by what is called the "pipeline" (composed of wholesalers and retailers). What happens at the consumer level is eventually reflected in activity at the factory, but the time lag is exceedingly long. Sales to wholesalers may be high, but the wholesalers may have large inventories in their warehouses because the product hasn't been selling well at the retail level. Furthermore, even if a manufacturer should eventually learn how sales are going to consumers, he may not know his brand's share of total sales compared to his competitor's. The best that these advertisers can do is to examine the number of wholesale shipments into each market and prepare their media plans on such a basis. The weakness of this technique should be apparent, though, because the relative number of shipments into a given market may not be equivalent to the sales potential of that market. Lack of sales volume and share, market-by-market, handicaps the media planner

Figure 5

SALES ANALYSIS BY MCA

S/M TLH MEANS SALES PER THOUSAND TOTAL HOMES AND IDX MEANS INDEX OF SALES TO TOTAL HOMES

MCA NO. MEDIA COVERAGE AREA	RANK	TOTAL HOMES	% OF U.S.	TV HOMES	% OF U.S.	SALES	% OF U.S.	S/M TLH	IDX	INDUSTRY SALES	% OF U.S.	S/M TLH	IDX	SHARE
243 HARRISBRG-LAN-LEB-YORK	24	226.9	.392	217.7	.399	1,003	.620	4.42	158	15,675	.574	69.08	146	6.3987
102 CHARLESTON, S C	25	123.6	.214	110.8	.203	544	.336	4.40	157	4,763	.174	38.54	82	11.4214
111 CHATTANOOGA, TENN	26	192.3	.332	173.7	.319	837	.517	4.35	156	8,580	.314	44.62	95	9.7552
129 COLORADO-SPRING-PUEBLO	27	129.1	.223	121.5	.223	552	.341	4.28	153	6,019	.221	46.62	99	9.1710
96 CEDAR RAPIDS-WATERLOO	28	231.4	.400	218.2	.400	977	.604	4.22	151	11,276	.413	48.73	103	8.6644
240 HANNIBAL-QUINCY	29	129.1	.223	121.7	.223	541	.334	4.19	150	5,535	.203	42.87	91	9.7742
90 CAPE GIR-PADUCH-HARRIS	30	230.8	.399	207.4	.380	961	.594	4.16	149	8,565	.314	37.11	79	11.2201
303 LANSING, MICH	31	139.0	.240	135.1	.248	576	.356	4.14	148	7,289	.267	52.44	111	7.9023
171 EAU CLAIRE, WISC	32	36.9	.064	35.4	.065	153	.095	4.15	148	1,620	.059	43.90	93	9.4444
522 TAMPA-ST PETERSBURG	33	491.4	.849	459.9	.844	2,026	1.252	4.12	147	24,311	.891	49.47	105	8.3337
438 RALEIGH-DURHAM, N C	34	234.4	.405	213.7	.392	963	.595	4.11	147	11,402	.418	48.64	103	8.4459
345 MEDFORD, ORE	35	36.3	.063	33.5	.061	149	.092	4.10	147	1,406	.052	38.73	82	10.5974
21 ALEXANDRIA, MINN	36	66.3	.115	58.9	.108	265	.164	4.00	145	2,359	.086	35.58	75	11.2336
564 WICHITA, KANS	37	307.7	.532	287.2	.527	1,237	.765	4.02	144	12,892	.472	41.90	89	9.5951
225 GREEN BAY, WISC	38	235.8	.407	229.5	.421	937	.579	3.97	142	13,080	.479	55.47	118	7.1636
318 LITTLE ROCK, ARK	39	280.2	.484	250.3	.459	1,108	.685	3.95	141	12,687	.465	45.28	96	8.7333
255 HAWAII	40	172.1	.297	153.0	.281	679	.420	3.95	141	10,386	.381	60.35	128	6.5376
159 DES MOINES-FORT DODGE	41	262.9	.454	249.6	.458	1,029	.636	3.91	140	12,637	.463	48.07	102	8.1428
48 BATON ROUGE, LA	42	131.4	.227	118.4	.217	514	.318	3.91	140	6,240	.229	47.49	101	8.2372
87 CADILLAC-TRAVERSE CITY	43	93.9	.162	88.4	.162	368	.227	3.92	140	3,648	.134	38.85	82	10.0877
249 HRTFRD-N H-SPRING-HOLY	44	717.6	1.240	692.2	1.270	2,791	1.725	3.89	139	35,240	1.291	49.11	104	7.9200
579 YOUNGSTOWN, OHIO	45	129.7	.224	126.3	.232	501	.310	3.86	138	7,571	.277	58.37	124	6.6174
144 COLUMBUS, OHIO	46	461.7	.798	447.7	.821	1,773	1.096	3.84	137	29,402	1.077	63.68	135	6.0302

Reprinted from *Media Decisions*, Jan., 1968, p. 25

---

in deciding in which markets to place his advertising. Nevertheless, many small advertisers simply cannot afford to purchase sales volume and share data from the syndicated research services. Shipments, or sales potentials determined through other ways may then have to be used.

One way that is available to almost all advertisers and their agencies is to use *Sales Management Survey of Buying Power* to help determine the sales potential of geographic markets. The Survey of Buying Power is published annually and is available to anyone at a relatively low cost. The data in the Survey is based on census measurements plus projections for updating.

The Survey uses a multiple factor index that is computed for every major metropolitan area in the country. Therefore, it is possible to examine the sales potential, in a general way, for every geographical market. A *factor* is some kind of market quality that affects sales. Generally, the more people in a market, the greater potential for more sales. Effective buying income, similar to disposable income, is another factor based on the amount of total income, less taxes, in a market.

35

Table 11
How a Buying Power Index Is Calculated*

Denver Colorado (10)					
	Percent of total U.S.		Weight		Total
Population	.6523	×	2	=	1.3046
Total retail sales	.7561	×	3	=	2.2683
Effective Buying Income	.7382	×	5	=	3.6910
SUM OF WEIGHTED FACTORS 10					7.2639

$$\text{Buying Power Index} \ldots \ldots \frac{7.2639}{10} = .7264$$

*Source: *Sales Management Survey of Buying Power,* July 8, 1974, pp. C-19-20.® 1974, further reproduction is forbidden.

A third factor in the Survey's index is Total Retail Sales. These three aforementioned factors are weighted to indicate that some factors are more important than others in making sales, although the weights are arbitrarily assigned. Population is weighted twice, Total Retail Sales is weighted three times, and Effective Buying Income is weighted five times. To show how the Index of Buying Power is calculated, see Table 11.

The indices above help the planner determine the relative value of each market. These values in turn, may be used to determine budgets or media weights. On the other hand, the indices may also be too general for certain kinds of products. These products are quite specialized in nature and may need additional or more specific marketing data. However, the information in *Sales Management Survey of Buying Power* may be used with data from other sources to provide a better and more selective index. An example could be the market for air conditioners. It would be possible to use Survey data and add on maximum annual average temperature, plus annual average humidity and create a special

Table 12
Buying Power Indices of Five Selected Markets*

Denver	.7264
Milwaukee	.7063
Tampa-St. Petersburg	.6478
Indianapolis	.5996
Memphis	.4019

*Source: *Sales Management Survey of Buying Power,* July 18, 1974, pp. B-22© 1974; further reproduction is forbidden.

index number for each market. Furthermore, weightings of factors could be made in any way that was necessary to get a better perspective of the relative value of each market.

One can use the Buying Power indices for a quick evaluation of alternative geographic markets. As an example, indices for five geographic markets are shown in Table 12.

Table 13
Demographic Data of a Market*

Dry Soup Mix Usage Data, Homemakers & Adult Women				
	Regular Users 1+ Packages/Month		Heavy Users 3+ Packages/Month	
	Percent of Each Category	Index To Market	Percent of Each Category	Index To Market
Total Homemakers (& Adult Women)	34.8	100	18.0	100
AGE				
Under 25	31.5	91	13.9	77
25-34	43.2	124	23.0	128
35-49	40.8	117	23.7	132
50-64	30.1	86	13.9	77
65+	19.2	55	7.3	41
HOUSEHOLD INCOME				
Under $5,000	23.0	66	12.0	67
$5,000-$7,999	38.3	110	19.7	109
$8,000-$9,999	41.9	120	22.3	124
$10,000+	47.9	138	24.5	136
HOUSEHOLD SIZE				
1-2	26.2	75	9.9	55
3-4	37.9	109	19.8	110
5+	43.0	124	27.3	152
EDUCATION				
Grade School or Less	21.4	61	11.5	64
High School But Not Beyond	37.4	107	19.9	111
College	46.5	134	22.1	123
COUNTY SIZE				
A	42.4	122	22.3	124
B	37.9	109	20.0	111
C & D	23.5	68	11.4	63
REGION				
NE	45.5	131	25.5	142
NC	34.2	98	17.6	98
S	20.6	59	9.7	54
W	46.0	132	22.6	126

*Source: *Advertising Age, Third Media Workshop*, 1967, p. 5-C

The question of where to advertise is based on research of sales, product usage or general sales potential, plus whatever marketing objectives must be met. The answer, then, is a synthesis of what is known in terms of opportunities and problems, plus the marketing goals.

Identifying target audiences. A media planner should also know who, precisely, are prospective purchasers of his brand, so that he can limit his choices of media to those which reach these prospects. Prospects are those who have purchased the product in the past. It is assumed, of course, that they will purchase it in the future. So the identification of prospects may be obtained from demographic descriptions of past purchasers. (The theory that past purchasers are the best prospects is a reasonable one, but non-prospects may, upon occasion, become prospects if a brand of product meets their needs and advertising reaches enough of them at the right time.)

Traditional use of demographic classification characteristics have been limited to a purchaser's age, sex, income, occupation, education, family size, race, and sometimes religion. The objective of using this kind of research data is to differentiate prospects from non-prospects. At times, there is so little differentiation that other classifications of prospects must be used. These other classifications fall under the heading of *psychographics,* and will be discussed later. Table 13 shows the demographics and appropriate index numbers for a given market.

Table 13 shows not only personal but geographic and heavy-user demographics of a market. Depending on the marketing objectives of the user, the demographics chosen for targeting (the target market) of a media plan will be those with the highest index numbers.

Creating a market profile chart. Instead of analyzing index numbers in tabular form, it is often more desirable to analyze them in a market profile chart where the best demographic segments can more easily be seen and compared with all others. In Figure 6, a market profile chart shows all index numbers over 100 to the right of the axis, and those under 100, to the left.

How product and media use data is presented in research reports. Product use and media use data is gathered from the same sample of respondents so that it is not necessary to match marketing data from one source and media data from another source. The two largest producers of continuous product-media data are the W. R. Simmons Company and Target Group Index (TGI) produced by the Axiom Market Research Company.

Essentially both companies use extensive questionnaires for obtaining their data, although Simmons collects its data through personal interviews, while TGI's is filled out by the respondent and mailed back to the company.

From time to time, companies get into the measurement business and some leave while new ones are being formed. Two of the largest such product and media use companies that have discontinued their services are the Nielsen Media Service and Brand Rating Index. Despite the apparent dissimilarity in reporting their data, most companies use about the same kind of classifications.

Figure 6

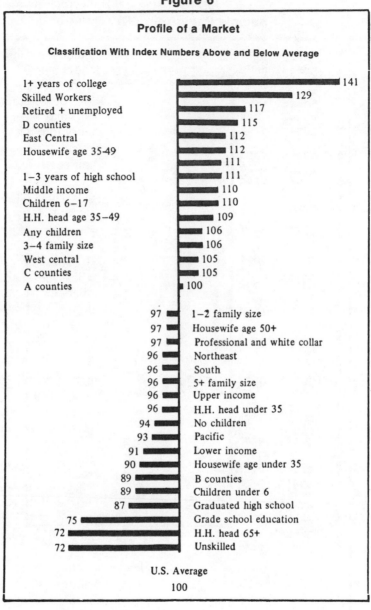

Profile of a Market

Classification With Index Numbers Above and Below Average

Classification	Index
1+ years of college	141
Skilled Workers	129
Retired + unemployed	117
D counties	115
East Central	112
Housewife age 35-49	112
	111
1–3 years of high school	111
Middle income	110
Children 6–17	110
H.H. head age 35–49	109
Any children	106
3–4 family size	106
West central	105
C counties	105
A counties	100

Index	Classification
97	1–2 family size
97	Housewife age 50+
97	Professional and white collar
96	Northeast
96	South
96	5+ family size
96	Upper income
96	H.H. head under 35
94	No children
93	Pacific
91	Lower income
90	Housewife age under 35
89	B counties
89	Children under 6
87	Graduated high school
75	Grade school education
72	H.H. head 65+
72	Unskilled

U.S. Average
100

Data users will find that the index numbers are an easy way to examine a large number of categories and make comparisons. If the raw numbers or percentages are needed they are usually provided so that users need not make any further preliminary calculations.

Figure 7 is a sample of a TGI page and Figure 8 is a sample of a Simmons' page.

DISH-WASHING LIQUID

Figure 7
Sample Page from TGI*

Demographics of Liquid Dishwashing Users

How to interpret this data

979,000 homemakers, aged 18-24, are Heavy users of dish-washing liquids

11.8% of all Heavy users are aged 18-24. (979 ÷ 8310 = 11.8%) Col. B totals 100% for each demographic segment

10.7% of all homemakers aged 18-24, are Heavy users. To find number of all homemakers, add all users: 8,342 + Non-users: 818 = 9160.

979 ÷ 9160 = 10.7%

This is an index number based on the top of Col. C.

10.7 ÷ 12.3 × 100 = 87.

	ALL USERS				HEAVY USERS				MEDIUM USERS				LIGHT USERS				NON USERS			
	A '000	B % down	C % across	D index	A '000	B % down	C % across	D index	A '000	B % down	C % across	D index	A '000	B % down	C % across	D index	A '000	B % down	C % across	D index
ALL HOMEMAKERS	57651	100.0	85.5	100	8310	100.0	12.3	100	16036	100.0	23.8	100	33306	100.0	49.4	100	9775	100.0	16.5	100
HOMEMAKERS 18-24	8342	14.5	91.1	107	979	11.8	10.7	87	2177	13.6	23.8	100	5186	15.6	56.6	115	818	8.4	8.9	62
25-34	12029	20.9	88.7	104	1425	17.1	10.5	119	2767	17.3	20.4	86	7355	22.1	54.2	110	1538	15.7	13.7	78
35-49	15710	27.3	86.3	101	2475	32.2	14.7	119	3801	27.4	24.2	102	8633	22.5	48.7	99	2498	25.6	15.6	95
50-64	13028	22.6	84.4	99	1700	20.5	11.0	89	3826	23.8	24.8	104	7507	22.5	48.7	98	2402	24.6	15.6	107
65 OR OVER	8542	14.8	77.2	90	1048	12.6	9.5	77	2071	12.9	26.0	109	4623	13.9	41.8	85	2320	23.8	22.8	157
NORTH EAST	13045	22.6	82.0	96	2715	32.7	17.1	138	3433	21.5	23.8	91	6877	20.6	43.2	88	2860	29.3	18.0	124
NORTH CENTRAL	13730	23.7	84.1	101	1659	20.0	9.3	75	4283	26.6	23.9	100	9302	29.4	54.9	111	2131	21.8	11.2	82
SOUTH	18731	32.5	85.8	100	3010	36.2	13.8	112	5646	35.2	25.9	109	10074	30.2	55.6	112	3510	17.1	11.2	98
WEST	10146	17.6	85.8	100	925	11.1	7.8	63	2669	17.6	22.6	95	6952	29.7			1073		14.2	98
NEW ENGLAND	2000																	20.6		112
MID ATLANTIC	11763																	10.4		72
EAST CENTRAL	7621																	12.8		69
WEST CENTRAL	8796																	14.8		102
SOUTH EAST	10235																	13.4		92
SOUTH WEST	7778																	14.7		101
PACIFIC	9259																			
COUNTY SIZE A	22380				2443			74					7050	21.2	37.6	117	1634	16.7	14.2	98
B	13851						12.6	102					198	0.6	47.6	96	82	0.8	12.5	89
C	9955					0.6													10.9	
D	9464				1127		14.7	119	1036		23.9	100	3556	10.7	46.3	94	1165	11.9	15.2	103
SMSA CENTRAL CITY	18535																	15.8		109
SMSA SUBURBAN	21319																	14.6		101
NON-SMSA	17797																	15.0		89
GRADUATED COLLEGE	7425																	13.6		94
ATTENDED COLLEGE	10297																	15.4		101
GRADUATED HIGH SCHOOL	22526																	15.4		92
DID NOT GRADUATE HIGH SCHOOL	17404																	16.2		112
EMPLOYED FULLTIME	15313																			
PART TIME	6931																			
NOT EMPLOYED	35407																			
PROFESSIONAL/MANAGERIAL	4788	8.3	87.3	102	274	3.3		41							57.3	117		12.5		86
CLERICAL/SALES	10604	18.4	86.4	101	1111	13.4		76		15.2	20.1	84							19.7	136
CRAFTSMEN/FOREMEN	336	0.6	80.9	94	52	0.6		102	86	0.5	26.1	86	198							
OTHER EMPLOYED	6517	11.3	84.8	99	1127	13.6		119												

*Sample page reprinted by permission of Axiom Market Research Bureau

Figure 8
Sample Page from Simmons*

Users' Demographics of Powdered All-purpose Cleaners.

(IN THOUSANDS)

		AGE					EMPLOYMENT STATUS		EDUCATION			PRESENCE OF CHILDREN IN HOUSEHOLD			RACE	
	TOTAL FEMALE HEADS	18-24 YEARS	25-34 YEARS	35-49 YEARS	50-64 YEARS	65 YEARS OR OLDER	EMPLOYED	NOT EMPLOYED	ATTENDED/GRADUATED COLLEGE	GRADUATED HIGH SCHOOL	DID NOT GRADUATE HIGH SCHOOL	UNDER 6 YEARS	6-17 YEARS	NO CHILD UNDER 18	WHITE	BLACK
TOTAL	61330	7672	12086	16519	14921	10132	25349	35982	13238	24295	23798	14085	23050	31245	55381	4921
PCT. DIST.	100.0	12.5	19.7	26.9	24.3	16.5	41.3	58.7	21.6	39.6	38.8	23.0	37.6	50.9	90.3	8.0
USED ALL-PURPOSE POWDER CLEANER IN PAST MONTH	14819	1420	2975										5741	7568	13619	1043
PCT. DEM. COV.	24.2	18.5	24.6										24.9	24.2	24.6	21.2
INDEX	100	76	102										103	100	102	88
PCT. DIST.	100.0	9.6	20.1										38.7	51.1	91.9	7.0
AMOUNT USED IN PAST MONTH (16 OZ. PKG. EQUIVALENT) 1 OR LESS	7965	735	1349										2419	4777	7371	538
PCT. DEM. COV.	13.0	9.6	11.2										10.5	15.3	13.3	10.9
INDEX	100	74	86										81	118	102	84
PCT. DIST.	100.0	9.2	16.9										30.4	60.0	92.5	6.8
1 1/2 TO LESS THAN 3	3599	*397	687										1574	1679	3357	*172
PCT. DEM. COV.	5.9	5.2	5.7										6.8	5.4	6.1	3.5
INDEX	100	88	97										115	92	103	59
PCT. DIST.	100.0	11.0	19.1										43.7	46.7	93.3	4.8
3 OR MORE	3255	*287	939	1161	668	*199	1308	1947	474	1440	1341	867	1748	1112	2890	332
PCT. DEM. COV.	5.3	3.7	7.8	7.0	4.5	2.0	5.2	5.4	3.6	5.9	5.6	6.2	7.6	3.6	5.2	6.7
INDEX	100	70	147	132	85	38	98	102	68	111	106	117	143	68	98	126
PCT. DIST.	100.0	8.8	28.8	35.7	20.5	6.1	40.2	59.8	14.6	44.2	41.2	26.6	53.7	34.2	88.8	10.2
1 1/2 OR MORE	6854	684	1626	2334	1653	557	2825	4029	1284	3051	2520	1764	3322	2791	6247	504
PCT. DEM. COV.	11.2	8.9	13.5	14.1	11.1	5.5	11.1	11.2	9.7	12.6	10.6	12.5	14.4	8.9	11.3	10.2
INDEX	100	79	121	126	99	49	99	100	87	113	95	112	129	79	101	91
PCT. DIST.	100.0	10.0	23.7	34.1	24.1	8.1	41.2	58.8	18.7	44.5	36.8	25.7	48.5	40.7	91.1	7.4

DFHL

How to interpret this data

There are 7,672,000 female household heads, *aged 18-24*, in the country, or 12,5% of total female household heads (12.5% × 61,330,000 = 7,672,000)

1,420,000 female household heads, *aged 18-24,* used powdered all-purpose cleaners in the last month, or 18.5% of all female household heads, aged 18-24.

76 is the index number found as follows: 18.5 ÷ 24.2 × 100 = 76. Note that the 24.2% is the percent of total female household heads *of all ages* who used these cleaners

9.6% of total female household heads, *of all ages* (or 14,819,000) who used these cleaners in the last month were aged 18-24

* PROJECTION RELATIVELY UNSTABLE BECAUSE OF SMALL SAMPLE BASE - USE WITH CAUTION
** NUMBER OF CASES TOO SMALL FOR RELIABILITY - SHOWN FOR CONSISTENCY ONLY.
\+ MAY ADD TO MORE THAN TOTAL BECAUSE OF MULTIPLE RESPONSE.

W. R. SIMMONS & ASSOCIATES RESEARCH, INC. 1973

This report is the property of W. R. Simmons and Associates Research, Inc. and is distributed on loan to a limited group of clients, pursuant to contract, for their exclusive and confidential use. Any reproduction, publication, circulation, distribution, or sale of this report or disclosure of the contents thereof, in whole or in part, is strictly forbidden, and W. R. Simmons and Associates Research, Inc. will avail itself of every remedy in law and in equity respecting any unauthorized use.

*Reprinted by permission of the W. R. Simmons & Associates Research, Inc.

Up to this point, the discussion in this chapter has been on alternative kinds of research to use in helping make a decision of where and to whom to advertise. But only part of the answers can be found through this research. Other kinds of research may be used to help achieve better decisions. The planner can and, in some agencies, does, make decisions with much less data than discussed in this chapter. But ideally, he should be concerned with much more. The next chapter is concerned with different kinds of data that, to some extent, will help the planner make better decisions about demographic and geographic targets.

QUESTIONS

1. Why are counties usually preferred to cities as a basis for studying markets?
2. If you knew that 11.1% of all housewives between the ages of 18-24 had used a product within the last month, what other specific piece of information would you need to compute an index number?
3. In searching for demographic target segments, is the demographic segment with the highest index number always the best target? Explain briefly.
4. What is the value of knowing a Brand Development index number for a given market?
5. If 3.6% of the men who rented cars within the past year do about 90% of all car rentals, should the 3.6% be the only targets for advertising messages? Discuss.
6. In the Sales Management Survey of Buying Power index, each factor is weighted differently. Briefly explain why.
7. How could the data from Sales Management Survey of Buying Power be used to create one's own index for outboard motors?
8. Percentages are easier to use than raw numbers in comparing sales or usage data of two brands. But why should the user pay special attention to the bases on which two sets of figures were computed?
9. In studying sales or usage data it will be found that occasionally one simply doesn't have the kind of research that is needed most. What does a planner usually do when he doesn't have necessary data and he can't afford to buy it?
10. Why might a manufacturer who has national distribution for his product only want to advertise in the top 70 markets in the U.S.?

SELECTED READINGS

Committee on Research (Media Research Subcommittee) *Recommended Breakdowns for Consumer Media Data,* American Association of Advertising Agencies, Revised, 1973

Brown, Lyndon O., *Marketing and Distribution Research,* Ronald Press, 1955, Pages 437-439

Garfinkle, Norton, "The Marketing Value of Media Audiences—How to Pinpoint Your Prime Prospects" Speech: ANA Workshop, July 19, 1965

Maneloveg, Herbert, "Another Way to Look at Audience and Marketing Figures," *Advertising Age,* April 13, 1964, pp. 95-96

Media Decisions, "Is ADI the One?" Nov., 1969, pp. 42-45

Media Decisions, Jan. 1968, "How—Not Where," pp. 22+

Media/scope, "What's A Market to a Media Planner?" June, 1966, pp. 64-72

Nielsen, A. C. Jr., *A Brief Description of Nielsen Food Index and Nielsen Drug Index,* 1957

Sales Management, "New Ways to Measure Markets," Sept. 18, 1964, pp. 55-56

Sissors, Jack Z., "What Is a Market?," in *Journal of Marketing,* July, 1966, pp. 17-21

Sprague, Jeremy D., "Local Media Analysis Through Marketing Considerations" in *Journal of Marketing Research,* Jan. 1964, pp. 49-53

Tveter, Norman T., "What the Media Expert Gains from Studying Markets," in *Media/scope,* May, 1964, pp. 94-100

Van Bortel, F. J., "Applying What We Know About Marketing Segmentation" in *Perspectives in Advertising Management,* Association of National Advertisers, Inc., April, 1969, pp. 103-112

Yankelovich, Daniel, "New Criteria for Market Segmentation," in *Harvard Business Review,* Mar.-April, 1964, pp. 83-90

chapter 3

A Continuation of Market Analysis Needed for Media Planning

Use of psychographic analysis. The term *psychographic* is an adjective used to describe psychological characteristics of consumers. Psychographics are available to help marketing and media planners better discriminate between prospects and non-prospects, or to better differentiate kinds of prospects that are now being differentiated by demographic classifications.

Psychographic descriptions of purchasers have been sought for many years because demographic descriptions did not discriminate well enough between consumers. For example, a janitor may be reported in the same income class as a college professor, but their lives and purchasing habits are vastly different. Two adults may have graduated from college, but their life styles are radically different. Two men may be working in the same professional field, but demographic analysis would not show that they tended to buy different kinds of products. Market researchers, therefore, have long felt that the best way to go beyond demographics, would be to use some kind of psychological description of consumers.

In the past, many different kinds of psychological descriptions have been tried and discarded. Social class categorization was one of the first attempts at psychological-sociological discrimination. But it too was only minimally helpful. Later on, researchers used findings from various kinds of psychological tests to help find better discriminators, but without success. Even intelligence quotients (IQ's) were tried. In addition to the desire of market researchers to find psychological discriminators, media publishers also sought the same things, only as a means of differentiating media audiences. *Better Homes & Gardens* conducted some famous research in 1956 showing that the magazine's audience contained many "venturesome" type persons. A venturesome person was one who was first in his social group to try new products. Yet researchers were generally dissatisfied with most attempts at using psychological descriptions of consumers.

In recent years, one method of psychological analysis, called *life style research* has caught the attention of many marketing and media planners. Joseph T. Plummer, of the Leo Burnett advertising agency, is one of the leaders of this research.

He described life style research as follows:

"Life style is designed to answer questions about people in terms of their activities, interests and opinions. It measures their activities in terms of how they spend their time in work and leisure; their interests in terms of what they place importance on in their immediate surroundings; their opinions in terms of their stance on social issues, institutions and themselves; and finally, basic facts such as their age, sex, income, and where they live."[10]

In order to find consumers' life styles, samples of individuals are selected and administered questionnaires which ask respondents to check such things as:

"_____I like gardening
_____I do not get enough sleep
_____I enjoy going to concerts
_____A news magazine is more interesting than a fiction magazine
_____There should be a gun in every home
_____Instant coffee is more economical than ground coffee
_____I stay home most evenings
_____There is a lot of love in our family"[11]

These questions therefore cover activities, opinions and interests as well as media usage and preferences, and product and brand usage. Through life style analysis it has been found that television program audiences differ a great deal. Perhaps these differences can be used to predict who will watch one medium rather than another?

Plummer also found that, through cross-tabulation of respondents' cluster membership (through cluster analysis) and demographic analysis, broad categories of life styles emerged as follows:

For males

"(1) The active achiever
(2) The self-indulgent pleasure seeker
(3) The traditional homebody
(4) The blue collar outdoorsman
(5) The business leader
(6) The successful traditionalist"[12]

Other persons, however, seeking for psychographic dimensions of consumers have found different groupings of life style characteristics. Dr. Marvin Chotin, a member of the Consumer Opinion Research Panels (CORP) first analyzed consumers on the basis of three psychological characteristics: (1) personality characteristics (2) social role identification and (3) social aspirations. These characteristics then were the basis for a number of sub-categories of life styles as follows:

---

[10]Plummer, Joseph T., "Life Style Patterns," in *Journal of Broadcasting,* Winter, 1971-72, p. 79.
[11]Plummer, p. 81
[12]Plummer, p. 86

Female sub-categories

"1. The self-righteous social conformist
2. The family-oriented church goer
3. The downtrodden salvation seeker
4. The happy materialist
5. The blithe-spirited natural woman
6. The romance and beauty seeker
7. The fulfilled matron and
8. The liberated career seeker

Male sub-categories

1. The inconspicuous social isolate
2. The silent conservative
3. The embittered resigned worker
4. The highbrow puritan
5. The rebellious pleasure seeker
6. The work-hard play-hard executive
7. The masculine hero emulator
8. The sophisticated cosmopolitan"[13]

Target Group Index and Simmons both have audience measurements on the basis of psychographics. Target Group Index uses a measurement of *self-concept*, meaning: "how a respondent tends to see himself . . . . as a person in terms of basic dimensions emerging from a factor analysis of detailed self-concepts."[14] This research, therefore, reports 20 factors that reflect psychographic dimensions of consumers and media audiences as follows:

"1. Affectionate   8. Efficient   15. Reserved
2. Amicable   9. Egocentric   16. Self-assured
3. Awkward   10. Frank   17. Sociable
4. Brave   11. Funny   18. Stubborn
5. Broadminded   12. Intelligent   19. Tense
6. Creative   13. Kind   20. Trustworthy"[15]
7. Dominating   14. Refined

Self concept measurements are to be related to product and media oriented behavior as a method of finding the best media for a given brand.

The preceding three methods of analyzing consumers using psychographics are only a sample of many different ways of accomplishing the same goal. The most important question to be asked about these and any other is: how good are they for use in selecting media or for media planning in general?

[13]*Media Decisions*, "The New Six in Media Research," May, 1973, pp. 69-71
[14][15]Axiom Market Research Bureau, *Measuring Self Concept*, May, 1972, p.14

The answer is that they are somewhat helpful. Their best use, however, is in other areas of marketing and advertising. They may be helpful in better differentiating consumers, or learning more about how consumers buy. They also are helpful in devising creative strategies, especially for very selective kinds of products. But for selecting media, they tend to be weak; according to Leo Bogart, of the Newspaper Advertising Bureau.[16]

Another person who is skeptical about the use of psychographics in selecting media is Ed Papazian, media director of B.B.D.&O. He noted: "Psychographics has some way to go before it takes on real meaning."[17] Papazian asked about some media whose psychographics were supposed to give them an advantage over other media: "Even if the slightest psychographic edge really existed, how would it affect the reader's acceptance for the advertiser's message?" Furthermore, Papazian raised a question about the manner in which media audiences are measured: "Can adults who have sat through 50-page questionnaires, or three-hour interviews, answer questions about their psychological makeup, meaningfully and establish a relationship between their replies and the advertising or commercial impact?"[18] He felt that the answer was no.

When psychographics were first used, there was some feeling among experts that this was going to be a means of achieving a real breakthrough in media selection processes. Subsequent use and evaluation of psychographics indicates that it is helpful, but does not replace demographic bases for selection. More research on its advantages and limitations also seems to be needed before a final evaluation can be made.

Competitive Media Expenditure Analysis

The battle for consumers' loyalties and dollars, generally, is so fierce that media plans for large national brands are rarely made without assessing or considering competitors' media strategies. When competing marketing and media strategies are known, then plans may be made to best exploit their weaknesses while maximizing the advertiser's strengths. Furthermore, expenditure analysis may help explain why the leading companies and brands have been so successful, so unique or efficient.

While it may be difficult to obtain all of the data required in a situation analysis, it is relatively easy to learn, to some degree, how competitors spend their money in such major media as newspapers, magazines, network radio and television and spot television. Also, it is possible to learn something about expenditures in trade magazines and outdoor advertising, albeit on a relatively limited scale. Expenditures in major media listed above are measured by syndicated reporting companies on a regular basis, while other media expenditures may be found from association reports.

---

[16]*Editor & Publisher,* "Study Indicates Psychographic Data is Weak Media Buying Tool," Sept. 8, 1973, p. 8
[17]Papazian, Edward, "Buzz Words—Like Psychographics," in *Media Decisions,* Oct. 1973, pp 14-16
[18]*Papazian,* p.16

The regular reporting services, unfortunately, have some limitations. They do not provide a perfect picture of competitive media expenditures because it is economically unfeasible to measure every dollar spent in every medium. The task is simply too great. So expenditure analyses are therefore never quite complete. Furthermore, such analyses are not precise either, because the dollars reported do not show how much discount each competitor earned when he purchased space or time. Therefore there may be large variations between what the syndicated services report and what competitors actually spent. Finally, competitive reporting companies often do not distinguish between which two or three brands appeared in a single ad. In other words, one of the three brands may be given credit for appearing in the ad to the exclusion of the other two.

These limitations, however, do not render competitive media expenditure analysis invalid. It simply means that the data is not to be interpreted literally; but coupled with other marketing and media information, it will help provide a more complete picture of competitor's spending activities than would be possible without such data. In a sense, then, a study of media expenditures is part of the situation analysis—but of major consequence to the planner.

Brief Descriptions of Major Expenditure Data Sources

The following is a brief description of important contents of major media expenditure data sources. Before presenting these descriptions, it should be noted that the data is reported on expenditures of large national advertisers only. Neither small national advertisers nor retail advertisers of any size are represented. The user of such data should be aware that often he may be missing significant information simply because it is not reported by any of the services. In such cases, estimates or assumptions about spending must be made.

Media Records (Expenditures in Newspapers). *Media Records* are reports of expenditures by large national advertisers in about 60 major markets of the United States. While not all daily newspapers are included, most of the larger ones are, and the data represents a good cross-section of all daily newspapers throughout the country. It is published monthly, quarterly and yearly.

It should be noted that *Media Records* shows both the number of dollars and the lines purchased by each advertiser, broken into six product classifications for each of the newspapers listed. Each city is listed separately and data for all major daily newspapers in the city are shown by the following classifications: (1) Retail display advertising; (2) General display; (3) Automotive display; (4) Financial display; (5) Classified; and (6) Total. The term "display" means all advertising using either pictures and/or test matter and which appears in other than Classified sections of the newspaper. In addition, each of the six classifications are subdivided into specifc product classes. These product classes enable one to find which newspaper in a given market carried the most lines of a product class such as radio and television sets, women's clothes, food advertising, etc.

Section Two of *Media Records* is very significant because it categorizes advertising expenditures, first by product class and individual brand name, and then by market and newspapers which carried the advertising in that market. So it is possible to find a given product class such as soaps and detergents, and then find each brand of soap listed for which the advertiser spent money in the newspaper markets reported. The data is reported in the number of lines and dollars of advertising which ran during the quarter reported. See Figure 9.

Leading National Advertiser's Expenditure Analysis By Class, Company and Brand. The Leading National Advertisers Company provides a report of advertising expenditures in six media: (1) Magazines, (2) Newspaper supplements (3) Network television (4) Spot television (5) Network radio and (6) Outdoor. What is most important about this report is that it shows expenditures identified by brand. Therefore, each competitor's brands can be identified and compared directly with the planner's brand. Like most other reporting services, however, only leading national advertisers' brands are measured. It would be too expensive to measure all brand advertising. To further aid the planner, the data for product categories are summarized so that all brands that compete are listed together in a report titled: *Ad $ Summary.* Both *LNA Class/Brand* $ and *Company/Brand* $ samples are shown in Figures 10 and 11.

Leading National Advertisers Outdoor Advertising Expenditures. Expenditures in outdoor advertising are reported by companies and brands in major markets of the country. Division of expenditures are for posting and painted signs. Posting refers to sheets that are pasted on the boards in various locations throughout a given market. A sample of this report is shown in Figure 12.

Broadcast Advertiser's Reports (BAR) The Broadcast Advertiser's Reports covers three major areas: network and spot television and network radio expenditures. In the spot television section called "Barcume," expenditures are reported by parent company, individual brands, and quarterly expenditures for each month, plus a cumulative compilation (listed as YTD, or Year-to-date). In addition, one of the most important qualities reported are the number of markets in which spot television advertising is purchased, and the listing of individual markets by name. As a result, the planner can determine in which markets competitors are placing most money and then estimate the value of each such market to the competitor's entire marketing plan. A sample is shown in Figure 13.

Broadcast Advertiser's Report also covers network television expenditures with similar data to the spot television section. However, for network television, expenditures by individual markets are not shown and, if a planner wants to know how much was spent in each market comprising a network lineup he will have to estimate it. Such estimates are necessarily crude and generally unreliable for planning purposes. However, one important breakdown in the network data report shows expenditures by daytime and nighttime, in addition to breakdowns by networks. A sample page of network expenditures is shown in Figure 14.

Leading National Advertisers Magazine Analysis Service (Compiled for the Publishers' Information Bureau—PIB). This reporting service shows data for expenditures in consumer magazines for large national advertisers. It is released monthly. The data shows expenditures in magazines for each month and cumulatively. There are seven different volumes of this report, as there were for each of the other Leading National Advertisers Reports: (1) Apparel; (2) Business and Financial; (3) Drugs, Toiletries; (4) Food, Beverages; (5) General; (6) Homes and Building; (7) Transportation and Agriculture.

In any one of these seven volumes, each company which purchased advertising is identified separately. Figure 15. Then the magazines in which advertisements were purchased during a given month (or for previous months of the current year) are listed for each brand. Also listed are such data as: the size of advertisements; the position on either of the three covers, if applicable; whether color or bleed was used. A special edition of these reports contains expenditures in regional magazine data.

Unfortunately, this service does not cover expenditures in all magazines. Compared to other services, then, it is more incomplete than the other media expenditure service reports. A special problem in using this data occurs when more than one brand of product appears within the same ad. For example, a cake mix ad may show a yellow cake mix, a chocolate mix, and an angel food mix. Expenditures are not divided between the three mixes, but are credited to one of the mixes; therefore, it may be important to check the reprints or tear-sheets of advertisements to see which brands were featured, and apportion the cost of the advertisement between the various brands shown.

Data for regional advertising expenditures also are reported on a monthly, quarterly or yearly basis. Since there have been increased expenditures in regional edition advertising for some years now, it is also important to know to what extent competitors are concentrating their advertising efforts in certain marketing areas of the country.

Gathering and Assembling the Data

The first of two major tasks involved in studying competitive expenditures is gathering and assembling the data. The second task involves analyzing it.

What kind of data should the media planner seek? The most obvious answer is: find the amount of money which each competitor spends annually in each medium. Such data provides a bird's-eye view of the competitors' media activities. In order to make this data more meaningful, dollars should be analyzed by expenditures for individual brands which each company sells, rather than by total expenditures for the company. Each brand is competing with others for a proportion of the total market sales, so specific expenditures by brands are most meaningful.

In gathering expenditure data by brand, it is advisable to include the planner's brand as well as competitors' brands so that both are compared on the same basis.

Figure 9
Sample Page from Media Records

*** DAIRY PRODUCTS***

KRAFT CHEESE (CONTINUED)

CITY	NEWS PAPER	OCT.	NOV.	DEC.	QTR.	TOTAL
CLEVELAND PD	S		850		850	850
COLUMBUS O	S		850		850	850
DENVER P	S	850			850	850
DETROIT N	S		850		850	850
HOUSTON C	S	850			850	850
INDIAPOLIS S	S		850		850	850
JACKSVILLE J	E					1000
KANSAS CIT S	M				980	980
LOS ANGELS HE	S	850			850	850
LOS ANGELS T	S	1275			1275	1275
MIAMI H	S	850			850	850
MILWAUKEE J	E					850
MINNEAPOLS T	S		850		850	850
NEW YORK N	S					600
PHILA I	T					850
PHOENIX R	S	850			850	850
PROVIDENCE J	M					585
ROCHESTER D&C	E		850		850	850
SAN BERNAD S&T	M	850				300
SAN JOSE MN	S				850	850
SHREVEPORT J	F					1000
SHREVEPORT T	M					995
SYRACUSE HA	S	850			850	850
TAMPA T	S					1000

TOTAL ACCOUNT EXPENDITURES - QTR $100905 YTD $170030
TOTAL EXPENDITURE EXCL. SUPPLEMENTS $63423 $107631
PROJECTED 125 MARKETS $70039 $119722

KRAFT DAIRY PRODS

CITY	NEWS PAPER	OCT.	NOV.	DEC.	QTR.	TOTAL
BALTIMORE PRADE						
ATLANTA J	E				850	850
ATLANTA J&C	S				290	290
BALTIMORE S	S				288	288
CAMDEN CP	M				850	850
CINCINNATI E	S				995	995
CINCINNATI E	S				300	300
CINCINNATI P	E				306	306
DENVER P	E				300	300
HOUSTON C	E				380	380
						300

LAND O LAKES BUTTER (CONTINUED)

CITY	NEWS PAPER	OCT.	NOV.	DEC.	QTR.	TOTAL
SOUTH BEND PRADE						1190
ST PETERBG PRADE						2380
W PALM BEA PRADE						1615
WASHINGTON PRADE						2380
YOUNGSTOWN PRADE						2380
AKRON BJ	E					570
BALTIMORE S	S					2380
BOSTON HA	S					2380
BUFFALO CE	S					
BUFFALO N	E				850	5950
CHARLOTTE M	E	995			995	6975
CHICAGO T	S					345
CINCINNATI E	S					2380
CLEVELAND PD	S					2040
COLUMBUS D	S					2380
DALLAS M	S					2380
DETROIT N	S					984
ERIE T&N	E					2380
FT LAUDALE M	E					1995
HARTFORD C	S	425	425			394
INDIAPOLIS N	E			1200	1200	850
INDIAPOLIS S	S					1200
LONG ILAND N	S					2890
LOUISVILLE CJ	S					2380
MANCHESTER UL	D					1586
MIAMI H	M					1212
MIAMI H	S					400
MIAMI N	E					2380
MILWAUKEE J	E					400
MILWAUKEE J	S					960
MINNEAPOLS S	S					2380
NEW HAVEN JC	E					2040
NEW ORLENS SSI	E					1170
NEW ORLENS TP	M					525
NEW YORK N	S					525
PHILA I	S					1190
PROVIDENCE J	S					2380
ROCHESTER D&C	S	425	425		850	3315
SHREVEPORT J	E					2380
SHREVEPORT T	M					992
ST LOUIS GD	WE					988
ST LOUIS PD	S					2550
ST PAUL D	E	1200		1200	1200	1200

50

Figure 9 (Continued)
Sample Page from Media Records

INDIANAPOLIS N E
INDIANAPOLIS S M

				290
KANSAS CITY T	M			300
LONG REACH PTGI	EM			304
LOS ANGELES HE	E	300		300
MILWAUKEE J	E		680	1280
MILWAUKEE J	S	1275	1275	2265
MILWAUKEE S	M	680	680	680
MINNEAPOLS S	E			600
MINNEAPOLS T	M			590
NASHVILLE B	E	607	1602	4544
NASHVILLE T	M	596	596	3534
NEWARK SL	M			290
SAN DIEGO T	E			588
SAN DIEGO U	M			596
SAN FRAN E&C	S	995	1700	1700
SAN JOSE M	E			300
SAN JOSE N	E			206
ST LOUIS GD	M	1700		564

TOTAL ACCOUNT EXPENDITURES - QTR $19579 YTD $36689
TOTAL EXPENDITURE EXCL. SUPPLEMENTS $19579 $34989
PROJECTED 125 MARKETS $22961 $41468

LAND O LAKES BUTTER

AKRON	PRADE	2380
BALTIMORE	PRADE	2380
BINGHAMTON	PRADE	1190
BIRMINGHAM	PRADE	2380
BOSTON	PRADE	2380
BUFFALO	PRADE	2380
CHARLOTTE	PRADE	2040
CHICAGO	PRADE	2380
DAYTON	PRADE	2380
DETROIT	PRADE	2380
ERIE	PRADE	2380
FT LAUDALE	PRADE	2040
FT WAYNE	PRADE	2380
HARTFORD	P2ADE	2380
HOUSTON	PRADE	1530
NEW HAVEN	PRADE	2380
NFWARK	PRADE	2380
ORLANDO	PRADE	2340
PHILA	PRADE	2380
PITTSBURGH	PRADE	1190

MEDIA RECORDS BLUE BOOK - 1974   PAGE 225   PART II

ST PAUL

| | | PP | M | 1200 | | 1200 | 1200 |

TOTAL ACCOUNT EXPENDITURES - QTR $10291 YTD $364968
TOTAL EXPENDITURE EXCL. SUPPLEMENTS $10291 $238937
PROJECTED 125 MARKETS $11778 $269318

LAND O LAKES CHEESE

BOSTON G	E		2742
BOSTON	M		2748
BOSTON HA	M		2646
DENVER P	E		1533
HARTFORD C	M		3648
HARTFORD T	S	455	455	455
MANCHESTER UL	D		2400
NEW HAVEN JC	M	546	546	2751
NEW HAVEN R	E	546	546	4128
PROVIDENCE B	M		3612
PROVIDENCE J	GM		3600
QUINCY PL	E		2412
ST LOUIS GD	M		1000
ST LOUIS PD	E		1000

TOTAL ACCOUNT EXPENDITURES - QTR $1011 YTD $35486
TOTAL EXPENDITURE EXCL. SUPPLEMENTS $1011 $35486
PROJECTED 125 MARKETS $1193 $42133

LAND O LAKES DAIRY PRODUCTS

| HARTFORD FMKLY | 546 | 546 | 546 |

TOTAL ACCOUNT EXPENDITURES - QTR $366 YTD $366
TOTAL EXPENDITURE EXCL. SUPPLEMENTS
PROJECTED 125 MARKETS

LIGHT N LIVELY ICE CREAM

BALTIMORE S	E	2400
BALTIMORE S	M	2400
BOSTON G	E	2400
BOSTON G	M	2400
BOSTON HA	M	2400
HARTFORD C	E	3100
HARTFORD T	E	3148
JACKSVILLE J	E	1000
JACKSVILLE TU	M	2980
NEW ORLEANS SSI	M	2400
NEW ORLEANS TP	M	3100

*Reprinted by permission of Media Records, Inc.

51

Figure 10
Sample Page of LNA Class/Brand $

LNA CLASS/BRAND QTR $ (000)

BRANDS BY CLASSIFICATION	CLASS	6-MEDIA TOTAL	MAGAZINES	NEWSPAPER SUPPLEMENTS	NETWORK TELEVISION	SPOT TELEVISION	NETWORK RADIO	OUTDOOR
F142 OTHER FRUITS (INCLUDING FRESH NUTS)						CONTINUED		
*CALIFORNIA AVOCADO ADVISORY BOARD	F142-9	32.1	32.1	-	-	-	-	-
CALIFORNIA CANNERS & GROWERS	F142	163.5	163.5	-	-	-	-	-
FRUIT N HONEY CANNED FRUITS	F142-9	1,059.6	415.7	-	643.9	-	-	4.
*CALIFORNIA RAISIN ADVISORY BOARD								
CALIFORNIA STATE OF								
CALIFORNIA PRUNE ADVISORY BOARD	F142-9	4.5	-	-	-	4.5	-	-
CLING PEACH ADVISORY BOARD	F142-9	1,314.4	-	-	-	1,314.4	-	-
CALIFORNIA TABLE GRAPE COMMISSION								
GRAPE PROMOTION	F142	319.9	-	-	-	319.9	-	-
CASTLE & COOKE INC								
DOLE CANNED FRUITS	F142	350.0	350.0	-	-	-	-	-
COT FARM THE								
COT FARM DRIED FRUIT	F142	.6	.6	-	-	-	-	-
COT FARM NUTS	F142	.2	.2	-	-	-	-	-
COT FARM NUTS	F142	1,076.7	73.3	-	-	1,003.4	-	-
*DEL MONTE CANNED FRUITS	F142	712.3	92.5	91.4	-	528.4	-	-
DIAMOND WALNUT GROWERS INC								
DIAMOND WALNUTS	F142	74.5	74.5	-	-	-	-	-
DUCHE T M NUT CO								
DUCHE ALMONDS	F142	361.3	326.3	35.0	-	-	-	-
*HARRY & DAVID FRUIT & DELICACIES	F142	21.0	-	-	-	21.0	-	-
*JOAN OF ARC CANNED FRUIT	F142	.6	.6	-	-	-	-	-
*LANE WILSON PECANS	F142	.3	.3	-	-	-	-	-
*MASCOT PECAN MEATS	F142	16.5	-	-	-	16.5	-	-
*MASSACHUSETTS CRANBERRY PROMOTION	F142	.5	-	-	-	.5	-	-
*MICHIGAN CANNERS & FREEZERS ASSN	F142-9	168.7	-	-	168.7	-	-	-
NESTLE CO INC								
LIBBYS CANNED FRUITS	F142	19.8	-	-	-	19.8	-	-
*NEW JERSEY CRANBERRY PROMOTION	F142	88.0	-	5.4	-	82.6	-	-
NEW YORK & NEW ENGLAND APPLE INSTITUTE INC								
APPLE GROWERS OF NEW YORK	F142-9	41.8	-	-	-	41.8	-	-
OCEAN SPRAY CRANBERRIES INC								
OCEAN SPRAY FRESH CRANBERRIES	F142	45.5	-	-	-	45.5	-	-
*OREGON-WASHINGTON-CALIFORNIA PEAR BUREAU	F142-9	93.3	-	-	-	90.5	-	2.8
*PACIFIC BARTLETT PEARS	F142	180.5	-	-	-	180.5	-	-
PACIFIC COAST CANNED PEAR SERVICE INC								
CANNED PEAR BUREAU	F142-9	24.4	-	-	-	24.4	-	-
*PENNSYLVANIA APPLE PROMOTION	F142	7.7	-	-	-	7.7	-	-
SHURFINE-CENTRAL CORP								
SHURFINE FINE FRUITS	F142							
STOKELY-VAN CAMP INC	F142							

Figure 10 (Continued)
Sample Page of LNA Class/Brand $

Brand / Company	Class							Total
STOKELYS CANNED FRUITS & VEGETABLES PREMIUM OFFER	F142	--	--	--	--	--	72.9	72.9
SUN-MAID RAISIN GROWERS OF CALIFORNIA	F142	--	216.7	--	--	--	--	216.7
SUN-MAID RAISINS	F142	--	--	--	--	--	--	--
SUNNYLAND FARMS	F142	--	--	--	--	--	--	--
SUNNYLAND PECANS	F142	--	--	--	--	--	2.9	2.9
SUNSWEET GROWERS INC	F142	--	--	--	--	--	--	--
SUNSWEET PRUNES	F142	--	169.8	--	--	--	--	169.8
TENNECO INC	F142	--	--	--	--	--	--	--
HOUSE OF ALMONDS ALMONDS	F142	--	--	--	--	--	9.0	9.0
SUN GIANT CALIFORNIA RAISINS	F142	--	--	86.2	--	--	5.5	91.7
THAMES H M PECAN CO INC	F142	--	--	--	--	--	--	--
THAMES PECAN MEATS	F142	--	--	--	--	--	.2	.2
VIRGINIA STATE APPLE COMMISSION	F142	--	--	--	--	--	--	--
VIRGINIA APPLES	F142-9	--	--	15.4	--	--	--	15.4
*WASHINGTON STATE APPLES	F142-9	--	--	.4	--	--	--	.4
*WESTERN NEW YORK APPLE GROWERS ASSN	F142-9	--	--	7.4	--	--	--	7.4
F142 TOTAL		8.2	386.5	4,240.2	812.6	131.8	2,141.4	7,720.7
F143 VEGETABLES -------								
AMERICAN HOME PRODUCTS CORP		--	--	--	--	--	--	--
LUCKS CANNED VEGETABLES	F143	--	--	105.2	--	--	--	105.2
CALIFORNIA CANNERS & GROWERS		--	--	--	--	--	--	--
REDPACK CANNED VEGETABLES	F143	--	--	--	--	15.5	119.4	134.9
CALIFORNIA & WASHINGTON CO		--	--	--	--	--	--	--
C & W FROZEN VEGETABLES	F143	11.0	--	--	--	--	--	11.0
CAMPBELL SOUP CO		--	--	--	--	--	--	--
CAMPBELLS CANNED BEANS	F143	--	--	--	--	10.3	154.1	164.4
CAMPBELLS HOME STYLE CANNED PORK & BEANS PREMIUM OFFER	F143	--	--	--	--	9.1	--	9.1
CLOROX CO		--	--	--	--	--	--	--
B IN B MUSHROOMS	F143	--	--	81.2	281.1	--	--	362.3
MR MUSHROOM CANNED MUSHROOMS	F143	--	--	111.1	--	--	78.5	189.6
CURTICE-BURNS INC		--	--	--	--	--	--	--
BLUE BOY CANNED VEGETABLES	F143	--	--	--	--	--	4.9	4.9
SILVER FLOSS SAUERKRAUT SWEEPSTAKES	F143	--	--	--	--	--	22.6	22.6
*DEL MONTE CANNED VEGETABLES	F143	--	--	--	--	--	2,571.7	2,571.7
GENERAL FOODS CORP		--	--	--	--	--	--	--
BIRDS EYE AMERICANA RECIPE FROZEN VEGETABLES	F143	--	--	12.0	--	--	--	12.0
BIRDS EYE FROZEN INTERNATIONAL VEGETABLES	F143	--	--	329.1	226.6	--	243.8	799.5
BIRDS EYE FROZEN STIR-FRY VEGETABLES	F143	--	--	82.8	--	--	44.6	127.4
BIRDS EYE FROZEN VEGETABLES	F143	--	--	75.7	--	20.9	736.6	833.2
BIRDS EYE FROZEN VEGETABLES WITH SAUCE	F143	--	--	--	--	--	71.6	71.6
GENERAL MILLS INC		--	--	--	--	--	--	--
BETTY CROCKER INSTANT POTATOES	F143	--	--	48.0	--	--	--	48.0
CONTINUED								

106   *Company and Brand name are the same.   OCTOBER—DECEMBER 1974

*Reprinted by permission of Leading National Advertisers, Inc.

Figure 11
Sample Page of LNA Ad $ Summary

LNA AD $ SUMMARY–BRAND INDEX

BRAND NAME—CLASS CODE / PARENT COMPANY (SUBSIDIARY or DIVISION)	CODE	YTD $(000)	MEDIA USED
KENTUCKY BEAU BOURBON WHISKEY (KENTUCKY BEAU DISTIL C)	F330	6.3	M
RENFIELD IMPORTERS LTD	G330	11,946.1	M-N-S-O
KENTUCKY FRIED CHICKEN FOOD SERVICE	G330	1.9	M
KENTUCKY FRIED CHICKEN TV PROGRAM (KENTUCKY FRIED CHICK C)	G330		
MEUBLEIN INC	F330	28.9	M-O
KENTUCKY GENTLEMAN WHISKEY			
BARTON BRANDS LTD	B620	11.3	M
KENTUCKY INDUSTRIAL DEVELOPMENT (DEPT OF COMMERCE)	T432	25.6	M-O
KENTUCKY COMMONWEALTH OF			
KENTUCKY RESORT PROMOTION			
KENTUCKY COMMONWEALTH OF (DIV OF PUBLICITY)	T432		
KENWOOD STEREO RECEIVERS	H320	36.1	M
KENWOOD STEREO TUNER & AMPLIFIER	H320	3.8	M
KENWOOD TURNTABLES	H320	13.7	M
TRIO ELECTRONICS INC (KENWOOD ELECTRONICS IN)			
KENWORTH MOTOR TRUCK DEALERS	T121	3.8	O
PACCAR INC			
KENYA GEM JEWELRY (KENYA GEM DIV)	G211	1.3	M
DAY & FRICK INC			
KENYA RESORT PROMOTION	T432	16.0	M
KENYA TOURIST OFFICE			
KENYON MARINE HARDWARE	G430	2.2	M
KENYON MARINE STOVES	G430	2.2	M
KENYON NAVIGATION INSTRUMENTS	G222	2.2	M
OUTDOOR SPORTS INDUSTRIES IN (KENYON MARINE)			
KERNS BREAD	F161	58.4	S-O
KERNS BAKERY PRODUCTS	F101	.6	O
KERNS BAKERY OF VA INC			
KERR COUNTY TEXAS RESORT PROMOTION	T432	1.1	M
KERR COUNTY CHAMBER OF COMME			
KERR JARS & LIDS	H235	46.8	R
KERR GLASS MFG CORP			
KERR-MCGEE CORP GENERAL PROMOTION	T230	10.1	S
KERR-MCGEE MOTOR OIL	T211	10.9	S
KERR-MCGEE MULTI-PRODUCT ADVERTISING	T211	14.9	S
KERR-MCGEE CORP			
KESSLER BLENDED WHISKEY	F330	605.2	M-O
DISTILLERS CORP-SEAGRAMS LTD(KESSLER JULIUS CO)			
KESSLER SALES CORP SERVICE	B110	24.5	M
KESSLERS (MISCELLANEOUS)	G608	47.5	S
KESSLER H & CO			
KETCHUM FISH LURE	G410	4.0	M
KETCHUM H & CO			
KETCHUM FISHING PRODUCTS	D111	.3	M
KEY WEST CREAMS & LOTIONS	D113	.6	M
KEY WEST PERFUME			
KEY WEST FRAGRANCE & COS F I			
KEY WEST HAND PRINT FASHIONS (APPAREL-WOMEN)	G&O7	10.6	M
KEYLESS AUTO GAS LOCK	T154	6.2	S
RAFFLES CO			

BRAND NAME—CLASS CODE / PARENT COMPANY (SUBSIDIARY or DIVISION)	CODE	YTD $(000)	MEDIA USED
KINGS CRAFT YACHTS (KINGS CRAFT CORP)	G430	8.2	M
CLOROX CO	G608	2.7	O
KINGS DEPARTMENT STORES (MISCELLANEOUS)	G330	.8	O
KINGS FOOD HOST USA			
KINGS FOOD HOST S A INC			
KINGS INN SUN CITY CENTER	T431	2.5	M-O
M G DEVELOPMENT CORP			
KINGS ISLAND AMUSEMENT PARK	G320	182.0	S-O
TAFT BROADCASTING CO			
KINGS ISLAND COUNTRY RESORT PROMOTION	T432	13.5	M
KINGS LODGE OTISVILLE	T431	.5	M
KINGS RANSOM 6 HOUSE OF LORDS SCOTCH WHISKIES	F330	238.0	M
(WHITELEY WILLIAM 6 CO)			
MEUBLEIN INC			
KINGSBERRY HOMES	G605	3.0	M
BOISE CASCADE CORP (KINGSBERRY HOMES)	H515	19.7	M-P-O
KINGSDOWN CONVERTIBLE SOFAS	H120	22.5	S
KINGSDOWN MATTRESSES	H120	68.6	S
MEBANE CO			
KINGSFORD CHARCOAL BRIQUETS	H234	578.5	M-N-S
KINGSFORD CO			
KINGRAY LIQUOR DISCOUNT CENTER	G604	.5	M
KINNEY RENT-A-CAR SYSTEM	T414	1.2	M
SANDGATE CORP (KINNEY RENT-A-CAR DIV)			
KINNEYS SHOES (FAMILY)	G607	2,004.3	S
WOOLWORTH F W CO (KINNEY SHOE CORP)			
KIP SUNBURN SPRAY	D111	4.1	O
YOUNGS DRUG PRODUCTS CORP (RABIN-WINTERS DIV)			
KIRBY LUMBER PRODUCTS HOME	H513	2.4	O
SANTA FE INDUSTRIES INC			
KIRBY PRODUCTIONS GAMES	G450	1.0	M
KIRBY VACUUM CLEANERS	H215	7.1	S
SCOTT & FETZER CO			
KIRIN BEER (MITSUBISHI INTL CORP)	F310	27.9	M-O
MITSUBISHI CORP	B410	.7	M
KIRKBRIDE BIBLES			
KIRKBRIDE B B CO INC			
KIRSBERRY WINE	F320	117.4	S
KIRSCH BATH ACCESSORIES	H152	46.9	S
KIRSCH BEDSPREAD ENSEMBLES	H152	133.5	M-P
KIRSCH MULTI-PRODUCT ADVERTISING	H150	162.7	M
KIRSCH CO			
KIRSCHNER MEATS	F150	22.6	S-O
KIRSCHNER JOSEPH A CO INC			
KIRSTEN PIPES	G120	8.0	M
KIT BITS CAT SNACKS	G531	6.4	S
KIT KAT CANDY	F211	17.4	S
HERSHEY FOODS CORP			
KITCHEN BOUQUET	F114	53.3	M-S

Figure 11 (Continued)
Sample Page of LNA Ad $ Summary

Company / Brand	Code	$
KEYSTONE AUTO ACCESSORIES (ELECTRO CHEMICAL	T154 / IND I	< 1 0
INTERMARK INC		
*KEYSTONE MATERIAL HANDLING EQUIPMENT	B520	1.0 M
KEYSTONE PHOTO EQUIPMENT	G230	476.6 S
BERKEY PHOTO INC		
KEYSTONE PHOTO SERVICE (KEYSTONE PHOTO SERVICE	G220	5.0 M
ROYALTONE INC	T154	
KEYSTONE RIMS (ELECTRO CHEMICAL	IND I	56.8 M
*INTERMARK INC		
*KIDDER PEABODY & Co INC SERVICES	B152	9.9 M
*KIDDIE HOUSE	G450	2.3 M
MISCELLANEOUS RECORD ALBUMS	H330	23.9 S
KIKKOMAN SOY SAUCE	F116	45.9 M-p
KIKKOMAN TERIYAKI MARINADE	F116	7.6 M
KIKKOMAN INTERNATIONAL INC		
*KILLINGTON AREA RESORTS	T431	11.1 M
*KILLINGTON ADVENTURE CAMP RESIDENTIAL	B133	.3 M
KILLINGTON SKIING RESORT	T431	9.5 M
SHERBURNE CORP		
KILPATRICKS BAKERY PRODUCTS	F161	53.8 O
CAMPBELL TAGGART INC		
KIMBALL FURNITURE	H120	.5 S
KIMBALL PIANOS & ORGANS	H340	6.9 S
JASPER CORP		
KIMBERLY KNIT DRESSES WOMEN	A114	9.0 M
KIMBERLY KNIT PANTSUITS WOMEN	A119	9.0 M
KIMBERLY KNIT SPORTSWEAR WOMEN	A115	8.2 M
KIMBERLY KNIT SUITS WOMEN	A112	7.7 M
GENERAL MILLS INC (KIMBERLY KNITWEAR	A121 / INC I	4,665.0 M-N-S
KIMBIES DISPOSABLE DIAPERS		
*KIMBERLY-CLARK CORP	B133	2.8 M
KINDER CARE DAY CARE		
KINDER CARE LEARNING CNTRS I		
*KING & PRINCE HOTEL ST SIMONS ISLAND	T431	12.6 M
KING ARTHUR FLOUR	F113	40.1 S
SANDS TAYLOR & WOOD CO		
*KING BROADCASTING RADIO STATIONS	B430	24.8 O
KING COTTON MEAT PRODUCTS	F150	18.4 S-O
HOLIDAY INNS INC		
KING COTTON WINE	F320	12.5 S
KANE-MILLER CORP		
KING EDWARD CIGARS	G112	3.2 M
AMERICAN MAIZE-PRODUCTS CO		
KING KOIL MATTRESS	H120	154.0 N-S
KING KOIL SLEEP SETS	H120	25.3 S
U S BEDDING CO		
*KING KWIK MINIT MARKETS	F180	4.6 O
KING LOUIE SPORTSWEAR MEN	A115	.4 M
KING LOUIE INTERNATIONAL INC		
KING OSCAR SARDINES	F150	74.2 M
BJELLAND CHO DELICACIES		
*KING QUILL INC (APPAREL-MEN)	F180	187.6 M-p-S
KING SIZE INC	GA07	
KING SOLOMON WINE	F320	55.4 S
MICHIGAN WINERIES INC		
*MICHIGAN TABLE SYRUP	F111	22.8 S
INTERNATIONAL MULTIFOODS COR		
*KING VAN LINES MOVING SERVICE	B613	2.7 O
**KINGS CASTLE TAHOE	T431	2.9 O
KITCHEN BOUQUET PRIME CHOICE STEAK SAUCE	F116	244.6 N-S
CLOROX CO (GROCERY STORE PROD CO)		
KITCHENAID APPLIANCE DEALERS	H216	1.8 O
KITCHENAID APPLIANCE DISTRIBUTORS	H216	0
KITCHENAID COMPACTORS	H715	137.3 M-n-S
KITCHENAID DISHWASHER & COMPACTOR	H715	1,062.2 M-N-S
KITCHENAID DISHWASHERS & DISPOSERS	H715	22.7 S
KITCHENAID DISPOSALL UNIT	H215	29.1 M-S
KITCHENAID FOOD MIXERS	H720	34.8 M
KITCHENAID GOURMET RANGE	H212	.3 S
KITCHENAID HOT-WATER DISPENSER HOME	H521	11.7 S
KITCHENAID MULTI-PRODUCT ADVERTISING	H215	46.9 S
HOBART CORP (KITCHENAID DIV)		
KITTINGER FURNITURE	H120	40.0 M
KITTINGER OFFICE FURNITURE	B313	8.1 M
GENERAL INTERIORS CORP (KITTINGER CO INC)		
KITTY CANNED CAT FOOD	G531	42.3 S
NEW ENGLAND FISH CO		
KITTY CLOVER SNACKS	F212	75.9 S
FAIRMONT FOODS CO		
KIWANIS MAGAZINE	B420	3.0 M
KIWANIS INTERNATIONAL		
KIX CEREAL	F122	106.7 M
GENERAL MILLS INC		
KLAAS BOATS INC	G430	.7
KLAAS KEYS		
KLAUS BRASS YACHTS		
HADS KEYS		
*KLAUSNER ASSOCIATES REAL ESTATE	G520	1.1 M
KLEENGUARD FURNITURE POLISH	H432	67.6 S
ALBERTO-CULVER CO		
KLEENEX BOUTIQUE FACIAL TISSUES	D132	67.9 N-S
KLEENEX BOUTIQUE MULTI-PRODUCT ADVERTISING	H232	199.6 N-S
KLEENEX BOUTIQUE TOWELS	H232	53.5 M
KLEENEX FACIAL TISSUES	D132	1,287.6 N-S
KLEENEX THICK & THIRSTY PAPER TOWELS	H232	56.4 S
KLEENEX TOILET TISSUE	H732	13.1 S
KIMBERLY-CLARK CORP		
KLEFFNERS SUN VALLEY CAMP RESIDENTIAL	B133	.6 M
SUN VALLEY CO INC		
KLEIN SLEEP (HOUSEHOLD)	G605	243.1 M-p
KLEIN SLEEP PRODUCTS INC	F150	25.2 S-O
KLEMENT MEAT PRODUCTS		
KLEMENT SAUSAGE CO INC	Ga30	3.4 P
KLEPPER FOLDING BOATS		
KLEPPER-HANS GMBH	G230	2.2 M
KLINGCAMERA ACCESSORIES (KLING PHOTO CO)		
BERKEY PHOTO INC	H320	7.1 M
KLIPSCH STEREO SPEAKERS		
KLIPSCH & ASSOCIATES INC	A170	1.8 M
KLOPMAN FABRICS CHILDREN	A170	.6 S
KLOPMAN FABRICS FAMILY	A170	40.6 M-p
KLOPMAN FABRICS MEN	A170	89.4 M-p
BURLINGTON INDUSTRIES INC (KLOPMAN MILLS INC)		
KLUTCH DENTURE ADHESIVE	D121	42.0 M-p
PUTNAM I INC		
KNABE PIANOS	H340	1.8 M
AEOLIAN CORP (KNABE DIV)		
KNEISEL TRAVEL SERVICE	T420	16.5 M
NATIONAL TRAILWAYS BUS SYSTE(KNEISEL TRAVEL INC)		

*Company and Brand name are the same.

JANUARY–JUNE 1974

MEDIA USED: M–MAGAZINES,   S–SPOT TV,
P–NEWSPAPER SUPPS,   R–NETWORK RADIO,
N–NETWORK TV,   O–OUTDOOR

*Reprinted by permission of Leading National Advertisers, Inc.
*Reprinted by permission of Broadcast Advertisers Reports, Inc.

Figure 12
Sample Page of LNA Outdoor Advertising Expenditures*

PARENT COMPANY — BRAND — MARKET	CURRENT QUARTER			YEAR-TO-DATE		
	TOTAL	POSTING	PAINT	TOTAL	POSTING	PAINT
F330 LIQUOR	CONTINUED					
FOREMOST-MCKESSON INC						
MARTINS V V O SCOTCH WHISKY				CONTINUED		
CAL SAN FRAN-OAKLND-SAN JO	8.0	8.0	--	29.4	29.4	--
WIS MILWAUKEE METRO MKT	--	--	--	9.3	--	9.3
BRAND TOTAL	8.0	8.0	--	38.7	29.4	9.3
FOREMOST-MCKESSON INC						
MCKESSON & ROBBINS LIQUOR MULTI-PRODUCT ADVERTISING						
CAL SAN FRAN-OAKLND-SAN JO	8.9	8.9	--	21.2	21.2	--
FOREMOST-MCKESSON INC						
MOHAWK CORDIALS						
MICH DETROIT METRO MKT	--	--	--	21.2	--	21.2
GERMAN DISTILLERIES LTD						
ASBACH URALT BRANDY						
ILL CHICAGO METRO MKT	5.5	5.5	--	5.5	5.5	--
WIS MILWAUKEE METRO MKT	2.7	2.7	--	2.7	2.7	--
BRAND TOTAL	8.2	8.2	--	8.2	8.2	--
GLENMORE DISTILLERIES CO INC						
KENTUCKY TAVERN CAPTAINS QUART BOURBON WHISKEY						
ARK FT SMITH METRO MKT	--	--	--	1.4	--	1.4
GLENMORE DISTILLERIES CO INC						
MACKENZIE SCOTCH WHISKY						
ARIZ PHOENIX METRO MKT	--	--	--	2		
GLENMORE DISTILLERIES CO INC						
OLD KENTUCKY TAVERN BOURBON WHISKEY				SPECIMEN		
ARK LITTLE ROCK ST MET MKT	2.2	1.3	.9			
TENN CHATTANOOGA DISTRICT	1.3	1.3	--			
BRAND TOTAL	3.5	2.6	.9			
GLENMORE DISTILLERIES CO INC						
OLD MR BOSTON BOURBON WHISKEY						
MINN MINNEAPOLIS-ST PAUL ME	5.1	--	5.1	10.5	--	
GLENMORE DISTILLERIES CO INC						
OLD MR BOSTON CORDIALS						
MINN MINNEAPOLIS-ST PAUL ME	--	--	--	4.8	4.8	--
GLENMORE DISTILLERIES CO INC						
OLD THOMPSON BLENDED WHISKEY						
ILL ROCKFORD METRO AREA MK	--	--	--	5.2	5.2	--
MASS BOSTON METRO MKT	25.5	25.5	--	91.8	77.1	14.7
LAWRENCE	1.4	1.4	--	1.4	1.4	--
LOWELL MKT	1.4	1.4	--	1.4	1.4	--
WORCESTER COUNTY MKT	1.8	--	1.8	4.6	--	4.6
OHIO CLEVELAND METRO MKT	--	--	--	14.8	14.8	--
BRAND TOTAL	30.1	28.3	1.8	119.2	99.9	19.3
GLENMORE DISTILLERIES CO INC						
YELLOWSTONE BOURBON WHISKEY						
ARK FT SMITH METRO MKT	1.0	1.0	--	3.5	3.5	--
LITTLE ROCK ST MET MKT	2.9	1.9	1.0	11.5	8.1	3.4
IND EVANSVILLE GREATER MET	3.2	3.2	--	4.4	4.4	--
KY COVINGTON & NEWPORT DI	2.4	2.4	--	4.8	4.8	--
LEXINGTON THREE COUNTY	2.4	2.4	--	5.4	5.4	--
LOUISVILLE METRO MKT	6.2	--	6.2	25.7	--	25.7
NEB OMAHA METRO MARKET	--	--	--	3.0	--	3.0
TENN NASHVILLE URBAN MARKET	--	--	--	5.3	5.3	--
BRAND TOTAL	18.1	10.9	7.2	63.6	31.5	32.1

*Reprinted by permission of Leading National Advertisers, Inc.

56

PARENT COMPANY — BRAND — MARKET	CURRENT QUARTER			YEAR-TO-DATE		
	TOTAL	POSTING	PAINT	TOTAL	POSTING	PAINT
F330 LIQUOR	CONTINUED					
GOULD ROBT CO INC						
JTS BROWN LIQUOR						
KY COVINGTON & NEWPORT DI	.3	- -	.3	4.7	- -	4.7
OHIO CINCINNATI METRO MKT	2.0	- -	2.0	7.8	- -	7.8
BRAND TOTAL	2.3	- -	2.3	12.5	- -	12.5
GROSS JOHN & CO						
MCCOLLS SCOTCH WHISKY						
N Y NEW YORK METRO MKT	2.4	2.4	- -	9.6	9.6	- -
GUILD WINE CO						
CEREMONY BRANDY						
CALI SACRAMENTO	3.1	3.1	- -	3.1	3.1	- -
ORE PORTLAND	2.8	2.8	- -	2.8	2.8	- -
BRAND TOTAL	5.9	5.9	- -	5.9	5.9	- -
GUILD WINE CO						
GUILD BLUE RIBBON BRANDY						
MINN DULUTH METRO MKT	1.7	1.7	- -	5.2	5.2	- -
MINNEAPOLIS-ST PAUL ME	8.5	7.6	.9	10.2	7.6	2.6
WIS APPLETON MARKET	- -	- -	- -	1.4	1.4	- -
GREEN BAY MARKET	- -	- -	- -	1.3	1.3	- -
MADISON METRO MARKET	2.5	1.9	.6	8.2	2.5	5.7
MILWAUKEE METRO MKT	7.7	6.0	1.7	15.5	7.5	8.0
RACINE MKT	- -	- -	- -	.5	.5	- -
WAUSAU-STEVENS PT-WIS	.4	.4	- -	.4	.4	- -
BRAND TOTAL	20.8	17.6	3.2	42.7	26.4	16.3
PAGE D-SAN JO	5.3	- -	5.3	18.1	- -	18.1
KET	1.4	- -	1.4	2.3	- -	2.3
ND TOTAL	6.7	- -	6.7	20.4	- -	20.4
OAKLND-SAN JO	- -	- -	- -	1.3	- -	1.3
HAAS BROTHERS						
ROYAL GATE VODKA						
CAL SAN FRAN-OAKLND-SAN JO	7.6	- -	7.6	37.7	- -	37.7
NEV RENO METRO MARKET	- -	- -	- -	1.4	- -	1.4
BRAND TOTAL	7.6	- -	7.6	39.1	- -	39.1
HAMILTON BARRETT INC						
T V VODKA						
ARK FT SMITH METRO MKT	.7	.7	- -	2.9	2.9	- -
LITTLE ROCK ST MET MKT	.5	.5	- -	2.4	2.4	- -
BRAND TOTAL	1.2	1.2	- -	5.3	5.3	- -
HEAVEN HILL DISTILLERS INC						
HEAVEN HILL BOURBON WHISKEY						
CAL SAN FRAN-OAKLND-SAN JO	- -	- -	- -	8.1	- -	8.1
KY LOUISVILLE METRO MKT	13.5	10.8	2.7	44.9	35.1	9.8
N J MONMOUTH COUNTY	.8	.8	- -	.8	.8	- -
OCEAN COUNTY	.8	.8	- -	.8	.8	- -
TENN KNOXVILLE METRO MKT	.9	- -	.9	3.6	- -	3.6
BRAND TOTAL	16.0	12.4	3.6	58.2	36.7	21.5
HEUBLEIN INC						
BLACK VELVET BLENDED CANADIAN WHISKEY						
CAL SACRAMENTO	3.3	3.3	- -	17.0	10.8	6.2
SAN FRAN-OAKLND-SAN JO	9.9	5.6	4.3	42.2	22.1	20.1
LOS ANGELES-SAN DIEGO	64.9	55.9	9.0	142.3	107.2	35.1
CONN HARTFORD MARKET	4.2	2.2	2.0	4.2	2.2	2.0
WATERBURY-MERIDEN METR	1.8	- -	1.8	2.4	- -	2.4
FLA JACKSONVILLE METRO MKT	5.0	- -	5.0	16.0	- -	16.0
CONTINUED						

Figure 13
Sample Page of Barcume National Spot TV Report*

SECTION 1 BRAND/PRODUCT INDEX TO PARENT COMPANIES

CLASS CODE	INDEX SEC 2	INDEX SEC 3	BRAND / PRODUCT	PARENT COMPANY	APR	MAY	JUN	QTR	YEAR TO DATE
H330		247	A & M RECORDS	A & M RECORDS		.5	2.2	2.7	4.8
F150	82	123	A & R MEATS-FRANKS	A & R MEATS INC	.3	.4		.8	4.7
F126	72	102	A & R MEATS-FRZN MEAT PIES	A & R MEATS INC					4.0
F150		123	A & R MEATS-VARIOUS	A & R MEATS INC					1.4
F221	108	172	A & W SOFT DRINK	UNITED BRANDS CO	65.7	51.4	144.5	261.5	290.9
B220	12	22	A A INSURANCE CO-ALL FORMS	AMERICAN AUTO ASSN		.3		.6	.6
B220	12	22	A A INSURANCE CO-AUTO	AMERICA* AUTO ASSN	.6	.2	1.2	1.7	4.4
B150	9	16	A A INSURANCE CO-FINANCING	AMERICAN AUTO ASSN	.6	1.6	.2	2.5	12.8
B220	12	22	A A INSURANCE CO-HOMEOWNERS	AMERICAN AUTO ASSN	5.4	8.5	3.5	17.4	23.9
B220	12	22	A A INSURANCE CO-PUBLIC SRVCE	AMERICAN AUTO ASSN	.3	.3	.4	1.0	1.0
F116	60	87	A B BARBEQUE SAUCE	DICK A B CO	1.6	3.8	1.0	6.3	6.3
B312	30		A B DICK OFFICE EQUIPMNT	GENERAL MOTORS CORP	59.4	114.4	57.4	231.2	246.6
T154	197	303	A C-OIL FILTER	GENERAL MOTORS CORP	1.9	134.7	47.9	184.4	184.4
T154	197	303	A C-SPARK PLUGS	GENERAL MOTORS CORP		.3		.3	.3
H541	181	284	A C M PAINTS				27.0	27.0	27.0
H330	156	247	A COUNTRY SUNDAY RCGTP	DYNAMIC HOUSE INC	101.1			101.1	337.0
H330	156	247	A LITTLE BIT/IRELAND ALB	DYNAMIC HOUSE INC					1.2
B410		32	A STROKE OF LUCK BOOK	CARLING-CKEEFE LTD					5.6
F310	178		A 1 BEER	HEUBLEIN INC	57.8	131.8	11.1	200.7	324.7
F116	60	87	A 1 SAUCE	A-1 KOTZIN CO					6.4
A115		2	A-1 WEARING APPAREL-MENS SLACKS	A-1 KOTZIN CO					3.8
H320		245	ABBOTT SOUND SYSTEM		1.4	19.8	14.8	35.9	64.6
F133	79	116	ABBOTTS DAIRY-ICE CREAM	FAIRMONT FOODS CO	.4	6.9	1.1	8.4	14.3
F131	76	108	ABBOTTS DAIRY-MIGHTY MILK	FAIRMONT FOODS CO	.8	1.3		2.1	5.1
F180	100	158	ABBOTTS DAIRY-NICE N LIFE PDTS	FAIRMONT FOODS CO					1.4
F180		158	ABBOTTS DAIRY-VARIOUS	FAIRMONT FOODS CO	2.1	3.2		5.3	10.1
H412	89	264	ABC LAUNDRY DETERGENT	H & W CHEMICAL CO	39.4	35.0	22.2	96.6	136.1
F161		140	ABELS BAGELS	ABELS BAGELS INC					114.1
H150	138	218	ABIGAIL ADDAMS LAMPS	QUOIZEL INC					2.0
D216		72	ABSORBINE PDTS-ARTHC PN LTN	YOUNG W F INC	.4			.4	2.2
D216		72	ABSORBINE PDTS-LINIMENT	YOUNG W F INC	.5			.5	6.1
B210	10	17	ACADEMY LIFE-CASH COMPENSATION	UNICOM INSURANCE GROUP					
B210	10	17	ACADEMY LIFE-HEALTH	UNICOM INSURANCE GROUP		18.1	2.9	21.1	21.1
R210	63	92	ACCENT PDTS-GRND BEEF EXTENDER	UNDERWOOD WILLIAM CO					
F114	58	85	ACCENT PDTS-SEASONING	UNDERWOOD WILLIAM CO	19.1	189.8	2.1	211.0	659.1

ESTIMATED EXPENDITURES (000)

58

Figure 13 (Continued)
Sample Page of Barcume National Spot TV Report*

Code			Product						
T570	204	321	AFCO SEEDS	1.5	.7	.5		2.7	44.1
A132	5	7	ACME BOOTS	.1	.1	.2		.4	1.2
H541	181	284	ACME QLTY PAINT&VRNSHES			4.6		4.6	4.6
H120	135	212	ACME SLEEP POTS-MATTRESS&BOX SPRING	1.6	1.5	2.1		5.2	9.9
D216	50	72	ACOINT ACNE REMEDY	.7	.7			.7	1.3
H133	138	217	ACRILAN FIBERS-PLUS/CARPETS	5.3		2.9		8.2	9.6
H235		235	ACTIC FAN COVER UP						.3
H420	169	266	ACTION DRY BLEACH	8.4	8.0	.6		17.0	28.4
G410	120	191	ACTION LURE FISHING LURE	6.8	6.2	6.2		19.2	32.1
A115	1	2	ACTION MENS KNITS					.7	.7
A16C	5	9	ACTIVS PANTYHOSE	13.0	165.7	7.4		186.1	363.7
H330	156	247	ADAM VIII LTD			.5		.5	.5
F131		108	ADAMS DAIRY CO						8.7
F211		163	WARNER-LAMBERT PHARMACEUTICAL CO						11.2
H120	135	212	SLEEPER LOUNGE CO INC	.9	.5			1.5	3.3
H310	154	242	ADMIRAL-COLOR TV	19.3		122.3		19.3	247.9
H211	138	218	ROCKWELL INTERNATL CORP	10.4	1.9			134.5	135.0
H216		224	ROCKWELL INTERNATL CORP						4.7
F114	58	85	CHESEBROUGH PONDS INC	74.8	142.2	99.0		316.0	.2
D141	36	55	GILLETTE CO		.4	.7			358.7
D111	20	39	ADRIAN ARPEL EGLGY FCL					1.1	1.1
H310		242	ADVENT CORP						.6
G410	121	191	INGERSOLL-RAND CO	8.7	3.8	2.1		14.6	29.4
B410	17	32	ADVENTURE&ITS MLTNSHP/TM	.4				.4	.4
F211	101	163	AERO BAR CANDY	.7				.7	2.6
H235	149	235	TANDY CORP	42.3	138.5	.1		180.6	246.6
D125	32	51	AMERICAN HOME PDTS CORP	2.6	17.1			19.7	26.5
H432	173	270	AMERICAN HOME PDTS CORP		.6			.6	.6
H432	173	270	AMERICAN HOME PDTS CORP	26.1	31.0	20.5		77.6	160.2
B220	22	22	AETNA LIFE & CASUALTY CO						3.5
B220	22	22	AETNA LIFE&CASUALTY INS-AUTO						8.3
B210	17	17	AETNA LIFE&CASUALTY INS-LIFE						.6
B220	12	22	AETNA LIFE&CASUALTY INS-PUBLIC SRVC	.7	13.1	11.1		35.0	2.1
D141	36	55	JOHNSON PRODUCTS CO INC	8.6	15.9	13.3		37.9	70.0
D141	36	55	JOHNSON PRODUCTS CO INC	10.8	21.0	18.5		50.2	47.0
D141	56	56	JOHNSON PRODUCTS CO INC	10.7	13.6	7.9		33.7	81.5
D141	36	56	JOHNSON PRODUCTS CO INC	12.1	.6			.6	47.2
D141	36	56	JOHNSON PRODUCTS CO INC						8.1
D142	20	39	JOHNSON PRODUCTS CO INC	11.2	9.9	12.4		33.4	54.1
D141	36	56	JOHNSON PRODUCTS CO INC						.3
A112	1	1	AFTER SIX FORMALS	5.7	5.2	1.9		12.9	41.2
H234		234	WILLIAMS COMPANIES THE	2.8		3.2		6.0	6.3
T540	203	317	AGRICO LAWN FOOD	.6					1.7
T540		317	AGRO INTERNATL					.6	.3
B220	12	22	AID ASSN FOR LUTHERANS-ALL FORMS	.3		.3		.3	1.3
3210	10	17	AID ASSN FOR LUTHERANS	.2				.5	.9
D121	25	46	LEVER BROTHERS CO	182.9	475.5	531.0		1189.4	1441.4
T413	200	311	CANADIAN NATIONAL RAILWAY CO	1.3	1.6			2.9	2.9
H522	178	279	JOHNSON CORP		1.0			1.0	1.0
T413	200	311	AIR FLORIDA INC	19.6	13.1	10.5		43.2	77.0
H150	138	218	AIR FLORIDA AIRLINES			5.8		5.8	5.8
T413	200	311	AIR FRANCE PARIS FRANCE	262.9	306.1	123.1		712.1	1084.6
T413	200	311	AIR INDIA AIRLINES		56.8	4.3		61.0	61.0

Code			Product
T570	204	321	AFCO SEEDS
A132	5	7	ACME BOOTS
H541	181	284	ACME QLTY PAINT&VRNSHES
H120	135	212	ACME SLEEP POTS-MATTRESS&BOX SPRING
D216	50	72	ACOINT ACNE REMEDY
H133	138	217	ACRILAN FIBERS-PLUS/CARPETS
H235		235	ACTIC FAN COVER UP
H420	169	266	ACTION DRY BLEACH
G410	120	191	ACTION LURE FISHING LURE
A115	1	2	ACTION MENS KNITS
A16C	5	9	ACTIVS PANTYHOSE
H330	156	247	ADAM VIII RECORDS
F131		108	ADAMS DAIRY-MILK
F211		163	ADAMS GUM
H120	135	212	ADJUST-A-BED
H310	154	242	ADMIRAL-COLOR TV
H211	138	218	ADMIRAL-REFRIGERATOR FREEZER
H216		224	ADMIRAL-VARIOUS
F114	58	85	ADOLPHS-MEAT TENDERIZER
D141	36	55	ADORN HAIR SPRAY
D111	20	39	ADRIAN ARPEL EGLGY FCL
H310		242	ADVENT STEREO EQUIPMENT
G410	121	191	ADVENTURE TACKLE BOXES
B410	17	32	ADVENTURE&ITS MLTNSHP/TM
F211	101	163	AERO BAR CANDY
H235	149	235	AEROMIST AEROSOL DSPNSR
D125	32	51	AFRO-SHAVE SHAVE CREAM
H432	173	270	AEROWAX PDTS-FURN POLISH
H432	173	270	AEROWAX PDTS-WAX
B220	22	22	AETNA LIFE&CASUALTY INS-ALL FORMS
B220	22	22	AETNA LIFE&CASUALTY INS-AUTO
B210	17	17	AETNA LIFE&CASUALTY INS-LIFE
B220	12	22	AETNA LIFE&CASUALTY INS-PUBLIC SRVC
D141	36	55	AFRO-SHEEN PRODUCTS-BLW OUT KT&COND
D141	36	55	AFRO-SHEEN PRODUCTS-CNR ES&GHR SP
D141	56	56	AFRO-SHEEN PRODUCTS-CNDTNR&HAIR SPRY
D141	36	56	AFRO-SHEEN PRODUCTS-HAIR SPRAY
D141	36	56	AFRO-SHEEN PRODUCTS-HAWK HANDLERS
D142	20	39	AFRO-SHEEN PRODUCTS-HND&BDY LOTION
D141	36	56	AFRO-SHEEN PRODUCTS-SHAMP&COND
A112	1	1	AFTER SIX FORMAL WEAR
H234		234	AGLOW FIREPLACE LUGS
T540	203	317	AGRICO LAWN FOOD
T540		317	AGRO PLANT CARETAKER
B220	12	22	AID ASSN FOR LUTHERANS-ALL FORMS
3210	10	17	AID ASSN FOR LUTHERANS-LIFE
D121	25	46	AIM TOOTHPASTE
T413	200	311	AIR CANADA AIRLINES
H522	178	279	AIR EASE HTG & CLG UNIT
T413	200	311	AIR FLORIDA AIRLINES
H150	138	218	AIR FOME TOILET SEAT
T413	200	311	AIR FRANCE AIRLINES
T413	200	311	AIR INDIA AIRLINES

BARCUME — NATIONAL SPOT TV — SECOND QUARTER 1974

BROADCAST ADVERTISERS REPORTS, INC.

*Reprinted by permission of Broadcast Advertisers Reports, Inc.

59

Figure 14
Sample Page of BAR Network TV Report*

SECTION 1 BRAND/PRODUCT INDEX TO PARENT COMPANIES

CLASS CODE	INDEX SEC 2	BRAND/PRODUCT	PARENT COMPANY	ESTIMATED DOLLAR EXPENDITURES (000)				
				APR	MAY	JUN	QTR	YEAR TO DATE
T154	128	A C OIL FILTER	GENERAL MOTORS CORP	44.2	110.3	161.9	316.4	316.4
T154	128	A C SPARK PLUGS	GENERAL MOTORS CORP	103.6	156.6	149.3	409.5	409.5
F116	151	A 1 SAUCE	HEUBLEIN INC		144.0		144.0	290.7
D216	325	ABSORBINE PDTS LINIMENT	YOUNG W F INC	132.5	11.3	51.3	195.1	685.2
F114	305	ACCENT PDTS SEASONING	UNDERWOOD WILLIAM CO INC	9.3	92.9	3.9	106.1	300.4
G212	51	ACCUTRON WATCHES&CLOCKS	BULOVA WATCH CO INC		494.3	32.7	527.0	527.0
F211	312	ADAMS GUM	WARNER-LAMBERT PHARMACEUTICAL CO	99.1			99.1	477.9
H310	266	ADMIRAL COLOR TV	ROCKWELL INTERNATL CORP					395.1
H211	266	ADMIRAL REFRIGERATOR FREEZER	ROCKWELL INTERNATL CORP		29.3	46.9	76.2	273.6
F114	61	ADOLPHS MEAT TENDERIZER	CHESEBROUGH PONDS INC	188.1	498.4	126.9	813.4	1551.1
D141	133	ADORN HAIR SPRAY	GILLETTE CO	37.1	20.8		57.9	170.0
V227		AERO MAYFLOWER TRANSIT MOVING SVCE	AERO MAYFLOWER TRANSIT CO					360.0
H432	9	AEROWAX PDTS WAX	AMERICAN HOME PDTS CORP	130.3	133.0	107.5	370.8	497.0
B220	2	AETNA LIFE&CASUALTY INS ALL FORMS	AETNA LIFE & CASUALTY CO		360.0		360.0	616.7
B220	2	AETNA LIFE&CASUALTY INS AUTO	AETNA LIFE & CASUALTY CO	131.2	110.3	10.0	251.5	616.7
B210	2	AETNA LIFE&CASUALTY INS LIFE	AETNA LIFE & CASUALTY CO			8.6		73.0
D121	186	AIM TOOTHPASTE	LEVER BROTHERS CO	12.0	357.7	282.2	651.9	778.4
H431	70	AJAX CLEANSER	COLGATE PALMOLIVE CO	99.7	101.7	209.0	410.4	492.4
H411	70	AJAX DISHWASHING LIQUID	COLGATE PALMOLIVE CO	80.1	79.7		159.8	829.5
H412	71	AJAX LAUNDRY DETERGENT	COLGATE PALMOLIVE CO	101.7	159.5	128.9	390.1	586.6
H431	71	AJAX LIQUID CLEANER	COLGATE PALMOLIVE CO	21.1			21.1	321.0
D142	2	ALBERTO BALSAM CONDITIONER	ALBERTO CULVER CO	45.6	80.2		125.8	245.8
D141	3	ALBERTO BALSAM HAIR SPRAY	ALBERTO CULVER CO	24.5			24.5	95.3
D111	3	ALBERTO BALSAM LOTION	ALBERTO CULVER CO					327.4
D142	3	ALBERTO BALSAM SHAMPOO	ALBERTO CULVER CO	144.8	199.2	149.3	493.3	517.0
D142	3	ALBERTO BALSAM SHMP&BALSAM CNDTN	ALBERTO CULVER CO	47.0	36.2	15.8	97.0	246.9
D141	3	ALBERTO VO5 CNDTNR HAIR DRSNG	ALBERTO CULVER CO	149.2	174.7	119.8	443.7	998.8
D141	3	ALBERTO VO5 HAIR SPRAY	ALBERTO CULVER CO	47.0	34.2	15.8	97.0	246.9
D142	4	ALBERTO VO5 SHAMPOO	ALBERTO CULVER CO					
V233	85	ALICE/WONDERLAND MOVIE	DISNEY WALT PRODUCTIONS	161.5			161.5	846.3
D213	204	ALKA SELTZER	MILES LABORATORIES INC	769.8	748.6	737.1	2255.5	5299.4
D213	204	ALKA SELTZER GOLD	MILES LABORATORIES INC		73.7		73.7	73.7
D212	205	ALKA SELTZER PLUS COLD TABLETS	MILES LABORATORIES INC					712.9
H412	186	ALL COLD WATER DETERGENT POWDER	LEVER BROTHERS CO		10.2	134.4	144.6	144.6
H412	186	ALL DETERGENT POWDER	LEVER BROTHERS CO	465.5	409.9	119.0	994.4	2045.4
H411	187	ALL DISHWASHER DETERGENT	LEVER BROTHERS CO	78.8	100.9	48.4	226.1	432.3
D212	230	ALLEREST DECONGESTANT TABS & CAPS	PENNWALT CORP	175.2	326.5	462.8	964.5	96.5
V227	5	ALLIED VAN LINES	ALLIED VAN LINES INC	119.0			119.0	658.8
B220	276	ALLSTATE INSURANCE ALL FORMS	SEARS ROEBUCK & CO	42.7			42.7	42.7
B220	276	ALLSTATE INSURANCE AUTO	SEARS ROEBUCK & CO	230.5	467.9	252.3	950.7	2600.9
B220	277	ALLSTATE INSURANCE GEN PROMO	SEARS ROEBUCK & CO	22.8	15.2	90.0	128.0	292.2
B220	277	ALLSTATE INSURANCE HOMEOWNERS	SEARS ROEBUCK & CO	346.1	57.2	160.8	564.1	1200.8

60

Figure 14 (Continued)
Sample Page of BAR Network TV Report*

Code	No.	Product	Advertiser						
B210	277	ALLSTATE INSURANCE LIFE	SEARS ROEBUCK & CO	60.8		90.1	60.0	210.9	527.0
F122	71	ALPEN CEREAL	COLGATE PALMOLIVE CO	265.7		171.1	243.1	679.9	898.1
G531	191	ALPO CANNED DOG FOOD	LIGGETT & MYERS TOBACCO CO	515.6		469.8	363.2	1348.6	3914.8
H212	261	AMANA RADAR RANGE OVEN	RAYTHEON CO	78.3				78.3	397.6
H211	261	AMANA REFRIGERATOR FREEZER	RAYTHEON CO	52.2				52.2	374.1
B150	5	AMERICAN BANKERS ASSN GEN PROMO	AMERICAN BANKERS ASSN	474.0		131.4		605.4	605.4
B110	8	AMERICAN EXPRESS CREDIT CARD	AMERICAN EXPRESS CO	184.7		49.5	20.0	254.2	950.4
B150	8	AMERICAN EXPRESS TRAVELERS CHEQUES	AMERICAN EXPRESS CO				461.2	461.2	461.2
B140	8	AMERICAN GAS ASSN GEN PROMO	AMERICAN GAS ASSN INC			262.1		262.1	1680.5
V233	192	AMERICAN GRAFFITI MOVIE	M C A INC						29.3
G561	9	AMERICAN HOME REGIONAL	AMERICAN HOME PDTS CORP			6.6	30.3	36.9	36.9
T111	23	AMERICAN MOTORS AUTOS GREMLIN	AMERICAN MOTORS CORP	144.3		175.2	439.8	759.3	1027.2
T111	23	AMERICAN MOTORS AUTOS HORNET	AMERICAN MOTORS CORP	81.7				81.7	142.2
T111	23	AMERICAN MOTORS AUTOS MATADOR	AMERICAN MOTORS CORP	334.5		197.1	33.0	564.6	1307.2
T111	23	AMERICAN MOTORS AUTOS VARIOUS	AMERICAN MOTORS CORP	768.0		849.5	249.3	1866.8	3547.8
B140	24	AMERICAN TEL & TEL GEN PROMO	AMERICAN TELEPHONE & TELEG CO	1045.3		632.3	453.9	2131.5	6362.2
G510	23	AMERICAN TOURISTER LUGGAGE	AMERICAN LUGGAGE WORK INC			43.8	332.2	376.0	376.0
T610	200	AMES PDTS GRDN TOOLS	MCDONOUGH CO	84.8				84.8	84.8
G430	25	AMF PDTS BOATS	AMF INC						231.6
G490	25	AMF PDTS BOWLING&SPRT EQPT	AMF INC						726.5
A116	25	AMF PDTS HEAD SPORTSWEAR	AMF INC						85.0
T610	25	AMF PDTS LAWN & GARDEN EQPT	AMF INC						119.0
T130	25	AMF PDTS SCAMPER CAMPERS	AMF INC						68.0
G440	25	AMF PDTS WHEEL GOODS	AMF INC						167.4
H433	25	AMWAY CORP GEN PROMO	AMWAY CORP	53.0		53.0	31.8	137.8	137.8
H433	25	AMWAY HOME PDTS	AMWAY CORP	21.2		21.2	53.0	95.4	95.4
D211	9	ANACIN TABLETS REGULAR	AMERICAN HOME PDTS CORP	985.1		1346.6	1465.1	3796.8	10705.8
D216	10	ANBESOL PAIN RELIEVER	AMERICAN HOME PDTS CORP	27.0		32.6	47.1	106.7	194.8
T154	26	ANCO PDTS WNSHLD WIPER	ANDERSON CO	16.2		9.0	17.2	42.4	190.3
G112	264	APPLE PIPE TOBACCO	REYNOLDS R J INDUSTRIES INC	33.4				33.4	199.9
D125	211	AQUA VELVA PDTS AFTER SHV LT	NABISCO INC	153.0		106.6	198.3	457.9	674.7
G120	276	AQUAFILTER DSPBL FILTER	SCOTT'S LIQUID GOLD INC	86.2		15.9		102.1	354.0
A141	80	ARIS GLOVES	CONSOLIDATED FOODS CORP	43.2		48.9		92.1	92.1
F119	63	ARM & HAMMER BAKING SODA	CHURCH & DWIGHT CO INC	706.9		507.6	203.3	1417.8	3418.1
H412	64	ARM & HAMMER LAUNDRY DETERGENT	CHURCH & DWIGHT CO INC						24.8
F150	140	ARMOUR FOODS STAR BACON	GREYHOUND CORP	22.9		41.8	58.7	123.4	364.6
F150	141	ARMOUR FOODS STAR FRANKS	GREYHOUND CORP	122.4		95.5		217.9	462.5
F150	141	ARMOUR FOODS STAR HAM	GREYHOUND CORP	97.7		45.9		143.6	235.6
T141	27	ARMSTRONG TIRES	ARMSTRONG RUBBER CO			46.3	6.7	53.0	53.0
M131	27	ARMSTRONG CARPET TILES	ARMSTRONG CORK CO	103.8				103.8	172.7
H512	27	ARMSTRONG CEILINGS	ARMSTRONG CORK CO	209.2				209.2	274.1
M132	27	ARMSTRONG PLACE&PRESS TILE	ARMSTRONG CORK CO	159.4				159.4	316.9
D124	57	ARRID EXTRA DRY ANTI PRPS	CARTER WALLACE INC	1021.6		1067.6	1126.9	3216.1	3672.6
D124	58	ARRID LIGHT PWDR EXTRA DRY	CARTER WALLACE INC						1050.2
A111	67	ARROW APPAREL MENS SHIRTS	CLUETT PEABODY & CO INC	239.5		223.8	27.5	490.8	490.8
D211	10	ARTHRITIS PAIN FORMULA	AMERICAN HOME PDTS CORP	145.1		255.8	159.3	560.2	988.3
D211	270	ASPERGUM	SCHERING-PLCUGH CORP	70.2				70.2	482.3
T161	28	ATLAS PDTS TIRES	ATLAS SUPPLY CO	21.8		436.3	385.7	843.8	843.8

NETWORK TV SERVICE FOR SECOND QUARTER 1974   BROADCAST ADVERTISERS REPORTS, INC.

*Reprinted by permission of Broadcast Advertisers Reports, Inc.

Figure 15
Sample Page from Publisher's Information Bureau (PIB)*

Foods•Beverages (1972)

JANUARY		FEBRUARY		MARCH		APRIL		MAY		JUNE	
Space	Dollars	Space	Dollars	Space	Dollars	Space	Dollars	Space	Dollars	Space	Dollars

ANHEUSER-BUSCH, INC., St. Louis, Mo.

						1 P4B	11,473				
						1 P4B	12,998				
						S4B	24,915				
								1 P4B	13,041		
						S4B	18,680				
						S4B	18,844			1 P4B	9,422
		S4BJ	57,351			1 P4B4	28,675			1 P4B	13,442
						1 P4B	13,442			1 PBs	2,992
1 P4s	4,540					1 P4B	42,845			1 P4B	11,130
				S4B	22,260					1 P4B	10,041
						1 P4B	9,562				
		S4B4	51,293	1 P4B4	26,996					1 P4BJ	43,919
				S4B4	87,837						90,946
			108,644		137,093		181,434		13,041		

ANHEUSER-BUSCH, INC., St. Louis, Mo.

								1 P4B	3,581		
										1 P4B	12,998
										1 P4B	10,505
								1 P4B	9,422	1 P4B	9,340
						1 P4BJk	8,119	1 P4B	10,041		
				1 P4B2k	9,039	1 P4B2k	9,039				
							17,158		23,044		32,843

ANHEUSER-BUSCH, INC., St. Louis, Mo.

2 P4Bh	6,506					1 P4B	7,577			1 P4B	7,577
280 L4Bh	2,167										
								2 P4B2g	63,151		
				1 P4B	42,845			2 C4B	42,845	2 P4B4g	59,993
						2 P4B3g	57,293			2 P4B4g	93,837
		1 P4BJ	43,919					1 P4B	2,285		
	8,673		43,919		42,845		64,870		108,281		161,407

ASSOCIATED BREWING CO. (Drewrys, Ltd., South Bend, Ind.), Detroit, Mich.

				½ P42s	8,637						
		1 P44s	13,683	½ P44s	8,138	½ P43s	8,498				
					16,775		8,498				

CARLSBERG BREWERIES (Carlsberg Agency, Inc., New York, N. Y.), Copenhagen, Denmark

| | | | | | | | | 1 P4s | 6,420 | | |

CARLSBERG BREWERIES (Carlsberg Agency, Inc., New York, N. Y.), Copenhagen, Denmark

										1 P4s	6,420
											6,420
						1 P4J	7,520	1 P4J	7,520		
											6,420

CHAMPALE, INC., Trenton, N. J.—See Iroquois Industries, Inc.

COORS, ADOLPH, CO., Golden, Colo.

½ P4Js	7,055	½ P44s	7,055	½ P42s	7,055	½ P4Js	7,055	½ P4Js	7,055	½ P4Js	7,055
										½ P Js	3,909
1 2 PJs	3,909	½ PJs	3,909	½ PJs	3,909	½ PJs	3,909	½ PJs	3,909	½ PJs	3,909
	10,964		10,964		10,964		10,964		10,964		14,873

FALSTAFF BREWING CORP. (Ballantine, P. & Sons, Newark, N. J.), St. Louis, Mo.

1 P4s	5,025										
1 P4s	6,625										
	11,650										

FALSTAFF BREWING CORP., St. Louis, Mo.

				¼ PJs	7,422						
				¼ PJs	7,422						
				¼ PJs	7,422						
				¼ PJs	7,422						
					29,688						

GENESEE BREWING CO., INC., Rochester, N. Y.

| | | | | 1 P4Js | 5,651 | | | | | | |

GOLD SEAL VINEYARDS, INC. (Tuborg Importers, Ltd.), New York, N. Y.

HEUBLEIN, INC. (Hamm, Theo., Brewing Co., St. Paul, Minn.), Hartford, Conn.

HOLTERBOSCH, HANS, INC., New York, N. Y.

						1 P4B4	8,941	1 P4B1	8,941	1 P4B4	8,941
						1 P4B2s	11,471	1 P4B2s	11,471	1 P4B2s	11,471
								1 P4Bs	17,903	1 P4Bs	17,903
						1 P4B2s	9,712	1 P4B2s	9,712	1 P4B2s	9,712
							30,124		48,027		48,027
						1 P44	7,520	1 P42	7,520	4 C42	8,272
									7,520		8,272
							37,644		55,547		56,299

*Reprinted by permission of the Leading National Advertisers, Inc.

Beer, Wine & Liquor—F300

MEDIA	JULY		AUGUST		SEPTEMBER		OCTOBER		NOVEMBER		DECEMBER		CUMULATIVE	
	Space	Dollars	Space	Dollars	Space	Dollars	Space	Dollars	Space	Dollars	Space	Dollars	Pages	Dollars
BEER														**F310**
BUDWEISER BEER											**$824,527 (1971)**			**F310**
Argosy (429)	1 P4B	11,473					3 C4B	8,910			3 C4B	8,910	4.00	40,766
Ebony (680)					1 P4B	12,998			1 P4B	12,998			3.00	38,994
Esquire (420)	1 P4B	16,610											3.00	41,525
Field & Stream (429)							1 P4B	13,041			1 P4B	13,041	3.00	39,123
Mechanix Illustrated (224)	1 P4B	9,340							1 P4B	9,340			4.00	37,360
Motor Trend/Sp. Car (420)									1 P4B	9,422			4.00	37,688
Newsweek (420)													3.00	86,026
Outdoor Life (429)							1 P4B	13,442			1 P4B	13,442	4.00	53,768
Playboy (420)	1 P4B	47,245	1 P4Bs	4,994	1 P4Bs	4,994	1 P4B	47,245					3.12	154,855
Popular Mechanics (224)							1 P4B	11,130					4.00	44,520
Sport (429)			1 P4B	10,041			1 P4B	10,041					4.00	39,685
Sports Illustrated (420)	1 P4Bl	26,996					1 P4Bl	26,996	1 P4Bj	9,539			5.35	141,820
Time (420)													5.00	131,756
Total		111,664		15,035		17,992		130,805		41,299		35,393	47.47	887,886
BUDWEISER MALT LIQUOR											**$412,042 (1971)**			**F310**
Car Craft (420)													1.00	3,581
Ebony (680)													1.00	12,998
Hot Rod/Rod & Cust. (420)													1.00	10,505
Mechanix Illustrated (224)													1.00	9,340
Motor Trend/Sp. Car (420)													1.00	9,422
Newsweek (420)													.17	8,119
Sport (429)													1.00	10,041
Time (420)													.24	18,078
Total													6.41	82,084
MICHELOB BEER											**$724,855 (1971)**			**F310**
Golf (420)													2.00	15,154
Golf Digest (420)					1 P4Bf	4,732								
Golf Digest (420)	1 P4B	8,755			357 Lf	4,023							5.51	26,183
Newsweek (420)	1 P4Bf	28,675											3.00	91,826
Playboy (420)													2.00	85,690
Sports Illustrated (420)													4.00	117,286
Time (420)													3.00	137,756
Yachting (420)					1 P4B	2,285							2.00	4,570
Total		37,430				11,040							21.51	478,465
CHAMPAGNE VELVET MALT LIQUOR											**$8,788 (1971)**			**F310**
Life (680)													.60	38,956
Life (680)														
Total													.60	38,956
CARLSBERG BEER											**$19,260 (1971)**			**F310**
Esquire (420)													.31	6,420
CARLSBERG BEER & MALT LIQUOR											**$69,495 (1971)**			**F310**
Esquire (420)													.31	6,420
Total													.31	6,420
New York Times Mag. (850)													2.00	15,040
Total													2.00	15,040
Grand Total													2.31	21,460
COORS BEER											**$216,723 (1971)**			**F310**
Life (680)	½ P42s	7,055	½ P42s	7,055	½ P42s	7,055	½ P4ls	7,055	½ P4ls	7,055	½ P4ls	7,055	1.20	84,660
TV Guide (182)													1.30	51,754
TV Guide (182)	½ Pls	3,909	½ Pls	3,909	½ Pls	3,909	½ Pls	4,222	½ Pls	4,222	½ Pls	4,220	2.50	136,414
Total		10,964		10,964		10,964		11,277		11,277		11,275		
BALLANTINE ALE											**$102,340 (1971)**			**F310**
Esquire (420)													.20	5,025
Playboy (420)													.10	6,625
Total													.30	11,650
FALSTAFF BREWING CORP., TV PROGRAM														**F310**
TV Guide (182)														
TV Guide (182)														
TV Guide (182)														
TV Guide (182)													.74	29,688
Total													.74	29,688
GENESEE BEER											**$52,697 (1971)**			**F310**
Life (680)													.09	5,651
TUBORG BEER														**F310**
Car Craft (420)											1 P4Bs	2,612	.57	2,612
Motor Trend/Sp. Car (420)											1 P4s	6,328	.57	6,328
Total												8,940	1.14	8,940
APROPO' MALT LIQUOR														**F310**
Life (680)					1 P4Bls	4,649	1 P4Bls	4,649					.10	9,298
LOWENBRAU MUENCHEN BEER											**$268,387 (1971)**			**F310**
New Yorker (429)	1 P4Bl	8,941			1 P4Bl	8,941							5.00	44,705
Newsweek (420)			1 P4B2s	11,471	1 P4B2s	11,471							1.55	57,355
Playboy (420)	1 P4Bs	18,854	1 P4Bs	18,854			1 P4Bs	18,854					1.46	92,368
Time (420)			1 P4Bls	9,712	1 P4Bls	9,712							.70	48,560
Total		27,795		40,037		30,124		18,854					8.71	242,988
New York Times Mag. (850)	4 C4l	8,272	3 C4l	7,690									5.00	39,274
Total		8,272		7,690									5.00	39,274
Grand Total		36,067		47,727		30,124		18,854					13.71	282,262

© 1973 Publishers Information Bureau, Inc.

Compiled and Published by Leading National Advertisers, Inc. (Dollar figures in bold face type appearing with class numbers represent previous year expenditures.)
MAGAZINE NAMES SET IN CAPITAL LETTERS DESIGNATE PUBLICATIONS AFFILIATED WITH THE COMPANY/BRAND ENTRY

Furthermore, in analyzing expenditure data, it is important not only to show dollars spent in each medium, but the percent of each competitor's total annual expenditures for each medium. Thus, it is possible to learn the proportion of each competitor's total expenditures in each medium, which makes comparisons easier. See Table 14. One of the problems of making comparisons on the basis of percents occurs when the bases differ widely. Ten percent of a brand's total budget spent in newspapers, for example, may not be equivalent to a competitor's 10% spent in newspapers if the base of one percent was $3,000 and the base of the other, $3,000,000.

Table 14
Competitive Media Expenditure Analysis for a Product Class

Brands	Magazines %	Supplements %	Newspapers %	Network TV %	Spot TV %	Outdoor %	Totals %
A	9.8%	12.8%	50.3 %	19.8 %	.02%	7.3%	100%
B	36.7	11.5	43.1	8.7			100
C	.5	5.9	47.8	45.3		.5	100
D	5.4	2.9	5.9	80.6	5.2		100
E	.6		9.6	20.2	69.6		100

Annual expenditures is only one study which may be useful in analyzing competitors' marketing and media strategies. Another useful analysis may be made by comparing expenditures of a brand with its competitors on a market-by-market basis. Through this technique it may be helpful in learning which markets were most important to the competitors, and the analysis may serve as one basis for weighting media in a given market. The location of these markets is easy in *Media Records* but difficult in LNA network television service or LNA magazine service. It may be possible, however, to estimate which markets were used and relative weights placed in these markets. (Note: the number of dollars spent in each market represents the "weight" or importance of the market.)

Still another kind of analysis may be made of the dollars spent in each medium by a brand and its competitors, correlated with the number of audiences delivered for the dollars spent. Through this technique, it may be possible to make a quick analysis of the relative effectiveness of competitors' media deliveries. Plans for a brand's reach and degree of repetition, or frequency may be made as a result of such an analysis.

Finally, it is important to learn how much money was spent in each medium during each month (and perhaps each quarter) of the year. Most brands have peak selling seasons and vary the weight of their advertising according to the importance of a given time period. This kind of analysis helps to establish timing and scheduling plans for the media selected later in the planning process.

Problems in analyzing media expenditure data. Other than the fact that most such data is incomplete; does not show discounts and covers only large advertisers, there are still analyzation usage problems remaining. One problem deals with the age of the data. It is rare that any data is less than one month old, and, as a result, the nature of the data is historical rather than contemporary. The question arises whether this data has very much meaning, especially if a competitor does not use the same media in the same ways he did in the past. If a competitor uses media in a consistent pattern so that one might be able to predict his media usage behavior, then additional data may be of little value. If he constantly changes media-usage, one must keep abreast of new data. Probably the best use of an expenditure analysis is as part of an organized intelligence system where other kinds of marketing information are added to it to form a clear picture of competitors' strategies. Some advertising agencies tend to deprecate the use of expenditure analysis as not being worth the investment in money or time necessary to make the analysis, but most large agencies feel that it is valuable if used properly.

One worthwhile use is to examine expenditures by those advertisers who lead in share-of-market. Those with smaller shares might want to learn which media, markets and audiences are most important to the leaders. Sometimes it is possible to find that leading competitors ignore one or two media entirely. In such a case, it may be possible for those with lesser shares to pre-empt a medium for themselves. Occasionally, all of the share leaders may feel that they need to be in network television. Then, a planner may select radio as a medium in which his brand can be very significant because of its isolation from the others.

Probably the greatest danger may come from simply copying the leaders in a rather blind fashion. If a leading share competitor places 10% of its budget in market A, then other competitors may follow the leader. But the followers' products and market strategies may not lend themselves to such weight in market A. Furthermore, the share leader may establish its weight proportions for its own reasons, which are quite different from those that followers ought to use. There have been times when some advertisers copied the share leaders market by market and medium by medium based on competitive expenditure analysis. It is obvious that such tactics are not reasonable.

So an expenditure analysis is helpful as a means of knowing what competitors have done, but not necessarily as a means of knowing what to do as a result. Occasionally these analyses will show that a competitor is test marketing a product, and this information may call for a revised market strategy to combat the situation. Intelligently used, it may be worth the time and money invested in following large advertiser activities.

Sources of Marketing Data

Size and share of market for a brand and its competitors, and other information that comprise a situation analysis may be obtained from a number of syndicated research services. Other data may be obtained from periodicals, association reports, the government, and media.

65

The most widely used syndicated research services are those of the A. C. Nielsen Company, the Market Research Corporation of America (MRCA), Audits and Surveys, Inc., Selling Areas - Marketing, Inc. (SAMI), the W. R. Simmons Company and Axiom Marketing Research Bureau, Inc. producers of Target Group Index (TGI). Numerous other research companies exist but space does not permit a complete listing here.

The A. C. Nielsen Company provides a national brand store-audited service comprising almost every product sold in food and drug stores. Each of these product categories is audited in a national sample of retail stores every 60 days. The service provides share of market data based on sales to consumers at the retail level, in addition to average retail prices, wholesale prices, inventory, out-of-stock, dealer support (displays, local advertising and coupon redemption) and major media advertising. The sample data is then projected in order to obtain national and regional data. It is further broken down by county size, store type, (chain and independent) brand, package size and product type.

The method of making an audit is to count a store's inventory of a given product no matter where it is stored. Sales for a given period are found by subtracting the total stock on hand at the close of a period from the total available for sale at the beginning. Since only a sample of stores is audited, it becomes necessary to project average per-store sales to a national figure and to geographical regions, city-size groups, etc.

Market Research Corporation of America (MRCA) maintains a consumer panel of 7,500 families who keep continuous diaries of their purchases. The panel members keep records of food, grocery and personal care items they purchased during any given week and then mail their diaries to the company for tabulation. Diaries include quantities purchased, package sizes, prices paid and the kind of retail outlet through which purchases are made. Other information includes effects of promotional activities such as coupons, one-cent sales, or combination sales of different products. Through such tabulations it is possible to learn the share of market for many different brands and varieties of food products.

Audits and Surveys measures the national total market based on a sample of client's product class distribution. The sample of stores to be audited is drawn *only* from the types of outlets in which the client has distribution. Information on sales, inventory, distribution, out-of-stock and the number of days stock is on hand is provided. This data is projected to the total U.S. and client's sales regions. Audit and Surveys telephones a flash report to the client at the close of the audit followed by a formal report two weeks later, compared to Nielsen's 45 to 60 days for reports to reach a client.

Target Group Index and W. R. Simmons provide marketing as well as media data on a regular basis. Each company reports how often products and/or brands are used so that a planner can identify heavy and light users, demographically. In addition, each company reports how heavy and light users were exposed to either network television programs or national magazines. As a result, the planner can select the media which not only have the largest audiences, but the largest audiences of heavy users of a given product or brand. Special studies are also available on a custom basis.

Other sources of data.   The preceding sources of data provide specific and pertinent data for a situation analysis, but are relatively expensive. In fact the cost of these services may be too high for many small manufacturers, so it becomes necessary to find substitute sources of data. There are a number of such sources, which are relatively inexpensive, but do not provide the detail, especially about competitors' sales and distribution practice. When the data is incomplete, assumptions will have to be made about the missing data. These assumptions, however, can often be checked by an astute observer of the marketing action of both his own company and competitors. The following list, meanwhile, may be helpful in locating data for the situation analysis.

Sales Management Survey of Buying Power.   Marketing and media planners often find the *Sales Management Survey of Buying Power* a convenient source of three kinds of data about markets; (1) population and household data for all major markets in the United States; (2) income and spending statistics about markets; and (3) retail sales data by broad product classes. The classes reported on are: (a) Food sales; (b) Eating and Drinking Places; (c) General Merchandise; (d) Apparel; (e) Furniture and Household Appliances; (f) Automotive; (g) Gas Stations; (h) Lumber, Building and Hardware; and (i) Drugs.

No individual brand sales are shown, and there are no other classifications of consumers other than by population and income. However, the periodical is very convenient in locating and evaluating geographical markets by state, standard metropolitan statistical area, by county or by city. Furthermore, each of the three factors (population, income and retail sales) have been combined into a multiple factor index number for each market which makes comparisons between markets easier. To also facilitate comparisons between markets by each of the nine retail product categories, convenient tables are presented in which markets are ranked by sales potential. So if the market or media planner is trying to find and evaluate markets for a drug product, he will find a table which ranks markets from best to poorest on the basis of sales of drugs. *Sales Management Survey of Buying Power* is published annually.

Standard Rate and Data Service (S.R.D.S.).   The Standard Rate and Data Service publishes media rate books for all major media. In their local media books (newspaper, spot radio, and spot television) are market data sections similar to those in the *Survey of Buying Power*. It too shows geographical markets by state, standard metropolitan statistical areas, counties and cities, but not in the detail as the Buying Power book. Retail sales too are shown by seven different categories: (a) Food; (b) Drug; (c) General Merchandise; (d) Apparel; (e) Home Furnishings; (f) Automotive; (g) Service Stations. Convenient ranking tables are also provided showing markets for the seven sales product types. Local media rate books are published monthly, but the market data is revised annually.

67

Editor and Publisher Market Guide. This annual periodical contains geographical market data similar to that of the preceding two. Markets are also ranked by population, total income, total retail sales, total food sales, and by per household income. Individual descriptions of markets are provided in the text matter.

Census Data. The U. S. Department of Commerce publishes many census analyses that are helpful in marketing planning. Most useful have been the *Census of Business,* and *Census of Population.* But other census data, too numerous to list here, are available for special industries. The *Statistical Abstract,* published once a year has been considered helpful as a quick source of data for media-market planning.

Media Studies of Special Markets. Often local and national media conduct special market studies which may be quite helpful in learning about geographical as well as special markets. While, ostensibly the purposes of these reports are to show a given medium in a favorable light, the researcher should not assume that all such studies are biased. Often a medium will sponsor a study which represents a significant contribution to the understanding of markets and media. Many times the only research available on a special problem of markets and media is to be found in these studies.

One of the most widely used sources of market data, and one of the few which shows brand share of markets, are brand preference studies conducted by local newspapers and provided free of cost to agencies. These studies are named differently by different newspapers but they are essentially home inventories of brands of many different kinds of products which have been purchased recently. The *Milwaukee Journal* has one of the most well-known of such studies and reports on brands of face soaps, coffees, packaged meats, and almost a hundred other items. The data is tabulated and the percent of total sales which each brand has are computed so that, in effect, one may have a share of market for a given product in that area. Since there are a large number of such studies in existence, it is possible to get some idea of the relative share of market for a brand in various parts of the country by comparing data from a composite selection. Unfortunately, these studies are conducted but once a year and some newspapers do not repeat their studies each year. Furthermore, there may be differences in the degree of control exercised in the collection and reporting of such data, so that it is difficult to know how precise the data is. Then too, since the data is collected only once a year, there is no measure of volume purchased since an individual may just happen to have purchased a given brand at the time the study was made, but never buy it again.

Advertising Age is the source of much market data of varying kinds. It regularly publishes some kinds of data, such as advertising expenditures by media classes, and occasionally publishes other kinds of data such as market shares for a particular product class. Occasionally, special studies for various media are announced in this publication and may be obtained by writing to the source.

Associations as sources of data. There are many trade associations which report market data for their members. In some cases, this data shows sales by brands, but in others it tends to be rather general. In any case, since there are so many different trade associations in the country, it is advisable to determine whether they can be of aid in compiling the situation analysis.

Miscellaneous sources of data. There are still other sources of data which are available at relatively low cost to the market-media planner. Federal, state and local governments all produce various kinds of research which may be helpful. Federal data may be found by writing to the Government Printing Office in Washington, D.C.

Chambers of Commerce, both national and local, may be helpful in finding the right kind of data needed for marketing situation purposes. Obviously this kind of data will tend to be rather general, but may be necessary for preliminary portions of the analysis.

Finally for analysis of products and product values, both *Consumer Reports* (published by the Consumer Union of U.S., Inc.) and *Consumer Bulletin* (published by Consumer Research, Inc.) provides monthly and annual publications for a small cost. Both of these organizations put various branded products through rigorous tests to determine quality and the best buy for the money. Not all brands or models are tested, but many of the most popular brands on the market are analyzed. Ordinarily, this kind of information is very difficult to obtain except by special research services, so these two publications make the job of finding product values relatively easy.

In conclusion, then, the situation analysis is a very important document in the media planning area. To the extent that it is done thoroughly and with accuracy, it can help the media planner make more effective decisions because he has a complete picture of the marketing situation not only for his brand but for competitors.

QUESTIONS

1. Why are demographic analyses of consumers often felt to be inadequate as a basis for finding target markets?
2. What is meant by "life style research," and how does it differ from other kinds of psychological research?
3. What are the main limitations of using Competitive Media Expenditure Analyses for media planning?
4. What can an advertiser learn about competitors' marketing strategies by using competitive expenditure data?
5. What can an advertiser learn about competitors' media strategies by using competitive expenditure data?
6. Briefly explain whether it would be incorrect to compare your brand's media expenditures, where you know media discounts that have been allowed to you, and competitors' expenditures taken from competitive expenditure research data where discounts have not been noted?
7. Following are two methods of looking at expenditure data for three competitors. Which of the two methods is the most meaningful for media planning purposes?

Method 1

Competitor	Magazines	Supplements	Network TV	Spot TV	Newspapers	Spot Radio	Outdoor	Totals
A	20%	40%	—	15%	10%	15%	—	100%
B	10	10	50	20	10	—	—	100%
C	5	20	—	40	10	20	5%	100%

Method 2

	Magazines	Supplements	Network TV	Spot TV	Newspapers	Spot Radio	Outdoor	
A	57%	57%	—	20%	33.3%	43%	—	
B	29	14	100%	27	33.3	—	—	
C	14	29	—	53	33.3	57	100%	
Totals	100%	100%	100%	100%	100%	100%	100%	

8. What is the purpose of a Nielsen Food and Drug Audit?
9. If you wanted to find which counties were in a given Standard Metropolitan Statistical Area, where would you go to find this information?
10. Discuss the ramifications of making media decisions without the necessary research background.

SELECTED READINGS

Advertising Age, "Newspaper Bureau Promotes Psychographics," Sept. 10, 1973, p. 6.

Editor & Publisher, "Study Indicates Psychographic Data is Weak Media Buying Tool," Sept. 8, 1973, pp. 8-9

Media Decisions, "What's the Competition Doing?" Sept., 1973, pp. 64+

Media Decisions, "How Nestles Uses Psychographics," July, 1973, pp. 68-71

Media Decisions, "Beyond Demographics," Feb., 1968, pp. 22-23+

Media Decisions, "The Campaign that Psychographics Built," April, 1974, pp. 64+

Nelson, Alan R., "New Psychographics: Action-Creating Ideas, Not Lifeless Statistics," in *Advertising Age*, June 28, 1971, pp. 1-34+

Ostrow, Joseph, (Competitive Media Expenditure Analysis) in *Media Decisions* Dec., 1971, p. 52

Papazian, Edward, "Buzz Words Like Psychographics," in *Media Decisions*, Oct., 1973, pp. 14-16.

Peterson, Robert A., "Psychographics and Media Exposure," in *Journal of Advertising Research*, June, 1972, pp. 17-20

Plummer, Joseph T., "Life Style Patterns," in *Journal of Broadcasting*, Winter, 1971-72, pp. 78-89

Shiffman, Phil, "Psychographic Data Could Be the Base for Both Copy and Media," in *Media Decisions*, Aug., 1973, pp. 80-82

Wells, William D., (Ed.) *Life Style and Psychographics*, American Marketing Assn., Chicago, 1974

Wells, William D., "Psychographics: A Critical Review", in *Journal of Marketing Research*, May, 1975, pp. 196-213

Zeltner, Herbert, "Is Competitive Media Expenditure Information Worth Anything?" in *Media/scope*, Aug., 1962, pp. 8-10

Ziff, Ruth, "Psychographics for Market Segmentation," in *Journal of Advertising Research*, April, 1971, pp. 3-10

Zeisel, Hans, *Say It With Figures*, Harper & Brothers Publishers, N.Y., 1957

chapter 4

Marketing Strategy and Media Planning

The Marketing Strategy Plan

Once the facts about a marketing situation have been gathered, the data then should be analyzed in order to learn where problems and opportunities lie. An opportunity may be defined as a marketing activity which, if adopted, may result in an advantage over the competitor. An example of an opportunity might be a situation where a manufacturer has improved his brand so that it is superior to competitors' brands; but he may have communicated this advantage to only 10% of potential consumers. Increased sales may be achieved if the manufacturer is able to raise the awareness-level of this advantage to 40% or 50% of consumers.

Problem areas, on the other hand, demand that some action be taken to correct the situation. A problem area might be one where a brand does not have a competitive advantage, or one where a brand has been steadily losing its share of market for a multitude of reasons. Finding the causes for the decline is a first step in changing the situation. Most situation analyses turn up more problem areas than opportunities; but the delineation of each is a necessary preliminary step to marketing and media planning.

Market strategy planning consists of setting marketing objectives which will solve the major problems and take advantage of the opportunities. In effect then, a marketing strategy plan is a blueprint for action geared to sell the product. The ultimate goal of such action is to gain an advantage over a competitor who, in a sense, is the enemy.

Perhaps the weakest part of many advertising campaigns is the lack of a sound selling strategy, said Arthur Tatham, formerly chairman of the Board of Tatham-Laird & Kudner advertising agency. "Brilliant copy and art will never make a weak selling strategy succeed. But . . . once there is a sound selling strategy, then, good copy and art will multiply its effectiveness." Tatham's statement also applies to media selection and use. Without a sound method of selling, media planning may represent wasted effort. In fact, media planning is a service function of marketing and selling. It does not exist as activity unrelated to marketing. The fact that media is often selected and used without being based on a sound selling strategy demonstrates poor logic and inefficient modes of operation. This selling strategy, then, is the heart of a market strategy plan.

Major goals in a marketing strategy plan are: (a) setting objectives that will help solve existing problems and take advantage of opportunity and problem areas (b) deciding how the product should be sold (c) determining to whom the main selling effort should be directed (d) determining what role various elements of the marketing mix should play in the sale of a brand (e) determining what adjustments should be made in the package shape or sizes (f) determining how much should be spent.

Importance of the marketing strategy plan. Most often, the marketing strategy plan is written by someone other than the media planner. But because the latter is not directly involved, does *not* mean that he is less important than the market planner. There are a number of reasons why the marketing strategy plan is a significant document to media planners.

The foremost reason is that it serves as a single unifying and organizing force for all activity within an agency on a given brand's marketing and advertising plans. This means that the market researchers, account executives and creative people, as well as media planners, are all working from a single source of information. In such a case, there is great possibility that the plan will serve as a coordination effort in reaching the same goals. Large advertising agencies often have so many persons working on so many different accounts that it becomes difficult to communicate efficiently with each one. The media planner, especially, needs to know that his decisions will be directed toward the same objectives as others on the agency team.

But secondly, once the plan has been written, it becomes easier to visualize the whole scheme of operations on a given brand. All proposed plans can be evaluated for their logic and completeness. There should be no gaps of information or contradictions in planning. If a marketing plan existed in someone's mind, or in bits or scraps of memoranda, then it may be difficult to see where serious errors exist, because no one has an overview of the entire operation.

Perhaps the key to the success of a marketing strategy plan is the degree to which all tactics are spelled out, rather than stated generally or haphazardly. Herbert Zeltner cautioned that many marketing strategy plans are "either glossed over in the rush of hammering together a marketing program, or merely slapped together as a collection of ponderous cliches."[19] He noted:

"To be truly useful, the market strategy statement should not merely reflect some happy generalities about an increase in volume or share of market for the coming fiscal period.

---

[19]Zeltner, Herbert, "Marketing Strategy Statement," in *Media/scope,* August, 1964, p. 10.

"But establishing the requirement that a specific percent volume increase to be achieved—through the expenditure of a precise sensible sum of money—and that this increase can most realistically be expected through more aggressive development of certain stated territories or segments of the market . . . is the type of statement which gives a properly astute media planner the challenge he needs to create both a perspective and workable media recommendation."[20]

So the media planner needs specific direction, explicitly stated, in order to begin decision-making. The media plan grows directly out of the marketing strategy whenever advertising is to be used. The various segments of the strategy statement, however, are not all equally significant to the media planner. Some are much more important than others. Foremost in importance are: (a) the marketing objectives; (b) the basic selling idea; (c) sources of business; (d) overall sales strategy; and (e) spending strategy. Each of these will be discussed on the following pages. See Figure 16 for an outline of a basic strategy statement.

Figure 16
Outline for Basic Strategy Statement*

Advertiser _____ Brand/Product_____

I. *Major Strategy.*

This should be the briefest possible statement of the major one or two strategies you are going to recommend for the planning period, with just enough statement of the problem to explain the strategy.

If you can write this section in one or two sentences or paragraphs, do so. If it takes you more than a single-spaced page, it is probably too long.

II. *Basic Objectives*

A. Short Term (applies to next coming fiscal 12 months, unless otherwise stated, e.g., six months):

1. Increase share of total market.
2. Arrest decline in share.
3. Develop added volume.
4. Increase total market.
5. Profit goal.
6. Reduce losses.

Translate objectives into approximate sales and/or profit goals.

B. Long Term (applies to any prescribed period beyond the next coming planning period):

1. Increase share of total market.
2. Increase total market.
3. Increase profits.
4. Position goal, i.e., gain leadership.
5. Develop and establish a brand or corporate image.
6. Expand line of service or products.

Translate objectives into approximate sales and/or profit goals.

III. *The Basic Selling Idea.*

A one- or two-sentence statement of the key selling idea. This is the base from which the creative strategy evolves.

[20]Zeltner, Herbert, "Marketing Strategy Statement," in *Media/scope,* August, 1964, p. 10.

IV. *Presentation of the Basic Selling Idea.*

This is the creative strategy in its briefest form.

V. *Use or Uses for which the Product Will Be Advertised*

   A. Major.
   B. Minor.

VI. *Sources of Business and Relative Importance of Each.*

   A. Consumer Sources - What are the characteristics of the people who are the best prospects?
      1. Regional factors.
      2. City size.
      3. County size.
      4. Income groups.
      5. Age of housewife.
      6. Occupation of head of household.
      7. Family size.
      8. Seasonal.
      9. Sex—men, women, children.
         b. Who is principal purchaser?
   B. Dealer Sources—What is relative importance of various types of outlets?
   C. Competitive Sources—Important competitive brands or companies—national, regional, local.

VII. *Overall Sales Strategy*

   A. Relative importance of price.
      1. To the consumer.
      2. To the trade.
   B. Relative importance of personal salesmanship.
   C. Relative importance of dealers.
   D. Relative importance of advertising.
   E. Relative importance of promotion.
   F. Relative importance of publicity.

VIII. *Product Strategy.*

   A. The need for product improvement—Analysis of product superiorities and weaknesses compared to competitive products.
   B. The need for related products.
   C. The need for adding new sizes or deleting unprofitable sizes.
   D. The need for improving:
      1. Packaging.
      2. Package design.

IX. *Spending Strategy.*

   A. Is there a need for higher or lower margins?—What effect will this have on price, quality, quantity of the product?
   B. What is the proper amount to spend:
      1. On introduction?
      2. On re-introduction?
      3. On going basis?
   C. Is an extended payout plan indicated, and if so, what is the optimum time?

X. *Facts and Documentation.*

The pertinent facts needed to define the problems and to document the strategies outlined in the strategy sections.

---

*Reprinted by permission of the Leo Burnett Co., Inc.

Marketing Objectives and Media Planning

The marketing goals which the company and agency agree upon may, if achieved, result in the solution of a marketing problem. Marketing goals are measurable in most cases, and provide a means of determining whether the strategy employed has been effective. For the media planner, the objectives will undoubtedly affect the kinds of media selected and how media is used. In a sense then, marketing objectives serve as controls for media planning. It is media management through the use of objectives.

Most marketing objectives relate directly to share of market for a brand while others relate to communication objectives. Shown below is a sample of marketing objectives for different brands (taken from various strategy statements):

"To increase share in an expanding segment of the "x" market.

"To regain lost volume—increase sales a maximum of 5% and, in turn shoot for a 14% share of market.

"To acquire a 20% share of the market the first year after national introduction, 25% the second year, and 30% the third year.

"To increase share of market so that the product enters the select five brands on the market.

"To introduce the product so that we have at least 5% share in each sales division.

"To increase share of the market and save the morale of the sales force in the face of many competitive new product introductions.

"To find and convince new customers for our product.

"To maintain national coverage.

"To provide regional and local impact where two-thirds of sales are made.

"To increase the overall visibility of the product name against the people and the trade across the country."

Obviously some of these objectives do not meet Zeltner's requirements as discussed previously.

Whenever marketing objectives require advertising in specific geographical areas, then media must be selected which best reaches those areas. Sometimes the objectives call for added promotional effort to a geographical region such as the west coast, or the east central part of the country. Other times, the objectives may call for special advertising effort in a given market such as Los Angeles or any other large city. Such objectives limit the number of choices of media which can be used, because few media are available in some specified areas. At other times, objectives will call for advertising efforts to specific markets of children, or women ages 29 to 39. Again the marketing objectives provide direction for the planner in selecting media and he will have to find media which best *delivers* children or women from ages 29 to 39.

When marketing objectives call for increases in share of market with special effort directed at only prospects, then the media planner may be called upon to increase the number of his messages to known prospects. In such cases media selection is secondary and methods of using media is the primary consideration. One such method may be to increase the frequency of exposure of advertising messages to prospects.

Occasionally, objectives deal with some other area than market share, for example: the requirement "To increase the image of authority among adults." In the latter situation it was felt that adults, especially those from ages 21 to 44 were not buying the product, yet they were good prospects. In fact, the situation analysis noted that the 45-year age group had already been purchasing the product. So the marketing objective influenced media selection through the use of adult-appeal media, such as magazines and Sunday supplements, and the use of well-known television announcers whose personality images were strong in the 21-to 44-year age group.

The Budget, Marketing Objectives and Media

Once the marketing objectives have been stated, it is necessary to know how much money will be required to attain them. It is not realistic to make grandiose marketing plans and then find that the advertiser is unwilling or unable to provide the sufficient funds to make the plan successful. (The subject of budgeting and allocations to markets and media will be discussed in a later chapter.) But at this point, the media planner may be called in to help estimate (or cost-out) the marketing strategy plan even before the main portion of the media plan has been started. If there is not enough money available to accomplish a given set of objectives, then the objectives may have to be reduced or revised.

Estimating the cost of a marketing plan usually involves two separate activities: estimating media costs, and then production costs. Media costs may be ascertained by checking published reference books which show media rates or phoning media representatives to obtain general costs. Production costs may be estimated either by arbitrarily taking a given percentage of the total budget to be allocated for that purpose, or if the advertising is relatively simple, by estimating specific kinds of production pieces that are needed. In the latter case, engravings, art work, typography, video tape or film costs can be estimated.

The main problem in estimating marketing costs is determining whether any given amount of money spent for advertising will accomplish a given set of objectives. Marketing and media planners most often rely on their experiences with other brands and products as a basis for making these estimates. But it should be noted that competitors' advertising may influence the marketing budget. A new product introduction may require very heavy investments to get it off the ground. Brands which have to defend their share of markets against inroads of competitors, or those which aspire to increase their brand shares, may have to spend heavily, and determining the exact amount, however, is by no means a scientific matter. It is based mostly on experience. Experiences in obtaining one Nielsen share point increase is usually based on past increases. If, for example, an advertiser increased his national share of market, 3 percentage points, and he spent $10,000,000, it is then estimated that it will cost $3,333,333 to raise the share one percentage point.

Often, the planners recommend a given amount of money to be spent which is clearly beyond the means of the advertiser's ability. In such cases, the objectives may have to be changed. Sometimes, no matter what sum is recommended, the advertiser already has a preconceived notion of the maximum amount he can profitably spend and will not listen to requests for larger amounts.

Creative Strategy and Media Planning

Part of a marketing strategy plan consists of explanations of how the product will be sold or a statement of the basic selling idea. This section of the plan may be the most important single influence on the planner in the media selection process. Many times the creative strategy provides the most specific single direction which the planner should take so that he will select a given medium, or possibly it may require a limited number of different kinds of media.

Where color is an integral part of the creative strategy, then magazines, direct mail, newspaper supplements, or color television may be required. With the advent of fine rotogravure printing which may be inserted in newspapers (called hi-fi color or spectacolor) new alternatives in the use of color become available to the media planner. In some cases, where the creative strategy calls for the use of cartoon characters, then either comic strips or television may be most appropriate. Magazines also may be considered. Again, direction is given in the selection process. Where a strategy calls for demonstration, one might first think of television; yet it is possible to demonstrate the use of a product in print media through the use of a number of panels showing various steps in the use of the product. Sometimes the creative strategy may call for the use of an announcer or salesman who can exude a feeling of warmth and sincerity. Either television or radio may be required here, since each is a means of conveying emotional impact. If the creative strategy calls for music, media choices may be limited to radio or television. A novel alternative to using music might be to record the music and advertising message on thin vinyl records and have them inserted into a magazine. But in the latter case, while the creative strategy is important, of equal importance is the budget, which may not tolerate the expense of recording and inserting the record.

Occasionally, creative strategy calls for illustrations which are very large and dominating. This suggests billboards to the media planner, although alternatives of direct mail or a two-page center spread in newspapers may be equally acceptable.

Some advertising messages may seem to have more impact on consumers in one medium than they do in another. Traditionally, then, advertising for this brand of product is limited to one or two media. If the creative strategy is similar to that of previous years, then the media planner may have to meet the impact requirement. It should be noted, however, that the definition of "impact" generally is hazy and not precise. Impact is assumed, to mean that advertising does something to audience members, such as make the message memorable, change attitudes toward the brand, impart significant bits of information, or perhaps serve as a motivating factor in selling. The assumption is not always valid because there is often little proof that what is claimed to happen, actually does. In any case, where creative strategies call for traditional media, the planner may find it difficult to break tradition.

So, the creative strategy is an integral part of media planning, perhaps the most integral of all. The planner cannot make a decision without first knowing what is to be said and how it is to be presented to consumers. Only then can he think of media alternatives.

Consumer Targets: The Market

While marketing objectives and creative strategy obviously affect media planning, they are only two major factors which affect media decision-making. A third factor is the definition of media targets or sources of business.

A question which media planners must ask early in planning is: "To whom should we advertise?" Should we advertise to consumers who use the product? Or to those who buy the product? Or to those who have never used the product and who might be considered good prospects? Generally the answer is: advertise to influencers of purchasers, if they can be found and identified demographically. Unfortunately, this is easier said than done. Many times the influencer and the purchaser are the same person. Other times, the degree of influence which each family member has on a person is almost impossible to ascertain. So most often, advertising is addressed to purchasers. Purchasers are, therefore, the markets.

That being the case, it is important to determine who, demographically, is the market for the brand under consideration. If the Situation Analysis as described in the previous chapter was done carefully, the demographic classifications of purchasers for a product class will be delineated. But, there may be demographic variations within a product class for each brand on the market. So it is the responsibility of market planners to learn which segments of the market are most responsive to his brand. Once this has been done, then it is simply a matter of finding media which best reaches these segments of the market. These segments, then, are called "media targets" because they are the individuals who may pay most attention to advertising and who are most likely to buy the product. The process of finding media to reach these targets is called "matching markets with media," and will be discussed in detail at the beginning of the next chapter.

Selecting Geographical Markets

The practice of matching media with markets is primarily a function of the media planner; but the marketing strategy planner is often called upon to make decisions about which geographic markets ought to be used in the media plan. Obviously, most advertising budgets are not large enough for a planner to select media that reaches everyone in the United States, so the problem arises: In which individual markets should advertising appear? The planner may, through the process of analyzing sales potential in each market, compose a list of markets ranked from the best to the poorest. The list then may be reviewed by a media planner for use in ascertaining which media reaches key geographic areas.

There are some guidelines that planners use in selecting markets. Foremost would be to select and advertise heaviest in those markets where sales have been good.[21] The question arises: "Have these markets been exploited fully through advertising to maximize their potential?" In other words, why sell and advertise in new markets until those markets which have already shown themselves to be productive have been fully exploited? Brown, Lessler and Weilbacher noted: "It is always good sense to "fish where the fish are."[22] So, the best markets in terms of past sales should be selected first and additional money invested there before any other areas are selected.

The markets in which competitors have been selling best should be those considered next. Here the risk of failure becomes a little greater. Obviously competitors have been able to establish their own brands as the leading sellers in such markets. For a new brand to succeed by stealing customers from competitors may be rather presumptuous. Of course, there are times when a new brand is superior to competitors' and the superiorities can be easily demonstrated through advertising. Then competitors' markets might be considered more quickly. At times a weaker brand will have to advertise much more often in competitive markets in order to be visible and to make some dent in competitors' sales.

Finally, the greatest risk is to select new markets where neither a brand nor competitive brands have been exploited through advertising. These markets may have great sales potential, but may also be difficult in which to sell a given product. It also might be assumed that if these markets really had great potential, the competitors would have known about it too, and would have made efforts to exploit it. In any cases, these markets constitute considerable risk.[23]

Aside from these three basic guides for market selection, there are other factors which should be taken into consideration. One of the foremost, concerns selecting at least one or perhaps more markets in each of the client's sales territories. Almost all nationally-distributed product companies divide the country into sales territories, and these in turn may be sub-divided into smaller groups. The names of such territories varies somewhat from company to company. Some use the terms "divisions and districts," others use "regions and divisions" or other designations. No matter what they are called, it may be necessary to include at least one market in each of these divisions, depending on

[21]Brown, Lyndon O.; Lessler, Richard S.; and Weilbacher, William M., *Advertising Media*, The Ronald Press, N.Y. 1957, p. 323
[22]*Brown, et al*, p. 323
[23]*Brown, et al*, p.324

the needs of the company. The weights (or quantity of advertising used) in these areas may vary a great deal, however, so that the better markets will receive more dollars of advertising than will the poorer markets.

Other than the preceding, there are still other ways of selecting markets in which to place advertising:

Selecting markets on the basis of total sales volume for a brand.   Using the guidelines discussed previously, it is possible to select markets on the basis of how many dollars (or units) that each market generates in sales. In such a case, the markets are ranked from the largest volume markets to the smallest. The problem with using this method is that often a manufacturer does not know precisely how many dollars or units have been sold in all markets because his records only show sales to distributors. However, local market sales data may be purchased from the large research services, such as Nielsen. The total sales of all major competitors in each market comprises the basis for selection. Largest potential markets may be considered the best.

Selecting markets on the basis of share of markets.   This technique may be better than the preceding one because it is based on the relative strength of sales in each market. In such a case, the manufacturer arbitrarily may decide to use only markets in which his proportion of sales is above a given percentage. Where his brand is the leader such markets would automatically be on the list. This technique, like the preceding one, however, requires share-of-market information, which must be purchased from the research service companies.

Selecting markets on the basis of population, income, or retail sales potential.   Often a manufacturer cannot afford to buy sales data, and must rely on some other means of evaluating markets. In such a case he could obtain from such books as *Sales Management Survey of Buying Power,* or S.R.D.S., the population, income and retail sales of broad product classes in areas by which he can select markets.

Selecting markets on the basis of shipments to distributors in markets.   There are times where a manufacturer ships his products to a different distributor in each market, so that he can study his records to learn which markets received the largest dollar volume or number of units in shipments. From this data he can rank his markets from best to poorest. At times, however, this method doesn't work very well because the distributor may also sell to retailers in other markets and trans-ship to those markets. In such a case, the manufacturer's records may not show where the product is being shipped.

Some other methods of selecting markets may be on the basis of: (1) heavy users versus light users of a product. In such a case, special research data is necessary to inform the planner which markets have a large number of heavy users of the brand. (2) Special demographic segments such as large numbers of college educated families or very high upper-income families may constitute the basis on which markets are selected. (3) Profit per market. The more sophisticated advertisers who know just how profitable it is to sell in every market can prepare a list ranking each market.

Determining Cut-Off Points on Market Lists

In selecting markets for advertising, it is often difficult to know which markets should be eliminated at the bottom of the list. The place at which a decision is made to divide the list into those markets which are selected from those rejected is called the cut-off point.

One way to establish cut-off points is to select markets on the basis of some arbitrary number, usually in multiples of 10, 25 or 50. This is a widespread practice in industry, and it may be used only as a starting point for selecting markets, or it may actually be the prescribed length of a list. So whichever market appears as number 51 on down, may be eliminated. Most media planners agree that there isn't much difference between the 50th market on the selected list from the 51st market on the rejected list.

A more logical way to cut-off would be to determine how much weight in terms of dollars should be assigned to the best markets. Once these dollars have been allocated to the best markets, then all remaining money is distributed to the poorest markets based on a weighting system. Usually such a weighting system is composed of a minimum amount of money, below which it is not felt worthwhile to advertise. In using weighting systems, markets may be divided into three or more groups titled "A," "B," and "C." "A" markets might receive a given number of dollars of advertising; "B" markets receive somewhat less, and "C" markets receive much less.

At times a system of gross-rating points are used to determine how much money will be spent in a market. (See Chapter 5 for a further explanation.) The money is allocated from the top of the list down, until it runs out, which establishes the cut-off point.

In many cases, media planners and client representatives have, through experience, developed a minimum number of markets which *must* be on any list. Additional markets may be added if there is enough money left after allocating money to the basic list.

One of the problems in establishing cut-off points is that many times, a small number of markets account for a very large percentage of sales. For example, 25 markets might account for 75% of a brand's sales. But the next 25 largest markets only account for 8% additional sales; so, by adding the next 25 (or a total of 50 markets), only 83% of sales have been accounted for. Should the planner limit himself to the next 25 more and dissipate his budget? Usually, media planners prefer to have fewer markets, but have enough money to fully exploit the markets that have been selected.

Often too, there are marketing objectives which affect the length of a list. For example, if an objective is "to protect the brand's share of market from inroads of competitors," then more money may have to be added wherever competitors are trying to sell against the brand. Usually these are a brand's best markets, so that the list may have to be reduced somewhat in order to allocate extra money at the top of the list.

The whole process of selecting markets and determining cut-off points is not only the responsibility of the media planner, but may be shared by the account executive and a representative of the client. In such cases, decisions are made by compromise as well as by logic. One media planner explained:

"This give and take process between the account executive, the client and myself is often logical, but sometimes ludicrous. For example, I'll have both Rochester and Albany on my market list. The account man may take Albany off but leave Rochester in. But the client puts Albany back in and removes Rochester. Why? Well it could be that we can't afford both, or the client feels that he has to back a stronger sales force at Albany. But the whole process of selecting markets is an 'editing' operation, in which we each edit the others recommendations until a market list takes shape."

In summary then, market lists and cut-off points are established on the basis of subjective factors as well as objective criteria. The most important criteria are sales and money necessary to do a good job in each market. Experience, compromise and some arbitrary factors also influence the process at various times.

Dealers and Distribution

A major factor in media decision-making is distribution to dealers. It makes sense, then, to limit advertising to areas where the product is distributed. To do otherwise is to waste effort and money. There are, of course, exceptions, such as times when a manufacturer will advertise in areas where his product is not distributed in an effort to "force" distribution on the dealers in that area. It may be that dealers refuse to handle a new brand because they already have too many of a product class on their shelves. In fact, some grocery chains even refuse to handle a new brand unless the manufacturer removes an existing brand from his shelves. This is called a "one-for-one" policy. But by advertising in an area where his product is not yet distributed, the manufacturer hopes that the advertising will create such a terrific demand for the product that the grocery companies will be forced to carry the brand.

In most product categories, however, advertising is limited to areas where the product is distributed, and even then to only the most productive markets in terms of sales.

It is important then to note that dealers are sources of business, and important ones at that. The ability to select media which best communicates with dealers represents another aspect of the planners' operations. The most frequent method involves using the trade press, but there are other ways such as through direct mail or trade shows and conventions.

In some cases, the major problem in selling a product is not advertising to consumers, but to dealers instead. Such a case was discussed by T. Norman Tveter as follows:

"The problem was to sell a top-quality model train to fathers through boy salesmen, or the sons of those fathers. A sales analysis by the media director, based on sales for the two previous years, was the basis for planning advertising and promotion. Only then did strong points as well as weak show up concerning such factors as availability and rate of sales.

"Using a state-by-state breakdown of two boy age groups . . . as measures of potential, the analysis shows that sales were radically out of line with market potential. Also a breakdown in dollars of shipments to various outlets—such as department stores, specialty chains and premium distributors—showed that 50 cities accounted for 78% of the shipments. Seventeen better-producing cities alone, accounted for 62% of the shipments, and the two best producing areas: 28% to 30%. This left about 135 metropolitan areas accounting for approximately 22% of the shipments, simply because there were not enough dealers handling the product.

"From this it was concluded that more effective use of media to develop dealers' business was needed. Fewer publications with larger, dramatic advertising to impress dealers were indicated. There were more than 100 metro areas where just one act of getting the right dealer with the proper cooperation, could swing all negative factors to positive and score many hundreds of thousands of dollars in new retail sales. In other words, an impressive, primary dealer merchandising campaign in general media was indicated to take precedence over smaller-copy, more frequency, straight-consumer type of sell."[24]

The preceding case illustrates the importance of dealers in the scheme of getting products sold, and also indicates how media plays a role in communicating to dealers.

Dealers also affect media decisions because of their importance in selling at the local level. They are at the firing-line and often know which medium is best in their market. At times they communicate with the agency indirectly through distributors, or wholesalers or salesmen. Their influence may be very important for their own markets. Furthermore, they often dislike media choices of agency planners, feeling that the media planner, being distant from the scene of action could not possibly know which local or national medium was best.

In any case, the media planner must pay a great deal of attention to both dealers and importance of distribution in his planning. Often his decisions may affect the success of a marketing strategy plan by giving major consideration to these areas when they have been judged significant.

Competitive Sources of Business

There is no question that an advertiser has to consider the kind of media and the way media is used by competition in making marketing/media plans. Sometimes the problem is that competition varies so that the planner may have to deal with national, regional and local competitors as well. His first job is to know just who they are and, secondly, to what extent they affect his sales. When he buys

---

[24]Tveter, T. Norman, "What the Media Expert Gains from Studying Markets," *Mediascope,* May, 1964, p.96, p.100

Nielsen or MRCA market date, there is little problem in finding such information. But there is quite a problem of finding who competitors are when these research services are not purchased. At times this information may be obtained from competitive media expenditure analysis, but locally produced and sold products may not be identified very well, especially if they do not do much advertising. Other sources of this information, however, may be local media salesmen, media representatives, local media research departments or the company's own salesmen.

In determining the effect of competitors' media plans and strategy to counter such effects, probably the key factor will be the share of the competitor's market compared with the advertiser's brand. The brands which are leaders or close behind, may pose a threat. As far as media planning is concerned, the question is: "Shall we use the same media competitors use, or make special efforts to use different media?" Why not advertise in the media which the leading competitors advertise? Or vice-versa? Another question deals with the weight which should be applied to advertising in a market in order to counter competitor's advertising effects?

The answer to these and other questions about competitors depends to a great extent on the marketing objectives, and an evaluation of what effect competitors may have in preventing the attainment of such objectives. Each case, then, may be different. Whether to use the same media competitors use may not be as important as answering the question of, "Which medium or media best reaches the kind of prospects who are likely to buy my brand?" In such a case, the media which best reaches "my" brand may happen to be identical with competitors. But the media planner, while considering competitors, is not likely to imitate them simply because they happen to have larger shares of markets than his brand has.

Planners too will try to assess weaknesses in competitors' media tactics. Perhaps they are not using a media properly, or they have dissipated their advertising money in too many media, or they are missing an important segment of the market. These errors represent "opportunities" in media selection and use, and should be exploited. So the question of competitor's effects on a brand is not a matter of copying their tactics, but assessing their strengths and weaknesses in the light of marketing objectives. Plans for attaining the objectives, then, are not led by competitors, but are made on the basis of "problem" as well as "opportunity" situations.

In essence then, the planner must at least know the following information about competitors before he makes his own plans:

    a. Which media are used? Which are most significant?
    b. How much is spent in each medium?
    c. In which markets are media concentrated?
    d. How much weight is placed in each market?
    e. Which issues, broadcasts, times, are used? In other words when do competitors use various media and how are they used?

When this information is obtained and analyzed, then the planner is ready to determine whether or not he needs to imitate competitors, or when he must be different. To ignore competitors is almost like saying that it is possible to fight the enemy without knowing where he is or how he is deployed.

Overall Sales Strategy

Each element of the marketing mix should be examined by the media planner to determine how it might affect media selection and use. Foremost, of course, is advertising. It is conceivable that advertising could play a minor role in attaining objectives. Perhaps sales promotion may be more important. Advertising, however, usually plays a significant role in the marketing strategy, and its role should be defined. The more specific these definitions are, the better the media planner can plan his strategy. Generally, advertising is assigned a communication task which must be accomplished before a product can be sold effectively. (See Russell Colley, *Defining Advertising Goals for Measured Advertising Results,* for details on setting advertising objectives.)

When pricing tactics are important in marketing strategy, special media effort may be needed either to announce the price or keep the news in front of the consumers. Special prices to dealers also may require special trade media selections and use.

Sales promotion too, commonly has special significance to media planners. Many promotions call for inserts in magazines or newspapers. Inserts take the form of coupons, booklets, samples of fabrics, tinfoils or even plastic phonograph records. All of these require careful planning by media decision-makers, especially in estimating cost and timing. Marketing or creative plans might require gate-folds, die-cuts, or special inks, all of which require additional media considerations. Furthermore, the media planner must often select media which announces and keeps a special promotion in front of consumers. Contests, special cents-off deals and premiums, may lose their impact if they are not noticed by consumers. In fact, the general media strategy is to buy media in such a way as to get the largest reach possible. Trying to build large reach, then, is a difficult but necessary task of the media planner.

In other sales promotion practices, it may be necessary to tie-in local store information with national advertising so that the audience in any given market knows where to buy a given advertised national brand. The names and addresses of such stores are listed at the end of commercials, or at the bottom of newspaper or magazine ads.

Other parts of the marketing mix such as personal selling, public relations or packaging are of less importance in media planning than the above named. But the planner should know as much about the whole marketing strategy as possible in order to maximize the effectiveness of his decisions.

Test Marketing

Whenever a marketing strategy plan calls for the use of test marketing there is likely to be media involvement. For example, a test marketing situation might be required in three markets for testing the following objectives (1) to gain a substantial share of each market's sales; (2) to determine whether the total market for the product can be expanded (3) to determine how many repeat purchases will be made for a brand (4) to accomplish the above objectives within a reasonable length of time at a reasonable profit. It is then that special media planning will be required.

With these objectives, a new brand may be introduced in each of the three markets under varying marketing conditions. In Market A, fifty percent of the households may be given a free sample premium. Market B, 100 percent of the households may be given a free sample while in Market C, a coupon could be used in local newspapers offering a free sample redeemable at their stores. In each case, local advertising may be required to call attention to the offers, but especially to the coupon offer. Then measurements of sales would be made and compared market-by-market to see which performed best.

Another example of media planning being affected by test marketing would involve media weight varied in each of three test markets. Market A might receive 100 television GRP's a week, Market B, 150 a week and Market C, 200 a week. Sales would then be measured to see which weight affected volume the most.

Still another method of varying weights in test markets would be where each market received a specified advertising weight for a limited period of time and sales would be measured for that period. Then a "heavy-up" weighting might be applied to each market equally or in different proportions. In some cases, heavy-up weighting might simply be a doubling of expenditures in each market, and then measuring sales for a given time period. (For more details on Test Marketing, read Chapter 14.)

So test marketing strategy usually affects media planning in some ways whether in simple dissemination of advertising or in special testing situations within all or portions of the test markets.

In summary then, the market strategy plan will affect the media planner's operation in many ways. The media plan itself will grow out of a marketing plan. It is inconceivable for the media planner to operate without first having some kind of marketing strategy as a basis on which to select and use media. The ideal situation occurs when the marketing strategy plan is written and available for all personnel who work on a product or brand within the agency. The plan then serves as a unifying force and directs action toward a common goal.

QUESTIONS

1. What is the role of a marketing strategy plan in media planning?
2. Give some examples of marketing objectives and some marketing strategies that could be used to attain each objective.
3. What is the difference between a marketing objective and "the basic selling idea" in a marketing strategy plan?
4. Why may it be advisable to place more dollars in markets where a brand has been selling well, rather than in a new or undeveloped market that has good sales potential?
5. Why can't a manufacturer of cereals look at his sales records and know how well his brand is selling at any local (retail) level?
6. Why may it not be a good idea for a national advertiser to select local markets in which to advertise only on the basis of shipments?
7. Suppose that a planner intends to advertise in only the top 60 markets. How much difference should there be between the 60th and the 61st market on his list?
8. How can an advertiser "force" distribution sometimes in a market where his brand is not distributed?
9. In what ways does a sales promotion plan affect media planning?
10. Suppose that a planner feels that television is best for a given brand, but the creative people insist that an ad appear only in four colors in print. Whose judgment will probably be most significant?

SELECTED READINGS

Advertising Age, "Know Market Goals, Then Pick Media, AMC Exec Says," May 8, 1972, p. 32

Advertising Age, "Bolte Tells of 12 Criteria to Check Marketing Approach," May 16, 1966, p. 98

Blair, William, "Does Profile Matching Work?" in *Media/scope,* Sept., 1965, pp. 82-86

Bogart, Leo, "Relating Media Strategy to Sales," in *Sales Management,* Nov. 1, 1971, pp. 26+

Bruno, A. V. et al, "Media Approaches to Segmentation," in *Journal of Advertising Research,* April, 1973, pp. 35-42.

Chait, Lawrence, *"Targeted Marketing,"* Lawrence G. Chait & Co., Inc., 1965

Colley, Russell H. *Defining Advertising Goals for Measured Advertising Results,* Assn. of National Advertisers, Inc. 1961

Garfinkel, Norton, *"New Measurements of the Value of Marketing Targets and Media Vehicles,"* Speech delivered to the Advertising Research Foundation 12th Annual Conference, 1966.

Greene, Jerome D., "Media Exposure As A Demographic," in *Media/scope,* Nov., 1966, pp. 116-118

Grey Matter, "Media Market Planning," Speech given by Edward H. Meyers, reported in *Grey Matter,* Vol. 41, May, 1970, Grey Advertising Agency

Honomichl, Jack J., "How Research Relates to the Marketing Process," in *The New World of Advertising,* Nov. 21, 1973, pp. 52+

Joyce, Timothy, "Target Weighting Gives Boost to Consumer Studies," in *Advertising Age,* July 15, 1974, pp. 27+

Lodish, L. M. "Considering Competition in Media Planning," in *Management Science,* Feb., 1971, pp. 293-306

Media/scope, "How Media Strategy is Developed in the Marketing Concept," *Media/scope,* May, 1960, pp. 45-48

Ostrow, Joseph, "Let's Become Objective," in *Media Decisions,* May, 1972, p. 64

Peckham, James O., "Can We Relate Advertising Dollars to Market Share Objectives?" in *Advertising Research Foundation 12th Annual Conference Proceedings,* 1966, pp. 53-57

Setar, John W., "How to Solve the Problem of Problem Markets," in *Television Magazine,* Sept. 1959, pp. 56+

Sissors, Jack Z., "Matching Media With Markets," in *Journal of Advertising Research,* Oct., 1971, pp. 39-43

Wolfe, Harry D., "The Dimensions of Media Audiences," in *Evaluating Media,* National Industrial Conference Board, Business Policy Study No. 121, 1966, pp. 31-41

chapter 5

Basic media Planning Concepts, Measurements and Terminology

Media planning involves the use of large quantities of research data. In fact, the amount of data seems to be growing at a faster rate than it can be used. Part of this may be due to the lack of time available to completely understand the new data, and part to the fact that too much is produced through the use of computers. In a sense, the media planner is drowning in a sea of data. There are so many numbers available to the planner, and they may be used in so many different ways, that a problem exists of how to make best use of them in decision-making.

The solution, however, does not involve better or quicker techniques of decision-making but understanding better the concepts of media planning and how data may be used to implement the concepts. A concept is an idea. It is often the ideas involved in planning which are little understood, making the data confusing to the user. When, however, the underlying concepts are understood, the need for certain kinds of data becomes apparent immediately. Not only should the planner then understand the concept, but the measurement devices which provide the data too.

Along with concepts and measurement methodology should come an understanding of the terminology of media. The terms used in media planning and research can be confusing. The meanings of certain terms like coverage and reach are changing, and if the changes are not understood it will be difficult to implement the concepts with data. The following discussion, therefore, concerns all three essentials which should be understood before starting to plan.

Matching Markets with Media

After the market has been identified demographically, it is the job of a planner to match markets with media. The matching process is both a concept and an activity. The concept is that once the planner knows which demographic classifications best represent the market, he can search media audience data to find which media best reaches the market. The process of matching involves making comparisons between the audience sizes of alternative media to see which has the largest number of prospects. Prospects may be found through an analysis of media audience composition.

When one uses this concept he makes a number of assumptions about the data. These assumptions ought to be reevaluated from time to time to determine whether or not they still hold because the validity of the concept depends on them. One assumption is that the research is based on bonafide controls so that the findings are both reliable and valid. If market research is poorly done while media audience research is carefully done, the matching process is subject to question. Another assumption is that the samples of both markets and media are representative of the consumer and media universes. At present, only W. R. Simmons and Target Group Index provide marketing and media data from the same research sample, each using its own sample. Still another assumption is that most measuring instruments of consumers and audiences are valid. Occasionally there have been questions raised about one or another measuring instrument, but the better ones usually have a long life, because they are reliable and valid.

Assuming that both kinds of research are valid, the matching process involves search of media alternatives first. Table 15 shows a comparison of five magazines which might be considered for Brand X, a product used by men only:

Table 15
Matching Alternative Media Choices with Prospects for Brand X*

Classification showing highest consumption	Newsweek	Time	U.S. News and World Report	Sports Illus- trated	Playboy
			Audience Sizes (000's omitted)		
Men 18-24 ages	3,449	4,631	1,432	3,284	6,983
Graduated college	3,368	5,190	2,869	2,634	3,744
A counties	6,227	10,238	3,581	5,291	9,575
$15,000+ income	5,657	8,187	3,766	4,332	7,373

*Source: *Selective Audience Guide for Magazine Planning,* (1972 Updated Simmons) *Saturday Review,* 1972, pp. 4, 14, 19, 28.

Which medium is best according to the matching process? A first answer is: the one with the largest audience of prospects. Later analysis may confirm or nullify this conclusion because audience sizes are not the only consideration. Relative cost is a factor too. But the first step in making a selection decision will probably center on the matching process.

The Concept of Audience Measurements

One of the difficulties in matching markets with media is that there is no single measurement that can be used for determining the audience sizes for all media. Therefore, it is difficult to make intermedia comparisons (such as comparisons between the audience size of a television program and a magazine). The reason is that audience size numbers do not mean the same thing because they are measured on different bases.

Actual or potential audience size measurements. Those who use media audience research should be careful not to confuse data that shows the actual size of a vehicle's audience with other data that looks similar, but only shows potential audience size. The division of audience measurement data into classifications of actual vs. potential (or vehicle distribution vs. vehicle exposure) occurred because measuring techniques have changed. Before statistical sampling was widely accepted, media owners simply used distribution counts of their vehicles as evidence of audience size. Newspaper circulation is one of the older measurements that is still being used. But it only represents audience size potential because one unit of circulation indicates nothing about the number of readers of that unit. After sampling measurements were accepted, some media, like newspapers, retained potential audience size measurements, while others, magazines began to be measured on the basis of both potential and actual audience size measurements. However, all measurements are only estimates, not complete counts.

Planners, therefore, should understand the differences. Brown, Lessler and Weilbacher suggested three different classifications of audience measurements to help differentiate their meanings as follows: (a) gross potential audience, representing vehicle delivery; (b) net potential audience, representing a modification of gross potential audience by H.U.T.'s (households using television) or page traffic scores and (c) program or vehicle delivery representing actual vehicle audience size measurements.[25] The following table shows various media measurements and where they fall within the three classifications.

Table 16
Classification of Media Audience Measurements

Measurement	Vehicle gross potential audience*	Vehicle net potential audience*	Vehicle exposure (actual) audience size*
Newspaper or magazine circulation	√		
Newspaper or magazine page traffic		√	
Newspaper or magazine readership			√
Radio-TV station coverage	√		
Network program coverage	√		
Homes-using-television (H.U.T.)		√	
Outdoor coverage			√
Radio-TV Ratings			√
Audience accumulation measurements			√
Heavy-user measurements			√

*Estimated

[25]Brown, Lyndon O.; Lessler, Richard S.; and Weilbacher, William M.; *Advertising Media,* The Ronald Press, N.Y., 1957, pp. 84, 100, 104

The Concept of Audience Accumulation

There is an important underlying principle for counting the number of persons in a medium's audience, called "audience accumulation," which means that each audience member of a vehicle will be counted only once, no matter how many other times he was exposed to the medium. If a reader looked into one issue of *Readers' Digest* five times during a week, or 20 times during a month, he would only be counted once for a given issue. If a television viewer tuned-in to show X each Sunday night during a month he would be only counted once. As a result, audience accumulation measures the number of different persons that have some contact with a medium. The so-called "contact" with a medium are *exposures* for print media, and *tune-ins* for broadcast media.

Magazine (or print) audience accumulation is represented by a measurement called the "total audience" which is the total number of readers who were exposed to the magazine. Time and place have no bearing on this measurement. In other words, the total audience does not specify when and where the magazine was seen. It may have been in the home where someone paid for a subscription, or it may have been in a doctor's office, a beauty shop, or in a friend's home. Other measurements, however, are concerned with place of exposure, such as in-home or out-of-home.

The following table shows the total audience of adult readers for three magazines:

Table 17
Total Audience of Adult Readers for Three Magazines*

	Time	Playboy	National Geographic
Total adults	20,354,000	20,470,000	16,634,000

*Source: 1972 Updated Simmons Audience Data, *Saturday Review*, p. 3

Data for the total audience of a magazine is broken down by demographic classifications so that media planners can find the number of prospects within the audience size. Comparisons between magazines should not be made on the total audience basis, but on the audience size of demographic segments which match market demographics for a brand.

Table 18 shows the total audience of adult readers broken down by selected demographic classifications for three magazines.

In broadcast media measurements, audience accumulation is quite different from that of print media. Time *is* considered in the measurements. In other words, it is possible to measure the number of households that tuned-in to a program at least once over a four week period. The four-week period is an arbitrary time consideration. Audience accumulation could be measured for shorter or longer periods. But four weeks is a standard bookkeeping and business-planning period that is suitable for comparative purposes. Such a

Table 18
Some Demographic Breakdowns of Total Audiences*
(000's omitted)

	Time	Playboy	National Geographic
Adults 18-34	9,112	13,620	5,978
Adults 35-49	6,090	4,551	5,222
Adults 50-64	3,797	1,900	3,580
Graduated College	5,190	3,744	4,671
Attended/Graduated College	10,164	8,920	8,582
High School Graduate or better	17,000	16,554	14,322

*Source: Updated Simmons Audience Data, *Saturday Review,* pp. 6, 7, 8, 14, 15, 16, 1972

measurement is called the "reach" of a program, although it is sometimes called a "cume" or "cumulative audience." Reach is reported by measurement services for a four-week period. It may either be expressed as a percent of all television homes or as a number of homes that tuned-in for the four-week period. Shown in Table 19 are the four-week reaches of a number of television programs.

Table 19
Reaches of Selected Television Programs*

Program	Percent of TV homes reached in four weeks	Number of different homes reached four weeks
Mary Tyler Moore	51.9%	31,190,000
ABC Movie of the Week	57.1	34,320,000
Let's Make A Deal	34.7	20,850,000
Wonderful World of Disney	59.9	36,000,000

*Source: Nielsen Television Index, Program Cumulative Audiences Report, Jan. 25-Feb. 21, 1971, pp. 7-8.

Each of the above programs were broadcast once each week, and the fact that the four-week reach was higher than the average one-week reach is due to different homes tuning in during each of four weeks.

The Coverage Concept

Coverage is an audience measurement term that has a number of different meanings, depending on which medium it is applied to. Ideally, coverage should mean *the degree to which a medium reaches a market*. Therefore, coverage would be expressed as a percentage of the market exposed to a medium. An analogy might help clarify it, by thinking of the top of a water glass as the universe of a market, and a person's hand as a medium. When a person's hand is placed over the top of the glass, then it covers the universe 100 percent. If the glass (or market) is larger than a hand, then the hand may represent a percentage of the market covered.

In magazines, coverage is used in an ideal manner. If there are 12 million households in the United States that own a cat and magazine "A" reaches six million of them, then magazine A's coverage is fifty percent. This fifty percent represents actual exposure to the medium.

But in newspapers and television, coverage only represents potential degree of reach, not actual reach.

Since coverage can mean a number of different things, it is important for the user of this term to know and understand its alternative meanings. The following is a discussion of how coverage is defined in specific media.

Newspaper coverage. Most newspapers measure the number of copies sold or distributed and call this "circulation." Newspaper coverage represents the number of copies of circulation compared to the number of households in the trading community. Under this plan of terminology, coverage represents *potential* rather than actual exposure since everyone who receives a copy of a newspaper does not necessarily read it.

If the circulation of a newspaper is 500,000 and the number of households in the trading area is 2,000,000, then the coverage is 25 percent. The assumption is made that each unit of circulation equals one household covered. No exposure to the medium is necessarily assumed. So coverage based on circulation is a very rough comparison of newspaper audience size related to the size of the market reflected by the total number of households in that area.

When using newspaper coverage in planning media, it is sometimes felt that a minimum coverage level in any individual market should be no less than 50 percent. If it can be assumed that not all persons in all households will be exposed to any given edition of a newspaper, then 50 percent is the lowest limit that seems practical. Perhaps only two-thirds of that 50 percent will be exposed. Some media planners often set much higher limits on local market coverage such as no less than 70 percent. In such cases, it may take two or even three newspapers in that community to attain a 70 percent unduplicated coverage.

In planning newspaper coverage, the final selection of a newspaper in a market is that of the buyer. The planner's responsibility is to state the coverage level that he thinks necessary to accomplish an objective. Once the coverage level is set, the buyer will attempt to implement the plan inasmuch as it is possible, for the money available.

Coverage in newspaper planning, therefore, is not the same as it is in magazines and in other media. The limiting factor is the kind of research that is available. When a newspaper has research of its total audience size and provides a breakdown of that audience by demographic segments, then coverage will mean something different. It will then mean the number of individuals exposed to newspapers compared to the total number of *individuals* (rather than house-holds) in the market. In fact, it will mean the same as coverage for magazines. Since such measurements are not always available on a regular basis, newspaper coverage usually means potential exposure.

Magazine Coverage. An example of magazine market coverage is shown in Table 20.

Table 20
Market Coverage of Paper Napkin Users of Selected Magazines*
(For adult female heads)
(000's omitted)

Used Paper Napkins Within Last Month	No.	Percent
Total Users	42,339	100%
Family Circle	9,255	21.9
Ladies Home Journal	9,386	22.2
McCall's	9,953	23.5

*Source: Selective Markets and The Media Reaching Them, *1973 Marketing Report, W. R. Simmons & Associates Research Inc., p. A04*

In Table 20, the market was defined as all female household heads who had used paper napkins within the last month, or 42,339,000 women. Each magazine may have a proportion of that market, representing its market coverage. If a market is defined demographically, then coverage of a magazine represents a proportion of a demographic segment base.

Another way to look at magazine market coverage is based on total users of a given product class. If, for example, one of the syndicated research companies reported that 42,339,000 female household heads used paper napkins within the last month, then that figure would represent the size of the total market. If 9,953,000 readers of *McCall's* used paper napkins within the last month, then that number would represent 23.5% market coverage. (9,953,000 ÷ 42,339,000 = 23.5%).

Local television and radio coverage. Coverage in spot radio and television means the number of homes within the signal area of a given station that can tune-in to that station because they can pick-up the station's signal. The term "can" refers to persons in homes with television sets who are able to tune in to a station because their home is in the signal area. Whether or not they choose to tune in depends on a number of factors such as: (a) whether the programming of the station is interesting enough to attract them (b) the power of the station. More powerful stations can cover more homes than weaker stations. Also the height of a station's antenna and the height of the home's antenna affect reception of signals. Another consideration for television reception is the number and nature of obstructions which prevent the signal from being received. Such obstructions could be bridges, tall buildings or mountains.

Television stations produce an engineering contour map based on its signal strength in a market. Such maps indicate how wide an area the station's signal covers. The strongest signal is designated "Grade A" (or one which covers the primary market area surrounding the station). The next strongest signal is "Grade B" (or secondary area coverage). These measurements, however, are not as useful in determining coverage as those which estimate the number of homes covered regardless of whether they are in either Grade A or B areas. It has been shown through research that some homes outside of the A or B areas can and do watch certain stations.

In order to find the coverage of a station, therefore, research companies send out mail questionnaires to a carefully selected sample of homes located within and outside of the A and B signal areas. These questionnaires ask respondents to list the stations they view regularly. From the returns, estimates are made of how many homes in each county are covered by a television station's signal. Such measurements, then, are the starting place for determining the maximum potential audience to a given television station. The criterion for being included in a station's coverage statistics are that the home must be able to receive the signal.

Spot radio or television coverage in multiple markets. When an advertiser buys spot announcements in a number of markets located in various geographical regions of the United States, he may be interested in knowing what percent of all television (or radio) homes in the United States he is going to reach. Perhaps he has selected 50 of the largest markets in the country. In order to determine this percent coverage, it is only necessary to learn the percent coverage of each station in a plan and add the figures to find the percent coverage of the entire plan. For example, it has been shown that by buying spot announcements in the top 50 markets, planners can potentially reach 70% of the television homes in the country. He knows then that the maximum audience size (expressed in terms of homes which can tune in to a station's signal) is no larger than 70%. Since not everyone in those 50 markets will hear his commercials, the exposure to his commercials will be lower than 70%. Shown below is a list of percent coverages of the largest markets.

Table 21
Percent Coverage of Top U.S. Markets by Using Spot TV*

	Percent coverage
Top 10 markets	34%
Top 20 "	45
Top 30 "	55
Top 40 "	62
Top 50 "	68
Top 75 "	79
Top 100 "	86
Top 150 "	98
Top 209 "	100

*Source: *N.W. Ayer Media Fact Book,* 1974, p. 5 (Arbitron)

In network television, coverage is defined as the number and percent of all U.S. television households that are able to receive a given program. The degree of coverage is affected by the number of stations in a network lineup. The more stations, the more coverage.

Television and radio circulation. The term *circulation* is sometimes used to mean the same thing as coverage; but it has a different meaning. Circulation means the number of radio or television households who *can* and *do* tune-in to a station a minimum number of times. These times may be once a month, once a week, or once during a given daypart. Therefore, circulation is used to describe the potential audience size of a network or a station over a period of time. The reason that circulation is a potential audience measurement is that the minimum tune-in required to be counted is generally for a broad time period, rather than a specific day and time such as for a given program. One other way of thinking about circulation is that it is a special kind of coverage.

In practice, there seems to be little difference. It is important, then, to remember that both coverage and circulation are measurements of the gross potential audience. The term "gross" refers to a crude estimate, and "potential" means that the numbers deal with opportunities rather than actual audience tune ins to a program. Opportunities for tune-in vary by time of day.

Outdoor coverage. The coverage of billboards is based on the traffic that has developed, either by automobiles or by persons passing a given numbered showing. A number 100 showing theoretically is a certain number of billboards, which, in a 30 day period, is passed by 100 percent of the mobile population. A numbered showing does not deliver precisely 100 percent, but somewhere in the 90 percent to 100 percent range. A number 50 showing, theoretically, should deliver 50 percent of the mobile population.

Practically, however, coverage in outdoor means the same as reach because it includes exposure to the medium. Coverage is the number and percent of people in cars who pass, and are exposed to, a given showing of billboards in a 30 day period.

To show how effective outdoor advertising is in reaching various audiences, the following table is shown with data from the Simmons report:

Table 22
Average Coverage (Reach) for a 100 and 50 Outdoor Showing*

	100 Showing		50 Showing	
	Reach	Frequency	Reach	Frequency
Total adults	89%	31	87%	16
Adult males	90	34	90	17
Adult females	88	28	85	14

*Source: *N. W. Ayer, 1974 Media Fact*, p. 20 (Simmons)

Circulation is another term used in outdoor media planning. It means the total number of people who pass the poster panels in a given showing during a specified time period (12 hours for a daylight showing and 18 hours for illuminated panels). Circulation represents the gross potential audience of the medium and does not assume exposure.

Different Meanings of the Term "Coverage"

Kind of Coverage	Meaning	Uses
General Concept (more accurately called "Market Coverage")	The number of prospects delivered by a given medium. Coverage expressed as a percent of the universe of prospects.	Serves as a goal in planning. Used to determine whether media selected are delivering enough prospects.
Newspaper Coverage	The number of circulation units as a percent of the number of households in an area	For local markets. A goal to determine whether enough households are reached with one or more newspapers. This represents *potential* audience size
Magazine Coverage (Sometimes called reach)	Same as the general concept. Prospects are demographically defined.	Same as the general concept. This represents estimated *actual* audience size.
Spot TV and Radio Coverage (local market)	The number of TV (or radio) homes within the signal area of station that can tune in to that station	Serves as a basis for potential delivery in planning. Indicates the maximum size of the *potential* audience of radio or TV homes
Spot TV Coverage for a national campaign (also for spot radio)	Total number of TV homes in all markets that are part of a campaign, that can tune in (or be reached)	It can show how much of the country's TV homes may be *potentially* delivered by a spot plan. Maximum number and percent of potential exposure
Network TV Coverage	The number and percent of all stations in a network carrying a given program compared to total TV homes in U.S.	An indication of the maximum *potential* of TV homes that a TV program can reach
Outdoor Advertising and Transit Coverage	The number of people in cars who pass, and are exposed to a given showing of billboards in a local market, expressed as a percent of the total of all people in the market.	To determine the size of an audience that actually does look at each showing of billboards.

The gross rating point concept. In planning for the use of spot television it was found to be difficult to describe the total number of ratings that various commercials would be expected to produce. For example, if a planner wanted to buy two commercials, each with a 10 rating, and four commercials, each with an eight rating, it would be awkward to describe his decision in words. But if the ratings were multiplied by the number of insertions and added together, then it would be very convenient to say he was planning for 52 gross rating points. Here is an example:

Per week

2 commercials, each with a 10 rating = 20 gross rating points
+
4 commercials, each with an 8 rating = 32 gross rating points

TOTAL = 52 gross rating points

While gross rating points in television are usually discussed as part of a weekly package, they can be used to describe a monthly package of commercials as well.

One hundred gross rating points then is not the same as 100 percent of an audience reached, because it includes duplication. The term "gross" refers to duplication, so 100 gross rating points is the equivalent of 100 duplicated rated points.

Planners have used gross rating points in television for many years. In recent years they have expanded the concept to other media such as magazines, newspapers and outdoor.

In magazines, for example, gross rating points would equal the percent of market coverage of a target audience times the number of insertions of ads that are required. An example would be as follows:

McCall's target reach of paper napkin users	=	23.5%
Number of ads to be placed in *McCall's*	=	× 5
Gross rating points		117.5 or 118 GRPs

Another way of using gross rating points for magazines (or newspapers) is to add the target reaches for a number of magazines as shown below:

Target reach in *McCall's*	=	23.5%
Target reach in *Good Housekeeping*		20.6
Target reach in *Time magazine*		14.2
Target reach in *Woman's Day*		22.5
Gross rating points =		80.8 or 81 GRPs

In January, 1973, The Outdoor Advertising Association of America, Incorporated, adopted the basic unit of sales the term "100 gross rating points daily." The basic standardized unit of poster sales is the number of poster panels which is required in each market to produce a daily effective circulation equal to the population of the market. Other units of sale would be expressed as fractions of the basic unit: 75 gross rating points daily, 50 gross rating points daily and 25 gross rating points daily. This change in no way alters the 30-day period of sale.

Audience size related to cost efficiency. One of the principles of media planning stated earlier was that media should be selected on its ability to reach the largest audience of prospects at the lowest cost. Matching markets with media helps accomplish one part of this principle. The search for media with large audiences of prospects, rather than large total audiences is in recognition of the fact that media costs are too high to permit advertising to those individuals who are not likely to buy the product.

But the other portion of the principle is equally important. This requires that media be selected which reaches the largest number of prospects at the most efficient cost. Cost efficiency simply means that audience size must be related to media costs.

Rather than compute a single unit cost, the advertising industry prefers to compute a cost-per-thousand. These may be computed for a printed page, or broadcast time, and the audience base may either be circulation, homes reached, readers, or number of audience members of any kind of demographic classification.

Cost-per-thousands are a comparative device. They enable the planner to compare one medium with another to find those that are the most efficient. Its main use is for intramedia rather than intermedia comparisons.

Shown below are various formuli which may be used for making comparisons on the basis of cost-per-thousands (or abbreviated CPM):

a. *For print media (when audience data are not available)*

$$\text{CPM} = \frac{\text{Cost of 1 page (black and white*)} \times 1000}{\text{Circulation}}$$

Since many print media do not have audience research data for them, this formula is often used. But it tells nothing about the audience.

b. *For print media (when audience data is available)*

$$\text{CPM} = \frac{\text{Cost of 1 page (black and white)} \times 1000}{\text{Number of prospects reached}}$$

c. *For broadcast media (based on homes reached by a given program or time period)*

$$\text{CPM} = \frac{\text{Cost of 1 unit of time} \times 1000}{\text{Number of homes reached by a given program or time period}}$$

d. *For broadcast media (when audience data is available)*

$$\text{CPM} = \frac{\text{Cost of 1 unit of time} \times 1000}{\text{Number of prospects reached by a program or time period}}$$

e. *For newspapers only where circulation is the base, and the agate line rate is used: (Called the Milline Rate)*

$$\text{Milline rate} = \frac{\text{Cost of 1 agate line} \times 1 \text{ million}}{\text{Total circulation}}$$

The procedure for using any of the above formuli is to compare media on the basis of the two variables: audience and cost. The lowest cost-per-thousand medium is the most efficient, other things being equal. It is obvious that wherever precise demographic classifications of the audiences are available, that data should be used in the denominator of the formula. Generally, the medium (or media) with the lowest cost-per-thousands are selected; but not always. Whenever a very special kind of target audience is required, and there are few or no media which reach them exclusively, then the cost-per-thousand comparisons may be ignored. In the latter situation, media selections are based on the principle of reaching the largest number of targets, regardless of cost.

For example, there are times when individuals with very high incomes (over $50,000 annually) are target audiences. A few media reach a small proportion of these audiences, but even if many such media were used, the total number of persons reached might be relatively small. On the other hand, a very large number of these persons might be reached with mass media such as a network television program or a national magazine. It is obvious that either of these two media would also include a large amount of waste, so that when cost-per-thousands are computed, they will seem unduly high. Yet the waste and the high cost-per-thousands might have to be ignored in order to maximize the size of target audiences reached.

Mass produced and consumed products, such as cigarettes, cold cereals and automobiles, usually have target audiences for whom media are selected primarily on a cost-per-thousand basis. Specialized products such as yachts, private airplanes and classical phonograph records would have specialized target audiences which may require that less attention be paid to cost efficiencies and more to audience sizes.

Cost per rating point. A relatively new method of comparing the cost efficiency of media has grown in popularity along with the concept of gross rating points. It is called cost per rating points (CPRP) or sometimes, cost per gross rating point (CPGRP). The formula for calculating CPRP is as follows:

$$\text{Cost per rating points} = \frac{\text{Cost of a commercial}}{\text{Rating per cent}}$$

If the cost of a prime time spot commercial was $1000 and the rating for that spot was 10, then the CPGRP would be $100.

Essentially, a CPRP is a planning rather than a buying tool although it can be used for both. The concept was first used by media buying service salesmen, who would tell clients, they "could get a rating point for $20, whereas the agency was paying $30."[26] In other words, a CPRP is a short-cut way of talking about media cost efficiency with little advantages over the CPM other than convenience, perhaps.

How does a CPRP compare with a CPM for the same station and commercial? The following shows the differences:

---

[26]*Media Decisions*, "CPGRP or CPM?" Feb. 1973, p.90

CPRP	CPM
Cost of 30-second commercial: $110	Cost of 30-second commercial: $110
Metro rating, 2 p.m.: 8	No. H.H. delivered 2 p.m.: 77;000
$110 ÷ 8 = $13.75	$110 × 1000 ÷ 77,000 = $1.43

The two kinds of cost efficiencies are obviously different and cannot be compared. Is there any preference for either in planning?

The answer is that a CPRP may be useful in the planning stages, where they can be memorized and recalled easily for quick answers to general questions. Conceivably, a planner could be called upon to give an answer to the question: "About how much would it cost to buy x number of spots at prime time in this market?" Or another one, "How much would a prime-time network program cost, generally?" However, it is doubtful that it would have the same value in buying as in planning. In buying, it would be better to know the actual cost and a cost-per-thousand for a target audience; yet some media buyers do use CPRP in their work.

CPRPs may also be used in planning for other media such as magazines, radio or outdoor. But its best use seems to be for quick broadcast comparisons. Meanwhile CPMs will probably remain as the standard means of determining relative cost efficiencies.

Problems in Market-Media Matching

There are many problems related to the market-media matching process which were not obvious from the examination of preceding data. One has to do with determining how much waste is in a medium's audience. Waste represents media audiences who are non-prospects. The latter are not likely to buy the product or brand no matter how much advertising they see or hear. It is conceivable that the best media, according to the matching process and to relative cost comparisons, may also have large amounts of waste in them. Should this waste be accepted, or other media selected which has less waste? The answer is not simple.

In very selective markets, such as for airplanes, yachts, or even fine high-fidelity radios, it may be necessary to expect more waste exposure because it is so difficult to reach these markets. The consumers in these markets are distributed within the masses in such a way that they may be hard to reach. They may live in no single concentrated area, and no one medium reaches many of them. In less selective markets, waste may not be tolerated.

Another serious problem deals with the lack of precise data on prospects. Many small advertisers do not have a complete market profile on which to base market and media matching. Or they have some data, but not enough to furnish a completely adequate picture of prospects. On the other hand, there are times when some minor media do not have enough audience data to be used in the matching process. Furthermore, it is assumed that the data about markets as well as media audiences will be gathered in a scientific manner so that there are no biases introduced in the data which might affect its accuracy. Some pieces of market-media research are not valid, or are unacceptable for methodological reasons.

Still another problem deals with looking at media audiences in obvious ways which may be deceiving. Advertising a women's product, such as shampoo or hand lotion, might seem ideal in a woman's magazine. But careful examination of general magazines or nighttime television program audiences may show that either or both reach larger numbers of women than do the women's magazines. Of course, cost considerations may make the women's magazine a best buy if waste circulation is to be avoided. But at least the obvious solution is not always the best one until other factors in the selection process are taken into consideration.

Then there are other problems which deal with products that are not differentiated by demographic data. The case of upper-income persons who read *Harper's* and *Atlantic Monthly* magazines might be cited. A study was made of upper-income persons' buying habits for selective products such as bourbon or scotch, or for activities such as attending concerts, football games, or buying swimming pools. Through a demographic analysis of users, a market profile was constructed of likely purchasers of these products or users of these services. Then attempts were made to match magazine audiences with the market statistics. But it was found that the demographics did not account for the size of market to be found in *Harper's* or *Atlantic* audiences, so that a large proportion of such market was overlooked. William S. Blair, formerly President, Harper-Atlantic Sales characterized the situation as follows:

> . . . given the choice between demographic data and market data, you should always choose the market data. Selecting a medium on the basis of knowledge as to how its readers behave, what kinds of things they own, when they buy, and what they do with their spare time, is always more reliable a process than going through the elaborate round-about method of matching demographics. I should add two qualifications at this point: first, I am assuming the statistics that you have are reliable and meaningful; and secondly, I should add that these remarks apply particularly to the field of selective marketing areas in which the discretionary element is particularly high.[27]

Blair therefore recommended that media planners use market data showing which kinds of products his audience members own, rather than demographic data alone.

Or, there are possibilities that two or more media have almost the same kind of audience profiles. Which medium should be selected? If the relative costs are almost the same, there would have to be some other measurement that could distinguish one medium from the other.

---

[27]Blair, William S., "Does Profile Matching Work?" Visual presentation made by *Harpers-Atlantic* Magazine, Fall, 1964

The final problem of market-media matching is the failure to cross-tabulate all classifications of marketing and media data. The usual procedure is to evaluate each demographic classification separately, with the exception of age and sex (which most research companies provide in their reports). Income, occupation, education and family sizes of consumers and audiences are not usually cross-tabulated with age-sex classifications. For example, women whose ages range from 18 to 34 are tabulated separately from women whose ages range from 35 to 49. But what is needed are multiple cross-tabulations which report how many women 18 to 34, with a given income level, with a given educational level, within a given geographical area, are exposed to a medium or are part of a given market.

While such cross-tabulations are possible to make, they are not always made because it is too time-consuming to do it by hand. Now that market-media data is available on computer tapes it is possible to make a large number of cross-tabulations. But when data is compiled by hand, only the most simple kinds of tabulations are made. The hand-matching process based on only one cross-tabulation then, is not the best method of efficiently matching markets with media.

A final problem confronting those who do market-media matching is that of using data obtained from two independent sources, with the consequence that the technique may not be logical. If the demographics of the market obtained through sampling research are not precisely representative of the market, then they should not be matched with media audience demographics. Market data usually is obtained by sampling of the general population. Media audience data may be obtained the same way, but from a different sample. The two samples, however, may not come from the same universe, unless both were selected on a purely random basis. The assumption underlying the matching process is that the demographic classification of the market *is* obtained from the same universe as the demographic classification of a given medium's audience. While there may be similarities between the two universes, they usually are not identical. To be identical, every person in both universes should have an equal chance of being selected for each kind of research. But, for reasons of cost, time and effort, such random samples are not made. As a consequence, the matching process may not be entirely valid.

In recent years, media research companies such as W. R. Simmons and Target Group Index have obtained marketing and media data from the same sample of persons, which eliminates parts of the objection. However, even here, the sample is not selected on a purely random basis, and may not be representative of the entire universe.

Despite all of the preceding problems, the matching process is the most reasonable way known, at present, of locating the correct media alternatives. It is the responsibility of the media planner to keep in mind the limitations of this technique, and at the same time, make the best use of it. The end result of the process is a list of media alternatives which may reach the desired demographic segments of the market. Best media alternatives are compiled into a list, while poorer ones are disregarded.

QUESTIONS

1. In media planning, why would it be undesirable to make comparisons between alternative magazine total audiences rather than on some other bases? What is the most desirable basis for making comparisons?
2. An advertiser is considering the use of the top newspaper in a given market, but finds that it only has 40 percent household coverage. Why might he conclude that 40 percent is not enough?
3. A planner finds that a television program he is interested in using has a 98 percent coverage nationally. Can he assume that because the program has a large coverage it will also have a large audience? Briefly explain.
4. Why aren't magazines measured on the basis of a four-week reach as are television programs?
5. A planner intends to buy 100 gross rating points a week in a given market. Why doesn't a 100 gross rating points equal 100 percent reach in that market?
6. Although reach and frequency are inversely related, how is it possible for a planner to have both high reach and high frequency in his media plan?
7. Why should a planner use a different basis for computing CPMs when he intends to buy four-color ads in an advertising campaign?
8. If a planner is considering the use of a magazine that reaches 65 percent of a target market, and he intends to buy only one ad, how many gross ratings points is he planning for?
9. Why isn't newspaper circulation a measurement of its audience size?
10. What, precisely, is the meaning of this sentence? "We will have a 75 percent coverage in a spot television buy, if we buy the top 60 markets in the United States."

SELECTED READINGS

Broadcast Rating Council, *Maintaining Ratings Confidence and Credibility,* July, 1972

Bogart, Leo, "Isn't It Time to Discard the Audience Concept?" in *Journal of Marketing,* Jan., 1966, pp. 47-54

Ephron, Erwin, "Good Media Plans Grow Out of Great Research," in *Media Decisions,* Oct. 1970, pp. 40+

Ephron, Erwin, "Confused? Six Commonly Held Beliefs About Media Planning That Are Not So," in *Media Decisions,* Aug. 1972, pp. 48-102

Gerhold, Paul, "Seven Fallacies in Audience Measurements," in *Papers from the 1960 American Assn. of Advertising Agencies Region Conventions,* pp. 15-22

Greene, Jerome, "Personal Media Probabilities," in *Journal of Advertising Research,* Oct., 1970, pp. 12-18

Keller, Paul, "Patterns of Media Audience Accumulation," in *Journal of Marketing,* Jan. 1966, pp. 32-37

Hope, John, "Gross Rating Points Become Official for Outdoor Showings," in *Media Decisions,* Feb., 1973, p. 82

Lucas, Darrell, "How Valid Are Media Measures?" in *Media/scope,* Jan. 1960 pp. 40-43

Maneloveg, Herbert, "Media Research Future: Is There Any?" in *Advertising Age* July 15, 1974, p. 23

Media Decisions, "Rating Points for Newspapers," April, 1971, pp. 44-47

Media Decisions, "Which Is Best for Buying—CPGRP or CPM?" Feb. 1973, pp. 48-49

Papazian, Edward, "Setting Priorities," in *Media Decisions,* Dec. 1973, pp. 16-18

Shocker, Alan D., "Limitations of Incremental Research in Media Selection," in *Journal of Marketing Research,* Feb., 1970, pp. 101-103

Smith, Stewart, "Criteria for Media Comparisons: A Critique," in *Journal of Marketing Research,* Nov., 1965, pp. 364-369

Simmons, W. R., "We Can Believe *Most* of the Numbers *Most* of the Time," in *Media/scope,* Sept., 1967, pp. 46-49

Stanton, Frank, "A State of the Art Appraisal of Advertising Research Measurements," in *Perspectives in Advertising Management,* April, 1969, Assn. of National Advertisers, Inc., pp. 237-245

chapter 6

Decisions About Television

In planning for the use of television (and radio to some extent) special problems arise that are peculiar to the medium and require an understanding of basic information. Matching coverage areas with sales areas, modifying coverage data by H.U.T. data and selecting television programs represents problems that will be discussed in this chapter.

How broadcast coverage figures are used in strategy planning. When the media planner knows the market areas that he would like to reach with television, he needs to know the upper limit, or maximum number of television homes that he might reach with his advertising. He will not be able to reach all of the television homes in a given market. The question which faces the media planner is; how can he maximize this coverage statistic? The answer: by careful selection of markets and stations which reach a precise geographic marketing area.

An example of the use of coverage figures in planning for spot television might be where a national advertiser had divided the country into sales territories on the basis of county lines. It may so happen that the television station he selects to broadcast his advertising may not cover the counties in his best sales territories as well as some other station. He would then go to the coverage data books to

Table 23
Number of Homes Covered Weekly by Chicago Television Stations or Selected Counties*

| County | Stations | | | |
	A	B	C	D
Cook	1,692,000	1,689,500	1,673,200	1,503,400
Lake	102,800	105,100	102,800	92,700
Will	74,000	74,800	74,100	71,299
McHenry	31,400	31,100	32,800	28,700
TOTALS	1,900,200	1,900,500	1,882,900	1,696,000

In order to be counted in this statistic, persons in each home must listen to the station at least once a week.

*Source: Arbitron, 1974 County Coverage Study

find out which stations best cover his sales territories. Shown is an example of how four television stations cover selected counties surrounding Chicago. (Note that while the coverages for each station are similar, they are not identical.)

Modifying coverage data by H.U.T. data. Coverage data in television only represents audience potential. So, if a station has a coverage of 1,410,000 TV homes, this does not mean that an advertiser will reach all of those homes if he buys a commercial on that station. But what determines how many homes he will reach? To a great extent, the H.U.T. at any time of day will provide a clue to the possible tune-in. H.U.T. is a measure of the net potential audience, and indicates what percent of households with a television set are turned on at any given time of day, such as morning, early afternoon, later afternoon, prime time or late evening. The statistics are also reported by fifteen minute segments to allow a closer examination of tune-ins during various times of the day. Figure 17 shows how audience sizes vary by time of day.

Figure 17 also shows that television viewing is affected by living habits. In the morning the only persons available for viewing are housewives and young children, so the tune-in tends to be low. However, when children return from school, about 4 p.m., the tune-ins rise dramatically, and after 6 p.m. when many husbands have returned from work, the rise in tune-ins is even greater. After 10 p.m., viewing drops as expected.

The planner can study H.U.T. data and estimate his potential audience size better than by studying coverage figures alone. In the early evening hours there are more viewers available than at any other time of day, since children and parents are usually at home. But there are variations in viewing not only during a single day, but during a given week, and month. During the summer, for example, when many persons are out-of-doors, television viewing is much smaller in some viewing periods than it is in winter. These variations therefore, affect the size of audience that can be obtained.

Shown in Table 24 are data indicating the variations in viewing for different time periods.

Table 24
Variations in Viewing by Time Periods and Seasons[*]
(Percent of Total TV Households Tuned in)

	Spring	Summer	Fall	Winter
Daytime (Mon.-Fri.)	21%	24%	22 %	25%
Afternoon (Mon.-Fri.)	28	29	31	33
Early Fringe (Mon.-Fri.)	42	37	51	48
Prime Time (Mon.-Sun.)	54	46	62	64
Late Fringe (Mon.-Sun.)	31	31	30	33

[*]Source: A. C. Nielsen Company, *Audience '74*, pp. 18-25

Figure 17
Percent of Households Viewing Television by Hours of the Day*

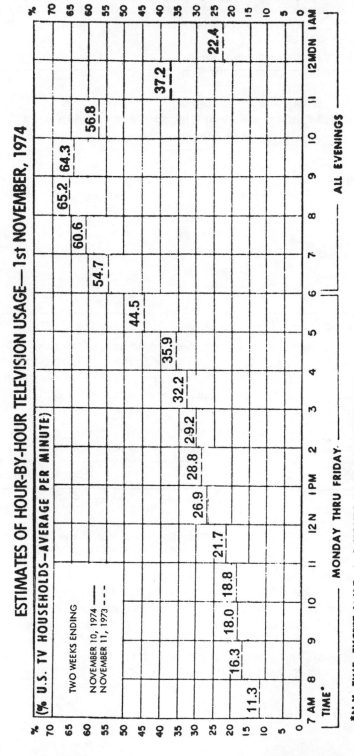

ESTIMATES OF HOUR-BY-HOUR TELEVISION USAGE—1st NOVEMBER, 1974

(% U.S. TV HOUSEHOLDS—AVERAGE PER MINUTE)

TWO WEEKS ENDING

NOVEMBER 10, 1974 ———
NOVEMBER 11, 1973 – – –

*N.Y. TIME, EXCEPT N.Y.T. + 3 HOURS IN PACIFIC TERRITORY.

MONDAY THRU FRIDAY. ALL EVENINGS

*Reprinted by permission of the A. C. Nielsen Company (from NTI)

The media planner, knowing that variations in viewing exist, must refine the coverage data to learn the approximate size of an audience that he can reach with an advertisement. In order to understand how the potential audience size may be interpreted in the light of tune-in variations by time periods, the following example is shown.

If a planner intends to buy spot television time on a local station, he would find the coverage reported in Table 25 (for Station A, Chicago):

Table 25
Potential Audience Size in Chicago Metropolitan Area
For Station A*

Counties which comprise the Chicago metro. area		Number of homes reached at least once a week
Cook	(Illinois)	1,692,000
Lake	"	102,800
McHenry	"	31,400
Kane	"	73,800
DuPage	"	142,300
Will	"	74,000
Lake	(Indiana)	160,200
Porter	"	24,300
TOTAL		2,300,800

*Source: Arbitron, *1974 County Coverage Study.*

The advertiser who might select Station A could never hope to reach all of the 2,300,800 households at one time because some of them will prefer other local stations. However, from Nielsen or Arbitron, it is possible to determine how large the net potential audience is. Table 26 shows this data for Station A.

Table 26
Average Number of Homes Reached for Station A*

Morning (Mon.-Fri.)		Afternoon (Mon.-Fri.)		Evening (Sat.-Sun.)	
6-9	9-Noon	Noon-3:30	3:30-6:30	6:30-8	8:10
25,000	102,000	174,000	1,340,000	470,000	28,000

*Source: *Nielsen Station Index,* NSI Average Week Estimates, Four Weeks Ending, March 6, 1974

These figures would be much lower if the planner were studying data for the months of July or August because fewer persons watch television during these months. Furthermore, there are also differences between the net potential audience of Station A and other Chicago stations. In any case, these figures help the advertiser learn about his potential audience size.

Program ratings will have to be used after potential audience sizes are examined in order to learn the estimated audience size for a given program.

Selecting a Television Program

There are a number of considerations that must be reviewed in selecting a program in which to place commercials. One consideration is to find a program whose entertainment or editorial content is compatible with the nature of the product being advertised. This means that the action of the program should in no way reflect unfavorably on the product or the brand. A cereal manufacturer might not want to select a crime or horror show because the action does not reflect favorably on the personality of breakfast or cereals. On the other hand that manufacturer might more likely accept a situation comedy, adventure story, or even a western program without fear of negative connotation. The compatibility of program with product, however, is more opinion than fact. There is little research to substantiate the fears about incompatibility. Some advertisers are simply more concerned than others.

Program types. A second consideration is based on the need for a planner to know which types or kinds of programs are preferred by audiences who are of various ages. Will a program appeal to men as well as to women, teen-agers or children? Rating services provide data showing audience sizes broken down by these various categories as shown in Table 27.

Table 27
Average Audience Estimates by Program Types*

Audience	Situation Comedies	Westerns	Informa-tional	Suspense-Mystery	Feature Films	Variety	General Drama
Men	14.1%	13.1%	8.8%	13.8%	12.9%	12.9%	12.3%
Women	17.3	14.9	9.5	15.2	16.3	16.3	16.8
Teens	11.1	12.3	3.9	10.1	13.3	11.8	11.9
Children	14.3	16.3	3.6	10.1	9.6	14.0	13.2

*Source: Nielsen National TV Ratings, Two Weeks Ending Feb. 19, 1974, pp. 2-3

From an examination of data such as shown in Table 27 the planner can quickly eliminate all but two or three kinds of programs from which he can make a final choice. Sometimes the kinds of programs he would like, simply are not available, in which case, he will have second and third alternatives in mind.

Once he has chosen the kind of program he wants, he now must examine broadcast ratings to determine the audience sizes; to be followed by reach and frequency analysis for the programs under consideration. The process of program selection at this point is one of eliminating kinds that would obviously not be suitable.

Ratings as a measurement of audience size. A previous discussion pointed out that the basis for measuring the television audience was the home where a set was tuned to a given program. The assumption is made that there are people actually watching a television program. It is conceivable, however, for a set to be turned-on, and yet not have anyone watching it, even though the set has been counted in a rating measurement. Ratings are not to be considered absolute measurements of audience size, but are estimates made by sampling procedures. As in all statistical sampling, a certain margin of error is possible. Ratings are used not as absolutes, but as relative measures where it may be possible to compare the audience of one program with that of another. Even then, the degree of statistical error based on different sample sizes is known and reported by the syndicated research companies. Table 28 shows the sampling errors reported by Arbitron:

Table 28
Sampling Errors of Television Ratings*

Rating situations	Size of sample		
	300 sample	1,000 sample	2,500 sample
Daytime program, 5 rating	±2.0	±1.1	± .7
Fringe time program, 10 rating	±2.8	±1.5	±1.0
Prime time program, 20 rating	±3.7	±2.0	±1.3
50 GRPs scattered, in daytime	±6.4	+3.5	±2.2
100 GRPs scattered in fringe time	±8.8	±4.8	±3.8

*Source: *Media Decisions,* "Arbitron Sampling Error by Sample Size" May, 1974, p. 144

These sampling errors may be interpreted to mean that in 955 cases out of 1000 estimates based on a sample size shown, the rating will differ from a complete census by more or less rating points as shown. If the sampling error is known, then the planner can judge whether or not he should use any given rating for comparative purposes.

The two most important ratings used for estimating audience size are the national and the local market ratings. The national rating is obtained by measuring a national probability sample of homes. The local ratings are obtained from probability samples related to the sizes of each local market being measured. Figure 18 shows a page from the National Nielsen TV Audience Estimates, for a Monday evening. Figure 19 is from Nielsen Station Index (NSI) for a time period that is relatively close to the national figures. By examining the same programs nationally and locally one can see that the same programs have different ratings. This difference should be kept in mind when planning to use television in both kinds of markets.

The Total Audience Rating (a measurement of program delivery). This rating represents the percent of homes (or individuals) of a sample who have tuned to a particular program for a minimum listening period of five or six minutes. In other words, if individuals in a home have tuned to a program for at

110

NATIONAL *Nielsen* TV AUDIENCE ESTIMATES — EVE. MON. OCT. 28, 1974

TIME	7:00	7:15	7:30	7:45	8:00	8:15	8:30	8:45	9:00	9:15	9:30	9:45	10:00	10:15	10:30	10:45 11:00

ABC TV

TOTAL AUDIENCE (Households (000) & %) — The Rookies: 17,260 / 25.2; 21,990 / 32.1

AVERAGE AUDIENCE (Households (000) & %) / SHARE OF AUDIENCE % / AVG. AUD. BY ¼ HR. %

The Rookies:
- 14,520 / 21.2 / 32 / 20.1
- 20.5* / 31* / 20.9 / 21.6
- 21.8* / 33* / 21.9 / 19.2 / 33 / 18.7

ABC NFL Football Game "LOS ANGELES VS. SAN FRANCISCO" (9:00-12:00MD)(1):
- 19.2* / 29* / 19.7 / 20.6
- 20.9* / 32* / 21.2 / 22.8
- 22.4* / 35* / 22.0 / 19.4
- 19.1* / 32* / 18.8

CBS TV

TOTAL AUDIENCE (Households (000) & %) — Gunsmoke 17,540 / 25.6; Maude 17,670 / 25.8; Rhoda 18,700 / 27.3; Medical Center 16,170 / 23.6

AVERAGE AUDIENCE / SHARE OF AUDIENCE % / AVG. AUD. BY ¼ HR. %

Gunsmoke:
- 14,860 / 21.7 / 33 / 21.7
- 21.7* / 33* / 21.6 / 21.8
- 21.8* / 32* / 21.9

Maude:
- 15,760 / 23.0 / 35 / 22.6 / 23.4

Rhoda:
- 17,470 / 25.5 / 39 / 25.5 / 25.6

Medical Center:
- 13,430 / 19.6 / 33 / 19.5
- 19.6* / 32* / 19.7 / 20.2
- 19.5* / 34* / 18.8

NBC TV

TOTAL AUDIENCE (Households (000) & %) — Born Free 13,360 / 19.5; 16,290 / 26.7

NBC Monday Night At The Movies "THE GREATEST GIFT" (9:00-10:59PM) (3)

AVERAGE AUDIENCE / SHARE OF AUDIENCE % / AVG. AUD. BY ¼ HR. %

Born Free:
- 10,340 / 15.1 / 23 / 13.8
- 14.0* / 21* / 14.3 / 15.8
- 16.2* / 24* / 16.7

NBC Monday Night At The Movies:
- 12,740 / 18.6 / 30 / 18.3
- 18.6* / 28* / 18.9 / 18.6
- 18.4* / 28* / 18.3 / 18.6
- 18.7* / 30* / 18.8 / 18.3
- 18.8* / 33* / 18.7

| TV HOUSEHOLDS USING TV | WK 1 | 61.5 | 62.7 | 63.8 | 65.9 | 66.3 | 67.6 | 68.0 | 69.3 | 69.3 | 68.9 | 67.9 | 66.6 | 60.7 | 58.2 | 55.3 | 51.0 |
| (See Def. 1) | WK 2 | 61.4 | 63.1 | 63.3 | 64.0 | 65.1 | 65.8 | 66.9 | 67.4 | 66.2 | 66.6 | 66.0 | 65.3 | 62.0 | 60.8 | 58.5 | 55.3 |

U.S. TV Households: 68,500,000   * Half-hour ratings (for immediately preceding and subject quarter-hours).   (R) Repeat, see page B.   (OP) See Other Programs Section: Page A-34.

(1) FOR REAL RATINGS SEE OP PAGES.
(2) TOWERING INFERNO, NBC, (10:50-11:00PM)(SUS.).
(3) FILL, NBC, (10:55-11:00PM)(SUS.).

EVE. MON. NOV. 4, 1974

*Reprinted by permission of the A. C. Nielsen Co.

Figure 19
Sample Page from the Nielsen Station Index for Chicago*

NSI Average Week Estimates—4 Week Period Ending March 6, 1974

MONDAY
7.30PM–11.00PM

AVERAGE QUARTER-HOUR AUDIENCES
STATION TOTALS (000)

STATION / PROGRAM	METRO AREA % HOUSEHOLD RATING (1)	METRO AREA % SHARE (2)	DMA CURRENT HOUSEHOLD RATING (3)	DMA CURRENT SHARE (4)	PRE-POST GUIDE SHARE & HUT NOV'73 (5)	SHARE & HUT JULY'73 (6)	SHARE & HUT MAY'73 (7)	TOTAL HOUSEHOLDS (8)	TOTAL PERSONS (9)	TOTAL ADULTS (10)	WOMEN TOTAL (11)	18-34 (12)	18-49 (13)	25-49 (14)	25-54 (15)	50+ (16)	MEN TOTAL (17)	18-34 (18)	18-49 (19)	25-49 (20)	25-64 (21)
RELATIVE ERROR THRESHOLDS, 50% & OVER (See Table 8, Page 3)	LT		LT					8	9	8	8	10	9	8	8	7	8	11	10	9	8
7.30																					
WBBM GUNSMOKE	14	24	14	23	25X	25	23	386	593	478	262	41	93	84	174	169	216	49	89	84	152
WFLD LUCY SHOW	3	7	3	7	2	6	5	77	130	43	29	8	16	16	22	13	14	7	11	5	7
WGN REG/PRES NIXON	4	7	4	7	7	6	12	118	188	129	88	25	41	32	64	47	41	16	18	9	26
124 MOD SQUAD	4		5					126	194	135	85	25	41	33	63	44	50	18	21	9	31
MLS ROOKIES	21	34	20	33	40X	32	33	547	1137	710	395	171	269	180	284	126	315	144	216	151	223
WMAQ MAGICIAN	20	32	19	31	26	20	21	508	1071	693	390	173	259	202	259	131	303	121	201	161	241
WTTW REG/EVENING-POPS			1					26	34	29	19		5			11	10	1		3	8
124 BOOK BEAT	1	1	1	1				14	11	11	9		2		6	2	2				2
HUT & TOTALS *	61		61		58	41	54	1662	3153	2082	1183	418	683	519	814	500	899	338	538	413	657
8.00																					
WBBM HERES LUCY	18	27	18	27	21X	30	30	479	857	518	342	99	170	131	215	172	176	42	82	69	121
WFLD MERV GRIFFIN	2	3	2	3	2	5	4	68	85	79	48		9		31	39	31	3	10	7	20
WGN REG/PRES NIXON	4	6	4	6	8	14	12	114	163	114	76	25	35	27	49	42	37	13	16	9	22
124 MOD SQUAD			4					119	163	112	77	25	35	27	53	41	36	13	13	8	23
MLS MON NIGHT MOVIE	21	31	20	30	36	26	26	527	1077	749	406	171	290	208	288	116	343	139	234	175	256
WMAQ MON AT MOVIES	22	33	22	32	34	18	18	580	1077	853	438	178	275	204	307	163	415	171	287	225	324
WTTW REG/DAY AT NIGHT								36	53	51	30	10	16	9	17	14	21	9	13		12
123 SPECIAL OF WEEK	1	2	1	2	2	7	3	35	58	35	34	13	19		18	15	21	1	9	7	13
HUT & TOTALS *	65		66		69	44	57	1804	3288	2354	1341	483	795	587	907	546	1023	375	639	492	755
8.30																					
WBBM DICK VAN DYKE	17	26	16	25	19	29	27	439	727	474	309	98	158	124	207	151	165	55	86	65	116
WFLD MERV GRIFFIN	3	5	3	5	2	5	4	74	97	97	61		8	8	34	53	36	10	10	7	21
WGN DRAGNET	4	6	4	6	8	14	15	127	185	141	82	16	35	21	42	47	59	13	32	21	35
MLS MON NIGHT MOVIE	20	30	20	30	38	26	26	526	1028	749	406	168	290	216	296	116	343	137	226	169	255
WMAQ MON AT MOVIES	22	33	21	33	34	19	17	579	1064	872	443	186	289	216	314	154	429	181	304	238	335
WTTW REG/CONSUMER GME								42	66	61	37	12	20	12	20	17	24	10	12	8	12
123 SPECIAL OF WEEK	1	2	1	2	3	6	2	41	70	64	43	17	25	15	25	17	21	10	10	8	11
HUT & TOTALS *	65		66		69	45	57	1786	3169	2394	1338	483	800	597	913	538	1056	404	670	509	774
9.00																					
WBBM MEDICAL CENTER	22	32	21	31	24	35	30	574	948	709	474	162	269	222	336	205	235	82	137	105	166
WFLD MERV GRIFFIN	5	8	6	9	4	3	4	61	90	86	55	24	13	13	29	42	31	3	12	9	20
WGN PERRY MASON	6	8	6	9	7X	14	15	176	257	222	123	24	41	26	70	99	99	24	49	40	66
MLS MON NIGHT MOVIE	19	28	19	29	37	23	24	499	973	730	396	162	278	201	283	139	334	134	222	166	249
WMAQ MON AT MOVIES	21	30	20	29	33	17	17	550	996	837	426	171	287	201	306	139	411	186	302	230	314
WTTW REG/U-C ROUNDTBL								38	59	54	34	13	18	14	17	16	20	8	11		12
134 SPECIAL OF WEEK	1	2	1	2	2	2		41	66	61	40	17	23	21	21	17	21	10	13	8	13
HUT & TOTALS *	69		69		70	50	61	1898	3323	2633	1508	548	906	692	1041	602	1130	437	733	558	827
9.30																					

112

Note: The following is a large multi-column audience data table, printed rotated on the page. Row labels are station/program names; data are arranged in 21 numbered columns (the audience-estimate columns are the most legible; the left-hand rating columns are partially illegible). Values are given to best reading.

Station	Program																					
WBBM	MEDICAL CENTER	22	22	22	24	32	37	24	581	745	973	493	178	292	244	355	201	252	93	154	115	178
WFLD	BILL BURRUD TRVL	2	2	2	2	9	14	7	57	79	87	50	14	14	13	28	36	29	5	4	4	13
WGN	PERRY MASON	5	6	3	7	8	23	37	176	219	253	122	26	45	29	28	77	29	23	47	39	66
MLS	MON NIGHT MOVIE	19	18	9	37	27	14	33	492	716	951	390	160	274	201	282	116	326	132	217	162	242
WMAQ	MON AT MOVIES	21	21	23	33	30	21	33	553	857	1010	428	189	289	216	304	139	429	195	317	244	331
WTTW	REG/KILLRS/U-CHG	2	1	3	2	2	5	2	32	49	53	29	13	15	14	12	14	14	13	11	8	11
34	SPECIAL OF WEEK	2	1	3	2	2	7	3	38	66	66	41	13	28	12	12	13	20	13	11	8	12
	HUT & TOTALS *	69	69	69	70	49	60		1891	2665	3327	1512	565	929	710	1050	583	1153	456	753	572	842

10-30

Station	Program																					
WBBM	REG/MED CENTER	17	16	16	24		17		438	626	723	363	121	211	183	257	152	263	98	174	141	199
124	TV 2 NEWS-10	16	16	16	23				424	597	697	331	108	197	174	242	134	266	97	181	150	213
WFLD	MISSN IMPOSSIBLE	2	3	2	3		6	5	59	71	71	29	18	29	24	28	10	32	20	25	18	24
WGN	10.00 PM NEWS	6	6	9	10		14	15	183	280	317	145	29	77	68	100	68	135	29	68	59	100
MLS	REG/MON-MOVIE	23	23	20	33	9X	31	31	612	978	1195	546	189	404	305	398	142	432	178	306	251	339
134	FLYNN & DALY-NWS	21	21	21	30	39			539	838	952	444	189	324	262	346	120	394	162	281	233	314
WMAQ	REG/MON-MOVIES	20	19	10	28		27		559	829	886	431	191	232	192	315	199	398	120	194	194	309
124	NEWSFIVE			1	1	31		3	519	779	820	409	126	201	162	287	208	370	107	206	166	274
WTTW	REG/DAY AT NIGHT	1	1	1	1				15	22	25	14	14	4	5	4		4	6	9	5	5
34	SPECIAL OF WEEK	1	1	1	1				15	23	24	14	14			8						4
12	DAY AT NIGHT								15	12	16	8	14					8	4	9	4	4
	HUT & TOTALS *	69	69	69		65	56	61	1866	2806	3238	1538	563	962	775	1103	576	1268	451	808	666	976

10-15

Station	Program																					
WBBM	TV 2 NEWS-10	16	16	15	23	16X	16	19	397	580	638	331	108	196	168	234	135	249	91	168	148	205
WFLD	MISSN IMPOSSIBLE	2	2	2	3		6	6	55	71	88	37	18	28	24	31	34	34	20	20	20	27
WGN	10.00 PM NEWS	6	6	6	10	9X	15	14	175	265	303	145	32	74	62	94	64	127	26	63	54	94
MLS	REG/MON-MOVIE	23	23	20	35	41	31	32	603	963	1165	545	205	409	304	398	136	418	175	271	239	325
134	FLYNN & DALY-NWS	20	20	19	32		27	25	534	841	955	459	205	339	269	355	107	382	161	271	220	297
WMAQ	NEWSFIVE		1	1		31X	3	2	514	756	797	394	138	197	162	291	120	362	196	196	165	275
WTTW	REG/FIELDS/SP-WK	1	1	1	1				19	35	35	22	13	17	5	11	5	13	6	9	5	10
12	DAY AT NIGHT								15	16	16	9	13	5	9	5	4	13	6	6	5	7
	HUT & TOTALS *	66	65	65		63	55	58	1763	2670	3026	1467	539	921	736	1059	546	1203	429	755	631	936

10-30

Station	Program																					
WBBM	REG/TV 2 NEWS-10	11	11	10	22	14	17	19	278	383	448	229	93	154	129	174	75	154	70	118	92	120
124	CBS LATE MOVIE	11	11	11	23		4	3	281	384	452	226	100	164	134	177	62	158	77	126	97	125
WFLD	MISSN IMPOSSIBLE	2	2	5	4	6	4	3	131	68	85	34	18	25	21	28	20	28	20	25	20	27
WGN	WGN TV PRESENTS	5	5	5	10	12X	23	21	131	183	215	87	37	65	50	60	87	106	44	70	56	73
MLS	REG/MON-MOVIE	13	13	10	27	46	16	23	338	527	617	310	138	223	169	226	87	217	87	123	123	162
134	WRLD-ENTERTAINMT	11	11	10	23		37		270	413	433	177	106	164	132	187	137	176	78	124	99	134
WMAQ	REG/NEWSFIVE	16	16	14	34	26		29	432	591	632	331	146	194	156	242	137	260	76	138	121	201
124	TONIGHT SHOW	15	15	14	31		6	2	389	529	554	292	104	161	128	211	131	237	52	115	107	187
WTTW	REG/NANA	2	2	2	4				46	72	75	36	18	26	10	24	10	36	13	24	13	23
124	ADVOCATES	-3	-3	-3																		
	HUT & TOTALS *	48	47	49		49	38	42	1280	1824	2072	1027	420	687	543	754	340	797	310	528	425	606

10-45

Station	Program																					
WBBM	CBS LATE MOVIE	9	9	9	22	15	17	18	242	331	393	198	80	136	110	151	62	133	64	103	78	102
WFLD	MISSN IMPOSSIBLE	2	2	2	5		3	2	56	67	86	17	17	24	21	28	13	34	13	26	20	28
WGN	WGN TV PRESENTS	5	5	5	12	12X	23	22	140	198	219	92	42	72	21	67	20	106	51	80	58	75
MLS	REG/EYE NWS/RPT	9	9	9	22	45	15	22	246	372	397	206	97	206	130	169	63	152	52	105	88	119
14	WRLD-ENTERTAINMT	10	10	14	24	25X	35	29	244	367	370	206	91	143	110	159	63	161	52	108	84	124
WTTW	TONIGHT SHOW	15	15	14	35		34	29	389	531	565	303	118	184	141	215	119	228	78	131	111	173
124	REG/NANA	2	2	2	4		1	2	48	72	75	35	17	18	18	23		37	13	24	16	24
124	ADVOCATES	-3	-3	-3																		
	HUT & TOTALS *	42	42	41		43	34	37	1121	1571	1735	881	571	604	474	653	277	690	277	469	371	521

| Column numbers: | 1 | 2 | 3 | 4 | 5 | 6 | 7 | 8 | 9 | 10 | 11 | 12 | 13 | 14 | 15 | 16 | 17 | 18 | 19 | 20 | 21 |

* Totals include only stations reportable in this market (including satellites/affiliates, if any). HUT includes all viewing to reportable and non-reportable stations (columns 1, 3, 5-7 & 39-40).
# Other Programming or Off-the-Air.   X Previous programming same as current report.   ISR Insufficient Sample for Reporting. See Section III.   NR Station Not Reportable.   — Special Event deleted.
— Below Minimum Audience Standards. See Table 4.   Estimates based on 2 or 3 out of 4 measured weeks have larger sampling errors. See Table 7.
Note: "Blanks" should not be interpreted as connoting zero audience levels. See Section III.   LT Less Than 1.   40

TIME PERIOD AUDIENCES

*Reprinted by permission of the A. C. Nielsen Company

least five minutes (or six, as required by some services) they may be counted as having watched the program. These ratings are reported for 15-minute segments of each program, so that if a set in a home has been tuned to a program for the whole half-hour, the measurement will cover at least 10 minutes of that time. The rating is reported in percent of the sample tuned to the program. Thus, if 45 percent of the sample tuned in to a given program, this would mean that the program had a 45 rating.

Rating services translate such percents to whole numbers by projecting the percentage to the total number of television homes in the country. For example, if there are 65,000,000 television homes in the United States and a program has a 45 rating with a 90% coverage of television homes, then 45% × 90% × 65,000,000 would represent 26,325,000 homes estimated to have tuned sets to the program. (See Figure 20 for an explanation of how ratings might be made for a sample of 10 homes).

The total audience rating for all programs broadcast on a network at the same time, *plus percentage of homes in the sample where the set has not been turned on* should add up to 100%.

The total audience rating is a measurement of the audience size for a one-week period. Although ratings may be shown for each week of a given month, the services will average them to indicate the average tune-in for a typical week in that month.

In studying ratings, one should remember that the measurements are of program delivery, meaning the audience size of the program. There is no measurement of the audience size of a commercial within the program. However, since the placements of commercials may vary, the rating may be assumed to be a *rough indication of audience size,* because it covers a five or six minute tune-in period. Since ratings are used for comparative purposes, the planner will find as many available suitable programs as possible and then make comparisons on the basis of the size of the ratings. Although a rating percent is a quick way for making comparisons, it is often secondary to a projection that shows the number of homes tuned in (or a simple projection of the rating percent to the base). Then numbers may be compared and the cost efficiencies calculated.

The Average Audience Rating.   The A. C. Nielsen Company provides a special rating for planners which represents the percent of homes tuned in to the average minute of a program. It is called the Average Audience Rating. Bernard Ober characterized the difference between the average audience rating and the total audience rating as follows:

"Consider a revolving door through which a number of persons pass. A count of the total number of different persons passing through this revolving door might be considered analagous to the total audience rating . . . In contrast, a count of the number of persons in the revolving door at any time might be considered analagous to the average audience rating of a program."[28]

---

[28]Ober, Bernard H., *"Measuring Television Audiences,"* A.C. Nielsen, 1959, p.3

Figure 20

Computation of Total Audience Rating for Sample of 10

Home No.	Channel No.	Name of Program
1	Ch 2	Program A
2	Ch 5	Program B
3	(set off)	Set not on
4	Ch 7	Program C
5	Ch 2	Program A
6	Ch 5	Program B
7	Ch 2	Program A
8	(set off)	Set not on
9	Ch 7	Program C
10	Ch 2	Program A

SUMMARY OF TUNE-INS

Name of Program	Number of Sets Tuned in	Total Audience Rating
A	4	40
B	2	20
C	2	20
Total of Homes Using TV	8	(H.U.T.) 80%
Sets not on	2	20%
Grand Total	10	100%

115

Table 29
Tune In To The Average Minute of a Program

	Minutes in a Program														
	1	2	3	4	5	6	7	8	9	10	11	12	13	14	15
Percent Tuned in	30	30	30	31	31	31	31	32	32	32	33	33	33	33	33

Total of percents tuned in for the 15 minutes = 475

$475 \div 15 = 31.7$; the average tune-in for 15 minutes

The average audience rating is particularly useful because it includes not only those who tuned in to the program for the five or six minutes (as the total audience rating did), but those who tuned in for only a minute. There are many individuals who will tune to a program for a few minutes and then switch to another channel because they are looking for a program more to their liking. Conceivably, they may have been exposed to a commercial during those few minutes, so the average audience would take such minimal tune in into consideration. Thus, the average audience rating may serve as a measure to a commercial placed somewhere within the framework of a fifteen minute segment.

But there is another advantage of this rating over the total audience rating. It better reflects the size of audience when comparing a half-hour program with an hour program. A total audience rating can remain the same or go up during the length of a program. Therefore the longer a program is broadcast, the more likely that its total rating will go up. An average audience rating, however, because it is an average, may go up, down, or remain the same during a program. But it does not penalize a program for being shorter as a total audience rating does. Therefore the average audience rating is a better statistic than the total audience rating for comparing programs of unequal length.

Share of Audience Rating. This rating reflects the percentage of homes tuned in to a program based *only* on those homes that had their sets turned on rather than based on all television homes, as in the total audience rating. If all total audience ratings for a fifteen-minute segment were added together, the sum would represent the H.U.T. The H.U.T. always is a proportion of all television homes. But the sum of all share of audience ratings represents only those homes tuned in. Homes that had their sets turned off are never figured in the base. The formula for computing share is as follows:

$$\text{Share} = \frac{\text{Rating}}{\text{H.U.T.}}$$

In practice, share data compared to average audience ratings are illustrated in Table 30.

Table 30
Difference Between the Average Audience Rating and Share

Programs being broadcast during same 15 minute period	Average Audience Rating	Share of Audience Rating
A	20%	33.3%
B	10	16.7
C	30	50.0
TOTALS	60% (H.U.T.)	100.0%

In Table 30, the sets not turned on totals 40%. When the 40% is added to the H.U.T., the total is 100%. Share was computed by dividing the average audience rating by the H.U.T. The sum of total audience ratings equaled the H.U.T., or 60%. But the sum of share of audience ratings is 100%.

The value of share rating is that it enables the media planner to compare two programs broadcast at radically different times of the day, week or year; or any time where the H.U.T.s for different programs are radically different. To illustrate the use of share data, Table 31 shows ratings for a sample program and its shares.

Table 31
Program "X", Ratings vs. Share

Month of year	Average Audience Rating	H.U.T.	Share of Audience Rating
January	36.3	72.2	50.3
April	34.2	68.3	50.1
July	28.9	53.5	54.0

If the media planner had made decisions about this program based only on the average audience rating, he might have concluded that this program was losing its audience. After all, ratings were declining. But a study of H.U.T.s shows that they, too, were declining as might be expected when comparing H.U.T.s for January and July. When share ratings were computed, however, the numbers showed that the program was not only doing well, but actually improving from January to July.

The best use of share ratings, therefore, is wherever making comparisons based on radically different H.U.T.s. In other words, when the bases for ratings differ, share may be most appropriate.

Considerations beyond ratings. The purpose of broadcast measurements, whether of homes or individuals, is to have a device whereby audience sizes may be compared. The process of comparison, then, should lead to a ranking of programs with varying audience sizes. But the ranking should always be followed by cost efficiency comparisons and in fact, such comparisons are more significant than simple audience-size comparisons. If it costs too much money to reach a target audience, then a program with fewer targets and better efficiency may be needed.

Even then, there is another, more important, consideration, especially when a program is to be purchased for a consecutive period of three or four weeks or more. That consideration is the size of the target audience over time. Either a rating or a demographic audience size for a program may represent a one-week measurement. The more important question is: how large is the unduplicated target audience over a four-week period? Conceivably the audience size for one telecast may be large, but subsequent telecasts may be smaller so that the unduplicated audience over a four-week period is not very large. It is for this reason that the reach of television programs comprise an additional measurement to be considered in program selection.

Reach and Frequency Considerations in Planning

When a medium such as television develops reach over a four-week period, it will be found, through measurement devices, that some homes tuned in to a given program only once during that time, while others tuned in two, three or more times. Reach is a measurement that shows the number who tuned in at least once. Another statistic is necessary to show how many times the homes in the sample being measured tuned in. That statistic is called the "frequency" of a program. Frequency represents the average number of times homes in a sample tuned in. Reach and frequency, then, are two measurements which tell the media planner how the audience tuned in to the program. Both are useful in planning to achieve marketing goals.

It is necessary to understand, however, that reach and frequency occur at the same time, but at different rates. If a program develops large reach, it will probably develop relatively small frequency. On the other hand, if it develops large frequency (or repetition of tune-ins) it will probably develop small reach. The principle is that reach and frequency are inversely related for a given program. In order to make this concept clear, it is necessary to first understand the formula for frequency, shown as follows:

$$\text{Frequency} = \frac{\text{Total number of duplicated tune-ins to a program in a four week period (called gross rating points or gross reach)}}{\text{Reach}}$$

Table 32 shows the inverse relationship for the mythical program "A" in which a sample of only 10 homes were measured. In this sample, a home is counted once if it tunes in to a program during a four-week period, no matter how many other times it tunes in. In the first four-week period, reach and frequency are measured. In the second period, frequency was raised so that reach would decline from the first period. In the third period, reach was raised so that frequency would decline when compared with the first period.

Table 32
How Reach and Frequency are Inversely Related

(Tune-ins to Program A During Three, Four-Week Periods) (X = home tuned-in)

Sample Home No.	Period One				Period Two				Period Three			
	1	2	3	4	1	2	3	4	1	2	3	4
1	x				x	x	x	x		x		
2											x	x
3		x	x	x	x	x			x	x		
4									x			
5		x	x									
6										x		
7	x		x		x	x	x	x			x	x
8									x			
9	x			x								
Ratings	30	20	30	20	30	30	20	20	30	30	20	20
GRP's	100				100				100			
	Reach 50 - Freq. 2				Reach 30 - Freq. 3.3				Reach 70 - Freq. 1.4			

Example of Reach, Frequency and Gross Rating Points	Reach declines Frequency rises	Reach rises Frequency declines

Table 32 shows that in Period One, the reach is 50% and the frequency is 2. The gross rating points (or the sum of each week's ratings) is 100. In this period, Home No. 1 was counted once, Home No. 3 was counted once (even though it tuned in three times during the period), and Homes No. 5, 7, and 9 were counted once each for a total of 5. Since there was a reach of five out of 10, the reach is 50%. Since gross rating points add to 100, then 100 divided by 50 equals two, the frequency.

In Period Two, the total tune in had not changed from the first period. It is still 10 tune-ins. But reach has gone down to 3 out of 10 homes or 30%. Since reach and frequency are inversely related, frequency should go up. It is 3.3, or 1.3 points higher than it was in the First Period.

But in the Third Period, Reach has gone up because seven out of 10 homes tuned to the program compared to only five who tuned in for the First Period. The reach, therefore, is 70%. Frequency, however, dropped to 1.4 as a consequence of the rise in reach.

It is imperative, then, in planning to remember the inverse relationship. The most significant implication of the relationship is that it is impossible to have both high reach and high frequency within the same program. One must be sacrificed for the other.

Which programs develop reach or frequency? Programs which develop reach are those whose contents tend to change either during a given telecast, or from week to week. As the contents change, so do audience types. When movies are broadcast, where one week a drama is shown and the next week a comedy, two different audiences are likely to develop (with some overlap, of course). Movies, therefore, tend to develop more reach than frequency. But a soap opera, broadcast daily, five days a week, or 20 times a month, will tend to draw a relatively smaller sized audience, but one with greater frequency of viewing. Shown in Table 33 is a typical comparison between a drama telecast once each week compared to a soap opera broadcast 20 times a month:

Table 33
A Comparison of Frequencies for
Two Different Kinds of Programs

	Daytime soap opera broadcast 20 times a month	Nighttime drama, broadcast once a week
Total audience rating per telecast	9.7	19.4
Four week reach	25.4	40.0
Frequency	7.6	1.9
	$\dfrac{9.7 \times 4 \times 5}{25.4} = 7.6$	$\dfrac{19.4 \times 4}{40.0} = 1.9$

Table 33 indicates that the drama had a much larger reach than did the soap opera, but the soap opera had a much larger frequency than did the drama. Part of the reason for the larger frequency was the frequency of telecasts. The more often a program is broadcast, the more likely it is that it will have a larger frequency. Spot television, for example, is a means of buying a large number of commercials within a given market in order to build large frequency.

But there are other factors than program content which affect reach and frequency. One is the size of ratings, and the other is the number of broadcasts. Programs with high ratings initially will probably have high reach because they already have a high reach in the first week's rating. A total audience rating for one telecast then, is a one-week reach. If that one-week reach is high, the four-week reach cannot go below that figure. It will most likely rise.

There is, therefore, some relationship between the ratings and the number of times a program is broadcast, and reach. Dr. Seymour Banks, Vice President of Leo Burnett Co., Inc., explained this as follows:

" . . .reach is not directly proportional to either ratings or the number of telecasts. Rather, as ratings increase or as the number of telecasts used increase, reach also rises but at a decreasing rate. This is more easily understood when we consider that the companion of reach is frequency. And when the rating or the number of telecasts increase, some of this increase goes towards boosting reach, while some of it contributes toward an increase in frequency."[29]

The reason for the declining rate of reach is that, up to a certain point, it is relatively easy to build reach. By selecting television programs of a different nature in which to place commercials, it is possible to reach different kinds of people. But there is a point of diminishing returns, where each attempt to build more reach by selecting more and different kinds of programs results in reaching the same persons over and over again, with an increase in frequency rather than in reach. Some homes never tune in their television sets during the period of a month, or they are almost impossible to reach. So as ratings and number of telecasts increase, reach will increase, but begin to decline in rate (not total) over time.

A reminder: frequency is an average. Users of reach and frequency data often forget that frequency is an average and not an absolute number. It is subject, therefore, to the same characteristics of all statistical averages. For example, averages are affected by extreme scores in a distribution. A few very high numbers may pull up the entire average of all other scores. The only way to guard against being deceived by a frequency statistic, then, is to look at a frequency distribution and see whether some segments of a sample are getting proportionately more frequency than others. Table 34 shows a sample divided into fixed quintiles and each group's reaches and frequencies.

The distribution of frequency is obviously unequal in Table 34. Some of the quintiles are getting much more frequency than others. This phenomenon is called "unbalanced frequency." To make it more dramatic in effect, Figure 21 shows the frequency in graphic form.

---

[29]Banks, Seymour, *How to Estimate Reach and Frequency,* Leo Burnett Co., Inc. p. 5

Table 34
Quintile Analysis of Tune-Ins for Program X

Divisions of sample	Reach	Frequency	GRPs
Heaviest 20% viewing	18%	11	198
Next 20%	16	6	96
Third 20%	17	5	85
Next 20%	16	3	48
Lightest 20% viewing	18	1	18
TOTALS	85	26	445

Reach of entire sample: 85. Frequency of entire sample: 5.2. Gross rating points: 445.

Figure 21
Graph of Frequency Distribution for Program X

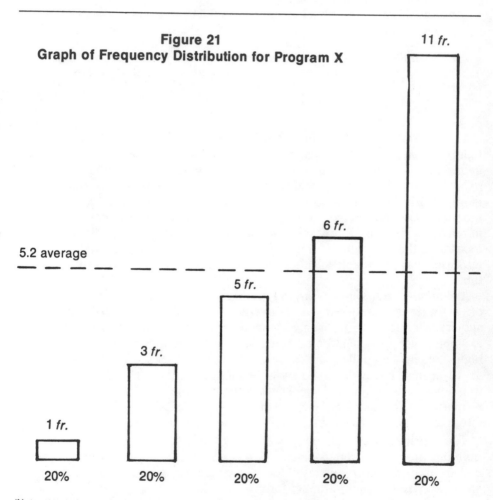

(Note: the average number of times each group tuned in to Program X is shown at the top of each column).

122

While Program X had a 5.2 average frequency in Figure 21 some segments were receiving too much frequency at the expense of other segments. But the average frequency of 5.2 does not indicate the disparity. The planner may have been deceived by the frequency level of Program X, thinking that every home in the sample tuned to the program 5.2 times during a four week period. But the illustration shows otherwise.

The problem of television viewing levels and target audiences. Another problem facing planners who want to use television is that of matching target audiences with the proper viewing level. Since television viewing audiences are composed of heavy and light viewers, the question arises of whether the lightest viewers happen to be the heavy users of a product type. If such is the situation, then much of the advertising is wasted since heavy television users are not likely to buy the product. The goal is to reach the heaviest users with the medium that provides the most exposures. To explain the problem in more detail, Table 35 is shown, dividing the population into quintiles of viewing.

Table 35
Population Divided into Viewing Quintiles*

Population divided into fifths	Percent of viewing by each fifth of the audience
Heaviest 20% viewing	36%
Next 20%	24
Next 20%	15
Next 20%	13
Lightest 20% viewing	12

*Source: Advertising Age Media Workshop, 1972, *Organization of a Media Plan,* p. 37

Table 35 illustrates the fact that there is considerable difference between the lightest and heaviest quintiles. The important question is: are the target markets also the heaviest viewers? If they are, then perhaps the correct selection of vehicles has been made. If not, then a problem exists that will have to be solved. If a target market is composed of heavy soap users, then a computer analysis can be made to determine how heavy users watch television as Table 36 shows.

Table 36 shows that the heaviest soap users are also the lightest television viewers, indicating that if the problem is ignored, then the targets will not be getting as much advertising exposure as they should.

If the targets can be identified by demographic segments, then a computer analysis of cross-tabulated target segments matched against viewing levels would be appropriate as Table 37 shows.

Table 36
Index of Heavy Soap Users Compared to Television Viewing Levels*

Daytime viewing levels	Totals	Average of Soap Usage	Light Soap Users (3 or less)	Medium Soap Users (4 bars)	Heavy Soap Users (5+ bars)
Heaviest 20%	100	85	97	88	70
Next 20%	100	93	98	90	93
Next 20%	100	93	95	94	96
Next 20%	100	106	89	108	125
Lightest 20%	100	111	114	101	117

*Source: Advertising Age Media Workshop, 1972, *Organization of a Media Plan*, p. 40

Table 37 shows that the better-educated persons watch television less than those who had not graduated from high school. However, since the target market can be defined as younger female household heads and those who are better educated, then again, the problem is that the target market happens to be composed of the lightest viewers. Additional analysis could be made to determine how other demographic characteristics of targets match viewing levels, but there is enough evidence that can be derived from the two preceding tables to take steps to remedy the situation.

Table 37
Index of Age and Education Compared to
Television Viewing Levels*

Daytime viewing levels	Total	Ages 18-49, Graduated high school or beyond	Ages 18-49 but did not graduate high school	Ages 50+, Graduated high school or beyond	Ages 50+, but did not graduate high school
Heaviest 20%	100%	72	134	79	129
Next 20 %	100	96	108	98	109
Next 20%	100	92	98	100	106
Next 20 %	100	115	90	111	77
Lightest 20%	100	121	75	112	80

*Source: Advertising Age Media Workshop, 1972, *Organization of a Media Plan*, p. 42

There are a number of alternative ways of correcting the situation such as adding additional media vehicles other than television programs. Magazines, radio or perhaps newspapers might be added to the schedule. Or, perhaps, television "specials" could be used, because they tend to attract many light viewers. The goal, however, is to find the vehicles that deliver the optimum or largest number of targets matched with appropriate viewing levels.

Ed Papazian media director at B.B.D. & O. found through computer analysis that; "On the average, a brand that was purchased regularly by 10% of all women in the country, which spent almost all of its dollars in TV, could expect no particular advantage in brand share by quintiles."[30] In other words, heavy viewing did not contribute much to the sale of a product, even if the viewers were also heavy users of the product. Papazion suggested that, perhaps, much advertising works to cancel out the impact of other advertising, so those who are heavy television viewers will be heavily exposed to every advertiser's schedule. This would suggest that perhaps an advertiser selling in a product field where most competitors use advertising, should switch to some other medium rather than television. So even if heavy viewing is matched to heavy usage of a product, the net effect may not be helpful. Papazian, however, pointed out that there is little research to completely validate his point of view.

Audience turnover and its relationship to reach.   It is possible to get another dimension of perspective about reach if one knows how many times during a four-week period a program gets a new audience. Every time it gets a new audience it "turns over" its audience. Turnover then, shows the rate of change for tune in during a four-week period. If a program is broadcast four times a month, it will have a turnover range from 1 to 4. If the same homes tuned in to a program and no new ones tuned in, the program would have a turnover of 1. But if, each week a new group tuned in to the program and the old groups did not, then the turnover would be 4.

Turnover is computed by the following formula:

$$\text{Turnover} \quad = \quad \frac{\text{4-week reach}}{\text{1-week rating}}$$

Programs with high turnover rates do not necessarily have high reach. Such programs may have relatively low ratings made by individuals who tune-in to a program to see whether they like it, and finding they do not, do not tune in again. Meanwhile, other individuals are doing the same thing during a monthly period. As a result, the turnover rates of such programs may be high. The following table shows the ratings, reaches and turnover rates of various programs:

---

[30]Papazian, Edward, "The Sixth Quintile," in *Media Decisions*, Sept., 1973, pp. 12-14

Table 38
How Program Ratings, Reaches and Turnovers Vary

Program	Kind of Program	Total Audience Rating	4-week Reach	Turnover
A	Situation Comedy	40.0	60.0	1.50
B	Drama	30.4	55.1	1.81
C	Mystery	25.7	49.0	1.91
D	Audience Participation	19.0	37.7	1.98

Probably the key considerations in turnover are program content and time of broadcast. Programs broadcast in prime time may have less turnover than others. The size of ratings too may be a factor in turnover, although rating sizes do reflect the attractiveness of program content to some extent.

Network and spot overlap. When network television is used as an umbrella in order to achieve national coverage and spot television is used to heavy up certain key markets, it becomes necessary to determine standards of rating performance, market by market. A first consideration is to determine the number of gross rating points needed in key markets. This decision will come from experience, from studying competitive levels of gross rating points, from the budget that is available, and from the minimum job that television is supposed to perform. Next step is to study network ratings in each key market to determine how well the vehicle is doing locally. If the network ratings are below the level set for the market, then additional spot gross rating points will have to be planned for, to bring the message weight up to the required level. In some markets, the network ratings may be above the arbitrary level of gross rating points needed. In such cases, no spot weight need be added.

Sometimes planning is not done on a gross rating point level, but on a reach and frequency level, market by market. If, in key markets, a given level of reach and frequency has been set, then the number of gross rating points to bring about those goals can be planned for in each market comprising the network ratings plus any additional gross rating points needed to attain the required reach and frequency.

Gross Impressions. Gross impressions are statistics that are occasionally used by planners to describe with one number, the entire delivery for a media plan. One impression equals one exposure by a media vehicle. But because of the way impressions are calculated, they most often are duplicated rather than unduplicated exposures.

An example of how impressions are calculated for various media is shown as follows:

Television: Assume that a planner will buy 20 commercials in his media plan for a national ad campaign on network television. The estimated rating for program commercials on a given show is 25. (Total U.S. TV Households = 71,600,000)

$$71,600,000 \times 20 \times .25 = 358,000,000 \text{ Gross Impressions}$$

Magazines: Assume that a planner will buy the following number of ads in three magazines:

Magazine	No. of targets reached	No. of ads to be purchased	Gross impressions
A	5,000,000	X 5	= 25,000,000
B	2,100,000	X 3	= 6,300,000
C	7,000,000	X 2	= 14,000,000
Total gross impressions 45,300,000

The number of impressions delivered by a media plan usually runs into the millions, and because the number is so large, it is called a box-car figure. Its value, however, is debatable. Alone, impressions have no meaning. But if they can be related to some measure of campaign effectiveness such as sales volume, brand awareness levels, or competitive media plan effectiveness, they may be of value.

QUESTIONS

1. Briefly explain why H.U.T. figures for a given time period (such as a Monday evening in February) do not change very much from year to year.
2. Many newspaper columnists who are television critics tend to disparage broadcast ratings with a statement such as: "Well, no one ever called me to ask which program I was watching." Briefly explain: is this statement valid?
3. If you added all the ratings for a given time period (such as 7 to 7:30 p.m., on Monday night), to what would the sum be equivalent?
4. Why are television ratings not fully satisfactory measurements of the audience size to commercials?
5. In comparing alternative television program ratings, when is the most appropriate time to use *share* calculations for comparison?
6. Which kinds of television programs tend to develop more reach than frequency? Which kinds tend to develop more frequency than reach?
7. Why is it likely that a television program with a high initial rating will probably also have a high four week reach?
8. Why is *unbalanced frequency* possibly a poor media strategy?
9. If it is found that heavy users tend to fall mostly in the lightest viewing quintile, how can the planner correct the situation?
10. Why can't we add the ratings for each week in a four-week period to find that program's four week reach?

SELECTED READINGS

Barz, Edward, A Fresh Look at Cumulative Audiences, *Advertising Research Foundation, 15th Conference Proceedings,* 1969. pp. 8-12

Ephron, Erwin, "Are the People You Want Watching?" *Media/scope,* Oct. 1967, pp. 46[a]

Friedman, Lawrence, "Calculating TV Reach and Frequency," in *Journal of Advertising Research,* Aug. 1971, pp. 21-26

Keshin, Mort, "Ins and Outs of TV Audience Cume," in *Media/scope,* May, 1968, pp. 11[a]

Mayer, Martin, "A Writer Looks at TV Ratings," in *Journal of Advertising Research,* Oct. 1972, pp. 3-10

Media/scope, "Cox's Case for Cume," Sept., 1968, pp. 99-140

Mills, Martin, "How to Estimate Network TV Audiences," in *Media/scope,* Mar., 1966, pp. 90-93

Orenstein, Frank, Newspaper Researcher's View of TV, *Media/scope,* March 1968, pp. 79-82

Papazian, Edward, "The Sixth Quintile," in *Media Decisions,* Sept., 1973, pp. 12-16

Papazian, Edward, "Will the Real Average Minute Viewer Please Stand Up?" *Media/scope,* June, 1967, pp. 51-54

Towers, Irwin M., Goodman Leo A. and Zeisel, Hans, "What Could Nonexposure Tell the TV Advertiser?" in *Journal of Marketing,* July 1963, pp. 52-56

Twyman, W. A., "A Technique for Measuring Program vs. Commercial Audiences—New Findings from British Television," in *Advertising Research Foundation, 15th Annual Conference Proceedings,* 1969, pp. 32-38

chapter 7

Decisions About Print Media

Use of circulation data in planning. Measurements of circulation are available for most newspaper and magazine vehicles, but this data is of limited usefulness in making selection decisions because it is too crude. It does not provide the planner with precise enough information that he needs to select the best media to reach targets.

Circulation data is crude because it does not reflect the number of readers in a vehicle's audience. One unit of circulation means one copy of the periodical distributed. But for every copy distributed there may be as many as six different readers. Therefore one cannot know the size of a vehicle's audience by looking at its circulation; it is the audience size that is one of the major considerations in media selection. In addition, circulation data tells the planner nothing about the demographics of the audience, whereas his planning is based on reaching precise targets defined demographically.

As a result, circulation data is not used much in planning for magazine selection. However, it is often used in making decisions about newspapers because there is little or no audience data available. Circulation data, while admittedly crude, is still valuable, but on a limited basis.

When circulation data must be used, then measurements verified by the Audit Bureau of Circulation (See Figure 22) are the most reliable. The accuracy of ABC audits are widely accepted throughout the advertising industry. The ABC is a non-profit, cooperative association of about 1,100 advertisers, advertising agencies, and 2,800 daily and weekly newspapers, business publications, magazines and farm publications in the United States and Canada. It audits and reports circulations of these publications at regular intervals.

ABC data will include paid circulations categorized for newspapers by city zone, trading zone, and outside both areas. In addition, circulation is categorized for newspapers by Standard Metropolitan Statistical Areas. Therefore this data may be used to determine how the distribution of circulation matches selling and marketing areas of advertisers.

Magazine data from ABC shows the circulation categorized by size of metropolitan areas, by regions of the United States, and by other geographical divisions, all aimed at helping the planner choose the medium which best reaches geographical targets. But no demographic data of the reading audience is available from ABC.

Figure 22
Sample Page from an ABC Magazine Publisher's Statement*

COSMOPOLITAN

CLASS, INDUSTRY OR FIELD SERVED: Young women, married or single interested in self-improvement, careers, clothes, beauty, travel, entertainment and arts-with special emphasis on the world outside the home, edited to help young women realize the very most of themselves.

1. AVERAGE PAID CIRCULATION FOR 6 MONTHS ENDING DECEMBER 31, 1974:

Subscriptions:	123,773
Single Copy Sales:	1,808,361
AVERAGE TOTAL PAID CIRCULATION	1,932,134

Average Total Non-Paid Distribution   5,539

1a. AVERAGE PAID CIRCULATION of Regional, Metro, & Demographic editions.

Edition & Number of Issues		Edition & Number of Issues	Edition & Number of Issues
Eastern Region (6)	843,912		
Central Region (6)	527,644		
Western Region (6)	560,578		

See Paragraph 12(a)

2. PAID CIRCULATION (Total of subscriptions and single copy sales) BY ISSUES:

Issue		Issue		Issue	
July	1,945,949	Sept.	1,953,208	Nov.	1,862,254
Aug.	2,167,732	Oct.	1,916,751	Dec.	1,746,910

3. U. S. PAID CIRCULATION BY ABCD COUNTY SIZE based on August, 1974 issue:

January, 1973 issue used in establishing percentages.

Total paid circulation of this issue was 12.19% greater than average total paid circulation for period.

County Size	No. of Counties	% of U.S. Population	Subscription Circulation Copies	% Total	Single Copy Circulation Copies	% Total	Total Circulation Copies	% Total
A	135	41%	62,777	51.97%	964,723	52.02%	1,027,500	52.02%
B	271	27%	34,511	28.57%	526,128	28.37%	560,639	28.38%
C	554	17%	14,266	11.81%	258,150	13.92%	272,416	13.79%
D	2,113	15%	9,241	7.65%	105,522	5.69%	114,763	5.81%
	3,073	100%	120,795	100.00%	1,854,523	100.00%	1,975,318	100.00%
Alaska-Hawaii	33		735		18,045		18,780	
Unclas-sified					103		103	
TOTAL U.S.	3,106		121,530		1,872,671		1,994,201	

*Reprinted by permission of Cosmopolitan Magazine

Figure 22 (Continued)
Sample Page from an ABC Magazine Publisher's Statement*

4. GEOGRAPHIC ANALYSIS OF TOTAL PAID CIRCULATION FOR THE August, 1974 issue:

Total paid circulation of this issue was 12.19% greater than average total paid circulation for period.

STATE	Subs.	Single Copy Sales	TOTAL	%
Maine	285	8,969	9,254	
New Hampshire	333	11,229	11,562	
Vermont	234	3,257	3,491	
Massachusetts	3,124	65,019	68,143	
Rhode Island	573	7,659	8,232	
Connecticut	2,054	31,792	33,846	
NEW ENGLAND	6,603	127,925	134,528	6.21
New York	12,939	212,389	225,328	
New Jersey	5,631	71,023	76,654	
Pennsylvania	7,246	107,139	114,385	
MIDDLE ATLANTIC	25,816	390,551	416,367	19.21
Ohio	6,035	78,131	84,166	
Indiana	2,529	36,502	39,031	
Illinois	7,364	102,764	110,128	
Michigan	4,360	83,860	88,220	
Wisconsin	2,150	40,938	43,088	
EAST NO. CENTRAL	22,438	342,195	364,633	16.82
Minnesota	1,828	32,458	34,286	
Iowa	1,634	13,435	15,069	
Missouri	2,806	24,297	27,103	
North Dakota	180	4,433	4,613	
South Dakota	248	4,760	5,008	
Nebraska	1,073	11,090	12,163	
Kansas	1,239	17,791	19,030	
WEST NO. CENTRAL	9,008	108,264	117,272	5.41
Delaware	373	5,553	5,926	
Maryland	2,381	21,585	23,966	
District of Columbia	858	40,168	41,026	
Virginia	2,923	18,242	21,165	
West Virginia	511	8,678	9,189	
North Carolina	2,351	30,299	32,650	
South Carolina	1,062	12,916	13,978	
Georgia	2,684	39,695	42,379	
Florida	5,907	75,765	81,672	
SOUTH ATLANTIC	19,050	252,901	271,951	12.55
Kentucky	1,555	14,146	15,701	
Tennessee	2,060	25,014	27,074	
Alabama	1,481	17,385	18,866	
Mississippi	979	4,671	5,650	
EAST SO. CENTRAL	6,075	61,216	67,291	3.10
Arkansas	574	11,839	12,413	
Louisiana	2,061	22,496	24,557	
Oklahoma	937	20,172	21,109	
Texas	5,235	93,045	98,280	
WEST SO. CENTRAL	8,807	147,552	156,359	7.21
Montana	244	7,019	7,263	
Idaho	294	7,695	7,989	
Wyoming	173	3,134	3,307	
Colorado	1,599	30,711	32,310	
New Mexico	421	8,020	8,441	
Arizona	1,137	22,884	24,021	
Utah	391	8,451	8,842	
Nevada	511	17,163	17,674	
MOUNTAIN	4,770	105,077	109,847	5.07
Alaska	210	6,393	6,593	
Washington	1,908	40,067	41,975	
Oregon	1,133	21,331	22,464	
California	15,187	257,444	272,631	
Hawaii	525	11,662	12,187	
PACIFIC	18,963	336,887	355,850	16.42
Miscellaneous		103	103	
Unclassified				
UNITED STATES	121,530	1,872,671	1,994,201	92.00
Possessions & Other Areas	138	5,160	5,298	0.24
U.S. & POSSESSIONS, etc.	121,668	1,877,831	1,999,499	92.24

	Subs.	Single Copy Sales	TOTAL	%
Canada	1,194	137,977	139,171	6.42
Newfoundland	17	805	822	0.59
Nova Scotia	30	4,218	4,248	3.05
Prince Edward Island		276	276	0.20
New Brunswick	13	2,823	2,836	2.04
Quebec	121	15,341	15,462	11.11
Ontario	622	60,649	61,271	44.03
Manitoba	76	6,479	6,555	4.71
Saskatchewan	45	3,561	3,606	2.59
Alberta	85	15,426	15,511	11.14
British Columbia	169	27,925	28,094	20.19
Northwest Territories	14	188	202	0.14
Yukon Territory	2	286	288	0.21
CANADA	1,194	137,977	139,171	100.00
Foreign	922	12,147	13,069	0.60
Unclassified				
Military or Civilian Personnel Overseas	599	15,394	15,993	0.74
GRAND TOTAL	124,383	2,043,349	2,167,732	100.00

3a. CANADIAN PAID CIRCULATION BY ABCD COUNTY SIZE based on August, 1974 issue:

Total paid circulation of this issue was 12.19% greater than average total paid circulation for period.

County Size	No. of Counties	% of Canadian Pop.	Subscription Circulation Copies	% Total	Single Copy Circulation Copies	% Total	Total Circulation Copies	% Total
A	46	61%	892	75.21%	100,120	73.03%	101,012	73.05%
B	47	16%	133	11.21%	15,708	11.46%	15,841	11.46%
C	56	11%	78	6.58%	13,138	9.58%	13,216	9.56%
D	111	12%	83	7.00%	8,131	5.93%	8,214	5.93%
Unclassified					8		880	888
TOTAL	260	100%	1,194	100.00%	137,977	100.00%	139,171	100.00%

*Reprinted by permission of Cosmopolitan Magazine

131

ANALYSIS OF THE TOTAL NEW AND RENEWAL SUBSCRIPTIONS
Sold During 6 Months Period Ending December 31, 1974

5. AUTHORIZED PRICES and total subscriptions sold:

(a) Basic Prices: Single Copy $1.00. See Par. 12(b)
   Subscriptions: 1 yr. $15.00, 2 yrs. $30.00, 3 yrs. $45.00, 4 yrs. $60.00, 5 yrs. $75.00 42,018
(b) Higher - than Basic Prices: Par 12(c) ....
(c) Lower - than Basic Prices: Par. 12(d) 4,081
(d) Association Subscription Prices .... None

   Total Subscriptions Sold in Period 46,099

6. DURATION OF SUBSCRIPTIONS SOLD:

(a) For five years or more 677
(b) For three to five years 1,850
(c) For one to three years 43,153
(d) For less than one year 419

   Total Subscriptions Sold in Period 46,099

7. CHANNELS OF SUBSCRIPTIONS:

(a) Ordered by mail 39,460
(b) Ordered through salesmen:
   1. Catalog agencies and individual agents 3,681
   2. Publisher's own and other publishers' salesmen 2,780
   3. Independent agencies' salesmen 32
   4. Newspaper agencies 1
   5. Members of schools, churches, fraternal and similar organizations 145
(c) Association memberships .... None
(d) All other channels .... None

   Total Subscriptions Sold in Period 46,099

8. USE OF PREMIUMS:

(a) Ordered without premium 46,099
(b) Ordered with material reprinted from this publication .... None
(c) Ordered with other premiums .... None

   Total Subscriptions Sold in Period 46,099

ADDITIONAL CIRCULATION INFORMATION

9. ARREARS & EXTENSIONS: Average number included in PAID (Par. 1) which represents:

(a) Average number of copies served on subscriptions carried in arrears not more than three months .... None

10. COLLECTION STIMULANTS .... None

11. BASIS ON WHICH COPIES WERE SOLD TO RETAIL OUTLETS & BOYS:
   Fully returnable 100.00%

12. EXPLANATORY:

Latest Released Audit Report issued for 12 months ending June 30, 1973.

(a) Par. 1(e): In addition to total circulation, advertising is available in any one or combination of three regional areas. Basic editorial content is the same in all regional areas.

(b) Par. 5(a): In a single copy price test 215,304 copies of the December, 1974 issue was sold at $1.25 per copy.

(c) Par. 5(b): Higher Than Basic Prices: Subscriptions: Canada, 1 year $17.00, 2 years $34.00, 3 years $51.00, 4 years $68.00, 5 years $85.00. Pan American and Foreign Countries, 1 year $19.00, 2 years $38.00, 3 years $57.00, 4 years $76.00, 5 years $95.00. Single Copy: Canada, $1.25 per copy.

(d) Paragraph 5(c): Lower Than Basic Prices: Employes, 1 year $7.50; Transportation Companies, 1 year $7.50; 2 years $1500. Combination Sales Prices: Prices for combination sales of this publication with other publications were 80.52% to 86.89% of combined basic prices or publications in combinations. Combination sale prices were $139.50 to $212.57 in actual amounts.

We hereby certify that all statements set forth in this statement are true.   04-0225-0

COSMOPOLITAN, published by, The Hearst Corporation, 959 Eighth Avenue, New York, New York 10019

ALBERT A. RACHOI   FRANK R. DUPUY, Jr.

   Vice President & Director of Circulation   Publisher

   Date Signed, January 30, 1975.

*Reprinted by permission of Cosmopolitan Magazine

The Total Audience Concept. The total audience concept, was introduced earlier. It represents the idea that all readers of a magazine should be counted as part of a media vehicle's audience, no matter where readers come in contact with the magazine. Most readers of most magazines have regular opportunities to come into contact with their favorite magazines because they live in a household where someone paid for a subscription, which are delivered regularly to a household. Readers who live in such households are called "primary" because they are first to see the magazine and they have a regular opportunity to see it. It is often presumed that primary readers are the ones who should be counted first and who should comprise the target audience. All other readers are called "secondary" and they are often considered less important than primary readers because they do not have a regular opportunity to see the magazine. Secondary readers are composed of pass-along readers who come into contact with magazine in doctors' offices, barber or beauty shops, or at newsstands, or in the home of the original subscriber.

Not all media planners believe in the total audience concept; some prefer to use only primary audience data in planning and, if they use secondary audience data, they may discount the latter group.

Heavy-user data matched to magazine readership. Most planners prefer to use demographic breakdowns rather than total audience data for selecting magazines. However, many others are relying on heavy-user data matched to magazine readership as another means of finding the best alternatives. If it can be shown that heavy users of a given product tend to read one magazine more than some other, this provides further evidence that aids in making a final decision. Figure 23 shows how the data looks in a product market, with heavy-user readership.

The value of secondary (or pass-along) audiences. Since the primary audiences have a regular opportunity to see a given magazine and secondary audiences do not, then primary audiences should be more valuable to the media planner. In a study, called Printed Advertising Rating Methods (PARM) it was found that primary readers were more valuable than secondary readers; not necessarily because they had a better opportunity to see the magazine, but because they paid more attention to advertisements than did secondary readers. Furthermore, the PARM study showed that, for the Gallup-Robinson (Aided Recall) Measuring Technique, fewer of the out-of-home pass-along readers were able to recall ads than other secondary readers. Table 39 shows some of the findings that support the conclusion that primary readers are more valuable than secondary readers.

Although there were differences between Starch and Gallup-Robinson, each method found less recall among pass-along audiences than primary audiences.

Audits and Surveys Research Company conducted a study for *Look Magazine* and found the following differences between primary and secondary audience recall as shown in Table 40.

Figure 23
Sample Page from Simmons*

AVERAGE-ISSUE AUDIENCE
PAPER NAPKINS — HOUSEHOLD USAGE BY AMOUNT AND BRAND
TOTAL FEMALE HEADS
(IN THOUSANDS)

	U.S. TOTAL	AMERICAN BABY	AMERICAN HOME	BETTER HOMES & GARDENS	COSMOPOLITAN	FAMILY CIRCLE	FAMILY HEALTH	FAMILY WEEKLY	GLAMOUR	GOOD HOUSEKEEPING	HOLIDAY	HOUSE BEAUTIFUL	HOUSE & GARDEN	LADIES' HOME JOURNAL	LIFE	MADEMOISELLE	MC CALL'S	MODERN ROMANCES
TOTAL	61330	757	6520	15498	3664	11958	1151	7903	3053	11645	1315	2846	3697	12330	11335	2284	13024	1987
PCT. MKT. COV.	100.0	1.2	10.6	25.3	6.0	19.5	1.9	12.9	5.0	19.0	2.1	4.6	6.0	20.1	18.5	3.7	21.2	3.2
USED PAPER NAPKINS IN PAST MONTH	42339	504	4975	11655	2742	9255	906	5627	2112	8734	992	2164	2800	9386	8300	1553	9953	946
PCT. COMP.	69.0	66.6	76.3	75.2	74.8	77.4	78.7	71.2	69.2	75.0	75.4	76.0	75.7	76.1	73.2	68.0	76.4	47.6
INDEX	100	97	111	109	108	112	114	103	100	109	109	110	110	110	106	99	111	69
PCT. MKT. COV.	100.0	1.2	11.7	27.5	6.5	21.9	2.1	13.3	5.0	20.6	2.3	5.1	6.6	22.2	19.6	3.7	23.5	2.2
AMOUNT USED IN PAST MONTH (60 NAPKIN PKG. EQUIVALENT) LESS THAN 3	25178	228	2756	6645	1606	5054	540	3385	1233	4885	502	1146	1530	5483	4804	924	5830	618
PCT. COMP.	41.1	30.1	42.3	42.9	43.8	42.3	46.9	42.8	40.4	41.9	38.2	40.3	41.4	44.5	42.4	40.5	44.8	31.1
INDEX	100	73	103	104	107	103	114	104	98	102	93	98	101	108	103	99	109	76
PCT. MKT. COV.	100.0	.9	10.9	26.4	6.4	20.1	2.1	13.4	4.9	19.4	2.0	4.6	6.1	21.8	19.1	3.7	23.2	2.5
3 TO LESS THAN 6	9359	*147	1220	2615	620	2148	*165	1403	443	2015	333	465	664	2068	1765	333	2215	**121
PCT. COMP.	15.3	19.4	18.7	16.9	16.9	18.0	14.3	17.8	14.5	17.3	25.3	16.3	18.0	16.8	15.6	14.6	17.0	6.1
INDEX	100	127	122	110	110	118	93	116	95	113	165	107	118	110	102	95	111	40
PCT. MKT. COV.	100.0	1.6	13.0	27.9	6.6	23.0	1.8	15.0	4.7	21.5	3.6	5.0	7.1	22.1	18.9	3.6	23.7	1.3
6 OR MORE	7801	*129	1000	2395	516	2053	*201	838	436	1834	157	553	607	1836	1730	297	1908	*207
PCT. COMP.	12.7	17.0	15.3	15.5	14.1	17.2	17.5	10.6	14.3	15.7	11.9	19.4	16.4	14.9	15.3	13.0	14.6	10.4
INDEX	100	134	122	122	111	135	138	83	113	124	94	153	129	117	120	102	115	82
PCT. MKT. COV.	100.0	1.7	12.8	30.7	6.6	26.3	2.6	10.7	5.6	23.5	2.0	7.1	7.8	23.5	22.2	3.8	24.5	2.7
3 UR MORE	17161	276	2220	5010	1136	4201	366	2241	878	3850	489	1018	1270	3904	3495	629	4123	328
PCT. COMP.	28.0	36.5	34.0	32.3	31.0	35.1	31.8	28.4	28.8	33.1	37.2	35.8	34.4	31.7	30.8	27.5	31.7	16.5
INDEX	100	130	121	115	111	125	114	101	103	118	133	128	123	113	110	98	113	59
PCT. MKT. COV.	100.0	1.6	12.9	29.2	6.6	24.5	2.1	13.1	5.1	22.4	2.8	5.9	7.4	22.7	20.4	3.7	24.0	1.9

W. R. SIMMONS & ASSOCIATES RESEARCH, INC.
1973

This report is the property of W. R. Simmons and Associates Research, Inc. and is distributed on loan to a limited group of clients, pursuant to contract, for their exclusive and confidential use. Any reproduction, publication, circulation, distribution, or sale of this report or disclosure of its contents thereof, whole or in part, is strictly prohibited. W. R. Simmons and Associates Research, Inc. will avail itself of every remedy in law and in equity respecting any unauthorized use.

*Reprinted by permission of the W. R. Simmons & Associates Research, Inc.

* Reprinted by permission of the W. R. Simmons & Associates Research, Inc.

Table 39
Recall of Ads Using Starch and Gallup-Robinson*

Type of Audience	Percent recall using Starch	Percent recall using Gallup-Robinson
Primary	20.0%	3.2%
Out-of-home pass-along	17.9	2.5

*Source: Advertising Research Foundation and Alfred Politz Research, Inc., *A Study of Printed Advertising Rating Methods,* N.Y. 1956, Vol. III

Table 40
Percent of Respondents Who Were Able to Recall Advertisements*

Type of audience	Verified Recall Average
Subscribers (primary)	27.4%
Non-subscribers (secondary)	17.8

*Source: Roth, Paul, "Why We Discount Out-of-Homes by 50%," in *Media/scope*, March, 1967, p. 64

Here again, fewer secondary readers were able to recall ads than were primary readers.

These research studies provide some clues about the value of secondary, pass-along audiences. If the secondary audiences are deemed less valuable, then it seems reasonable to discount them in some way. But few media planners would ignore them entirely.

Dr. Seymour Marshak, manager of advertising and distribution research of the Ford Motor Company, felt that simply discounting the secondary audience was not correct.[31] Instead it would be better to determine the value of a secondary reader on the basis of how important an individual is in the target audience and determine what opportunities he had to see a given advertisement in a given medium. For example, secondary readers may even be more important than primary readers when they receive only one or two exposure-opportunities compared to primary readers who might receive over 20 opportunities. This assumes that large frequencies (or many exposure opportunities) are not automatically good media strategy. Each marketing-media situation may be different. Foremost in this kind of evaluation is the fact that secondary readers are the most important target audiences and had to be reached if the advertising messages were to have the proper effect.

[31]Marshak, Seymour, "Forum Question: Generally speaking, what value do you place on the secondary or pass-along reader?" in *Media/scope,* Feb., 1970, p. 26

Marshak cited two examples of different ways of determining the value of a pass-along reader:

"1. The product is advertised in only one medium. The secondary reader has a regular source for obtaining the medium and he is a member of the target group. His value should be equal to the value of a primary reader.

2. The product . . . is advertised in many small circulation magazines (e.g. Camping and Fishing magazines plus others). The secondary reader, by chance, sees the ad for a product in media Z while waiting in a pizza parlor. The reader has already seen, or had the opportunities to see the ad in 20 other media. The value of this 21st exposure within a short time period may be very low."

Marshak, therefore, felt that the value of the secondary audience depends on a number of things: (1) whether it is possible to reach the target audience through primary readers; (2) the relative importance of targets where, perhaps, one demographic group may be as much as three times as important as some other demographic target; and (3) whether the planner feels that he needs some other measurement on which to base his decision.

In conclusion then, there seems to be good evidence for not using secondary audience data at full value. The method of discounting the secondary audience should be based on logic and research evidence rather than on subjective judgment alone.

One method for discounting the secondary audience. One method that could be used for discounting the pass-along secondary audience is simply to cut their numbers in half. If Medium A has a 37,000,000 total audience of which 75 percent are primary and 25 percent are secondary (out-of-home) readers, then the latter are discounted 50 percent. Shown in Table 41 are examples where the secondary audience is first treated at full value and then 50 percent discounted value.

Table 41
Two Bases for Analyzing the Audiences of Magazine "A"

Full Value Basis		Out-of-home Audience Discounted 50% Basis	
Primary audience	27,750,000	Primary audience	27,750,000
Out-of-home audience	9,250,000	Out-of-home audience	4,625,000
Total Audience	37,000,000	Total Audience	32,375,000

The example shown in Table 41, however, is based on the total audience. Typically, media planners would use the discount basis on only the demographic group that comprised the target audience such as men ages 18-34, or women who graduated high school, etc.

Reach and Frequency in Print Media

Time is not a consideration in the measurement of the reach of a magazine. One does not speak of the four week reach of Magazine A because it would be too difficult to measure. Conceivably the reach of a magazine continues to grow as long as the magazine is in existence. Perhaps National Geographic magazines printed in the 1920's would have enormous reaches if time were a consideration in measurements.

An issue of a magazine is the basic measuring unit. Therefore the reach of magazines can be expressed in a number of different ways as follows:

1. Total audience
   or
   Target audience
   } of one issue of a magazine. Example: the reach of the July 1st issue of *Newsweek*

2. Total audier/e
   or
   Target audience
   } of multiple issues of the same magazine. Example: the net reach of July 1, July 8, July 15, July 22, and July 29 issues of *Newsweek*

3. Total audience
   or
   Target audience
   } of single issues of different magazines. Example: the net reach of July issues of *McCall's, Ladies Home Journal, Reader's Digest* and *Better Homes & Gardens*.

Frequency, on the other hand, is based on the same principle as for broadcast media. It is the relationship between the reach of a magazine and the duplicated audience. If the target reaches of *McCall's, Ladies Home Journal, Reader's Digest* and *Better Homes and Gardens* for one issue are added, the sum is the duplicated audience. Therefore, the formula for frequency is the same as it was for broadcast as follows:

$$\text{Frequency} = \frac{\text{Total duplicated audiences}}{\text{Reach (or net reach)}}$$

Table 42 shows that it is possible to build reach by buying advertisements in subsequent issues of a given magazine. The reach that way is relatively slow, especially when using monthly magazines such as *McCall's* or *Reader's Digest*. On the other hand, it is possible to build reach faster with weekly magazines.

Another implication of Table 42 is that frequency is also built slowly. In fact, a magazine is not considered to be a high-frequency medium, with some obvious exceptions such as when using *TV Guide* (a magazine with four issues per month).

In order to determine the net reach of multiple issues of the same magazine, special research is required. The research will show the amount of duplication that exists, and the net unduplicated audiences of combination issues.

Table 42
Net Unduplicated Audiences and Frequencies of Selected Magazines*
(Total Female Household Heads. U.S. Population Base: 61,330,000)

						NUMBER OF ISSUES						
	1	2	3	4	5	6	7	8	9	10	11	12
TV Guide												
Reach %	29.5	39.5	45.1	49.0	51.8	54.0	55.8	57.3	58.6	59.8	60.8	61.7
Frequency	1.0	1.5	2.0	2.4	2.9	3.3	3.7	4.1	4.5	4.9	5.3	5.7
Reader's Digest												
Reach %	32.6	40.1	44.1	46.8	48.8	50.3	51.6	52.7	53.6	54.5	55.2	55.8
Frequency	1.0	1.6	2.2	2.8	3.4	3.9	4.4	5.0	5.5	6.0	6.5	7.0
Good Housekeeping												
Reach %	19.0	27.7	33.2	37.0	40.0	42.4	44.3	46.0	47.5	48.7	49.9	50.9
Frequency	1.0	1.4	1.7	2.1	2.4	2.7	3.0	3.3	3.6	3.9	4.2	4.5
McCall's												
Reach %	21.2	27.8	31.6	34.2	36.1	37.7	39.0	40.1	41.1	41.9	42.7	43.3
Frequency	1.0	1.5	2.0	2.5	2.9	3.4	3.8	4.2	4.7	5.1	5.5	5.9
Woman's Day												
Reach %	20.0	27.8	32.3	35.5	37.9	39.8	41.4	42.8	44.0	45.0	46.0	46.8
Frequency	1.0	1.5	1.9	2.3	2.7	3.0	3.4	3.8	4.1	4.5	4.8	5.2

How to Read This Table: For TV Guide, 29.5% of all female household heads were exposed to one issue, and 39.5% were exposed to either the first, second or both issues, but they were counted only once.

Also the 29.5% exposed for TV Guide were exposed to only one issue, but the 39.5% were exposed to an average of 1.5 issues (not 1.5 times).

Source: 1973 Simmons Magazine Audience Report Supplement. Net Unduplicated Average Issue Audiences, pp. D020-D021

Net Unduplicated Audiences of Combinations of Different Media

It is possible to determine the net reach (or net unduplicated audiences) of combinations of different media such as for three different magazines, or two different television programs and one magazine. The concept for measuring them is the same as for individual programs or magazines: if an audience member is exposed at least once, or has contact with the medium at least once, he is counted once no matter how many other times he has contact with the medium.

To illustrate the concept of net unduplicated audiences for three magazines or television programs, Table 43 is shown.

Table 43
Net Unduplicated Audience of Three Media

Reader Number	Reach of Magazine A	Reach of Magazine B	Reach of Magazine C
1	x	x	
2		x	x
3			
4	x	x	x
5			x
6			
7			
8	x	x	x
9			
10		x	x

x = Reader was exposed to the magazine at least once

According to Table 43, reader No. 1 is counted once. Reader No. 2 is also counted once, even though he read two magazines. Reader number four was also counted once even though he was exposed to all three magazines. Counting each reader for only one exposure, then, the net unduplicated audience is 6 out of 10 or 60%. The duplicated audience totals 13 which, when divided by the net reach (6), will show a frequency of 2.3 average issues exposed.

If a media plan calls for a large reach and one individual medium cannot supply that reach, then multiple media will be necessary. Generally those media which are unlike in editorial or entertainment contents will have the smallest amount of duplication and consequently, the largest reach.

Although Table 43 shows three different magazines, the same principles hold true for three different television programs, newspapers, or any other combination of media where duplication is measured.

How to think about the net reach of multiple magazines. Some students have a little difficulty conceptualizing the net reach of a combination of magazines. In order to help clarify this concept, one must remember that the net reach of two magazines includes the entire reach of A and only the new reach (unduplicated reach) added by B. Therefore, the reach of A and B magazines include those who read only magazine A and those who read only magazine B, plus those who read both A and B *with the following exception:* those who read both are counted only once. Figure 24 illustrates the concept.

Special opportunities in magazines. Media planners who want to reach special or limited markets may find that magazines can be adapted to meet their needs. This is because special demographic or geographic editions have been devised by some media for just that purpose. Table 44 is a list of some of the demographic breaks that are available in major consumer and business magazines.

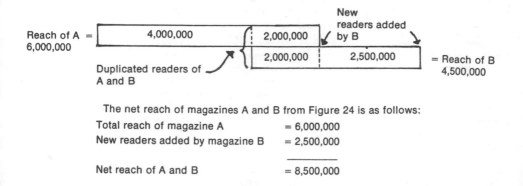

Figure 24
Net Reach of A and B

The net reach of magazines A and B from Figure 24 is as follows:

Total reach of magazine A	= 6,000,000
New readers added by magazine B	= 2,500,000
Net reach of A and B	= 8,500,000

In addition to offering special demographic and geographic breakouts as discussed above, most magazines offer two-way (and in some cases even four-way) copy splits. Among these is *Reader's Digest,* which can distribute special copy to one out of every four subscribers across the nation through the use of zip coding and computers. This trend towards increased flexibility and specialization is expected to continue.

When magazines reach their audiences. Magazine audience data provides information on how many readers of varying demographic segments read a given magazine. Generally a planner is apt to forget that all magazines do not reach their audiences at the same time. The timing then of magazines may be important if the marketing considerations demand quick message assimilation. But there is evidence to show that the nature of a magazine may affect its timing ability to reach prospects. For example, *TV Guide* is a magazine that would be read quickly and reach its entire audience in about a week. On the other hand, some magazines, with large pass-along readership, take a longer period of time to reach their audiences. This might include *Business Week* and *Sports Illustrated.* Ed Papazian, media director of B.B.D.&O. reported the degree to which some magazines reached their audiences by certain time periods in Table 45.

Some considerations about newspapers for national advertisers. National advertisers tend to use magazines, radio and television more than they use newspapers, but this in no way limits the value of the medium. The primary uses of newspapers for national advertisers are: (a) to support new product introductions with immediate and broad market coverage; (b) to deliver local advertising that requires specific printed information, for example, price advertising; (c) to provide local dealer support in connection with availability of new merchandise or models; for example, auto advertising; (d) to provide local print advertising that requires a reader response as in the use of coupon ads; and (e) to provide advertising support for products which are prohibited in broadcast media.

Table 44
Some Demographic Editions of Magazines

Publication	Demographic Edition	Name of Edition
Better Homes & Gardens	High income, New home market	Super spot, Movers Edition
Esquire	Upper income male home-owners	Homeowners Marketing edition
Fortune	Mfg.	Mfg. Edition
	Financial	Financial Demo. edition
McCall's	Top income	V.I.P./Zip
Nation's Business	Industrial top management executives	Industrial Edition
Newsweek	Students	Student Edition
Reader's Digest	Affluent Subscribers	Reader's Digest, Demo. 1
Time	College Student	College Student Edition
	Educators	Educators Edition
	Doctors	Doctors Edition
	Businessmen	Time "B"

But some exciting uses of the medium is in Hi-Fi or Spectacolor printing where four-color fidelity is very high. Although both of these techniques are very expensive, they may be just the kind of local medium that is needed for special impact.

Some newspapers allow the use of Flexform Advertising. A flexform ad is one which is designed in free-form shapes and floated within a page. Editorial material surrounds it. Because the shape of flexform is so unusual, it may attract a great deal of attention. However, not all newspapers allow flexform because it represents a rather difficult problem in arranging editorial material around it. Most newspapers who allow it are in B and C counties. (smaller population counties).

Table 45
How Long Some Magazines Take to Reach Their Audiences*

Time period	Sunday Supplement	TV Guide	Reader's Digest	Typical women's service monthly
First day	90%	50%	20%	10-15%
1 to 7 days	100	90	45	40%
1 to 14 days	—	97	65	60
1 to 21 days	—	100	70	65
1 to 28 days	—	—	75	70
1 to 35 days	—	—	80	75
1 to 42 days	—	—	85	80
1 to 49 days	—	—	89	85
1 to 56 days	—	—	93	89
1 to 63 days	—	—	96	93
1 to 70 days	—	—	98	97
1 to 77 days	—	—	100	100

*Source: Papazian, Ed, "How Fast Does a Magazine Reach Its Total Audience?" in *Media/scope,* Jan., 1966, p. 64

Another Consideration in Print Media Planning: Qualitative Values

As stated earlier in the text, media selection is based mostly on the ability of media to reach precise target audiences at low cost efficiency with little waste. Some other considerations in planning might be the total cost of the media plus the reach and frequency to be generated. Before a final decision for or against any medium is made, however, the planner ought to consider the qualitative values of each medium and how important they are for his plan.

A qualitative value of a medium is some characteristic of that medium that would enhance the chances of an advertising message carried within it of being effective. It is based on the assumption that media are not simply passive carriers of advertisements; they are active carriers. A medium is an environment with a personality of its own that may rub off on its advertisements and make them more effective in disseminating advertising messages. Social Research Company defined this environment as follows:

"Think of a magazine similar to a geographic location, a neighborhood, or a section of town. There are certain meanings that are generally associated with the location, and these meanings usually are known and taken for granted by most people living in the community. When an advertiser buys a lot in that location, he automatically buys whatever connotations the neighborhood carried. The building he erects on this site (or the ad he places in this magazine) is responded to in terms of its own merits. But the edifice is also thought of in connection with its location, and this will either add to or detract from the impression the building makes."[32]

A medium's environment, therefore, may represent a qualitative value which could affect each advertisement carried within it. William Weilbacher, vice president of Dancer, Fitzgerald, Sample agency defined a qualitative value in a more specific way as follows:

"... Qualitative media value is the total increment to advertising message effect contributed by the medium or medium vehicle. This qualitative medium value includes such individual contributors ... as the special characteristics of the audience attracted to the medium or vehicle, and whatever personality characteristics are attributed to it by its audience members.

Implicit in this usage of the terms qualitative value is the notion, that, beyond individual and definable source ... such as demographic and attitudinal characteristics, the medium may also contribute completely undefined, even unanticipated values to the advertising process. . . "[33]

Weilbacher warned, however, that his concept of a qualitative value did not include such general media characteristics as the image and prestige of each medium because these, although easily measured, did not necessarily add to advertising effectiveness. He preferred to deal with qualitative values that affect individual advertisements, specifically.

Weilbacher's warning, however, focuses attention on the kinds of problems planners face in using the concept of qualitative values for media planning. Because it is so easy to measure the image of a magazine, it is often done. One way to measure the image is to compile a list of adjectives that could describe a magazine and ask respondents in a study which best represents the medium being studied. Such adjectives are: interesting, learned, dynamic, timely, modern, alert, etc. Then the findings may be presented in a graphic form as shown in Figure No. 25. Shown at the bottom of the graphic in boxes are the percents of respondents who felt that the adjective in question best described the magazine.

The problem with studies of magazine images is: what does one do with the results? Because one magazine has a different and presumably better image than another magazine, does this have anything to do with advertising effectiveness? There is very little evidence to suggest such a relationship. Therefore image studies, though a form of determining a qualitative value, have little importance in media planning.

[32]Social Research, Inc., *Advertising Impact and Business Magazines,* Chicago, 1959, p. ii
[33]Weilbacher, W.M., "The Qualitative Value of Advertising Media," in *Journal of Advertising Research,* Dec. 1960, p. 14

Figure 25

Graphic Profile of a Magazine's Image*

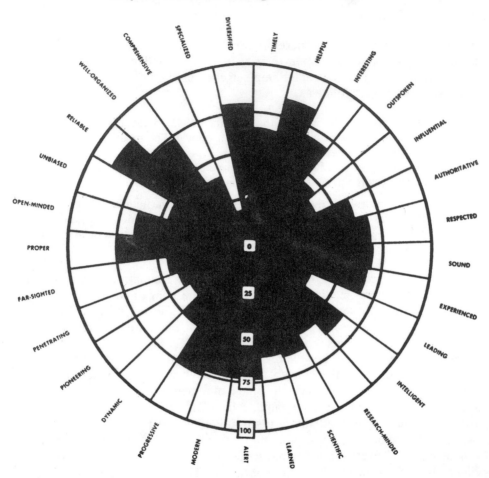

*Reprinted by permission of the Marsteller Co., Inc.

The kind of research needed to prove that media have qualitative values is that which tests the effectiveness of the same advertisement in two or more media. If all variables are held constant, then differences in reactions to the same advertisements may be due to qualitative values.

Alfred Politz studied responses by women to 12 advertisements appearing in *McCall's* versus responses to the same 12 advertisements place in *Life* and *Look* magazines. In order to isolate the qualitative media effects of each medium he solicited responses from his sample first with no exposure to the ads to determine what respondents knew about the brands without them having seen the ads.

Then he exposed the ads to the respondents in all three magazines, after which he measured responses again. Any differences between the no exposure and one exposure were attributed to the qualitative differences of the medium as they affected readership of ads within them.[34]

Shown in Table 46 are some of Politz's findings from the study:

Table 46
Some Findings from the Politz Study*

Percent of respondents who:	McCall's	Life/Look
1. Were familiar with the brand:		
a. With No Exposure	16.3%	15.0%
b. With One Exposure	20.6	18.2
2. Believed claims found in ads:		
a. With No Exposure.............................	17.0	16.5
b. With One Exposure	19.4	17.8
3. Considered advertised brand to be one of the "very highest quality:"		
a. With No Exposure.............................	17.6	17.8
b. With One Exposure	21.4	18.8
4. Were interested in buying the brand:		
a. With No Exposure.............................	10.3	10.1
b. With One Exposure	13.2	11.6

*Source: Politz, Alfred and *McCall's, A Measurement of Advertising Effectiveness,* Nov. 1962, p. 11.

Not only were there differences in responses with no exposure between *McCall's* and *Life/Look,* but there were greater differences after one exposure between the two magazine measurements. Presumably these differences were the effect of the media.

Notwithstanding Politz's and others' research on qualitative values, there is still little consensus about the matter. The tendency in most advertising agencies is to rely very little on such evidence of qualitative values in media planning; but they do use subjective interpretations instead of objective evidence of qualitative values in planning. When they do they are apt to prepare the following kind of statement for their plans: "We feel that medium A reflects greater authority and prestige than other media and therefore recommend that we purchase X number of ads in it."

Other terms that are used in the same manner are: impact, mood, believability, atmosphere, authority, excitement, and leadership. In addition, print media are sometimes judged on the following qualitative values:

a. Reputation of media for attracting ads of only the highest quality products. It is assumed, therefore, that readers knowing this fact will be more favorably inclined toward products and brands advertised in these media than they would for products and brands advertised in other media.

[34]Politz, Alfred, and *McCall's,* "A Measurement of Advertising Effectiveness," Nov. 1962, p. 11.

b. New product editorial features. Some magazines are known for their editorial features wherein they cover the new product field. It is assumed, therefore, that readers know this and when they want to learn about the existence of new products they turn to such magazines in preference to some other magazine.

c. Advertising copy censorship. Some media have a reputation for examining the veracity of all advertising copy and claims and annually reject many dollars of advertising. They publicize this fact regularly. The assumption here is that readers, knowing of this practice, will prefer to read ads in these magazines in preference to magazines that do not publicize their censorship efforts.

d. Some magazines claim to have more innovators in their audiences than others. An innovator is defined as someone who is first to buy new products or new services before the masses do. Presumably advertisers with new products will want to advertise in a medium that has a large audience of innovators.

e. Reading days. How many days, totally, are alternative magazines read? If a magazine is opened at any time on given day, this could constitute a reading-day. If, for example, there is evidence that magazine A is read more total days than magazines B, C, D, and E (all under consideration) then the planner has one more qualitative reason to select A. More reading days represent more opportunities to see ads.

f. Reading time. In a similar manner, it is possible to measure the total or average number of hours spent reading magazines. These measurements may indicate that the magazine with the largest number of reading hours is simply more attractive than others. Therefore, it also may be assumed that audience members have more opportunities to see ads if they spend more time reading.

g. Page openings. It is possible to measure the number of pages opened in alternative magazines. A technique in which a tiny spot of glue is applied to pages containing ads may be used. Respondents may be given specially glued magazines on a given day. On the next day (or two) the interviewer may return and pick up the special copies. He then counts the number of pages pulled open. Another variation of page opening measurements is simply to count page traffic on all ad pages. Using a "recognition measuring technique" researchers count the number of pages where any ads on the page were noted by audience members who comprise a sample. Page traffic data is a measure of the net potential audience size of a magazine and may play a role in the final selection decision for or against alternative magazines.

h. Response to coupons, information or recipes. Measurements of the number of audience members who send in coupons, or ask for information, or recipes may constitute a qualitative measure that could help a planner differentiate one magazine from another. This information, however, is not public for all magazines and may be difficult, if not impossible, to obtain. In situations where an advertiser runs the *same* ad in more than one magazine, it is sometimes possible to learn which magazine pulled best.

i. Number of editorial special features. A magazines promotion director may keep records of the number of special features that his magazine runs in comparison with the number run by his competitors. For example, the number of articles on cakes, salads or furniture run yearly by one magazine may far outdistance competitors, providing the media planner with evidence that could lead to a favorable decision on behalf of the magazine with the largest number of articles.

The above list is by no means complete, but it does show how media planners might look at the qualitative values of various media and use them in planning.

Probably the most misused of all media qualitative value terms is that of "impact." Print media executives often claim their magazine has more impact than other magazines. If they mean that an ad in their magazine will sell more of the product than any other magazine, then they are exaggerating the power of their publication because it can't be proved. It is not possible to parse out the effect of a medium and an advertisement on sales. Conceivably, there could be a careful testing program conducted for one advertiser and, with strict controls, prove that more targets recalled a given ad in their magazine than any other. But recall and sales are quite different. How can one prove that it wasn't the price, the packaging, the distribution or the sales promotion that sold the product? It can't be. Yet some media are better than others, but not on the basis of impact, which is too vague to be used in media planning. Only when a clear-cut cause-and-effect relationship can be established for the brand and the medium on sales can the concept of impact be used. Any other use is simply too vague.

Guidelines in the use of qualitative values. Qualitative rationales for selecting media have a place in planning procedures. But there are some reasonable guidelines that ought to be kept in mind if they are used:

1. Qualitative, or subjective, rationales should never be a total replacement for quantitative substantiation. The reason is obvious.

2. Qualitative considerations come after quantitative analysis and thereby modify numerical relationships.

3. If possible, more than one person should contribute to making subjective analysis in order to reduce the possibility of individual bias.

4. Media sponsored research concerning qualitative values such as high impact, "liked-most," etc. should be considered highly suspect. Much of this kind of research tends to be highly promotional rather than objective. It is very difficult to transfer the findings from one medium to another.

In conclusion then, qualitative values of media are felt to exist, but they can't be used to any great extent in media planning. They are simply not objective enough to be used alone for decision-making. Perhaps ways will be found in the future to prove that one medium indeed has more impact than some others, but at present it cannot be proved. Experts can only agree that media are not passive carriers of ads. They do have qualitative values, and some can be used for planning purposes.

QUESTIONS

1. What is the value of having circulation audited by the ABC?
2. Why do some media planners feel that the primary audience of a magazine is more important than the secondary audience?

3. Explain why the four-week reach of a magazine is not measured as it is in television.
4. What is the advantage of having available special demographic editions of magazines?
5. Why would it matter whether a magazine reaches its total audience quickly or slowly in planning media?
6. What is the role of qualitative media values in making media selections of magazines?
7. Why did Alfred Politz measure the percentage of respondents who were familiar with a brand with no exposure to a magazine, and then, with one exposure? Would not a measurement of just one exposure have been sufficient?
8. How are pass-along readers of magazines discounted by planners who feel such readers are less valuable than primary readers?
9. If a planner wanted to build reach quickly, which of the three methods of building reach would he use?
10. Which kinds of magazines tend to develop large reach, and which develop large frequency?

SELECTED READINGS

Aaker, David A., and Brown, Phillip K., "Evaluating Vehicle Source Effects," in *Journal of Advertising Research*, Aug., 1972, pp. 11-16

Advertising Age, "Experts View Magazine Selling," Oct. 1969, pp. 111+

Agostini, J. M., "How to Estimate Unduplicated Audiences," in *Journal of Advertising Research*, Mar., 1961, pp. 11-14

Glenn, Norman R., "How Do Media Buyers See Newspapers?" in *Media Decisions*, June, 1972, p. 2

Joyce, Timothy, "The State of the Art in Media/Marketing Research," Speech given to Atlanta Media Planners Assn., and Magazine Advertising Representatives, May 13, 1974

Joyce, Timothy, *A Better Way to Measure Magazine Audiences*, Axiom Marketing Research Bureau, Inc., 1973

Kaatz, Ronald B., "Improving Agostini's Formula for Net Audiences," in *Journal of Advertising Research*, Sept., 1963, pp. 43-44

Lucas, Darrell B., "Can Total Magazine Audience Be Ignored?" in *Media/scope*, Nov., 1964, pp. 64-72

Marder, Eric, "How Good is the Editorial Interest Method of Measuring Magazine Audiences?" in *Journal of Advertising Research*, March., 1967, pp. 2-6

Marsteller, Rickard, Gebhardt and Reed, Inc., *Qualitative Media Measurements*, Chicago, 1959

Maneloveg, Herbert, "The Total Audience Concept for Magazines - Good if Understood," *Advertising Age*, Oct. 14, 1963, pp. 84-85

Media/scope Forum, "Question: Generally Speaking, What Value Do You Place on Secondary or Pass-along Readers?" Feb., 1970, p. 26

Bass, K. M., Pessemier, E. A., and Tigert, D. J. "A Taxonomy of Magazine Readership Applied to Problems in Marketing Strategy and Media Selection," in *Journal of Business*, July, 1969, pp. 337-363

McClathery, D. G., "Claimed Frequency vs. Editorial-Interest Measure of Repeat Magazine Audiences," *Journal of Advertising Research*, March., 1967, pp. 7-15

McDonald, Frank, "Needed: Better Magazine Audience Data," *Advertising Age*, Dec. 31, 1973, p. 19

Papazian, Edward, "Application of Audience Concepts in Print Media Planning," in *Media/scope*, Oct., 1964, pp. 67+

Roth, Paul, "Why We Discount Out-of-Home by 50%", in *Media/scope*, March, 1967, pp. 63-68

Roth, Paul, "What is the Value of the Pass-along Audience?" in *Media/scope*, Nov., 1963, pp. 84-87

Shiffman, Phil, "Special Significance of Newsstand Sales Data on Magazines," *Media Decisions*, July, 1973, p. 82

Swan, Carroll J., "In Magazines - Selectivity Within Within," *Media/scope*, July, 1968, p. 33

Weilbacher, William, "The Qualitative Values of Advertising Media," in *Journal of Advertising Research*, Dec., 1960, pp. 12-17

Wiener, Norman, "What's Wrong With Newsstand Distribution of Magazines?" *Advertising Age*, Oct. 16, 1972, pp. 59-60

Zeltner, Herbert, "Primary or Total Audience?" in *Media/scope*, July, 1962, p. 8

Zeltner, Herbert, "Ramifications of the Pass-along Question," *Media/scope*, July, 1964, p. 11+

Marketmath, Inc. *Advertising Reach and Frequency in Magazines*, Readers Digest, 1967

chapter 8

An Introduction To
Media Strategy Planning

One of the most frequently used words in marketing and advertising is "strategy." There is marketing strategy, pricing strategy, copy strategy and media strategy. What, precisely, is strategy; and where does it fit into the decision processes in media planning?

A strategy is a series of actions, usually planned ahead of time, to accomplish specific and stated goals. Whenever there are alternative ways of accomplishing a goal, then there is the need for strategy. In media planning there are many opportunities for the use of strategy, and inevitably a problem arises in trying to find a way to know, objectively, which course of action will be optimal? The mental process of weighing media strategy alternatives, however, presents a formidable task because there are many components of alternatives to think about, at any one time. A planner finds it difficult to think about audience sizes alone, because at the very same time, he must be thinking about cost efficiencies, availabilities of media units, discounts that could change his whole plan, the effect of competitors, his creative strategy and execution, the amount of money that is available and the time available to accomplish objectives—and these are only a partial list.

Although strategy may represent the best of all alternatives, the net total of a number of strategies to be included in a single plan *may not* represent a unified, or coordinated plan. A unified plan is an objective of good strategy planning. Perhaps the term *orchestrated* would be more pertinent than the term unified to explain this goal. It is reasonable to require that all media actions work together for the attainment of media and marketing goals. Contradictory or incomplete actions should have no place in good strategy.

Strategy also serves as a means of organizing the media plan. Strategy is neither the beginning nor ending of a plan. Media objectives should precede it and a series of lesser media decisions should follow it. So strategy represents a *frame of reference* on which the details of a plan should be based. If this function is not fulfilled, the lesser decisions may not fulfill the requirement of an orchestration of efforts, and the outcomes of the plan may be ineffective.

How is strategy to be judged? The answer is that, eventually, the strategy will be evaluated on what happens as a result of the planning. Someone will have to answer a question such as: "Were the marketing and media objectives attained as a direct result of the strategy or in spite of the strategy?" However, such questions really comprise post-evaluation, and they are far removed from the immediate problem of evaluating strategy in the short run.

There are several ways to evaluate strategy before a plan is implemented, as follows. One way is to determine the risks of doing or not doing something. This requires subjective judgment plus experience of having tried various strategies and found them not to be worth the risk. Another evaluation technique is a weighing of economy of effort and time. If a strategy takes too much effort, or is too time consuming to execute, it may not be worthwhile. If it costs more than the budget provides, then a question arises: Can one be sure that the extra money is worth the risk?

Another method of evaluation is based on estimating the probabilities of having it succeed. Unfortunately, beginners have no way of knowing whether a plan will succeed, especially if the marketing situation is very unique or new. The answers, however, are based on strong clues. One clue is based on the experience of others in an organization who have created plans or know of plans that are similar and have succeeded. Another clue may be found in published reports of competitors' strategies that have succeeded. The planner will have to determine whether their experience is directly translatable to the present situation.

Sometimes marketing and/or media consultants may have to be hired to provide expert opinion of whether a strategy will work. But other times testing and experimenting may be necessary to provide the answer. In addition, journals of marketing and advertising often provide information and/or theories that could be adapted to fit the needs of a given situation.

Finally, however, there is no substitute for good reasoning and logic. Even if the evidence is not available, the planner can make assumptions about how the marketing-media environment is operating. But the better planners go beyond making assumptions. They first attempt to check the validity of their assumptions by keen observation of what happens after a strategy has been tried, to determine whether or not it has been successful, and whether the assumptions were valid. But secondly, they are always challenging their own assumptions and changing them if necessary, as time progresses.

Once a strategy has been devised, it is the responsibility of the planner to prove that he has chosen the best of all alternatives, and he should be able to defend his decisions with as much evidence as possible, plus good judgment. For a continuation of this discussion on judging the adequacy of strategy, the reader is directed to Chapter 11, on response functions.

Media Decisions Must Be Organized Into a Plan of Action

It is possible, and one often finds it probable, that media planning is done in such a way as to end with a series of decisions remotely related to each other or to the proper antecedents. One might find, for example, that media was selected on the basis of cost-per-thousand, for target audiences reached, while the reach or frequency that resulted was neglected. Or, one could select media, but the decisions might have little to do with the marketing objectives. Or, a series of media decisons might represent a loosely organized plan of action. Sometimes, media are selected first, and then scheduled. Following this a strategy may be devised. Such practices, however, are inefficient.

It is important, therefore, for a planner to organize his thinking for media planning in such a way as to be logical and efficient. His goals should be as follows:

a. All media decisions should be based on marketing objectives and strategy. The goal of the planner is to select and use media to help attain either some objective or strategy.

b. Therefore, the first step in media planning after studying marketing objectives and strategy should be to create media objectives, whose purposes are, to implement its antecedents.

c. Media strategy should be created after the objectives have been written. It should consist of a series of broadly conceived decisions directly aimed at fulfilling media objectives. The reason media strategy should represent broad (or general) media decisions is that it is logical to procede from the general to the specific. Thus the strategy should serve as the basis for the next step in planning: tactics or implementation and finally media buying.

In order to see the relationship between the various general steps in media planning, Figure 26 is presented. Figure 27 summarizes some of the most important media variables that may be manipulated in planning, and Figure 28 shows the marketing objectives and strategies that affect the use of media variables (partial list).

Determining Media Objectives

The best way to plan media is to decide what goals are most important and then find ways to achieve them. Media objectives serve the purpose of deciding where one wants to go and strategy serves as the means of getting there.

Since media objectives are not ends in themselves, but are aimed at implementing either marketing objectives or strategy, a study of both marketing antecedents is necessary. But it is not obvious how such a study can lead to media objectives, nor is it possible to find an easy-to-use formula for creating media objectives. Perhaps the best direction that could be given to a media planner who wants to create objectives would be for him to first answer the following question as thoughtfully as possible:

"In what ways can I use media to help implement either a marketing objective, or some marketing strategy?"

The answer to this question must come from a thorough knowledge of media, research, and marketing, plus good judgment. And furthermore, there may not be one answer to the question, but a number of alternatives; each of which may have a greater or lesser degree of importance.

Figure 26
Steps in Media Planning

The following is a diagram showing the logical progression of steps leading to media strategy and planning:

Marketing Objectives	Marketing Strategy	Media Objectives	Media Strategy	(Tactics) Decisions Implementing Strategy	Media Buying
A number of marketing goals for a given brand. Presumably they are based on best opportunities for sales, or solving other marketing problems	A number of broadly conceived marketing decisions, organized into a unified plan of action aimed at attaining marketing objectives	A number of media goals, all related in some way to helping attain marketing objectives, or being related to marketing strategy	A number of broadly conceived media decisions, organized into a unified plan of action aimed at attaining media goals	A number of very specific decisions which implement the media strategy. In many instances, these decisions serve as a basis for media buying	Actual purchasing decisions involving the selection and use of media

EXAMPLES OF EACH

Marketing Objectives	Marketing Strategy	Media Objectives	Media Strategy	(Tactics) Decisions Implementing Strategy	Media Buying
Goal: to increase brand share of market by 5% over last year, nationally	Concentrate on stealing customers from competitors by using ads which show ways in which our brand is better than theirs	Goal: plan media selections so as to deliver at least 80% of both our and competitors' target markets. (Targets are defined demographically)	Plan search procedures of alternative media which deliver larger reach of target markets, being sure that reach is national. Sacrifice frequency for reach (because reach and frequency are inversely related)	Eliminate newspapers, spot radio, spot TV, and billboards from consideration. Use network TV or magazines. Find either which gives 80% net reach of targets at lowest CPM.	Make purchase of best alternative media according to the specifications laid down in strategy and tactical plans, and according to any other specifications (such as creative requirements)

If for example, one of the marketing objectives was to introduce a new brand of soap to a market, then a number of alternatives might be considered for media objectives, as follows:

    (a) Use media that reaches heavy users of soap

    (b) Use media that other soap manufacturers have used most often in the past (assuming, of course, that such media will reach heavy soap users)

Figure 27
Variables That May Be Manipulated in Media Planning

1. *Constraint variables*
   a. Budget size
   b. Creative strategy
   c. Nature of the product
   d. Nature of the brand
   e. Past use of media
   f. Competitive uses of media
   g. Competitive spending in media

2. *Media plan objective variables*
   a. Reach (or market coverage) needed
   b. Frequency needed
   c. Continuity patterns needed

3. *Media strategy variables*
   a. Strategy concept variables:
      concentration
      media dominance
      flighting
   b. Levels of reach needed
   c. Levels of frequency needed

   d. Weighting proportions:
      By geographical markets
      By demographic targets
      By heavy-user targets
      By season
      By gross rating point levels
   e. Schedule length
   f. Schedule patterning
   g. Cost efficiency standards
   h. Discounts
   i. Allocation of budget to media or markets
      or both
   j. Number of ads or commercials to be run
   k. Number of different media to be used
   l. Number of different markets to be used

4. *Other variables*
   a. Size of ads or lengths of commercials
   b. Kind of sponsorship in broadcast media
   c. Use of qualitative factors
   e. Availability of media units

Figure 28
Some Marketing Variables that Affect Media Strategy Variables

1. *Introduction of new products*
   a. Roll-out patterns
   b. Key market patterns
   c. Broad scale national introductions

2. *Increasing market share requirements*
   a. Steal from competitors
   b. Get present users to consumer more
   c. Expand the entire market

3. *Changes needed in brand image*
   a. Requiring new creative strategy
   b. Requiring new timing strategy

4. *Changes in corporate image*
   a. Requiring new creative strategy
   b. Requiring new timing strategy

5. *Changes in brand positioning*
   a. Requiring new creative strategy

6. *Reductions in the advertising budget
   caused by:*
   a. Attempts to increase profits
   b. Attempts to cut losses
   c. Production problems of all kinds

7. *Increases in the advertising budget
   caused by:*
   a. Movement into new markets
   b. New product introductions
   c. Need for any changes in communication

8. *Changes in sales promotion strategy*
   a. New relationship between sales
      promotion and advertising
   b. New or different sales promotion
      techniques required

9. *Test marketing situations*
   a. Testing various budget levels in
      different markets (same media)
   b. Testing various budget levels in
      different markets (different media)

10. *Changes in the life cycle of a product:
    growth, maturation, decline*

11. *Meeting competitive marketing
    strategies head on*

(c) Spend at least as much money in the same media as the manufacturer of the number one brand share does

(d) Try to reach as much, or more, of the market as the manufacturer who has the number one brand share.

Which of the above should become media objectives? The answer may depend on what other marketing objectives there are, how important, relatively, each is, and what strategy has been devised. After such considerations, perhaps one or all of the above may be adopted as media objectives.

Sometimes, however, media objectives are based on marketing strategy rather than marketing objectives. If, for example, the objective is to introduce a new brand to the market, and the market strategy is to use a roll-out pattern of introduction, then the media objective will specify the geographical areas where media is to appear first. Sometimes a roll-out pattern would be limited to the states in the northeastern section of the United States, and only after the brand is selling well, will it be introduced gradually to adjacent more western states. So media objectives could clearly indicate which states will receive media, and when such media may be used.

It is not possible to precisely explain how media objectives should be created. Instead, the "idea of a relationship" between media objectives and marketing objectives or strategy should serve as a guide in planning.

Budget constraints in setting media objectives. Even though the relationship of marketing-to-media objectives are clear, there are a number of constraints that temper the planner's decision. The size of the budget, if known ahead of time, is one such constraint.

Many times, the marketing budget is set ahead of time, before any media planning has taken place. In such a case, the media objectives will have to be written with that constraint in mind.

On the other hand, if no budget is available, then media objectives may well serve as a guide to setting a budget, at least as far as the cost of time or space is concerned. Once the planner has a general idea of his goals, then he is in a position to cost out his goals. Sometimes, a budget can't be set at the media objective stage, but must wait until the strategy has been worked out. In such cases, media objectives may have to be re-written later to accommodate the size of the budget. Perhaps a series of marketing-media priorities may have to be set so that the planner achieves those goals that are most pressing, while secondary goals may have to wait for another day. The size of the budget may be recommended by a media planner, but it may be reduced by the client after examining marketing-media objectives and strategy.

Creative constraints in setting media objectives. Creative strategy acts as a constraint in setting media objectives. The role of creative strategy in planning media was discussed earlier. Suffice it to say that a media planner would first study creative strategy before writing his objectives.

Media objectives usually concern reach and frequency. When a planner selects media he is, in effect, choosing those which will deliver a given number of target audiences. Delivery, however, is nothing more than potential exposures. Because all research data represents measurements taken in the past, they therefore only represent "estimates of exposures." The future may be somewhat different.

But the number of estimated exposures contracted for in a media plan may be patterned in such a way as to maximize either reach or frequency and, in some unusual cases, both. So media objectives should be set in such a manner as to

154

plan for whichever goal is sought. Brown, Lessler and Weilbacher called this pattern: the "Message Basket."[35] They meant that, without clear-cut, deliberate planning, all of the potential exposures planned for may represent a confused basket of numbers, some of which may even represent contradictory goals. Therefore, media objectives should be written in such a way as to bring control and order out of chaos in the basket.

More explicitly, media objectives should state whether reach or frequency are to be goals; and explain why each was, or was not needed. In addition, the level of reach and frequency should become objectives. Here, too, an explanation is needed to justify, logically, why any given level is desired.

Continuity as a media objective. It should be apparent that media objectives will affect the kind of strategies which later evolve. One very important goal, therefore, which will affect the timing of advertising during weeks and months of a year, is "continuity." Continuity may be defined as consistency of advertising placement. It, too, like reach and frequency, may result in many alternative contradictory patterns of placement if not controlled.

One pattern, for example, may consist of advertising appearing every day of the year, while another pattern may be limited to placing ads once a month. Which is better? The answer is relative. What are the brand marketing goals and strategy? Does it require a given pattern? Does the creative strategy require a different pattern? For example, if the creative strategy includes a very complex message in television commercials, will audiences be able to grasp the meaning if the commercials are shown once a month? Will a pattern of frequent showings be required?

Therefore media goals will have to be based, at least to some extent, on continuity.

What determines the pattern of continuity? The answer to this question is one of the most difficult in media planning. There is very little research available that is applicable to all products or services. Even for a given brand, the answer is not clear because there is also little research available. But there are some general guidelines available which may help the planner create media objectives that control continuity intelligently.

The first consideration is to plan continuity to match sales volume peaks during the year. It is logical to encourage consumers to buy a given brand at the same time consumers tend to buy the generic product type. Beer sales, for example, are very high during the summer; so special emphasis should be planned to advertise a given brand during the summer. If no emphasis is given, there is then the possibility that consumers may switch to the more heavily advertised brands.

A second consideration is the degree to which the product is sold throughout the year. While a generic product like soap may have very high volume of sales during the summer, it also has fairly good volume all during the year. Such a consistent sales pattern may require advertising to be placed continuously

---

[35]Brown, Lyndon O.; Lessler, Richard S.; and Weilbacher, William M.; *Advertising Media,* Ronald Press, 1957, p. 118

throughout the year. Perhaps ads need not be placed every day or even every week; but some degree of consistency such as advertising every other week may be required.

While the preceding guidelines are very general and may help decide how to plan continuity, some better basis is needed. The authors suggest another foundation that might supplant, or at least supplement, the other two.

This foundation is based on the answer to the following question for each brand:

"How long can this brand be on the market *without advertising* before some negative consequence (such as a loss of brand awareness) will result?"

The answer to this question, in turn, depends on the positive objectives hoped for through the creative strategy. If, for example, a communication goal is to build brand awareness from a present 45% to 85% of the market, then what will happen if advertising is spaced at various time intervals? Suppose that advertising were planned to appear three times a week, each week of the year. This pattern of continuity may have been based on the consumption pattern for the generic product class such as soap, beer, automobiles or television sets. If a longer interval of spacing ads were used, say every other week (but three insertions during each of those weeks) what would happen to the level of brand awareness? Would audiences forget about the brand during the week in which no advertising was done? Or would the rate of forgetting decline only minima"y? Still another question might be: "What would happen if a continuity pattern of three consecutive weeks of advertising were followed by two weeks of no advertising?"

The answer to these questions cannot be generalizations because it is most probable that each brand, in each generic product class would have different answers. Other factors which might affect any answer to these questions would be:

(a) How active are competitors in advertising while the given brand is out of advertising?
(b) How novel or interesting are competitive advertisements?
(c) How novel or interesting are our brand's advertisements?
(d) How unique a product is the given brand in comparison to others in the same generic class?
(e) How intensive is competitors' advertising, both while our brand is or is not advertising?
(f) In what marketing life cycle stage is the brand during the campaign?

These questions are complex and should not be answered subjectively. Their answers may depend mostly on carefully controlled experiments to serve as predictors of probable outcomes, or could depend on a very thorough analysis of a brand's history in the market-place under varying competitive conditions.

For these reasons, the answers to planning for continuity in media objectives is simply not clear nor easy. What is true for one brand may or may not be true for other brands. As a result this area of planning, while very important, must be done with a great degree of uncertainty. Specific research on continuity patterns for each brand offers the greatest potential for a viable solution.

Specification of market coverage levels. Coverage levels desired should be stated in media objectives, if possible. Coverage defined here, is the percent of a market that a combination of all media will reach. While the reach of a media plan might be defined as the cumulative audience of TV homes tuned to a given program for a four-week period, such information does not indicate how much of the total market has been reached, demographically.

To be more explicit, suppose the 4-week reach of television programs has been stated as 65% of all television homes in the country. The 65% does not tell the planner how many women, aged 18-34, have been reached, cumulatively, in a 4-week period. But if the market consists primarily of women aged 18-34, then it becomes important to know what percent of the market should be reached.

If the coverage consisted of only 30% of all women aged 18-34 that may be too low. Whether 30% is too low or high is a matter of marketing-media judgment however. But a coverage goal should be set. Furthermore, if both magazines and television are to be used, coverage goals should be stated so the net percent of accumulation by both media of the entire market are expressed. Coverage, therefore, represents a crucial goal on which the selection and use of media will be based.

It is also wise to justify the level of any coverage goals stated. In other words, if a media plan is supposed to deliver 75% of the market, the planner ought to be able to explain, reasonably, why he chose 75%. Why not 65% or 85%? Usually budget limitations affect coverage goals, but the amount of frequency also affects it. Finally marketing objectives probably constitute the main consideration in determining coverage levels. A coverage level gives the market-media planner a given number of potential exposures, many of which, hopefully, will be turned into buyers through exposure to the advertising message.

Specifications of media targets. To whom will advertisements be directed; users, persons who influence users, or both? The more specific a planner is in identifying targets by demographic or other means, the easier it may be in finding media that will reach those targets. Most media targets are defined demographically. Occasionally, some other description such as "psychographics" (or psychological descriptions of targets) are used. The goal, however, is to be specific rather than vague because the latter may mean wasted exposures on individuals who would never buy a given product or brand under any circumstances. Once media targets have been specified, than all subsequent decisions can be checked to see whether the correct targets are being reached by the media selected.

Where media targets live, geographically. Media objectives usually also include a statement indicating where targets are located geographically. Sometimes this information is stated in the strategy portion, rather than the objective portion, of the plan. The need for including geographical locations of targets is obvious and needs no elaboration here.

Cost efficiency as a media objective. Cost-per-thousand maximum levels may or may not be a part of media objectives. Usually, cost-per-thousand targets are needed to discriminate between media. But in past years, when media planning was often based on large audience figures (sometimes called box-car figures) representing crudely identified media audiences, maximum cost-per-thousand levels were usually stated in media objectives. For example, one media objective might have been written to warn buyers not to buy any medium that had a cost-per-thousand over $5 for total audiences. But in the present, and most likely in the future, maximum levels of cost-per-thousand may be meaningless. The reason is that cost-efficiency formulas are now used to help discriminate between the ability of various media to deliver prospects.

The actual practice of writing media objectives often results in statements that are mixtures of both objectives and strategy. The probable reason for this occurrence is that there are too few objectives, so both objectives and strategy are planned about the same time. In fact, there may be little difference between the two.

The following are examples of media objectives (with some strategy statements intermixed) taken from various advertising agency media plans:

Media Objectives from Plan A

"Television will continue to be "X"'s primary medium because of its ability to provide efficiently:

(1) Audience: the desired woman, or heavy user recognizing the role of women as the decision-maker regarding "X" type of food.

(2) Effectiveness: demonstration of "X"'s palatability, via sight, sound and motion.

(3) Schedule and Pressure Variation—based on these needs:

1. Continuity: year round support that can reasonably be expected to reach a significant number of established customers on a regular basis.
2. Impact: heavy pressure during certain flight periods affording the brand the opportunity to reach a large audience with a frequency substantially above the continuity level, the purpose being to help stimulate new trial.
3. Flexibility: to capitalize on geographic variation in existing market potential and to support major promotions.

Media Objectives from Plan B

Based on the outline of the problem, the specific objectives of the media plan are:

. . . to reach large families with special emphasis on the housewife, who is usually the chief purchasing agent.

. . . to concentrate the greatest weight of advertising in urban areas where prepared foods traditionally have greater sales and where new ideas normally gain quicker acceptance.

... to provide advertising continuity and a fairly consistent level of impressions throughout the year except for extra weight during the announcement period.

... to deliver advertising impressions over the entire country in direct relation to food store sales.

... to use media which will help to strengthen the copy strategy and put major emphasis on convenience, ease of preparation, taste and economy.

... to attain the greatest possible frequency of advertising impressions consistent with the need for broad coverage and the demands of the copy plan.

Since, as we have pointed out, the regional strategy normally stems from the national plan, we will outline first the campaign that is proposed for Phase II when full national distribution will have been attained.

Media Objectives, Plan C

1. Coverage of all housewives, with special emphasis against those in larger urban markets, in middle and lower-middle income groups and in larger families.

2. Maximum frequency, within budgetary limits, to match the relatively frequent pattern of purchase in this category.

3. Adequate time or space for a complete, thorough multi-reason sales message.

4. The opportunity to punctuate a continuous level of coverage with two crescendos of special weight, one in the summer in the south and one in the winter in the north.

5. Maximum efficiency for every advertising dollar spent—to combat higher competitive per-pound expenditures by buying more impressions per dollar than competition.

6. A corollary requirement, if it can be realized, is dominance of advertising weight in Brand X's markets can be made to appear more important than any competitor.

7. To reach housewives insofar as possible close to meal times; early morning, noon and dinnertime.

Determining Media Strategy

As a first consideration in planning media strategy, one should take a close look at the entire marketing-media situation, with special attention to competitors' marketing and media strategies. Perhaps one of the first steps should be to answer the question: "To what extent do I copy competitor's media selection or use?" At times in planning media strategy there may be the temptation to simply implement media objectives without first considering the strategies of competitors. But such temptations should be subdued by the logic that a brand does not exist in a vacuum, so strategy will have to be based, in some part, on what competitors are doing.

What should the planner look for in considering competitors? Perhaps the most important consideration is market-share position. What rank does a brand in question have in the market? If a brand is number one in share, then it is worthy of special study. Does it have the best product in its class? Is its distribution outstanding; its creative efforts in advertising superior; or is its selection and use of media better than others? Perhaps the answer is a combination of these and other considerations. In any case, brands in numbers two, three or lower positions cannot ignore the leader if they intend to make inroads in competitors' shares. If the leader(s) tend to limit their media choices to spot and network television, then brands below the leader must take this fact into consideration in planning their media strategies. One of the most importation questions relating to competitors' media selections may have to be: "Should I fight it out with competitors in the media they use, or shall I seek media which they do not use?"

The answer to this question depends on how much money a brand has budgeted to fight competitors. If a brand has a much smaller budget than competitors, then his advertising may be lost by comparison with competitors who can buy much more advertising. But even if a brand has a budget the same or similar in size to a leading competitor, another qualification for strategy must be considered. It is possible that the brand in question is perceptually superior to his competitor's brand, meaning that it is easily possible to demonstrate its superiority in advertisements. In such a situation, the brand may not require as much money as its competitor because the brand's qualities are so obvious. Advertisements may not have to work so hard to communicate essential information. Perhaps there may even be large word-of-mouth advertising.

Still another consideration would be whether a brand's targets for advertising are the same as his competitors'. If his targets are different, then strategy can be worked out using media different from that of competitors'. If, however, a brand's targets are identical to competitors', then he may have to use the same or similar media.

Finally, in answer to a study of competitor's strategies, it may be necessary to determine whether competitors are using their media effectively. If they are not, then even though a brand may have a smaller budget, it may succeed in the same media. An example of a competitor not using his media effectively is one where he is reaching the correct targets, but with not enough frequency to be optimally effective. In such a case, a brand may use the same media if it can match or surpass its competitor's frequency.

Media budgets and their effects on strategy. The size of the budget, as mentioned earlier, gives the planner a frame of reference, or limitation on what he can do to attain a media objective. Media planners know what it costs to buy a low or high impact level in 25 or 150 markets for spot television, or for a lineup of

200 stations on network television. They know about how much it takes to buy a full-page ad in the top 100 markets, or a number 100 showing in outdoor billboards in 50 markets. Secondly, the number of dollars available affects the choice of media and the depth of impact needed.

What happens when insufficient funds are appropriated for media use? There are, at least, four different courses of action, and possibly more. (1) Marketing objectives may have to be changed toward more modest and realizable goals for the amount of money allotted. (2) A series of priorities may have to be set up in which the greater part of the budget will have to be allocated to the most pressing objectives. Minor objectives will have to be ignored until more money is available. (3) It may be possible to obtain large discounts from media which will spread a small amount of money farther. This might be done by limiting advertising to one medium. In addition, the wave strategy could be used to spread a small amount of money over a longer period of time. (4) Finally, the client may be advised not to advertise until he does have enough money. The media planner is often responsible for giving this advice. If the agency proceeds to buy media with a budget which is known to be inadequate, then the client may later blame the agency for poor advertising performance.

In planning media strategy then, it is imperative to study the strategies of competitors before planning one's own. The results may be that one can proceed by ignoring competitors entirely because they are no threat.

How much reach is necessary?   Another question that rises early in strategy planning is how much reach is necessary? The question of reach and frequency may have arisen earlier when planning media objectives. The level of reach, however, may have depended on other aspects of strategy so this question may not have been answered until the strategy has been planned. The answer to the question requires a great deal of executive judgement based on experience with a given brand in the market-place.

Yet there are a number of guidelines that can help provide the answer. One is an understanding of the nature of reach. Generally, when a medium reaches 70% of a target market, it becomes difficult to add much more reach inexpensively. Ideally, a planner would like to attain 100% reach of a target market. Once he did, all additional effort would go into building frequency. But, most of the time, it is too expensive to reach everyone in a precisely defined demographic market. The reason is that there are usually some prospects who never see, hear, or are exposed to any media, or, perhaps they are exposed to very unusual media. As a consequence, it may be difficult, if not impossible, to reach them.

One may try to build reach by adding different kinds of television programs to a media plan assuming that different programs attract different audiences. But as one adds media, more energy is added to building frequency and very little is added to building reach (since reach and frequency are inversely related). The consequence of reach-frequency relationship may be that it is too costly to go beyond a certain level in building reach. So the planner must look at the size of the market and the characteristics of his target audience and estimate the probabilities of attaining various reach levels without adding more frequency (unless frequency is also desired). The optimum reach may be where any additional money spent beyond a certain point (70% for example) may turn into frequency instead of reach.

But another guideline to finding an optimum reach level depends on where the planner intends to find new customers for a brand if his marketing objective calls for increased brand share. If new customers are supposed to come from competitors' customers, then the reach level will depend on how many such customers are needed. Then plans can be made to reach a given level based on a conversion ratio of new customers reached related to the probable percent of those who will try or buy the brand in question. For example, it may be estimated that for every ten persons reached, four will try the product once and two will remain with the brand in future purchases.

But another guideline may be based on the degree of reach that past media plans have attained. Has the brand reached enough of its own target markets? Suppose that last year's brand only attained a 65% reach of targets. What would happen if that reach were raised to a 75% or even 85% level? Judgment based on experience for a given brand would have to be the deciding factor, unless experiments were conducted to test alternative reach levels.

If the marketing strategy called for attacking a given competitor head-on, using the same media as he did, then it would seem appropriate to have as much reach as he had. Perhaps it would be necessary to have more reach of target markets than competitors.

Still another consideration in deciding on the optimum reach is based on using more than one demographic variable. In planning media without the use of a computer, it is difficult to plan for target markets of more than two or three demographic variables. The size of each market is the number of individuals in each demographic variable. Conceivably, it may be possible to have large reach of one variable and smaller reach of others. Is it important to have large reach of all target markets, or is one or two much more important than others? If large reach is needed of all variables, then the cost may be too great to be practical. By limiting the market variables, it may be easier to make the decision on the proper reach level needed.

Finally, the level of reach may depend on how much frequency is also needed. If a media strategy requires large frequency, then reach will suffer. The question is, how low can reach be even if the desired frequency is attained? It might be easy to have 10 average frequency in television for four weeks, but the reach may be only 35%. So the amount of frequency needed affects planning for the desired level of reach.

The concept of effective reach. Another means of helping a planner determine how much reach is necessary is based on a concept called "effective reach." The planner must know at what reach levels his messages are most effective. The underlying basis for this concept is that each exposure to a medium and a message has different values. For example, one exposure most likely will have little effect on audience members. They may not be in the market for the product advertised, or they simply have not paid much attention to the ad,

162

being distracted by other things. But subsequent exposures may be perceived differently. There may be a point where most audience members begin to pay attention to the message so that brand awareness or recall of key message ideas rises dramatically. These first number of exposures may be called a "threshold effect of frequency."

Of course, the rate of accumulation will have declined somewhat at the point that frequency of exposures begins to have marked effect. But as the rate of accumulation declines, each additional exposure begins to have more value. The increase in effectiveness may continue until a point is reached where the message begins to wear out (be ignored) or become annoying.

If a media planner could find the reach level where each exposure begins to have marked effectiveness, and later where it begins to decline in effectiveness, that portion of exposures could be called "effective reach." See Figure 29.

While the concept of effective reach is reasonable, there is much that is unknown about its practical use. For example, is there an effective reach for all brands, or does it vary? Under what conditions would the effective reach vary? Assuming that levels of effective reach could be determined by test marketing experiments, could the results of such experiments be usable nationally? At

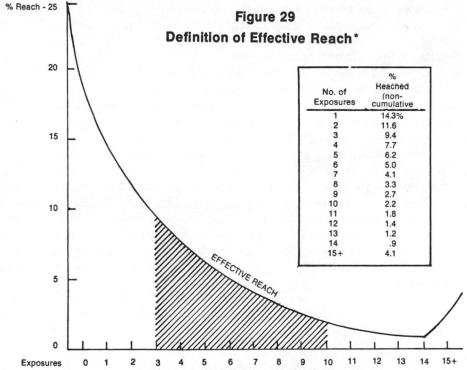

Figure 29
Definition of Effective Reach*

No. of Exposures	% Reached (non-cumulative
1	14.3%
2	11.6
3	9.4
4	7.7
5	6.2
6	5.0
7	4.1
8	3.3
9	2.7
10	2.2
11	1.8
12	1.4
13	1.2
14	.9
15+	4.1

*Source: J. Walter Thompson, *The Concept of Effective Reach*, Nov. 6, 1973, p. 6
In Figure 29 the audience in the three to 10 exposure (shaded) areas would be the effective reach. Although the one exposure reach was 14.3%, the effective reach (3-10 exposures) would range from 9.4% to 2.2%, non-cumulatively, or, 9.4 to 40.6 cumulatively (9.4 + 7.7 + 6.2 etc = 40.6)

present the concept may be considered as one more idea that can help the media planner, but that its practical application may need considerably more research verification.

How much frequency is necessary?   A great deal of experience and judgment is necessary in determining how much frequency is required for a media plan. A first guideline in helping the planner determine a frequency level is for him to know what effect frequency has on sales. For some brands, in some product markets, an optimum amount of frequency may lead directly to a given volume of sales. In other situations and for other brands, frequency has little relationship to sales. The media planner, therefore, must know what the relationship, is if any. These relationships may be learned by experience or by experimentation. Many times, various weighting levels are tried in different test markets to see if there are optimum levels of frequency that will lead directly to sales.

But another consideration may be the creativeness of advertisements for a given brand. The assumption is that the more creative and attractive the advertising, the less frequency will be needed. Often a television commercial is so unique and interesting that it becomes a topic of conversation among people and thus achieves additional communication effect through word-of-mouth advertising. Sometimes novelty is less important than the communication power of the advertisement to reveal a fact which, if widely known might bring about sales. In such a case, less frequency may be required than in normal situations.

Typically, however, a planner tries to match frequency with his competitors, especially those who have larger market shares than his brand has. On the other hand, if a brand is clearly and demonstrably superior to competitors' brands, there may be less need for high frequency. Or when a brand is so unique compared to other brands that most individuals have learned about it, less frequency may be needed. Such superior or unique brands may have built high word-of-mouth advertising volume in the past.

When a brand is being advertised in a market where there are many competitors, they may generate a very high noise level caused by a flood of advertising for all brands in about the same kind of media. As a consequence, planning for such situations requires that the planner have a frequency level that is at least as large as competitors' frequencies, or equal to or better than the number one market share competitor. The assumption is that, because there are so many advertisements being disseminated, the chances for prospects seeing a particular brand's advertisements may be slim or limited. Therefore a large amount of repetition increases the opportunities for exposure.

The question of optimum frequency levels, then, is a relative one. The answer probably differs with changes in the marketing situations and with experience in handling varying situations.

Media Dominance Strategy

In the media dominance strategy, the objective is to buy advertising exclusively in one medium, but for a relatively short period of time. Then, all advertising dollars may be moved entirely to another medium. In a sense, then, this is a form of concentration but one in which there is a shifting of emphasis. There is the feeling that a medium may "wear out" after a time and there is a need consequently to shift to some other medium. The length of time spent within any given medium may vary from three months to over a year. Each advertiser must decide for himself whether the medium, indeed, has worn out. Research, however, is lacking in proving "wear-out" or that this strategy is effective.

Wave Strategy

This involves arranging the media schedule so that advertising is placed intermittently on and off. Instead of advertising every week, with a relatively small budget, it is possible to arrange the schedule so that one may advertise every other week of the year. This week-in, week-out technique (also called flighting) thereby allows the advertiser to put *more* money into fewer weeks in which he advertises but, perhaps, make his messages more visible to his prospects as a result. Meanwhile his prospects usually do not forget about him during the intervening week because he has not been out of the advertising media too long. Considerations about whether to use the wave strategy depend on the budget, where there may not be enough money to do a good job in every period, especially when competitors are outspending the advertiser. It also depends on seasonal factors too, in that if he decides to concentrate on certain seasons of the year by using heavier weight during those periods than normally, he may be handicapped in competing with those competitors who advertise more regularly.

Some advertisers will advertise heavily right before the season begins, withdraw for a while, and come back in to close out the season. In that manner heavier than usual advertising may be placed at both times, rather than relatively lighter advertising on a regular and consistent basis. Wave strategy is also a good way in which to maintain consumer awareness by extending the time period necessary to make some kind of impression on the consumers. A limited budget, for example, might take an advertiser through a half a year; but with the wave technique, awareness may be maintained all during the year.

Other Considerations in Media Planning

After media objectives and strategy have been planned and written, there still remain other considerations before the detail work of specific decision-making starts. These may be thought of as major requirements on which decisions eventually will be based, but are not covered in either objectives or strategy. These considerations, then, serve as the ground rules for decision-making. Most often they are specifically concerned with media selection. The following is a discussion of such considerations.

Flexibility needs. One problem which may affect the strategy and objectives of a media plan is the need for flexibility. Media often is needed which can be changed at the last minute because the marketing situation has changed or because new opportunities in different media become available. But this isn't possible unless care is taken to select media which are flexible. Generally, local media such as newspapers, spot radio and spot television are flexible because they can be purchased in many different ways and at different times. For example, spot television may be purchased nationally, regionally or locally. Furthermore, it can be purchased in very small amounts (such as for two or three spots a week), or it may be possible to buy large volumes of time needed for a saturation campaign within a given market. Then too, spot television often can be cancelled at short notice, and sometimes reinstated (if there are time slots available).

Flexibility is needed mostly when the marketing situation may change and require subsequent changes in media selection or media use. Media selection for some large-budgeted products such as automobiles, however, may achieve flexibility in different ways. Instead of limiting themselves to local media, they can buy network television or national magazine media in what might be called an "umbrella" pattern. Through these two classes of media they reach a national audience; but they achieve flexibility through additional purchases of local media where they can make changes easily and relatively inexpensively. In most cases, however, advertisers cannot afford to buy both national and spot media and must limit themselves to those which are the most flexible.

The authority and prestige that each medium offers. Authority and prestige are qualitative aspects of media which are difficult to measure but which, experts feel, have some effect on audiences' awareness or perception of advertising. Some media such as the *New Yorker*, or *Fortune* magazines are felt to have considerable amounts of both qualities. But it isn't known precisely just how these, or other media, affect the audience and advertisements because research in this area is so meager. The fact that research has not been able satisfactorily to measure prestige does not mean it does not exist. While authority and prestige may not be the most important factors in media planning, they often become quite significant in helping the planner make a decision about two or more media which are very much alike.

Effectiveness of a medium throughout the year. In planning to use a medium, one might also consider how it performs during all seasons of the year. Summer months, for example, are a problem when using television because so many persons are out-of-doors and may miss advertising. Winter months, on the other hand, may not be as effective for outdoor advertising. Newspaper and magazine reading too, may vary to some extent during the summer months. Furthermore, there may be differences in the year 'round effectiveness of media locally. In some parts of the country, where there are extreme hot or cold temperatures, reading as well as viewing or listening may affect local media effectiveness. So, in planning media, the degree to which it is effective during key selling seasons becomes an important consideration.

Dramatic or creative use of media. Is it possible to select or use media in some bold and dramatic way? This consideration may be the most important one in years to come when media audiences are fragmented to such great degrees and the volume of advertising becomes deafening. It is at times like these that the planner should look for dramatic use of media, or use media more imaginatively. Some years ago, Shell Oil took all of their advertising dollars out of every medium except newspapers. Then it bought only full-page advertisements, continuously, for over a year. The very fact that it used newspapers only in an age when television was considered so dynamic was a dramatic move. The fact that Shell ran full page ads rather than half or small-page units also was dramatic. Consumers could not help seeing a Shell ad in newspapers during that campaign. But there are other examples of imaginative and dramatic media use.

Ford Motor Company once ran a 10-minute commercial on the network movie "The Robe." Celanese took 100 pages of advertising in a single issue of *Harper's* Bazaar. Greyhound went to the production time and expense to print and run 26 different two-page booklets in 26 regions of the country, each with its own travel rates. General Motors once bought all available time on all three networks to introduce its cars. Gulf Oil Company had an open-end contract with a network for automatic and instant sponsorship of Bulletins which break into regular programming when significant news is happening. UniRoyal bought 40 pages (a million dollar buy) in *Reader's Digest*. Advertisers now use gatefolds, pop-ups, perfumed inks, die-cuts, and aluminum foil paper in magazines and many other ways of using media dramatically and imaginatively.

Past media use. The question of whether to continue with media used previously, or switch to some other is certainly a factor in media planning. This means that there must be some evaluation of past media effectiveness. Do consumers expect to find ads in that medium? Are there any advantages to remaining with past media or using entirely new ones, or using some new and some older media? This question may be related to the need for a new, fresh and dramatic change in order to increase brand-name visibility.

Details of the Media Plan: Recommendations

After the objectives, strategy and other considerations have been stated, the planner is ready to make recommendations for the selection and use of media. Recommendations should be stated in detail for national media, but only market names and budget allocations should be shown for local media. For national media such as network television, the programs (or program types) on which commercials will be purchased and the names of specific magazines which are recommended should be shown. But in the case of local media, only the markets in which media will be purchased should be shown because the plan will be taken over by space and time buyers later on and these individuals will make the final selections of both specific newspapers, and/or stations. Buyers will be guided by the general recommendations and criteria for selections which will appear in the specific recommendations. The following details should also appear somewhere in the recommendations:

Specific class of media recommended: Both the class of media as well as the specific media are listed in the recommendations. In other words, not only might network television be recommended, but specific programs if possible.

Coverage levels.   If the planner has determined how many potential homes he hopes to reach with his plan, then such information should appear in the recommendations section. Coverage levels may be stated in terms of the number and percent of homes, households, men, women, or other demographic characteristics which the plan may reach.

Specific reach and frequency levels.   In media objectives, the planner usually states whether he intends to achieve reach or frequency; but no specific numerical levels are shown at that point. However, in the strategy section he should state the levels of reach and frequency the plan will develop, for example, "This plan should reach at least 70% of the television homes in the United States within a four week period with an average four-week frequency of 3.5."

Cost-per-thousand levels.   Since the media plan will serve as a guide for buyers, the recommendations should state just how high cost-per-thousands can go. In most cases, the cost-per-thousand for local media is stated as an average for the whole plan. When the buyer makes his selections of time and stations for spot television, he may not be able to find time spots at the cost-per-thousand figure stated in the plan. But he may achieve an average cost-per-thousand for the whole plan which is close to the level stated in the recommendations, by buying some spots at a higher price than he originally intended balanced by others which are lower priced. In any case, the levels of cost-per-thousand must be determined, usually by experience based on what is a reasonable figure, and this number should be stated in the recommendations.

Market list and budget allocations.   If the plan calls for local media, then a list must be made showing the names of all markets in which local media will be purchased. Not only should this list show the name of the market, but the approximate number of dollars budgeted for media in each market. The buyer uses these figures as guides in determining how much he can spend in each market.

Cost of media.   Somewhere in the recommendations, there should appear statements of the specific costs of each medium used. Not only should the unit cost be shown, but any discounts which have accrued and the total cost of the medium for each week, month and year should also be shown.

The Schedule.   Part of the recommendations, perhaps at the end, should consist of a schedule which shows the specific days, weeks and months on which advertisements are to appear. The sizes and color of the advertisements also should be shown.

A media schedule is one of the most important parts of a media plan because it shows, at a glance, the pattern of media selection and use for a year. This pattern gives a bird's-eye view of the entire recommendations. Because of its importance, the schedule may take two forms. One may be purely statistical with all of the data shown in great detail; the other, equally useful, may take a graphic form.

Figure 30
Sample Media Schedule

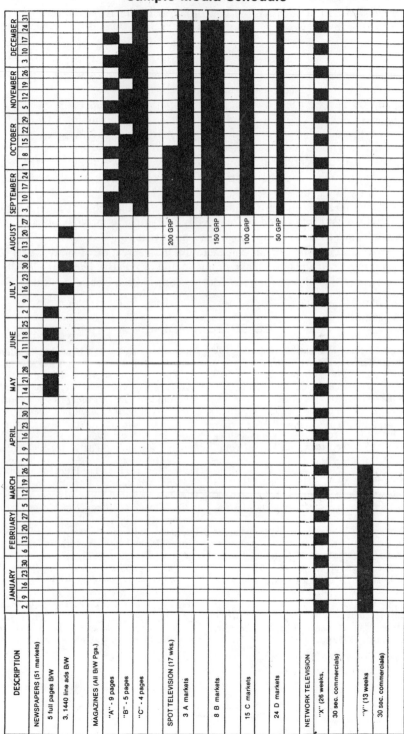

169

See Figure 30. The graphic form is helpful in that it enables one to quickly see the pattern of delivery of the entire plan.

Note: A sample media plan has been placed in the Appendix.

QUESTIONS

1. If a planner should decide that he "needs 70% reach of a target market" is he concerned with an objective or a strategy?
2. Explain the varying bases by which continuity can be planned.
3. Explain why there are no standards or formulae for determining how much reach and/or frequency a given media plan should deliver.
4. Explain how it may be possible for a competitor not to be using his media effectively.
5. Suppose that you create what is considered an excellent media plan but the total cost is much higher than the amount of money available for media. What are probably the best steps you can take to remedy the situation?
6. If the noise level of competitive advertising for a product class is high, what media strategy is most likely called for to remedy the situation for your brand?
7. What advantages are there in "flighting" advertising?
8. Why may *flexibility* be a major consideration in the creation of many media plans?
9. In what ways can a planner make dramatic and/or creative use of media?
10. What is the value of preparing a media schedule with a clear-cut pattern of media usage?

SELECTED READINGS

Advertising Age, "Hallmark-Armstrong Tell Media Strategies," Dec. 10, 1973, p. 30

Advertising Age, "Pulsing Schedules of Ads An Effective Technique," Oct. 20, 1969, p. 270

Frankel, Lester R., "Where Does Effective Exposure End and Irritation Begin?" *Media/scope,* Nov. 1957, pp. 40-41

Gomer, Frank J., "Problems in Media Planning and How to Solve Them," in *Media/scope,* Oct., 1963, pp. 49-73

Greene, Jerome, "Using Media Research to Help Build and Appraise the Media Plan," in *Perspectives in Advertising Management,* Assn. of National Advertisers, Inc., April, 1969, pp. 173-177

Jones, Richard P., "Building and Appraising the Media Strategy," in *Perspectives in Advertising Management,* Assn. of National Advertisers, Inc., April, 1969, pp. 185-195

Kanner, Bernard, "Building and Appraising the Media Strategy," in *Media/scope,* Sept., 1965, pp. 157-165

Krugman, Herbert, "What Makes Advertising Effective?" in *Harvard Business Review,* March-April, 1975, pp. 96-103

Maneloveg, Herbert, "How Media Men Buy Media—Six Factors for a Good Plan," in "The New World of Advertising," *Advertising Age,* Nov. 21, 1973, pp. 62+

McCann Erickson, *A Point of View on Advertising Strategy, White Paper I,* Oct., 1972

Media Decisions, "Why Reach for Frequency?" June, 1969, pp. 36-37

Media Decisions, "The Name-Callers" April, 1973, pp. 66+

Ochs, Malcolm B., "The Fight for Awareness," *Media/scope,* July, 1966, pp. 58-61

Papazian, Edward, "Structuring Media Plans for Maximum Effect," in *Media Decisions,* Mar., 1974, pp. 12-14

Papazian, Edward, "Creative Media - A Time and Place for Everything," in *Media Decisions,* Mar., 1973, pp. 12+

Ray, Michael, Sawyer, A. G., and Strong, E. C., "Frequency Effects Revisited," in *Journal of Advertising Research,* Feb., 1971, pp. 14-20

Vedder, Blair, "An Outline for Media Plans," in *Media/scope,* Aug. 1961, pp. 69-71

Vedder, Blair, "Smart Media Buying Begins With a Plan," in *Media/scope,* Oct., 1960, pp. 49-56

chapter 9

Problems, Practices and Techniques in Strategy Planning

In the selection and use of media, there are many decisions that can be based on a simple analysis of marketing and media data. No other considerations or computations beyond cost-per-thousands may even be necessary because the problem is relatively simple. But many times special considerations and/or computations are necessary because the problem is either so complex, or a simple analysis of the data does not reveal the best opportunities of vehicles or vehicle use. Sometimes these considerations involve calculations of data to bring out the most pertinent information. Other times, the considerations consist of judgments that have to be made about what to do, or how to do it. One such consideration is planning for weighting.

Use of Statistical Weighting

What is weighting? Weighting is a practice of giving extra consideration to one media alternative because it is more important than another alternative. If all alternatives were of equal value, weighting would be unnecessary. But one market or season is usually better than others. Those that are better should be given more weight.

There are two basic methods of weighting. One is a statistical method, and the other consists of adding emphasis somewhere in a plan, such as more dollars to a market, more messages, or more gross rating points.

The statistical weighting method is used often in media selection. In the selection process, weights may be assigned arbitrarily, or they may be assigned on the basis of statistical analysis that shows to what degree one media variable is better than another. To illustrate the concept of weighting for selection purposes, Table 47 is shown. Prof. Dennis Gensch proposed this idea in his book *Advertising Planning*.

Table 47
Weighting Demographic Targets*

Weights are arbitrarily assigned based on purchase rates.	
Purchase rate	Weight
30 cans a month	1.0
15 cans a month	.6
10 cans a month	.4
5 cans a month	.2
0 cans a month, but owns dog	.1
0 cans, doesn't own dog	0.0

*Source: Gensch, Dennis H., *Advertising Planning,* Elsevier Scientific Books, N.Y., 1973, p. 77.

If these weights are assigned to two media vehicles on the basis of audience delivered, the following could be the result:

	Vehicle A			Vehicle B		
Pur-chase rate	Number of targets delivered ×	weight =	Weighted audience	Number of targets delivered ×	weight =	Weighted audience
30	200,000	1.0	200,000	100,000	1.0	100,000
15	20,000	.6	12,000	50,000	.6	30,000
10	10,000	.4	4,000	20,000	.4	8,000
5	10,000	.2	2,000	20,000	.2	4,000
0+	5,000	.1	500	100,000	.1	10,000
0±	50,000	0.0	0	50,000	0.0	0
Totals	295,000		218,500	340,000		152,000

+ Owns a dog
± Does not own a dog

According to this table, Vehicle B delivers the largest number of targets, but Vehicle A delivers the largest number of *weighted* targets who are more important to the advertiser.

Using the same concept, but expanding the weighting technique to more demographics, N. W. Ayer weights all demographics, and variables within each demographic segment so that the optimum value of each vehicle is shown. Figure 31 is a brief overview of the Ayer weighting technique.

Timothy Joyce, president of Axiom Market Research Bureau has proposed another method of weighting, using his Target Group Index data (TGI).[36] Joyce suggests that weights be assigned by guessing at the per capita return on investments to be expected from various users of a given product and various users of a given brand.

---

[36] Joyce, Timothy, "Target Weighting Gives Boost to Consumer Studies," in *Advertising Age,* July 15, 1974, p. 27

Figure 31

How Ayer Applied Weights for a Corporate Advertiser*

1. Assignment was defined in writing as follows: To create favorable awareness of the industry and to influence public's attitude toward them. Target audience is the public at large, but with emphasis on those people who are influential in their business or community, and who are opinion formers.

2. Importance of demographic categories were established by weighting them.

Age	.70
Education	1.00
Occupation	1.00
Income	1.00
County size	.75

3. Desired audience weights within categories were then established. For example, by age of men:

Men 18-24	1.00
Men 25-34	1.00
Men 35-49	1.00
Men 50-64	.90
Men 65 & over	.70

4. Category weights and audience weights were combined to secure combined target audience weight. In the case of age (which had a category weight of 70) this was as follows:

Men 18-24	**(.70 × 1.00)**	.70
Men 25-34	**(.70 × 1.00)**	.70
Men 35-49	**(.70 × 1.00)**	.70
Men 50-64	**(.70 × .90)**	.63
Men 65 & over	**(.70 × .70)**	.49

5. Audience delivered by each possible media vehicle against each demographic segment was drawn from media audience reports. And then multiplied by combined target audience weight to determine weighted value of audiences offered by each medium. This whittled the total audience numbers offered by each medium down to those desired for the corporate campaign. In the case of age, four media shaped up as follows:

Magazine A	9,000
Magazine B	12,000
TV Program A	10,000
TV Program B	17,000

6. The weighted audience figures for each demographic category were then added and averaged, as follows:

	Magazines		TV Program	
	A	**B**	**A**	**B**
Age	9,000	12,000	10,000	17,000
Education	10,000	13,000	7,000	12,000
Occupation	9,000	11,000	9,000	15,000
Income	11,000	15,000	12,000	19,000
County Size	10,000	13,000	12,000	19,000
Weighted Value	9,800	12,800	10,000	16,400

7. The media choices were finally established in this order: TV Program B, Magazine B, TV Program A, Magazine A.

*Source: *Media Decisions,* "How Ayer Applies Weights to Media Plans,; Sept., 1972, p. 49

Before assigning weights to variables, one must determine the marketing cycle of a brand at any given moment. Joyce listed three marketing cycle situations, although it is conceivable that a planner might devise more:

a. Established major brands in a saturated market
b. A growing minor brand in a saturated market
c. A market leader in an expandable market.

If a product is used every day, then it would be assigned a weight of 28 (28 days in a month × 1). If a product is used once a week it would be assigned a 4 weight (4 weeks in a month) and if the product is used once a month, it would be assigned a 1, etc.

An example of the various weights that may be assigned for product and brand usage can be seen in Table 48.

Table 48
Estimated Return on Investment
for Advertising to Different Users*

	Product Category Use				Brand Use			
	Heavy	Medium	Light	Non	Sole	Primary	Secondary	Non
A. Established major brand in saturated market	28	4	1	0	1	4	4	1
B. Growing minor brand in saturated market	28	4	1	0	1	1	4	4
C. Market leader in expandable market	3	2	1	1	2	2	2	1

Now, the various weights can be combined by multiplication for any one marketing situation as shown in Table 49.

Table 49
Combined Targets Weights
for an Established Major Brand
in a Saturated Market*

		Product Category Use			
		Heavy	Medium	Light	Non
	Sole	28*	4	1	0
BRAND	Primary	112*	16	4	0
USE	Secondary	112*	16	4	0
	Non	28*	4	1	0

*The weights in the first column were obtained by multiplication: 28x1; 28x4; 28x4; and 28x1.

* Source: Joyce Timothy, "Target Weighting Gives Boost to Consumer Studies, Advertising Age, July 15, 1974, p. 27

There are a number of options open to the user of the weighted data in the planning process. He can check other data to find the demographic and psychographic characteristics of the heavily weighted users; or he can determine the present pattern of brand use of the weighted market; or best, he can build a schedule by using the weights projected against vehicles that contain demographics of his targets (as was done in the Ayer weightings) and compute cost-per-thousands to find the most efficiently weighted vehicles.

Applying pressure to key market areas. *Pressure* is a term used in media planning to denote extra effort applied to some demographic variables because it is more important than others. Pressure therefore is another form of weighting. A general principle of applying pressure or weighting is to use a ratio of 1 to 1 for the variable in question. If a geographic market contributes 7% of total sales, then it should receive 7% of the budget or weight. As a result, markets that contribute the most receive the most pressure. Demographic variables that show the most product or brand use also should receive the most pressure, at least at the beginning of planning.

There are, however, reasons for not using a 1 to 1 ratio in applying pressure. This would occur when there is reason to believe that any other ratio would be more profitable. To illustrate this concept, an example presented by Joseph Ostrow, media director at Young & Rubicam is shown.

Table 50
Problem: What kind of budget pressure should be applied to various demographics in order to maximize sales?*

Solution: Try two alternatives of pressure:

Demo-graphic	Sales percent made by ea. group	Ratio: 1:1		Ratio: 1:2	
		Ad Budget	Projected Sales	Ad Budget	Projected Sales
A	50%	$ 5000	$2500	$10,000	$5000
B	30	3000	900	0	0
C	10	1000	100	0	0
D	10	1000	100	0	0
Totals	100%	$10,000	$3600	$10,000	$5000

*Source: Ostrow, Joseph, "Some Problems in Profile Matching," in *Media Decisions*, Nov., 1972, pp. 72-74

It is obvious that disproportionate weighting produces more sales in the example shown than equal proportional weighting. Ostrow, however, said that one should watch for a point of diminishing returns in working with variable A because a saturation point may have been passed.

Some general guidelines in geographical weighting. There is no one formula used to determine weights applied in geographical areas. Weighting decisions are usually made as a result of many factors. The following guidelines comprise some of the more important considerations in weighting.

A general concept is that extra weight may be applied to markets where sales volume or market share is high. In a market-by-market analysis (discussed in Chapter 2) a planner might look at the BDI (brand development index) and compare it with a CDI (a category development index). Generally more weight is added to markets with high BDIs than those with low indexes. At times, however, when a CDI is high and a BDI is low for a given market, additional weight may be added to bring the market up to its potential (as shown in the CDI).

But market potential, as a basis for weighting, may depend on any one, or perhaps all, of the following considerations:

a. Past history of each market's responsiveness to advertising. If a local market historically did not respond well to advertising communication, then perhaps additional weight will not help.
b. History of profitability. While additional weighting in a local market may improve sales volume or market share, it may do so at an unprofitable level. Perhaps there is a point of diminishing returns in adding extra weight to a market relative to profit.
c. Pipeline problems. If distribution levels in a market are low, or difficult to increase, or there are any other marketing channel problems, then these facts may influence the amount of extra weight to be applied.
d. Sales force input. Some companies use their salesmen as sources of marketing intelligence at the local level. The input information from salesmen may affect the manner in which weighting is applied.
e. Local market idiosyncracies. In some local markets there are problems in communication and/or selling that may not be true of any other local market. One advertiser may find that an equal number of GRPs applied to large and small markets usually produces greater awareness in smaller markets regardless of other factors. If such idiosyncracies exist, then they should be accounted for in the weighting decision.
f. Competitive noise levels. If competitors advertise heavily in a market, the net effect of the noise level may require heavier weight in that market.
g. Cost efficiency of advertising in the market. Additional weighting may cost too much or result in cost inefficiency.

Once these considerations are evaluated, then the planner may want to decide on a course of action that could affect his final weighting. Does he want to defend his strengths in good markets? Improve weaknesses in problem markets? Or develop opportunity markets? After this decision, and taking other factors into consideration, weighting decisions for geographical areas, usually local markets, can be made.

Message weight distribution analysis. In reviewing an earlier media plan, or one that has just been completed, it makes sense to check on the relationship of message weight delivery to market share, not only for the brand in question, but for other competitors. The kind of relationships that are revealed will help the planner decide whether he has planned logically, or whether there are areas where he should increase or decrease the number and uses of vehicles according to general planning procedures. In Table 51, an analysis was made of nine competitors and their message weight deliveries:

Table 51
Message Weight Distribution for Nine Competitors*

Brand	Share of Market	Share of TV dollars	Share of TV H.H. Messages	Share of TV Messages to women 18-39
A	35%	25%	19%	19%
B	26	25	25	28
C	17	16	17	16
D	8	8	11	12
E	7	4	6	6
F	4	3	7	6
G	3	2	4	4
H	Not avail.	14	9	8
I	Not avail.	3	2	1
Totals	100%	100%	100%	100%

*Source: Roth, Paul, *How to Plan Media,* Media Decisions, 1974, p. 26

Table 51 shows that Brand A has 35% of the market but only spends 25% of total dollars in TV, and has a relatively lower percentage of message delivery than Brand B. One should ask, "Why?" Is Brand A inherently superior in quality to B? Does Brand A have better distribution? Better copy? There are many questions that should be asked about why Brand A's message delivery is so low compared to its share. But for most other brands, there is a high degree of consistency between market share and message share. Additional message weight analysis should be made of individual markets to see how they, too, are relating to market share.

Another Form of Weighting: Concentration

Concentration is another form of weighting strategy whereby heavy pressure may be applied to certain geographical areas; certain seasons of the year; certain demographic variables; or to certain media vehicles. It is not used as much for selection as for arranging elements of a media plan to function at an optimum level in attaining objectives.

Geographic concentration. This practice involves using media in only limited parts of the country to the exclusion of other parts, or it involves applying more pressure to limited parts of the country, even though media is used nationally. In a sense, this is spending strategy. Areas chosen for exclusive advertising or added pressure are those with very high sales volume or market share. Sometimes this geographical area is an entire region. If an advertiser's sales are large in the northeast, then media which are limited to only those portions of the country might be selected. If there is enough money available in the advertising budget, then other regions where sales are not quite so heavy, might be selected to receive advertising, so by concentrating dollars geographically, most the advertising money will be placed in regions where most of the sales take place.

Herbert Zeltner described a number of variables that may affect decisions to concentrate advertising geographically:[37] (a) "Differences in population size." The first variable is differences in "population-size and density among the various regions of the country." If sales are concentrated not by region, but in large urban or suburban areas, this will suggest special media which must be used to reach consumers who live there. (b) "Differences in sales development of an entire product category." When sales are well established for a product category in one part of the country and not in another, the section where it is established may become a concentration area. This, especially, may be true for new products but also for almost any product category. When sales are not equal in all parts of the country, then only those parts which are well established may be singled out for concentration. (c) "Sales development." In some cases, sales may be very low in a certain area, even lower than the national average for sales for that type of product; but if that area begins to show sales improvement, then dollars should be concentrated there. All that may be needed is extra media weight in the form of more dollars or messages, in order to bring sales up to the national average or even higher. (d) "Individual brand sales development." In some cases, competitors' sales are much higher than for other brands in certain areas of the country. Sometimes, but not always, more weight of advertising in those areas may pull a given brand's sales up to competitors', depending of course, on the natural attributes of the product. A product with few or no advantages over competitors' products can hardly hope to succeed for long, no matter how much money is spent in advertising. On the other hand, there are times when, normally, a brand sells very well in a certain area, but competitors have found this to be a poor sales area; then this may suggest the elimination of advertising effort so that the money may be used to boost sales elsewhere. (e) "Distribution." It does not make much sense to advertise in areas where the product is not distributed. At times, of course, it may be possible to force distribution by advertising in areas where the brand is not distributed, hoping that consumer-demand will force retailers to stock the product. (f) "Degree to

---

[37]Zeltner, Herbert, "Concentration I: Geographic Opportunities," *Medialscope*, June, 1965, p. 11

which national media efforts cause dislocations from market to market." At times a good network television program with high ratings does very poorly (and receives very low ratings) in certain parts of the country. In such cases, extra advertising efforts may have to be made to supplement such low-rated areas with local advertising. This may also be true of magazine distribution where circulation is high in certain areas, but unduly low in others. (g) "Degree to which important competitors vary their own weight—market by market—so that there is, in a sense, a different competitive selling situation in each area." If competitors outspend the media planner's brand, then he will have to decide whether to boost advertising effort up to competitors' expenditures, or suffer the possible consequences of losing share of market. The decision on how to deal with this situation is dependent on other factors such as history of success in the market or the need to place extra advertising money in other markets. The need for money to be spent in good markets may outweigh the requirement to meet competitors head-on in a given market.

Seasonal concentration. Another general method of using a concentration strategy involves planning for media on the basis of any kind of time variable. Perhaps the most well-known seasonal variation consists of advertising most heavily during those times of the year when, historically, more of the products tend to be purchased. In other words, for some products, it may be quite difficult to get consumers to buy products out of season. Temperature changes, for example, affect product purchasing. Tennis rackets, water skis and swimming suits are products which normally are sold during the summer months, (while sleds, anti-freeze, and snow tires would be sold mostly in winter months). Almost all products have sales periods during the year which are much better than others. Concentrating advertising during this period makes sense. In the case of food or other products purchased all year round, it may be necessary to advertise all during the year, in an almost even pattern. But even food products tend to be consumed more during various times of the year than other times, and it may be necessary, then, to concentrate advertising during these periods.

The media planner, however, should remember that temperatures are not the same throughout the country. While northern states might indeed be very cold, southern and west coast states might be very warm. In any case, media should be concentrated by placing advertisements at a time when sales volume is highest, so as to maximize the effectiveness of advertising.

Holidays are special seasonal variations during which media concentration strategy may be used. Christmas, for example, is a time, starting before Thanksgiving and extending to about a week before December 25, when a great many products are advertised more heavily than normally. Toys, gift items such as typewriters, radio sets, small appliances, and liquors might be a few of the products which would be featured. Other holidays where special advertising effort might be directed would be Mother's Day, Father's Day and Easter. Then too, there are traditional sales times such as January White Sales, August Fur Sales, and Back-to-School Sales.

Finally, there is the concentration of television media by time of day. During the summer, television may be placed in either the morning or late evening when it is possible to reach large numbers of viewers who are outdoors during most of the day. Sometimes radio can be employed to reach persons who do not watch television during the summer, but who may listen to radio either while they travel in the car, lie on the beach or sit in the back yard with transistor radios.

Also since much of the population is outdoors during the summer, a proportion of advertising might be switched to outdoor media to secure high visibility during these months.

Herbert Zeltner, noted, however, that seasonal concentration carries with it certain cautions that must be observed in order to maximize this kind of strategy. The first is that no matter what other factors appear to affect concentration, the most important factor must be "prospect interest." In fact, he suggests that there should be proof that consumers "will be more receptive to advertising messages during those periods."[38] Since it is likely that the company may not advertise at other times of the year, he must maximize his messages to the largest audience of prospects. A final caution is that the planner must remember that although he is concentrating his media efforts during one season, it is likely that his competitors are also doing the same thing. He noted:

> "For the advertiser of high-priced gift watches, for instance, chances are that many of his competitors are pressuring the consumer strenuously during the period before Christmas and before June graduation."[39]

This simply means that the creative effort embodied in the advertising messages will have to be superior to that of competitors in order to make the advertisements stand out and compete effectively for consumer attention.

Concentration by consumer characteristics: Most advertisers today use a concentration strategy, which simply involves trying to limit media to only best prospects for the market. This means that the media audience characteristics will have to be matched precisely to the demographic market characteristics. In fact, it may mean that media will be selected which reaches only that small segment of the market (based on demographic, or heavy-user characteristics) which will likely result in the most sales. Although conceivably the advertiser could buy media which reached large audiences, many of those audiences members are not prospects and the advertising may be wasted. The goal is to reach the largest number of prospects and to minimize waste.

Concentration by advertising medium. This strategy involves concentrating on selecting only a single medium. The idea has been most aptly expressed by one media expert who said: "When we buy media - we don't buy an ad here and an ad there, spreading out money in as many media as we can. We try to be as big as we can in a single medium. We want to be known and identified with this medium, and we feel that our money goes farther when used this way than with

[38]Zeltner, Herbert, "Concentration II: Seasonal Variations," *Medialscope*, July, 1965, p. 142

[39]Zeltner, p. 142

the spread type of strategy." Concentration by medium also has some practical advantages to the advertiser. Since he is buying so much space or time in a single medium, chances are that he will be able to earn large discounts—some reaching 50%—which will allow him to attain even greater advertising exposure than he previously thought possible.

In conclusion then, concentration is a strategy that may be necessary in order to make the best use of media, especially when the advertising budget is limited in any way. Probably the greatest danger lies in ignoring certain parts of the market while concentrating on others. As Zeltner noted: "It is conceivable that over the long haul, by ignoring half the country, half the seasons, half the market, you walk away completely from your best prospects and leave them open to the competition."[40]

Timing and Spending Strategy

The timing of advertising messages, and the manner in which spending is done by time period, is part of the overall media strategy planning. Generally, timing follows product usage or sales rather closely, with one major exception: that extra weight is usually applied during the best selling season. It has been found that almost every product has somewhat different selling seasons. Therefore, a planner should learn how the product is used and time his advertising messages to match this pattern with the heavy-up exception noted. To illustrate the concept of timing and spending, see Table 52.

Table 52
Timing Related to Product Usage for Deodorant Soaps*

Month of year	Percent of total Product Usage	Quarterly percent of product Usage	Brand X expenditures percent of total year	Brand X quarterly percent of total year
January	7.0%		6.7%	
February	7.5	22.1%	5.4	19.6%
March	7.6		7.5	
April	7.5		6.6	
May	8.1	24.2	7.5	25.5
June	8.6		11.4	
July	9.7		12.2	
August	9.8	29.3	13.2	35.0
September	9.8		9.6	
October	8.9		7.2	
November	8.2	24.4	6.7	19.8
December	7.3		5.9	
Totals	100.0	100.0	100.0	100.0

*Source: Advertising Age Media Workshop, 1972. *Organization of a Media Plan*, p. 31

[40]Zeltner, Herbert, "Concentration: Key to Effective Media Selection," in *Sponsor*, Feb. 15, 1965, p. 41

Table 52 shows the general principle of timing and spending. Brand X did not spend precisely the same percentage as product usage, but heavied-up the summer months where usage was higher. As a result, its spending in the poorer months such as January, February, October, November, and December were proportionately lower than product usage.

If, however, a new product were being introduced against Brand X, then its timing and spending strategy would probably be aimed at obtaining an advantage over Brand X by anticipating X's spending strategy. The new brand would probably heavy-up in the second quarter immediately before the heaviest usage summer season: To illustrate how a new brand might time its approach, see Table 53.

Table 53
Timing of a New Deodorant Soap Brand Against Brand X*

Quarter of Year	Product usage	Brand X's timing	New Brand's timing
First	22.1%	19.6%	15.0%
Second	24.2	25.5	40.0
Third	29.3	35.0	22.0
Fourth	24.4	19.8	23.0
Total	100.0%	100.0%	100.0%

*Source: Advertising Age Media Workshop, 1972, *Organization of a Media Plan*, p. 29

The new brand would have an advantage over Brand X by adding very heavy expenditures in the second quarter. Hopefully, consumers will try the new brand in the second quarter and repurchase it again in the third and fourth quarters at the height of the normally heaviest season. If the total number of dollars to be used by the new brand is considerably more than Brand X, then even though the heaviest selling season only receives a relatively small percent of money, the total amount may be greater than Brand X's allocation.

It should also be noted that a timing strategy used by most companies when introducing new products is to add very heavy weight in the first quarter. But in the example just shown, the first quarter does not warrant as much weight (because sales are lowest then) as the second or third quarters, so the second quarter became the main introductory effort. Usually, a very heavy introductory period is about 13 weeks in duration, although, at times, longer periods have been used by some companies.

Out-spending the competitor in new product introductions by ratios of anywhere from 1½-to-1 to 3-to-1 is common practice. See Chapter 13 for a further discussion of budgeting for new product introductions.

Considering Competitor's Reach and Frequency

In Chapter 8, a discussion was conducted about how much reach and frequency is necessary; and some guidelines were offered for determining levels of both. A study of the reaches and frequencies of competitors may play a major role in deciding how to accomplish one's own objectives. Each competitor that advertises has some kind of media strategy that is revealed by his reach and frequency. One cannot very well ignore what competitors do in planning.

Conceivably, a planner can adopt a defensive strategy in which he will tend to ignore what competitors are doing, because he doesn't have the money available to match his reach and frequency with theirs. So this planner will try to achieve his own objectives, regardless of what competitors are doing.

Most often, however, the competitor's strategies are taken into account. This could be called an *offensive* strategy, but the terminology is not correct. What the planner may do is to look for weaknesses in a competitor's actions, and plan to maximize his own opportunities to some extent at the competitor's expense, depending on his own marketing goals. In new product introductions, however, a planner may want to meet his best competitors head-on, and match or surpass their reaches and frequencies. No matter which kind of strategy is used, it makes sense to analyze the pattern of reaches and frequencies of competitors. An illustration of competitor's strategies is in Table 54.

Table 54
Competitive Reaches and Frequencies for Deodorant Soaps*

Brand	1st quarter Reach	1st quarter Freq.	2nd quarter Reach	2nd quarter Freq.	3rd quarter Reach	3rd quarter Freq.	4th quarter Reach	4th quarter Freq.
A	81	4.2	87	5.2	93	6.5	72	3.5
B	62	3.0	62	3.4	78	3.7	87	4.9
C	59	2.4	57	2.8	68	2.9	62	2.6

*Source: Advertising Age Media Workshop, 1972, *Organization of a Media Plan*, p. 37

Table 54 shows that Brand A must be spending more than the other two brands in order to achieve a leadership position in reaches and frequencies. Furthermore, all competitors heavy-up in the third quarter. However Brand B, for some reason, has an unusually high reach in the fourth quarter. Special research will be needed to determine why. In any event, a new brand being positioned against the three competitors will have to take Brand A into serious consideration because its reaches and frequencies are so high. Probably the new brand would want to, at least, meet these levels and, if possible, surpass them during the second and third quarters of the year.

Positioning of Ads Within Media

One part of media strategy that should be considered, perhap near the end of the planning period, is the positioning of ads within media. Assuming that the reaches and frequencies have all been estimated, the budget allocated, and a schedule worked out, media planning could end at this point.

Practically, however, questions are often asked by planners themselves and others interested in media: is there nothing else that can be done to help in the advertising communication process? Is reach and frequency all there is? The problem is to find ways for the media planner to go beyond delivery and not only get vehicles exposed, but ads within those vehicles exposed, and hopefully also get the ads read.

To a great extent, this last responsibility belongs to the creative people: planners, writers, and art directors who have special talents for getting advertising communication "through" to the reader. The copy people, for example, can write scintillating headlines and interesting and/or meaningful words. The art director can devise fascinating layouts. The creative people can ask for four-color ads, bleed pages, reverse printing, gatefold-size ads, two-page spreads; or they can require unusual papers such as printing on acetate or aluminum foil, or unusual inks such as day-glo or perfumed inks. These are but a few of the many options open to the creative personnel in getting ads noticed and read.

What, then, can the media planner do to help the situation? The answer is that he can ask for certain positions within media that are felt to be better than other positions. The evidence that these positions are better, however, is subject to questions that have kept position strategy from playing a more important role than it has.

Problems of positioning research.   There are a number of media positions that *seem* better than others. For example, the fourth cover of magazines is generally conceded to be the best place in a magazine for an ad. In fact, there is research that shows the fourth cover to be one of the best. But many media experts in this country question such research. Perhaps they would not question the value of a fourth cover position because there is some logic, even without research, to suggest that it is a valuable position. But for other positions, there is not as much agreement among experts. The reason for disputing the effects of other positions is that the research tends to be weak, and therefore inconclusive.

Perhaps the foremost problem of position research is that it is difficult to separate measurements of position from copy effects. Most research techniques that are used to establish the effects of position, are really a mixture of copy and position. In some pieces of research, another dimension is added: effects of different ad sizes. Perhaps measurements of varying ad sizes affects position? Then too, *averaging* data for position effects that contain widely varying degrees of copy effectiveness may not truly represent the effects of position because averaging tends to be unduly affected by extreme copy effect scores. Some media experts question whether there is any copy measuring device that is totally valid. But assuming that most are valid, there is still no way, through present-day measurements, to know the effects of position alone.

A solution would be to design experiments where the copy of ads are held constant and the only variable that is allowed to fluctuate is position. Since the same ads would be measured in different positions in different media vehicles, then the effects of position alone could be found. However, there is dissatisfaction with much research that is devised to measure position. It is often criticized for not being carefully controlled to eliminate bias. Research designs are often poor or non-existent. Samples are often non-random and selected haphazardly. Questionnaire design and interviewing controls are not always the best. As a result, much of position research is often suspect.

For these reasons, much of what is known about position is not considered as important as other kinds of media planning requirements such as reach, frequency or cost-per-thousands.

A brief list of some position effects. The following is a brief list of some position effects that some media planners accept. The reader is cautioned about accepting them as valid evidence. They are presented to show a sample of the kinds of positions that *may* affect the communication power of advertisements placed in vehicles.

Position in Magazines: (a) Fourth cover positions are usually considered better than any inside positions; (b) Second cover *and* page one positions are about equal and are the next best to fourth cover positions; (c) Front of the magazine positions (from page 2 to about page 20 are the next-best positions. (d) Right-hand pages are somewhat better than left-hand pages, but with some exceptions.

Position in Newspapers. (a) Ads near the front are considered better than those near the back, but the differences are small; (b) There is no significant difference between right and left hand pages; (c) Inside a newspaper section is better than the last page of the section; (d) There is little difference between ads above or below the fold; (e) Editorial environment affects the readership of ads. Ads for male products proved better on sports pages and ads for female products did better on women's pages; (f) Pre-print stuffers, while they cost about 4.6 times as much as ROP color, did about 3.8 times better in responses.[43]

Position in Television. (a) Attention is greatest during prime time and poorest in early fringe times; (b) Mysteries, spy adventure programs and movies do a little better than varieties and western programs in recall of messages; (c) Daytime is about 50 to 80% as good as nighttime recall; (d) A 30-second commercial is about 60% to 75% the value in recall of a 60-second commercial; (e) High-rated programs have higher attention levels than low-rated programs; (f) In-program commercials do better than between-program commercials in recall.

A major consideration in deciding whether to use for a special position in a vehicle is the premium cost. Some positions may not be worth the extra cost. Even if it seems to be worth the cost, there may be difficulty in supporting a decision one way or the other because the research is questionable.

---

[43]Jain, Charman L., "Newspaper Advertising: Preprint vs. R.O.P.," in *Journal of Advertising Research*, Aug., 1973, p. 32.

QUESTIONS

1. Why is weighting sometimes used in media selection strategy?
2. What is a general principle of applying weights to geographical sales areas in a media plan?
3. What possible explanations are there for a brand that has the largest market share, but has a much lower percent of media expenditures or message weight delivery to the market?
4. When would it be advisable for a national advertiser to concentrate all of his advertising in one or two geographical areas to the exclusion of all others?
5. When would it be advisable for the same advertiser to concentrate all of his advertising in only one quarter of the year?
6. What are the probabilities (or possibilities) of getting consumers to buy a brand out-of-season by advertising more heavily during that season?
7. How can an advertiser estimate the reaches and frequencies of his competitors who use television?
8. Suppose that valid and reliable research shows that a given position in a magazine has higher recall than any other position. Is this fact the only criterion you need for asking the medium to place your ad in that position?
9. If sales peak during the summer (third quarter) would it make more sense to add extra weight in the second or the fourth quarter (in addition to the third quarter)?
10. What special weighting considerations are often given to media plans for new product introductions?

SELECTED READINGS

Carter, David, "Newspaper Advertising Readership: Thick vs. Thin Issues," in *Journal of Advertising Research*, Sept., 1968, pp. 39-42

Frankel, Lester R., and Solov, Bernard M., "Does Recall of an Advertisement Depend on Its Position in the Magazine?" in *Journal of Advertising Research*, Dec., 1962, pp. 28-32

Graphic Communication Weekly, "Study Shows Reader Conflicts," Mar. 12, 1968, p. 13

Jain, Charman L., "Newspaper Advertising: Pre-print vs. R.O.P." in *Journal of Advertising Research*, Aug., 1973, pp. 30-32

Joyce, Timothy, "Target Weighting Gives Boost to Consumer Studies," *Advertising Age*, July 15, 1974, pp. 27+

Media Decisions, "How Ayer Applies Weights to Media Plans," Sept., 1972 pp. 48+

Media/scope, "Position in Broadcast Advertising," No. 1, Aug., 1962, pp. 50+. No. 2, Sept., 1962, pp. 41+. No. 3, Oct., 1962, pp. 48+. No. 4, Nov., 1962, pp. 46+

Media/scope, "Timing in Broadcast Advertising," Sept., 1962, pp. 46+

Media/scope, "How Important Is Position in Consumer Magazine Advertising?" June, 1964, pp. 52-57

Newspaper Advertising Bureau, Inc. *and* The *Minneapolis Star and Tribune* (Facts), *The Influence of Position, Size, Color, Creativity on Newspaper Advertising Readership*, 1972

Ostrow, Joseph, "Some Problems in Profile Matching," *Media Decisions*, Nov., 1972, pp. 72-74

Roth, Paul, How to Plan Media, *Media Decisions*, 1974.

Starch, Daniel, "Is Preferred Position Worth It?" in *Printers Ink*, Aug., 25, 1961, pp. 43-44+

Starch, Daniel, "Do Inside Positions Differ in Readership?" *Media/scope*, Feb., 1962, pp. 44-46

Zeltner, Herbert, "Concentration I. Geographic Opportunities," *Media/scope*, June, 1965, pp. 11+

Zeltner, Herbert "Concentration II. Seasonal Variations," in *Media/scope*, July, 1965, pp. 17+

Zeltner, Herbert, "Shifting Values in Magazine Positioning," in *Media/scope*, Jan., 1964, pp. 6-10

Zeltner, Herbert, "Concentration," in *Media Decisions*, November, 1970, pp. 44-50

Wheatley, John J., "Influence of Commercial's Length and Position," in *Journal of Marketing Research*, May, 1968, pp. 199-202

chapter 10

Problems of Intermedia Comparisons

One of the most difficult tasks in the media planning process is that of making comparisons between media of different classes, such as between television and magazines, or radio and outdoor. These kinds of comparisons are called "intermedia." Comparisons between media in the same class, such as between magazines A, B and C are called "intramedia." It is obvious that intermedia comparisons should be made before intramedia comparisons.

The main problem is whether it is logically correct to make intermedia comparisons on a statistical basis. In some situations it may be valid to compare media classes statistically, but in most others it is not. The reason that comparisons should not be made is that the numbers for one media class do not mean the same as they do for another class. Such comparisons are aptly called the differences between oranges and apples, or between readers, viewers and listeners. A reader is defined so much differently from a viewer that comparisons of numbers would be misleading. For example, would it be correct to compare the cost-per-thousand of a television program with a cost-per-thousand of a magazine? The answer is that it is partially correct. If one vehicle delivers more targets at better cost efficiency than another, in a different media class, the answer is correct to that point. But it is questionable whether a television commercial with its action and sound can be fairly compared with the stationary appearance of a four-color advertisement. Yet comparisons must be made whenever there are alternative choices that can be made between two different media classes. Figure 32 shows some of the differences between print and broadcast media.

While one might compare the circulation of a newspaper with coverage of a radio station, these intermedia comparisons cannot be made on a statistical basis and instead would have to be made on some subjective basis.

The basis of these latter comparisons, however, are not *entirely* subjective. They are founded on the idea that all media have inherent qualities that make them desirable. But the desirable qualities, even though they may be somewhat subjective on the part of various media planners, are some of the reasons why certain media are successful in disseminating news, entertainment, editorial and advertising material.

Figure 32

Differences Between Print and Broadcast Media

Print Media	Broadcast Media
Message must be read.	Message must be heard or read.
Message can be read at the reader's convenience.	Message is viewed/heard only when it is broadcast.
Message does not interfere with editorial or entertainment content.	Message often interrupts editorial or entertainment contents.
A reader is defined as one who was exposed to the medium.	A viewer is defined as one who has tuned in to the program.
Messages can be re-read as often as audience member	Message appears only once. Viewer has little idea when the same message will be re-broadcast.
Generally, one pays full or partial attention to medium while reading or even scanning.	It is possible to perform other tasks while program is on, so range of attention may be from none to full.
Placement of advertising message generally not controllable (with a few exceptions).	Placement of advertising message generally selected by the advertiser.
Reader can search for products in which he is interested.	Viewer has little idea when the product he wants will be advertised.
Color fidelity usually excellent.	Color fidelity ranges from one extreme to another. Some TV sets cannot show color at all.
Other than color, there are few emotional appeals in ads.	A great deal of emotional appeal possible in commercials.
Can be read in almost any location.	Viewing limited by the size and portability of TV or radio set.
Sold in space units.	Sold in time units.
Many production variables possible, such as gate-folds, pop-ups, day-glo inks, 3-D. etc.	Some different kinds of production variables possible: split-screen, cartoons, stop-motion, cut-ins, etc.

The following pages comprise a brief review of reasons for using major measured consumer media: newspapers, magazines, television, radio, supplements, direct mail, outdoor and transit. *The authors wish to emphasize that reasons for using a medium and their limitations are often a matter of a planner's perceptions and impressions rather objective evidence* and there are some media experts who may take exceptions to reasons and/or limitations stated here.

Reasons for Using Newspapers

Sense of immediacy. Readers tend to perceive newspapers as either the most, or one of the most, immediate media vehicles on the market. Every day a newspaper contains something new, and with the news come new advertisements. So newspapers may be thought of as having a "now" quality at all times. This quality is important when advertisers want to communicate something that must be known immediately. When manufacturers introduce new products to the market they usually include newspapers as one of the media that comprise the media mix.

Local emphasis. Almost all daily newspapers have a local quality which is important to advertisers. This means that while the advertiser may use a national medium such as network television, he may also want to use some medium with local impact. All selling is local and the newspaper helps emphasize this by exposing local merchants' names and addresses in national advertising.

188

Flexibility: both geographic and production. Newspapers are flexible because they may be used nationally, regionally and locally in a media plan. Even when a manufacturer's markets are widely scattered throughout the country, it is possible to reach them by using local newspapers.

Production flexibility means that the copy can be changed easily and quickly, or that some unusual production technique can be used to help get the message across. For example: some national advertisers want to have different prices for the same products in different markets. Or perhaps they want to include pre-printed inserts in the newspaper in only certain geographical markets. These and other production alternatives are possible with newspapers.

High fidelity color with Hi-Fi or Spectacolor. Through the use of either Hi-Fi or Spectacolor, it is possible for newspapers to compete favorably with magazines in given markets. Hi-Fi ads may be recognized by their wallpaper designs, while Spectacolor has a white margin border around the advertisement. Both of these techniques are produced by rotogravure presses which print only on one side of the page. The paper is not cut into pages, however; it is re-rolled and shipped to selected newspapers who print news on the back of the sheet and bind it into the regular newspaper edition for that day. The effect of rotogravure printing is to give the advertiser the possibility of brilliant life-like colors that can enhance his brand's advertisement.

Newspapers are a mass medium. Since newspapers are read by so many individuals in each market, its total reach per market may include many individuals in each family. When products are advertised to masses of people that include mom, dad and the children, then newspapers offer an ideal medium.

Catalog value. Newspapers have a quality of serving as a catalog for consumers searching for products they would like to buy. Often a consumer searches his daily newspaper before he goes shopping. The effect of such search is that often he is pre-sold on a product and a brand before he walks into the store to buy it. Some readers even cut out ads and bring them along as a reminder when shopping.

Newspapers reach black and ethnic markets. Although newspapers are considered mass media, they have selective power to reach black people or ethnic classes as well. If the local metropolitan newspaper does not reach these markets, then a special newspaper may do the job.

Limitations of Newspapers

R.O.P. color varies from newspaper to newspaper. When an advertiser buys advertisements printed in R.O.P. color he may find great variations in color fidelity from market to market. This variance means that his message may be more effective in one market than in another even though all markets have the same value.

Cost of buying national coverage is high. While newspapers are indeed a flexible medium, the cost of buying national coverage is very high and may be prohibitive for national advertisers with limited budgets.

National advertising rates are higher than retail rates. Most daily newspapers charge more for national advertising than for local. When national advertisers arrange with local retailers for cooperative advertising, the retailer may buy the advertising at lower (retail) rates and then send a bill to the national advertiser at the higher (national) rate. Through this technique the local cooperative advertiser pockets the difference in rates, which may be quite large.

Small pass-along audience. Newspapers are rarely passed along to other audiences as are magazines. This means that advertisements in yesterday's editions have a limited time value since relatively few persons will see the newspaper after it is read by family members.

Reasons for Using Magazines

Selectivity. Magazines are very selective in reaching certain kinds of audiences. There are an increasing number of magazines being started each year to meet the interest of special groups such as tennis or chess players, cooking enthusiasts, hobby fans, or even those wanting to know more about investing in the stock market. In addition, some magazines have demographic editions such as a physicians' edition, a college students' edition, or one limited to those whose annual income is over $15,000. Finally, there are geographic editions that enable the planner to reach broad or narrow markets. The selective nature of magazines, enabling the planner to use them in many different ways, means that they are flexible.

Fine color reproduction. Many magazines are able to reproduce advertisements in excellent color fidelity. The necessity for fine color reproduction is obvious for certain kinds of product advertising such as food, clothes and cars.

Long life. Magazines usually have a long life, at least for a week. But some last for more than a month and some for years. The effect of long life is that the advertiser can continue to build reach long after his present campaign has formally ended. While the product featured in his ads may even have been discontinued after a number of years, the effect of a person who reads an ad years after it originally ran is to build brand awareness for long periods of time. Reach built over long periods of time, however, may not help the planner attain short range goals.

Pass-along audience. Magazines usually have pass-along audiences who increase the reach. The size of the pass-along audience varies, however, from magazine to magazine, with some having a larger secondary audience than others.

Controlled circulation may pinpoint an audience. Because it is possible to locate and meet the needs of special interest groups, it is possible to have controlled circulation. In a controlled circulation arrangement, the publisher is able to identify a special group of targets, mostly by profession or occupation, and then send each of these individuals the magazine free of charge. He then turns to advertisers and informs them that he can guarantee a circulation or audience of a certain size. Most controlled circulation magazines are in the business field.

Limitations of Magazines

Long closing dates.   Some magazines require advertisers to have their engravings for four-color ads in their printing plants seven weeks before publication. The consequence of this requirement is that the marketing, creative and production work on the campaign must be completed so far ahead of publication date that the advertiser may lose the advantage of timeliness. It is even possible for a marketing situation to have changed by the time the ad appears in print.

Lack of immediacy.   Other than weekly news magazines, most lack a sense of urgency and immediacy. In other words readers may not even look at the latest issue of a given magazine until some time has elapsed after it has reached his home. Even news magazines do not have the sense of immediacy that newspapers have.

Reach builds slowly in some magazines.   Because some readers do not turn to their magazines quickly, reach tends to build slowly in this medium. Some readers read a small portion of a magazine immediately and then continue at later dates and times, whenever convenient. Active people who are always on the go sometimes will scan through a number of issues at one time to catch up with their reading. At other times, they just ignore a number of issues and will read only the most current one.

Reasons for Using Newspaper Supplements

Local market impact with a magazine format.   Newspaper supplements offer the advertiser the advantage of being able to reach local markets with a format that closely resembles magazines. Therefore, many of the qualities of magazines are also qualities of the supplement. Most important, however, is the ability of the planner to reach many local markets with a magazine format.

Good color fidelity.   Newspaper supplements are usually printed on rotogravure presses and therefore have high color fidelity.

Depth of penetration in covered markets.   Whereas magazines would have limited penetration in any market, supplements have high penetration. The reason is that magazines, because of their specialized natures, might have relatively small numbers of readers in any local market. But the supplement, distributed with newspapers, would naturally have large numbers of individuals who have access to it, and for whom the editorial features are broad and of general interest.

Circulation covers areas that do not carry supplements. One bonus of using supplements is that it is possible to reach some markets that do not carry the supplement. This is possible because large metro area newspapers will often have extensive area coverage far beyond the standard metropolitan statistical area. Consumers in these bonus markets may read their local newspapers on weekdays, but a large metro paper on Sunday.

Reach prospects on Sunday morning. When supplements are read, they will have little competition from other media because Sunday morning and afternoon typically offer freedom from special other media. Many readers are more relaxed on Sundays and can spend more time reading than on other days.

High readership. Since supplements have large penetration in individual markets, it is not surprising that they are widely read, especially by women. Working women especially tend to have the time to read this format, because it is available on Sunday, it is part of a newspaper, and because many features tend to cover women's interests.

Flexibility: geographic and production. It is obvious that supplements allow the planner to place advertising locally, regionally or even nationally. But some supplements even allow production flexibility such as the option of running a full-page ad in some markets, while at the same time running smaller-sized ads in other markets.

Limitations of Newspaper Supplements

Long closing dates for four-color. Because supplements are printed by the rotogravure process, the material for ads must be in the printing plant as long as eight weeks before publication date. This timing is even longer than that required for most magazines that are printed either by letterpress or offset process. Rotogravure is printed from copper cylinders that take an exceedingly long time to prepare. Furthermore, because it is so difficult to make corrections on rotogravure plates, greater care and time is taken in the preparation of the cylinders than would be true for other printing processes.

Little pass-along or secondary readership. Because supplements come with weekend newspapers, they inherit some of the weaknesses of newspapers. One of these is that supplements rarely are passed along to others. They usually are thrown away after the family has read them. In addition, one rarely finds supplements in barber or beauty shops or doctors' or dentists' offices as one would find magazines.

Reasons for Using Television

Sight and sound for dynamic selling. Audio-visual demonstrations are one of the best teaching methods known. By using the combination of sight and sound the advertiser may capitalize on a technique that comes closest to personal selling. If he could afford personal salesmen, he would do so. But television selling is very dynamic. It is also one of the best methods of demonstrating the uses or advantages of a given product.

Flexibility. Network television offers broad national coverage, while spot television allows the planner to use markets in any number of combinations.

Both selective and mass markets may be reached. Television may be used to attract both selective and mass markets through programming for either group.

When professional football games are being broadcast, the audience is almost all male. Children's programming on Saturday mornings, or daytime television tends to reach selective audiences. On the other hand, for some programming types such as movies, comedies, or special events, the audiences will consist of many different kinds and ages of people.

Good cost efficiency. Television can be very cost efficient at times. Daytime television, for example, usually has low cost-per-thousands as does fringe times. Though the costs are high, the audiences are large.

Limitations of Television

High total cost. The cost of commercial time can be beyond the means of some advertisers. The change from 60 to 30 seconds as the standard length for commercials reflects the advertiser's needs for lower total cost.

Short life messages. Although audio-visual messages may have the potential for high recall, the nature of television commercials is such that either the viewer pays attention or he may miss the message and therefore the commercial's life tends to be fleeting.

No catalog value. It is evident that viewers do not search for commercials when they are in the market for a product. While they pay greater attention to a commercial they happen to see for a product in which they are interested, they usually have little idea of the exact time such commercials will be broadcast.

Limited availabilities of good programs and time slots. Since television is a widely used medium, there is a limit to the number of programs with large audience following or time slots that are available and desirable.

Reasons for Using Radio

Radio reaches special kinds of target audiences. Radio is able to reach certain kinds of audiences very well. Through programming specialization where a radio station becomes known for its "sound," special kinds of audiences, such as men, women, teen-agers, farmers, ethnic populations, blacks, the elderly and shut-ins are attracted. Many nationalities have programs dedicated to interests of their own such as the Greek, German, Italian, Mexican or Polish. Religious groups, especially, have found radio to be an excellent communication medium. But the groups that are best known to be reached by radio are men, women and teen-agers.

A high frequency medium. Where a great deal of repetition is necessary, radio may be the ideal medium. The total cost is relatively low and there are usually many stations with time available to build a media plan with high frequency.

A good supporting medium. Because of the low cost and good reach of special target markets, radio is often used as a supporting medium in addition to some others. Often when a plan is predominantly print, radio can be added at low cost to bring sound into the plan.

Excellent for mobile populations. Since a large population of the American public owns an automobile and drives a great deal, radio becomes a means of reaching them while they are traveling. Many men drive long distances to and from work, and for some men the distances are getting longer, depending where they live in the suburbs. But listening to the radio in what is known as "drive time" has become a diversion to help pass the long commuting time and is an excellent means of reaching men.

But men aren't the only ones who travel every day. Women often take their cars to shopping centers that may be located far from their homes. They, too, will often turn on the radio to help pass the time while traveling. In fact, radio may be the last medium that a housewife is exposed to before she enters a retail store. Local retailers might very well carry on a campaign to communicate with these women before they arrive at the stores.

Summertime exposure. Related to the last advantage is the fact that since so many people travel during the summer months, radio would be an excellent medium to reach them while they are en route. This fact is sometimes disputed by experts who claim that radio tune-in is no higher in the summer than it is any other time, but their evidence is not conclusive.

Flexibility. Radio may be used locally, regionally or nationally, as television can be. There are not too many production advantages to radio, however. Copy can be changed quickly, and added or eliminated from a program quickly, but radio is still not regarded for its great production flexibility except for very simple commercials.

Local coverage available. Local radio is usually purchased because it reaches a given market very well. But radio signals may be carried far from the originating market into other geographical areas. This occurs at night when the "heavenside layer" (a natural phenomenon) broadly disseminates signals far beyond the local market. For the national advertiser who is trying to build brand awareness in many different markets, this added feature may be perceived as a bonus when buying radio locally.

Limitations of Radio

Many stations in any one market. In many large metropolitan markets there are so many radio stations vying for the audience's attention that only a relatively few reach a substantial number. In other words, radio reaches relatively small audiences. If one wanted to build large reach via radio it would be necessary to buy more than one station, and in some situations, many stations. In New York City there are 29 total AM and FM stations and another 34 in the New York metropolitan area. In Chicago there are 26 stations in the city and another 19 in the metro area. Another consequence of the large number of stations that are available is that of fragmentation of audiences caused by specialized programming. On the one hand, specialized programs do deliver little waste, because the program structure is not attractive to everyone. But on the other hand, it fractionalizes the audience especially for an advertiser who wants a mass—not class—audience.

Fleeting messages.   Like television, but even more so, radio messages are fleeting and may be missed or forgotten if only partially heard.

Reasons for Using Direct Mail

A very selective medium.   Direct mail can be the most selective of all media, provided that a list of names and addresses of a target audience are known, up-to-date and complete. When such a list is available there may be minimal waste, so the advertiser pays only for targets that are reached.

Response to advertising is easy to check.   It is relatively easy to learn whether a direct mail piece was effective. One simply counts the number of responses to an offer. The number of inquiries from direct mail may or may not be related to sales, but inquiries from direct mailings do constitute one form of measurement. Often alternative copy treatments are sent out by direct mail and the most effective one is checked easily. In a later chapter, the question is raised about how to measure the response function of media (Chapter 11). Although it is very difficult to measure response functions in most other media, the same cannot be said of direct mail.

A personal medium.   Direct mail can be a personal medium when addressed to a consumer bearing his name and address. Most advertising is very impersonal because it is difficult to talk to anyone by name. But direct mail, using specific names and addresses, comes closest to overcoming this problem. Of course, there is the problem of a stranger writing to a potential customer and calling him by name. But many people do appreciate seeing their names in print, and may read the offer when received.

Geographic and production flexibility.   Direct mail is probably the easiest of all media to tailor precisely to the geographic marketing needs of an advertiser. The beauty of this flexibility is that direct mail can be adjusted to very small markets, as few as needed, and also adjusted to as large an area as needed. The medium is also flexible for using varying production techniques. Almost any size and kind of paper and any kind of ink or special printing technique is possible. Advertisers with special creative problems may turn to direct mail because they can use the medium in more ways than they can with any other medium. Samples of a product can be mailed with ads, special die cut-outs can be made, special kinds of foldings; and special kinds of packaging are available only in this medium.

Some mailings have long lives.   When catalogs are received by consumers, they tend to keep them for long periods of time. Some educational materials also have the same quality. If the educational matter has value, such as a chart showing how to administer first aid, or a booklet on how to eliminate stains on clothing, then it may be retained for long periods.

Savings possible when direct mail inserted with bills. No special envelope, special addressing or extra postage is necessary when direct mail advertising is sent along with bills. The bill would have to be sent anyway, so the addition of a direct advertisement may not even cost extra postage. Printing costs , however, must be borne. Even when the total weight of the advertising enclosed with a bill is greater than the bill alone, there may still be substantial savings because there are no extra envelope and addressing costs. Meanwhile, the addition of the advertising may increase the cost only slightly.

Limitations of Direct Mail

It may be very expensive. There are two situations, at least, where direct mail is very expensive and perhaps more so than any other media: when a production technique requires the use of very heavy enameled or other expensive papers or when some unusual method of engraving, artwork, or printing is used and when very large mailings are made that cannot take advantage of bulk mailing privileges. It is unlikely that postage rates in the future will decline, and these high costs will continue to affect direct mail usage.

Problems of accuracy and completeness of lists. Without an accurate and complete mailing list, direct mail cannot succeed optimally. In this era when so many individuals move from one place to another, it may be difficult or too expensive to keep a list up-to-date or develop new ones. In an earlier era, it was possible to buy large mass mailings at low cost and not be concerned about the accuracy of the list. But today's high postage and production costs require that accurate and complete lists be used.

Delivery date may vary from person to person. Although a large mailing may be delivered to the post office on time, they may be delivered to various individuals at widely different times. If time is not of the essence in the marketing objectives, then it doesn't matter. But timing of an advertising message is most often critical and the direct mail user cannot control it very well. When direct mail is compared with other media, it comes off second best in respect to timing. When ads are placed in newspapers and magazines they are printed on the day requested. When broadcast commercials are purchased they are delivered not When ads are placed in newspapers they are printed on the day requested. When broadcast commercials are purchased they are delivered not only on the day, but the hour requested. In comparison, direct mail delivery dates to the entire market are unpredictable.

Reasons for Using Outdoor

Large coverage of local markets. Outdoor advertising is able to build large local coverage of the mobile population in many markets in a 30-day period. However, this coverage does not represent reading of the messages, only exposure to them.

Large frequency. Billboards also have large frequency of the mobile population of a market. It is in this area that billboards may be best. While the differences in reach of a 100 versus a 50 showing are not great, the frequency levels are quite different.

Largest size print ad available. Outdoor allows the advertiser to buy the largest size print ad available. The effect of size is one of attraction-power. The use of attractive color printing plus dramatic lighting and, at times, moving portions of a sign, all offer the advertiser great attention-getting power.

Geographic flexibility. Outdoor may be used locally, regionally and nationally. Even within any given market, it is possible to add emphasis wherever desired. Movable billboards enable an advertiser to concentrate his messages in many places, or to increase the potential for exposure.

High summertime visibility. Media plans will often include billboards for summer use because they increase the visibility of a brand name while many people are traveling. Warmer weather means that people often become more mobile, and as they take to their cars, it is possible to reach them through billboards and other outdoor signs.

Around the clock exposure. Since many billboards are lighted on main thoroughfares, anyone passing at any time of day or night can be exposed to the messages. As long as there is a mobile population, there is an opportunity for exposures to take place.

Good for simple copy theme and package identification. Where the message is relatively short and simple and the package is distinctive, this medium can be an excellent way to attract attention and build frequency for the message. Building brand awareness is a strength of the medium.

Limitations of Outdoor

Limited to simple messages. The best use of outdoor would be simple messages; it is obvious that complex or long messages cannot be used very well. This restriction means that the medium cannot be used in precisely the same manner as other print media.

High outdoor reach does not necessarily mean high recall of messages. Though outdoor may have high reach, and sometimes have good recall of ad messages, it is not necessarily true that high reach means high recall. The creativeness of the message is an important criterion in assessing the ability of the message to be recalled. But because of the nature of this medium, it is often possible that people look at billboards and are unable to recall what they saw.

A relatively high cost medium. Although the cost-per-thousands are low, this is a relatively high cost medium when compared to some other media. For a national effort of a 100 showing, the cost is over a million dollars for a month. Considering the fact that it is a medium whose position is often in the background, its requirement for very short messages, and that drivers' interests are primarily focused on the road ahead, this cost may be prohibitive for many advertisers.

Effectiveness (partially) controlled by individual plant operations. Because the number of boards necessary to provide varying levels of effective coverage in a given market may be determined at the discretion of the individual plant operator, a given showing may be more or less an effective advertising tool in different markets.

Reasons for Using Transit Media

Transit media involves interior displays on mass transit vehicles, exterior displays on the same vehicles, and terminal and station platform displays.

Transit provides mass coverage of a metropolitan area. When an advertiser wants to reach individuals in the heart of a market, then mass transit advertising may be desirable. It is primarily a vehicle for reaching adults either on their way to, or returning from, work. But its reach is extensive.

A high-frequency medium. Since this medium takes advantage of normal travel patterns that are duplicated many days throughout the year, there is an opportunity for a great deal of repetition of message delivery.

A relatively efficient medium. Based on potential exposures, this medium can deliver large numbers of individuals at low unit costs.

A flexible medium. An advertiser can select transportation vehicles in which to place his ads that reach certain kinds of demographically defined groups. He does not have to select all mass transit systems, only those that are known to have large numbers of his targets.

Opportunity to position messages to consumers on the way to their points of purchase. Local advertisers can buy messages that reach consumers on their way to their places of purchases. Therefore, it is possible that, for some consumers, the transit ads will be the last medium they are exposed to before making a purchase.

Limitations of Transit Media

Message space is limited. Most often, large or complex messages cannot be disseminated in this medium because there is not enough space available to carry such messages.

Competition from other media and personal activities may be high. Transit is not an intrusive medium—it competes for attention with other things such as attractiveness of scenery outside the medium; or things surrounding the medium (the nature of the transit vehicle) or other people. The person who travels to and from work on the same transportation vehicle may be tired, bored or interested in some other media vehicle he is carrying with him. For exterior displays, it is often necessary to devise something of extra creative pulling power in order to attract attention, a requirement that may be difficult to achieve.

Intermedia Comparisons for Non-Measured Media

Almost every medium in existence has some qualities that are useful for some advertiser. On the other hand, they also have some limitations too. The media planner then, in making intermedia comparisons involving non-measured media may have to rely even more on subjective judgments than he would for measured media. Sometimes non-measured media will conduct research that may be helpful for the media planner in making intermedia comparisons. Unfortunately most such research is suspected of being biased in favor of the company that pays for it, because it has a vested interest in the outcome. As a result, it is difficult to make intermedia comparisons even on a subjective basis for non-measured media except in simple, obvious areas.

Recall scores as an intermedia comparison technique. One way of seemingly solving the dilemma of non-comparable measuring techniques for intermedia comparisons is the use of response functions as a criterion of effectiveness. If it could be shown that an ad in one medium generates more recall than an ad in another medium, then the assumption may be made that the medium with the highest recall is better. However, the ad, or ads used for comparative purposes cannot be indiscriminately chosen. Nor can average recall of many ads be used in measuring recall of one medium versus another. The reason is that some products may be inherently more interesting than others and therefore generate higher recall scores. Or, perhaps some brands being advertised are inherently more interesting than others.

To prevent such bias, the same ad is usually measured in two different media. As a result, it is hoped that any variation in the recall scores is due to the effect of the medium rather than the ad. While this procedure seems to have solved the problem, it still is questionable whether it represents a valid means of intermedia comparisons.

The reason is much the same as mentioned earlier: when comparing print and broadcast, the differences in each medium are like comparing apples and oranges. If a cola product were being tested on television and the same ad were tested in a print medium, it would be difficult, if not impossible, to keep the copy and creative elements constant. A commercial for a cola drink usually would feature an announcer's voice, whether on or off camera. Most of the time the message would feature action, rather than still scenes. Then the audience members may receive it on many different-sized television screens, some in black and white, and some in color.

If the same cola ad were placed in print, the size of the ad would probably be constant from magazine to magazine, and there would be no sound whereby one could recognize a well-known personality's voice, and no music. Furthermore, if the print ad were placed in a magazine, there would be competition for attention from other ads, while the television program in which the commercial was placed would either be seen or not seen. (No competition for attention at the same time.)

199

Therefore, any results of recall measurements coult not be considered to be unbiased. Any one of the variables exclusive to the ad in a given medium could account for the greater or lesser recall scores. So while such techniques may be helpful for other purposes, they may not be entirely valid for use in intermedia comparisons.

Often a media class such as magazines will spend a great deal of money to prove that it is better than some other medium. While the results are interesting, they cannot be considered valid for intermedia comparative purposes.

QUESTIONS

1. Explain whether it is valid to compare a cost-per-thousand for a commercial on radio with a cost-per-thousand for an ad in magazines.
2. What are the general advantages of a print medium vs. a broadcast medium? What are the general advantages of a broadcast medium vs. a print medium?
3. Briefly explain the two kinds of flexibility that may be important in media planning.
4. How has the higher rate for national advertising in newspapers possibly affected the retailers' use or mis-use of cooperative advertising?
5. What is the most important reason for a publisher choosing to have controlled rather than paid circulation for his magazine?
6. What advantages does a Sunday supplement have over a magazine and vice versa?
7. Why may a media buyer who wants to build very high frequency choose radio rather than television for his media plan?
8. If a planner wants high level of brand visibility during the summer months, which media is he likely to choose?
9. Which medium is probably the most selective of all in reaching very selective target markets? What conditions must be met, however, before this medium can be called most selective?
10. If a motorist passes any outdoor billboard, is he covered by that showing for the month? Briefly explain.

SELECTED READINGS

Audits and Surveys, "Study of Advertising Communication," *Look Magazine,* Cowles Publishing Co., 1962

Coffin, Thomas E., "Total Effect" Is Called the Key to Meaningful Media Comparisons," in *Media/scope,* Feb. 1959, pp. 44-51

Editor and Publisher, "CBS-TV Claims Newspaper Ad Reading Time Is Under 6 Seconds," Sept. 5, 1970, p. 9-10

Forkan, James P. "Tele-Research Gives TV an Edge over Magazines in Latest Effectiveness Fight," *Advertising Age,* May 29, 1972, p. 6

Greenberg, A., "Point-of-View: Intermedia Comparisons," in *Journal of Advertising Research,* Oct., 1972, pp. 47-49

Grudin/Appel/Haley Research Corp., "Advertising Recall in Life vs. Television," *Life Magazine,* 1970

Keshin, Mort, "Apples and Oranges Revisited," in *Media/scope,* June, 1966, pp. 12-14

Kinley, Daniel L. "Inter-media Comparisons,"

in *Media/scope,* Sept., 1959, p. 28

Lodish, L. M., "Exposure Interactions Among Media Schedules," in *Journal of Advertising Research,* April, 1973, pp. 31-34

Life, "A Six-Step Inter Media Comparison," Spring, 1971

Media Decisions, "The Clutter Crisis," Dec., 1971, pp. 40+

Maneloveg, Herbert, "Television Isn't Alone in Commercial Clutter—Magazines, Newspapers Have It Too," Oct. 11, 1971, *Advertising Age,* p. 47

Media/scope, "No Simple Solution to Comparison of Media," in *Media/scope,* Mar., 1959, pp. 54-63

Orenstein, Frank, "When People Want to Know Where Do They Go To Find Out?" *Media/scope,* Oct., 1967, pp. 61-68

Roper Organization, The, *What People Think of Television and Other Mass Media* 1959-1972., Television Information Office, May, 1973

chapter 11

Beyond Reach and Frequency— Use of Response Functions in Planning

One of the most difficult problems facing a media planner is that of proving the effectiveness of a given plan. At present, a plan culminates in a given estimated reach and frequency of target audiences. The problem, more specifically, is to know what to do or how to go beyond reach and frequency goals. Alec M. Lee, Director of Operations Research for Trans-Canada Air Lines, aptly pointed out that there is nothing wrong with using reach and frequency to determine an optimum media schedule if the levels of reach and frequency are known that will attain a specific marketing objective.[45] But they are not known. They are intuitive estimates based on very little objective evidence.

At present, the quality of a media plan is judged subjectively, based on answers to a number of questions such as: (a) has the plan clearly defined the target audiences? (b) has it selected media vehicles that best reach those targets at good cost efficiency? (c) are the vehicles appropriate to the product and the message? (d) is the reach level and the average frequency level appropriate for the specified budget and copy considerations? (e) is the schedule matched to the best sales or communication opportunities? (f) and finally, does the plan help achieve the marketing objectives?

If the answers are all affirmative, then the plan may be judged effective. The answers, however, are based to a small extent on marketing and media data analysis, and to a greater extent on personal experience and subjective judgment of an individual (or advisory group). But there is little that can be judged on empirical evidence before the plan is implemented. It is not clear at all, that the plan is really effective because there are no effectiveness criteria other than logic or experience. Reach levels cannot be a criterion because there is no evidence that any given reach accomplishes a specific business objective. Frequency levels cannot be used as a criterion because there is too little evidence that they accomplish either a communication or marketing objective. In fact, there has

[45]Lee, Alec M., "The Search For Decision Rules for Optimal Media Scheduling," in *Advertising Research Foundation 8th Annual Conference Proceedings*, Oct., 1962, p.28

been no way to parse out the contribution of media vehicles selected, from the results of an advertising campaign. Perhaps the best that can be said about a plan is that, according to present-day practices in widespread use in sophisticated advertising agencies, and according to the state of knowledge about media planning, it represents what *appears* to be a good plan.

But media theoreticians have been thinking about and discussing this subject for a long time. What they consider to be most appropriate is a measurement of consumer response to a media plan. After all, a media plan is a combination of individual decisions. Without knowing the results of these decisions, it would be difficult to judge their adequacy. Therefore, the wisdom of a media plan should depend on what happens as a result of its proper implementation. If the results are observable then they should be measurable, and many of the results are observable.

The results are often called "response functions" to indicate that they are responses to media vehicle stimuli. In other words, people do things as a result of having been stimulated by advertisements presented in a certain media form (television, magazines, etc.) While it may seem desirable to measure the results of media stimuli alone, the effects of copy must also be considered. Presumably then, the same ad that is placed in two different media vehicles should have somewhat different degrees of responses. The reason that combination effects are recommended rather than media effects alone, is that the latter is too difficult to observe and, consequently, too difficult to measure.

The definition of a response function is: an effect on target audience members caused by an association of those individuals with media vehicles and ads in those vehicles.

For the convenience of thinking about, or discussing response functions, it may be advisable to divide them into at least two classes, or kinds. One kind of response is the result of a mechanical association of an individual and a vehicle, such as what happens when a person receives a magazine issue through the mail. He may unwrap it and lay it on a table. Perhaps he will never read it because he is too busy with other activities. This association is purely mechanical because it involves little interaction. On the other hand, if he opens the magazine and thumbs through it, that too is a mechanical interaction, but one of a higher level. If he should stop while thumbing through, and look at an ad or two, then an even higher level of mechanical response has occurred, called "ad page exposure."

But a different kind of response is one that is psychological. If a person opens a magazine, sees a given ad and, after questioning by an interviewer, says that he remembers having seen that ad, then the response is psychological because the action or effect involves something that occurred in his mind that resulted in an act of remembering. Of course, there are other kinds of psychological responses that might be measured, such as the kind of buying behavior that results from his having read an ad.

At present, most media planning is based on a very low level of mechanical response called vehicle exposure. One often hears statements (though not correct) that the media plan that delivers the most target exposures is best. Such a statement is an oversimplification.

The purpose of this chapter then, is to examine the concept of response functions and how they may be used in media planning evaluation. The objective is to discuss some of the more widely recommended response functions and help the reader see whether any of them can accomplish the goals discussed earlier.

It should be clearly understood by the reader that no single measurement of response exists in the industry by which media plans can be evaluated. The following portions of this chapter identify some of the response techniques employed by various firms or individuals within advertising. Knowledge of the various techniques, with their strengths and weaknesses, should aid in understanding how media planning criteria, beyond reach and frequency, sometimes serve as a basis for making media recommendations.

Different Kinds of Response Functions

Advertising recognition. Measurements of individuals who remember having seen ads in magazines or newspapers have been used as response functions from time to time. The measuring technique is very simple. A respondent is first qualified to be questioned further by an interviewer. Qualification means that the respondent, when shown the cover of a magazine, says that he remembers having looked inside it. If he is qualified, then the interviewer opens each page with a full-page or half-page ad on it; and asks respondent whether he saw a specific ad. Affirmative answers are considered as "noting" or "recognizing" each ad. Both terms mean the same thing. Recognition scores are tabulated for each ad in a magazine. The same ads can be measured in many different magazines, thus providing a rough measurement of a vehicle's ability to generate recognition levels.

Theoretically then, recognition scores should represent evidence that a certain percentage of individuals were affected by the vehicle and ads in it. If one vehicle has a higher average number of recognition scores than another, it may be a better vehicle. Alfred Politz called recognition scores a measurement of a magazine's efficiency, or performance in attracting readers to ads in each vehicle.[46]

Practically however, media planners do not accept, without some reservations, recognition scores as measurements of response functions. These reservations on using the data are as follows: (a) Many readers are confused about where they saw a given ad. There is no reason for them to remember that they saw an ad in one magazine, or that they saw the same ad in two different magazines. This confusion, therefore, affects the comparability of media by using the recognition technique. (b) Whenever bogus ads are inserted in magazines that are to be measured by this technique, there are always a number of individuals who claim they remember having seen those ads. This is an unusual response and casts

---

[46]Politz, Alfred, "What is Essential to Know from Magazine Media Research?" in *Media/scope*, April, 1959, p. 40

doubt on the validity of the measuring technique. Surely respondents should be able to remember that they did not see the bogus ads, some of which had never been printed in any magazine. Perhaps respondents want to empathize with interviewers and claim they read more than they really did. (c) In fact, there is no way to prove that respondents really did see the ads they claimed to have seen. How can a researcher know whether the respondent is telling the truth, especially when respondents are shown each ad directly? Is it not possible that some persons who saw few or no ads do not want to admit their actions? Since there is no penalty for misrepresentation, then it is possible that some recognitions are not correct. (d) Recognition measurements seem not to be based on memory. In a study conducted by the Advertising Research Foundation, called Printed Advertising Rating Methods (The PARM Study), recognition scores did not drop when the same respondents were measured after an interval of time, as shown in Table 54A.

Table 54A
Recognition Scores After Varying Time Had Elapsed*

Interviewing dates	Recognition scores
May 13 to 15	19.5
May 16 to 19	18.8
May 20 to 22	18.6
May 23 to 25	20.7

*Source: Lucas, Darrell B., "The ABC's of ARF's PARM," in *The Journal of Marketing,* July, 1960, p. 15.

Most experts felt that recognition scores should have declined because there had to be some loss of memory over time. (e) There is some question about what the technique really measures. To say that it measures recognition is not satisfactory to many who might use it for media evaluation. (f) Appel and Blum found that, using this technique, there were more false responses when people were very interested in the product types being advertised, or where a product had a high market share compared to similar products. They also found that some persons have a greater tendency to claim noting or recognizing ads than others regardless of whether they really did see the ads.[47]

In conclusion then, recognition technique measurements have varying degrees of acceptibility among media planners and should only be used with the understanding of the data limitations.

The Audience Concepts Committee's response functions. In 1961, the Audience Concepts Committee of the Advertising Research Foundation issued a report titled: *Towards Better Media Comparisons.* The essence of this report was that a special committee had discussed alternative response functions that could be used to compare media vehicles and had recommended one in particu-

---

[47]Appel, Valentine and Blum, Milton L., "Ad Recognition and Respondent Set," in *Journal of Advertising Research,* June, 1961, p. 14

lar, over others. The following is an introduction and explanation of the committee's response function discussion.

In order to compare media, the committee first recommended that an advertiser define his market so that prospects could be differentiated from non-prospects. Once prospects were identified, then it would be possible to compare media on the basis of which delivered the largest number.

The committee devised a model showing alternative response functions that could be used for comparative purposes. The model consisted of six stages of response functions, from a very mechanical, low-level response, to the ultimate or ideal response: sales contributed by media vehicles. Figure 33 shows a graphic of the model, and a discussion follows:

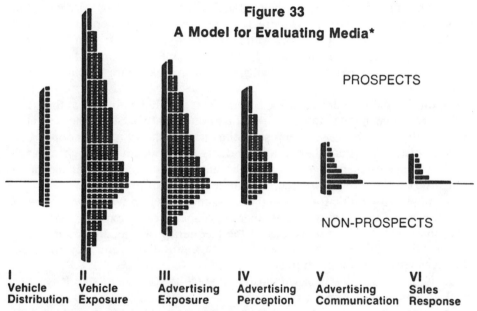

Figure 33
A Model for Evaluating Media*

PROSPECTS

NON-PROSPECTS

I	II	III	IV	V	VI
Vehicle Distribution	Vehicle Exposure	Advertising Exposure	Advertising Perception	Advertising Communication	Sales Response

*Reprinted by permission of the Advertising Research Foundation

Vehicle distribution as a response function. Stage one of the model represents the lowest level response. It is low level because it involves almost no interaction of a medium with an individual except that he receives a copy of a newspaper or magazine. In the case of television or radio, the individual has his set on, but no measurement is made of which program he is listening to. While media could be, and is, sometimes compared on the basis of vehicle distribution, it is much too crude a measuring device. It tells nothing about exposure to the medium, nor reaction of individuals to ads in that medium. It is obvious why this measurement is not generally employed as a means of evaluating a media plan, with few exceptions.

Vehicle Exposure. The second stage of the model represents a marked improvement over the first because here, comparisons of alternative media (or

205

plans) are based on the number of prospects who are exposed to the vehicle. Exposure is defined as open eyes facing the medium.

Even though this stage of the model represents a refinement over stage one, there are problems with it that limit its usefulness. For print vehicles, such as newspapers or magazines, exposure measurements are relatively easy to make. Respondents need only say, with assurance, that they looked into a given vehicle. On the other hand, broadcast media exposure is difficult to measure. The committee noted: ". . . that it is not conceivable that we shall ever be able to obtain any objective measure of the number of people whose eyes are confronted by a television commercial."[48] The problem is that of counting the number of individuals who are facing a television set when commercials come on. In diary measurements it is possible to count the number of persons in a room where a television set is on. Presumably they are facing the set watching a program; but who will count the number of individuals facing each commercial? The cost would be abnormally high to pay watchers, and even then, it is unlikely that enough diary keepers could be found to do the task for any amount of money. The same problem exists when trying to measure exposure to outdoor billboards.

In examining the model shown in Figure 33, it should be noted that there is a difference between the graphic form of stages one and two. Stage one is smaller in height than two, because it represents the fact that there are fewer copies of a medium distributed than there are individuals exposed. So the height of each graphic form represents the *reach* of the medium, suggesting that media be compared on their ability to reach a certain number of prospects.

But stage two graphic form is also multi-dimensional in width, with various sized bars representing a smaller number of prospects being exposed two times, three times, etc. These bars represent the frequency of a medium, suggesting that media should also be compared on the amount of frequency of target audiences each vehicle generates.

Media planning today is based mostly on stage two of the model. It is a low level, mechanical response function.

Advertising Exposure. In the two preceding stages, only a minimal involvement of individuals with media was counted. The result was that comparisons made by either measurement would not tell the planner much. Especially problematic would be a situation where a medium could have a large audience of individuals who were exposed to a vehicle, but had few individuals exposed to the ads. Stage three suggests that comparisons would be better if they were made on the basis of exposure to advertisements within vehicles. The graphic form for stage three also is smaller than that of stage two, suggesting that the numbers exposed to ads will always be less than the number exposed to the vehicles. Therefore, stage three, advertising exposure, is a better and higher level response function than stages one or two.

---

[48]Audience Concepts Committee, *Toward Better Media Comparisons*. Advertising Research Foundation, 1961, p. 18

Up to this point, the Audience Concepts Committee model suggested that response effects, while varying in value; (stage three was better than stage two, etc.) none of the three was ideal. Advertising exposure was best because to a limited, but important, degree, it represented some effect of a vehicle's editorial and/or entertainment format. Media vehicles differ in their ability to entice and hold audience members long enough for them to be exposed to the advertisements. The more holding power a vehicle has, the more likely audience members will see more of the ads. An example of holding power could be a television program where the entertainment is so attractive that audience members will not leave the room when commercials come on. Some viewers just won't take the chance of missing the continuation of the program after commercials and station-break interruptions.

But advertising exposure, as a response-function, is inadequate. One reason is that exposure cannot take into account the effects of different kinds and qualities of copywriting and artwork. It cannot be assumed that an exposure is equivalent to any other exposure. An attractively designed ad will usually obtain a different response than a poorly designed ad; but exposure measurements cannot differentiate between the two.

Exposure measurements also cannot account for different placement of ads within media vehicles. They cannot account for poor judgment in placing ads in inappropriate media. Some products are best advertised in one particular medium rather than most others. Some products need the dramatization of television, or the brilliant color fidelity of a magazine, or the source credibility of an announcer's voice on radio. Yet exposure measurements cannot account for these variations—one exposure unit is counted as equivalent to another, except for varying degrees of repetition. For that reason, the Committee developed three other response functions. The following three involve closer interactions of individuals and media vehicles.

Advertising Perception. The Committee suggested a refinement over stages one, two and three in a measurement of advertising perception. In this measurement, respondents are not only required to have seen ads in vehicles, but to remember that they have seen them. Perception involves the ability of audience members to recall that they saw specific ads. Therefore this response function is much better than exposure measurements because it involves more of an effect on the minds of audience members. See Figure 34 for a graphic drawing of how perception involves remembering and, therefore, more information enters the mind than in exposure.

There are two major ideas involved in perception response measurements. The first one is that this measurement involves the interaction of audience members and: (a) the effects of a vehicle's entertainment-editorial attraction and holding power (b) the image and reputation of a vehicle (c) attraction and message value of all advertisements in the vehicle. Yet the measurement itself is the smallest amount of communication received from all of the above media qualities.

Figure 34

STEPS TO LEARNING FROM MAGAZINE ADVERTISEMENTS*

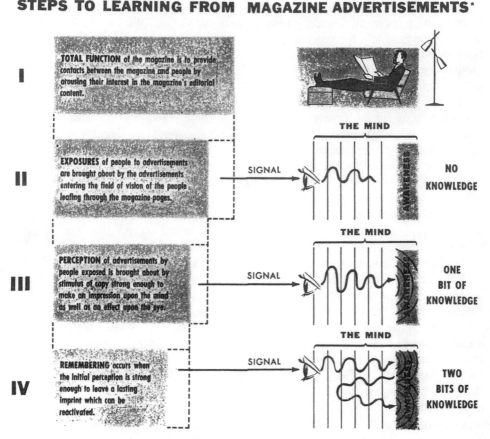

I
TOTAL FUNCTION of the magazine is to provide contacts between the magazine and people by arousing their interest in the magazine's editorial content.

II
EXPOSURES of people to advertisements are brought about by the advertisements entering the field of vision of the people leafing through the magazine pages.

THE MIND
SIGNAL
AWARENESS
NO KNOWLEDGE

III
PERCEPTION of advertisements by people exposed is brought about by stimulus of copy strong enough to make an impression upon the mind as well as an effect upon the eye.

THE MIND
SIGNAL
ONE BIT OF KNOWLEDGE

IV
REMEMBERING occurs when the initial perception is strong enough to leave a lasting imprint which can be reactivated.

THE MIND
SIGNAL
TWO BITS OF KNOWLEDGE

*Reprinted by permission of *Media/scope* Magazine.

The second idea is that the amount of recall of ads in media is so small that the number of persons who can remember having seen an ad will probably be much larger than if audience members were asked to recall more details of each ad. Consequently, this measurement does not penalize vehicles whose audiences just happen to have poor memories. Actually, there is no way to know the degree of memories audiences have; but it is a logical possibility that could exist. Figure 35 shows that perception measurements are a part of the communication process, and one where the least amount of memory of ads is required of audiences.

At present, there are no instruments available to measure perception. However, the effects of perception have been measured by a number of researchers, using varying techniques. None of these, however, is adequate for large-scale,

Figure 35

Relationship Between Perception and Degrees of Memory
on the Communication Continuum

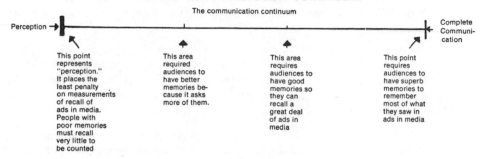

The communication continuum

Perception →

Complete Communication

This point represents "perception." It places the least penalty on measurements of recall of ads in media. People with poor memories must recall very little to be counted

This area required audiences to have better memories because it asks more of them.

This area requires audiences to have good memories so they can recall a great deal of ads in media

This point requires audiences to have superb memories to remember most of what they saw in ads in media

continuing use.[49][50][51][52] What is needed is a relatively simple, low cost instrument to provide the data.

Advertising communication. Stage five of the Committee's model is a measurement of the total amount of communication received from ads in media. The assumption underlying this measurement is that the medium that produces the largest amount of communication may be best. So the measurement is based on recall of information in ads, a very high level, and theoretically, an ideal response function. In fact, communication is more helpful than perception in making inferences about sales responses caused by ads. On the other hand, communication measurements are contaminated to some extent by each person's beliefs and attitudes. Therefore it is more difficult to control extraneous influences that affect communication than it is to control the same influences that affect perception. As a result, perception was preferred, at least at present, to communication.

Sales response. The final stage of the model represents the best way of making media comparisons if it could be proven that more sales were made by ads in one medium than any other.

Unfortunately, this kind of measurement would be "contaminated" by other sales motivating factors such as word-of-mouth effects, price, distribution and other marketing-mix elements effects. The committee noted that:

> "We have already considered certain aspects of sales response and noted some of the difficulties of attributing specific sales changes to advertising. We have said that such changes are the result not only of advertising but a variety of other factors. . . . as we progress from perception to measures of consumer

[49]Social Research, *Advertising Impact and Business Machines*, Chicago, 1959

[50]Politz, Alfred, and *McCalls*, "A Measurement of Advertising Effectiveness," Nov., 1962

[51]Politz, Alfred, and *Saturday Evening Post*, "The Rochester Study," Aug., 1960

[52]Winick, Charles, "Three Measures of the Advertising Value of Media Context," *Journal of Advertising Research*, June, 1962, pp. 28-33

responses of increasing importance to the advertiser we meet with a greater degree of contamination of our measure of advertising effectiveness by other factors."[53]

Since these other factors may not be controlled by the advertiser, it would be difficult to say with assurance that the ad in a given medium produced a given sales response.

Broadbent and Segnit's response function. Two British researchers have proposed a response function that is quite different from those reviewed earlier. They proposed the use of individual responses to different frequency levels of advertising, as criteria for comparing media.

Their definition of a response function is as follows:

"We take a response function to be a set of numbers defining the relative value to the advertiser of an individual in his target population receiving one, two . . . and so on advertising impressions."[54]

Some important considerations of their model not covered in their definition are as follows:

(1) Although their definition appears to be concerned with advertising impressions, meaning exposures to advertisements, their model could include any kind of exposure. One could use vehicle exposure, page traffic, ad page exposure, or even some kind of perception measurement. If low levels of measurement are used such as vehicle exposure, then any given number of exposures produces a number of *opportunities to see* (OTC) advertisements in a vehicle.

(2) The heart of their proposal is repetition (or frequency) of OTC, and it is based on a frequency distribution of exposures rather than an average frequency that media plans usually include.

(3) In order to show the value of various amounts of frequency, weighting is applied to the percentages of audience members who were exposed one, two or more times. *The weights are arbitrarily assigned, but they are based on the planner's judgment about how valuable any given number of exposures are.*

(4) If the weighted frequencies are added together they provide a single figure that they call the *effectiveness of a given schedule.*

The following illustration shows how they would use response functions to evaluate the effectiveness of two media plans:

	Reach	*Frequency*
Media Plan A	72	2.4
Media Plan B	79	2.1

[53]Audience Concepts Committee, p. 10

[54]Broadbent, S.R. and Segnit, S., "Response Functions in Media Planning," in *The Thomson Medals and Awards for Advertising Research,* 1967 London, pp. 37-86

A frequency distribution of the two plans for eight periods is shown below:

Table 55
Opportunities to See Ads at Various Frequency Levels*

| | Opportunities to see ads (OTC) for various frequency levels: number of exposures | | | | | | | | | |
	0	1	2	3	4	5	6	7	8	Total
Media Plan A	28%	20%	14%	8%	7%	9%	6%	5%	3%	100%
Media Plan B	21	30	10	14	13	7	4	1	0	100%

*Source: Broadbent, S. R. and Segnit, S., "Response Functions in Media Planning," in *The Thomson Medals and Awards for Advertising Research,* London, 1967, p. 38

The relative value of each exposure is arbitrarily determined. Broadbent and Segnit felt that the first exposure was only worth 50%. The second exposure was worth 75%. The third was worth 90% and each additional exposure was worth 100%. In essence, this means that a person who is exposed to a medium once is not likely to be affected very much, but when he is exposed four times, then the effect of the repetition will have been maximized. Every succeeding impression now received full value.

In order to find the effectiveness of the two plans then, each exposure level is the product of the percentage exposed times the weight, as follows, for Media Plan A: (28 x 0) + (20 x .50) + (14 x .75) etc. equalling 57.7 value. Therefore the effectiveness of A versus B is:

Media Plan A = 57.7 effectiveness
Media Plan B = 60.1 effectiveness

Weighting was cumulative rather than additive. To show the differences between the two approaches of weighting, see Table 56.

Table 56
Weighting Levels at Various Numbers of Exposures*

| Weighting Method | Weighting of Opportunities to See: (number of exposures) | | | | | | | | |
	0	1	2	3	4	5	6	7	8
Cumulative	0	.50	.75	.90	100	100	100	100	100
Additional	0	.50	.25	.15	.10	0	0	0	0

*Source: Broadbent, S. R. and Segnit, S., "Response Functions in Media Planning," in *The Thomson Medals and Awards for Advertising Research,* London, 1967, p. 39.

Other features of their model includes the fact that the campaign objectives may be given weights that correspond to their importance so that each response function could also be given these weights and a single weighted response function calculated.

It is assumed by the authors that the impressions evaluated are not of the total audience, but of prospect audiences, a concept that is a requirement for any contemporary media plan.

Finally, although they did not show it in their examples, they pointed out that qualitative media value weights could be included, as well as means of considering other media selection criteria such as heavy users, those more heavily exposed, and media effects, if known.

Theoretically, Broadbent and Segnit's model is very attractive, because it attempts to quantify responses, and then produces an effectiveness criterion by which alternative media plans can be judged. Practically, the authors admit that they do not know how to establish the relationship between exposures and effectiveness of an advertising campaign. In a sense, their concept does not replace the Audience Concepts Committee recommendation of "perception" as a measuring basis, but provides an addition or supplement. Both ideas can be used if measuring instruments and relationships can be found. (The reader should compare Broadbent and Segnit's concept with the Effective Reach Concept explained in Chapter 9.)

Response functions in computer media models. Many of the computerized media models have response functions that are similar to Broadbent and Segnit's. As an example of one in current use is the Mediac system's response function. In this system, "the user is asked to state his estimate of the value of multiple exposures in terms of the marketing objectives of the advertising campaign."[55] In effect then, the user is being asked to relate various levels of advertising exposure to his campaign goal. In order to do this, subjective judgment will have to be made on how his brand is sold, how much he spent to achieve various goals in the past, how much market share his past advertising produced, and anything that will help answer the question of how much is one exposure worth? Two exposures? Etc. At present, most computer models only allow increasing weights (cumulative, as in Broadbent and Segnit's) to higher levels of frequency. In the future, it may be possible to assign low weights to low frequency, greater weights to mid-range frequency and low weights again after a certain frequency level has been reached. If plotted on a graph, the latter method would produce an "S"-shaped curve where, after many exposures, the value of such high frequency would have reached a point of diminishing returns.

The weakness of computer media models using such response curves are that media values must be subjectively made. There is little evidence that can be used to prove the value of any given number of impressions. Obviously it would be inadvisable to judge media plans solely on such a basis.

---

[55]*Newsweek,* "A Report on Newsweek's Media/Market Systems," 1972, p. 35

Advertising involvement.   A different kind of response function was devised by Herbert E. Krugman, manager of Corporate Public Opinion Research at General Electric Company. His measurement is called advertising involvement. Involvement is a direct personal interaction of respondents with editorial matter and advertising. The interaction is defined as follows:

> "... the number of connections, conscious bridging experiences, or personal references per minute, that the subject makes between the content of persuasive stimulus and the content of his own life."[56]

These connections are not recall of specific information found in ads nor are they attitudes or opinions. They are mental incidents that have occurred while or after a person has read an ad.

Measurements are made by interviewing. Respondents are given editorial materials and advertisements which they are asked to read for a few minutes. Then the interviewer simply asks what thoughts came to respondent's mind while he looked at the ad. Some typical responses from Krugman's study were:

"It made me think of traveling there myself."

"It made me feel as if I would like to go on a vacation."

"My husband flies all the time . . . I think, wouldn't it be great to go?"

In the situation of measuring television, a few minutes of a program are shown to respondents before and after a commercial is shown. Questions are then asked following the showing.

Table 57 below shows how connections were made in measuring television versus magazines.

Table 57
Number of Connections for Television and Magazine Ads*

| | MAGAZINES | | TELEVISION | |
	Number Interviewed	No. of Connections†	Number Interviewed	Ave. No. of Connections
General editorial	14	1.9	20	.75
General Advertising	15	1.2	21	.43
Editorial environment:				
Serious/news	15	1.8	26	.65
Light/entertainment	14	1.3	15	.47
Product advertised:				
Airline	15	1.8	9	.67
Margarine	12	1.3	32	.56

†It is assumed that these are average number of connections; but research did not specify
*Source: Krugman, Herbert E., "The Measurement of Advertising Involvement" in *Public Opinion Quarterly,* Winter, 1966-67, p. 590

---

[56]Krugman, Herbert E., "The Measurement of Advertising Involvement," in *The Public Opinion Quarterly,* Winter, 1966-67, p. 584

While Krugman does not generalize from the research findings shown above, he has shown that a new kind of response measurement can be made. The results, because they discriminate between media vehicles, suggest that this measurement might be better than others for media plan assessment. Krugman also found that his findings showed no correlation between Starch noting scores nor between exposure time and involvements.

The conclusions to his research studies are quite significant to those who would use this measurement technique for media comparison analysis. They are as follows:

1. Involvement with magazines and/or television are highest when audience members' attention is directed to editorial environment, and less when directed to advertising. This may be interpreted to mean that audience members buy or expose themselves to media not for advertisements first, but for the editorial/entertainment formats.

2. When there is high interest in the editorial/entertainment environment, there is carryover to the ads. This would agree with those who say media differ in their ability to affect ads within them.

3. Magazines produced more involvement than did television. But Krugman would not go so far as to say that magazines were better than television; his research was of small sample sizes and it was exploratory in nature.

4. Involvement measurements are more sensitive than are recognition scores or measurements of exposure. This finding may mean that, perhaps, involvement measurements are more sensitive and consequently more valuable to the planner.

5. Involvement is affected by product types. Some product types (that audience members have little involvement in) tend to produce low connection scores. If audience members are highly involved with a product type, then their scores also are high.[57]

Can this measure be used as a response-function discriminator? The answer would have to be a qualified yes. From the small amount of evidence available, the technique has been shown to discriminate between vehicles. What is not known, however, is the relationship between connections and learning, or connections and buying. Without this kind of information, the technique has to offer only potential promise, not assurance that it is the best of all alternatives.

Other response-function alternatives. There are a number of other possible measurements that could be used as response functions. None of them, however, have been found completely satisfactory, for one reason or another. Media traffic scores, for example, have been proposed as a response-function. In radio or television, traffic could be measured by the number of homes using television or radio. In print media, page traffic scores could be used. A page traffic score indicates the number of individuals who looked at anything on a given page. The problem with these scores is that they are too low level to be useful. They

---

[57]*Krugman*, p. 596

represent the size of the potential rather than the actual audience. If the H.U.T. from 7 to 7:30 p.m. were 60%, that would in no way indicate the size of audience to any given program that was broadcast at that time. Conceivably, there could be great variation in audience size to the programs.

Another possibility for a response function could be coupon returns or inquiries generated as a result of ads in print media. But this measurement has minimal application because there is no guaranteed relationship between returns and sales. Furthermore, there are many individuals who do not return coupons and yet do eventually buy the product. Finally, there are many individuals who return coupons, not because they are interested in the product, but because they want to receive something in return through the mail, whatever the offer may be.

Still another possibility that has been seriously considered is measurement of attitude change caused by the combination of ads in media. If it could be shown that an ad in one medium produced more attitude change than the same ad in another medium, then this could constitute a response function for comparing alternative media. However, the entire area of attitude change is subject to so many questions that have no valid answers that the measurements are not considered viable. Some of the unanswered questions are: Does attitude change precede or follow behavior change? If behavior changes, is it due to attitude alone, or attitude and other variables that are difficult to control? Is it possible for consumers to have strongly negative attitudes and still purchase a brand regularly? Is it also possible for consumers to have strongly positive attitudes and yet not buy a given brand under any circumstances? Questions such as these have kept attitude change measurements from being accepted as a response function.

Finally, other mechanical kinds of response functions have been proposed and rejected for various reasons. Some of these methods have even been used to a limited extent, but not as a major method of evaluating media alternatives. They are: attention levels paid to media, time spent reading, amount of editorial material read, and a relatively new one: brain-wave measurements.

Attention level measurements play a minor role in media plan evaluation. Attention levels, however, have been limited to measurements of television program audiences. They cannot be used for measuring magazines. On the other hand, Simmons has been able to measure the amount of a given magazine that was read. But neither measure is applicable to both broadcast and print media. Validation of attention levels, too, is very difficult as William R. Simmons noted:

> "You can sit and talk to people but you can't always tell whether they're paying attention or not. It is almost a self-evaluation type of question. You almost have to read a person's mind to really know whether they are literally paying attention. . . . This sort of measure is not easily susceptible to any kind of clearcut test."[58]

Though planners may study attention level data paid to various television pro-

---

[58]*Mediascope,* "Roundtable on 1968 Simmons," Mar. 1968, p. 46

grams they would not consider such data as the most important factor in their decision to buy or not buy a program.

Time spent reading or viewing is also a response function that has been measured from time to time, but it is not powerful enough to be used as an evaluation technique for media planning.

Finally, brain wave measurements have been made not long ago, but it is much too early to tell whether or not it will be valuable for the purposes outlined previously. Much more research is needed to tell whether it can discriminate enough for various kinds of media. At present, it remains as a possibility that, some day may have a practical use.

In conclusion, it must be said that there is nothing available now that can serve as an industry-wide standard of determining the effectiveness of a media plan, although some of the alternative methods reviewed here offer some promise. Probably the ARF's *perception* measurement is logically the best of all alternatives, though not ideal. But, assuming that perception of ads in vehicles could be measured on a continuing basis, this measure would be much better than anything in existence. It cannot be stressed too strongly, that present methods of using vehicle exposure data is not the complete answer to comparing media vehicles, or the results of media plans.

QUESTIONS

1. Explain how one can judge the effectiveness of a media plan before it has been implemented.
2. Why aren't sales used as a response-function for media?
3. Since response-functions represent the contribution of an advertisement and a medium, how can one know how much of the function is attributable to each?
4. In measuring recognition of ads in magazines, what should one expect of results if the same sample of respondents are measured at two periods of time for the same magazines (six weeks apart)?
5. For all practical purposes, where is media planning as practiced today, on the six-step media model proposed by the Audience Concepts Committee of the ARF?
6. Why did the Audience Concept Committee recommend *perception* rather than *communication* as a response function?
7. Why, in Broadbent and Signits' model, does not an impression receive full value (1.00) until it is repeated four times?
8. Explain briefly what Krugman meant by the term "connection" in reference to advertising response functions.
9. Is a page traffic score in a newspaper the same as a noted score for an ad on a given page? Explain.
10. How could *attitude change* be used as a means of making media comparisons?

SELECTED READINGS

Appel, Valentine and Weiss, Tabor, "Sense and Non-sense in Attitude Change Copy Testing," in *Advertising Research Foundation 19th Annual Conference Proceedings*, 1973, pp. 54-58

Audience Concepts Committee, *Toward Better Media Comparisons*, Advertising Research Foundation, 1961

Banks, Seymour, "The Need for New Multi-Dimensional Measurements of Media," in *Advertising Research Foundations 5th Annual Conference Proceedings*, Sept., 1959, pp. 39-42

Banks, Seymour, "Media Performance vs. Copy Performance," in *Media/scope*, Aug., 1961, pp. 53-56

Broadbent, S. R. and Segnit, S., "Response Functions in Media Planning," in *The Thomson Medals and Awards for Advertising Research*, 1967, pp. 35-86

Caffyn, J. M., *Qualitative Aspects of Reader Data*, Institute of Practitioners in Advertising, London, April, 1964

Clunies-Ross, C. W., "The Practical and Theoretical Problems and Effects of Introducing Explicit Theories of Response Functions into Media Planning," in *Thomson Medals and Awards for Advertising Research*, London, 1967, pp. 125-130

Dodge, Sherwood, "What Readership Studies Really Measure," in *Media/scope*, February, 1961, pp. 44-49

Dodge, Sherwood, "Dodge and Simmons Debate Recognition and Exposure," in *Media/scope*, May, 1961, pp. 51+

Dodge, Sherwood, "Comments on the Current Scene in Copy Research," in *Perspectives in Advertising Management*, Assn. of National Advertisers, Inc., April, 1969, pp. 206-219

Eliasberg, Jay, "ARF Media Comparisons Report Supported by CBS TV Network," in *Media/scope*, Aug., 1961, pp. 58-61

Fuchs, Douglas A., "Two Source Effects in Magazine Advertising," in *Journal of Marketing Research*, Aug., 1964, pp. 59-62

Gerhold, Paul E., "Predicted Advertising Yield ARF Proposes An Outline of How Advertising Works," in *Advertising Research Foundation, 15th Annual Conference Proceedings*, Oct., 1969, pp. 46-50

Grass, Robert C., "Satiation Effects of Advertising," in *Advertising Research Foundation 14th Annual Conference Proceedings*, Oct., 1968, pp. 20-28

Gromer, Frank J. Jr., and Vedder, Blair G. Jr., "Another Look Beyond TV Ratings," from Association of National Advertisers Television Advertising Workshop Paper, June, 1964, pp. 1-24

King, Charles W., and Summers, John O., "Attitudes and Media Exposure," in *Journal of Advertising Research*, Feb., 1971, pp. 26+

Krugman, Herbert E., "Answering Some Unanswered Questions in Measuring Advertising Effectiveness," in *Advertising Research Foundation 12th Annual Conference Proceedings*, Oct. 1966, pp. 18-23

Krugman, Herbert E., "The Measurement of Advertising Involvement," in *The Public Opinion Quarterly*, Winter 1966-67, pp. 583-596

Krugman, Herbert E., "Brain Wave Measures of Media Involvement," in *Journal of Advertising Research*, Feb., 1971, pp. 3-10

Lee, Alec M., "The Search for Decision Rules for Optimal Media Scheduling," in *Advertising Research Foundation 8th Annual Conference Proceedings*, Oct., 1962, pp. 25-29

McConnell, J. Douglas, "Do Media Vary in Effectiveness?" in *Journal of Advertising Research*, Oct., 1970, pp. 19-22

Media/scope, "Roundtable on 1968 Simmons," in Mar., 1968, pp. 45+

Media/scope, "New Measures of Attitude Change," in Oct. 1967, pp. 127-130

Media Decisions, "Beyond Demographics," in Feb., 1968, pp. 19-26

Orenstein, Frank, "The Ad and the Market: Some First Results," in *Advertising Research Foundation 14th Annual Conference Proceedings*, Oct., 1968, pp. 10-13

Philadelphia Inquirer and Research Inc. of Ohio, *Exposure/Ratings of Measuring Newspaper Readership*, Philadelphia Inquirer, 1962

Politz, Alfred, "Media Performance vs. Copy Performance," in *Media/scope* Nov., 1960, pp. 61-63

Politz, Alfred, "What is Essential to Know from Magazine Research?" in *Media/scope*, April, 1959, pp. 39-44

Rothman, L. J., "The Role of Response Functions: A Discussion and an Alternative," in *Thomson Medals and Awards for Advertising Research*, 1967, pp. 89-122

Simmons, W. R., & Associates, Inc. *Commercial Impact Study for Golden West Broadcasters*, 1973

Stanton, Frank, "A State of the Art Appraisal of Advertising Research Measurements," in *Perspectives in Advertising Management*, April, 1969, pp. 238-245

Vitt, Sam B., "Editorial Environment" in *Hidden Media Values or Going Beyond the Numbers*, Papers from the 1964 American Assn. of Advertising Agencies Meetings, pp. 17-28

Zeltner, Herbert, "From Audience . . . to Attitude," in *Media/scope*, Oct., 1966, pp. 62-72

chapter 12

Media Costs and
Buying Problems

One of the major tasks of a media planner is to match markets with the best media for reaching those markets at the most favorable cost to the client. Earlier chapters have discussed how markets are defined in terms of people and their product consumption, geographic distribution and demographic characteristics. Those chapters also noted that individuals are exposed to media in varying degrees. For example, full-time housewives are more likely to watch daytime television shows and read women's service magazines than teenagers or men. Conversely, men are most likely to read sports magazines and the financial section of newspapers than women.

Each of these media alternatives has a different cost. The final media plan emerging from the marketing strategy should effectively maximize the delivery of the designated marketing target in a cost-efficient manner. Therefore, the media planner must not only be familiar with market definition but also must be fully versed in how people utilize various media. In some cases, the cost of media varies with supply and demand as is the case with television time. Other media, such as magazines and newspapers, tend to remain fairly constant in cost, therefore providing a high degree of predictability when developing costs for the media plan. The costs that go into the final media plan are always in a state of dynamic change. Estimating such costs is as much an art as a science and relies heavily on the experience and professionalism of the media planner. Media costs included in a plan which are way out of line with market-place realities can result in wrong media plan delivery. For example, if a planner estimates that 100 gross rating points of prime-time television can be purchased for $200,000, and the actual cost of that time is $300,000, the deliverability of the plan is seriously impaired. The client can then justifiably question the value of that media plan as well as the competence of the planner.

Estimating media costs is a complex task. In addition, different media have different problems connected with the buying process. The purpose of this chapter is to identify the importance of the planner's involvement in the media buying process which requires familiarity with both the cost of media and the problems associated with purchasing different media types.

219

Some Considerations in the Planning and Buying Process

The value of a media plan is related to how well the plan delivers the designated marketing targets at the lowest cost with the least amount of waste. The criteria for determining how well the plan accomplishes its mission are related to such concepts as reach and frequency and target market impressions delivered, such as women 18-49. The gross number of target market impressions, coupled with the reach and frequency associated with those impressions within the designated budget form the nucleus of an effective media plan. Therefore, the media planner must go through a calculated process of matching the cost of various media alternatives with the delivery of the plan to arrive at the optimal relationship between cost and delivery.

For example, the cost-per-thousand of women 18+ for daytime network is currently about $2.28 (:60 basis) while the cost-per-thousand for the same audience segment in nighttime network is approximately $6.03. Therefore, in terms of total impressions, daytime network will deliver 2½ times more women 18+ impressions than night network. However, for a $5 million budget over a six-month period of time, allocated to 30-second commercials, it is estimated that the reach for nighttime would be 21% more than the same budget in daytime as shown in Table 58.

Table 58
Average 4 Week Delivery Estimated for a $5MM Budget

	6-Month Period		
	Reach	Frequency	GRPS
Night Network	83%	4.5	371
Day Network	65%	13.9	906

Two ways of analyzing media costs used most often are to calculate cost-per-thousands on either a basis of gross impressions or net reach. No matter which is used, it is obvious that the cost efficiency of media delivery is important. It may be found that the medium with the largest reach or gross impressions is not necessarily the best buy because its cost efficiency is so low. Table 59 shows a rough comparison of alternative media deliveries and cost efficiencies.

An examination of Table 59 shows that different coverage levels are achieved by different media vehicles with certain cost-per-thousand implications. The media planner's task is to fully combine his familiarity with media costs and delivery dynamics with the goals of the marketing plan in reaching designated audiences. The planner must be careful to employ correct media cost assumptions in the development of the plan. In referring to Table 59, the reader can see where, if inappropriate cost assumptions were used in estimating daytime net-

Table 59
Alternative Media Deliveries by Time Periods*

| | Adv. Unit | National Equivalent Cost | Persons Reached | | | | | |
| | | | Women 18+ | | | Men 18+ | | |
			#(000)	%	CPM	#(000)	%	CPM
Night Network	:60	$56,900	9,432	14	$6.03	7,336	12	$7.76
Day Network	:60	8,700	3,820	5	2.28	976	2	8.91
Sports (Weekend)	:60	25,200	4,060	6	6.20	6,080	10	4.14
Fringe Network	:60	15,300	3,354	5	4.56	2,608	4	5.87
General Magazines	4CP	37,733	14,233	20	2.65	14,748	23	2.56
Women's Magazines	4CP	33,905	13,837	19	2.45	2,515	4	13.48
Shelter Magazines	4CP	30,890	12,192	17	2.53	3,794	6	8.14
Newspaper	FP—B&W	491,300	53,008	76	9.27	50,380	79	9.75

*Sources: A. C. Nielsen, 1973, Cost Per 1,000 Commercial Minute Report
Standard Rate & Data Service, June, 1974
Bureau of Advertising, January, 1973

work versus women's service magazine costs, it would be possible to include one media type in the plan to the exclusion of the other.

Following are some of the ways media planners can help insure correct and current media cost estimates.

1. The planner must maintain close contact with media marketplace cost mechanisms. For example, pricing for print such as magazines, newspapers and newspaper preprints tends to be related to the cost of producing the product. As paper, ink and wage costs increase, magazine and newspaper publishers will pass these costs on through to the reader, to some degree, and to the advertiser. Generally speaking, print costs have tended to grow at a relatively modest annual rate compared to broadcast as shown in Table 60.

Conversely, broadcast media costs, particularly television, are importantly in-

Table 60
Media Unit Cost Trends Indexed to 1970*

	Night Network	Day Network	Consumer Magazines
1970	100	100	100
1971	103	92	100
1972	125	105	97
1973	130	116	97
1974	145	122	101

*Source: Media Decisions, "1974-75 Cost Trends," Aug., 1974

fluenced not so much by the cost of the product but by the law of supply and demand. The mechanism by which the media planner assesses supply and demand in broadcast is to maintain constant contact with broadcast suppliers, that is, the networks and television station representatives. Maintaining these contacts permits the planner to have a feel for what is transpiring in the market and thus be able to forecast changes (upward or downward) in broadcast pricing.

2. Intelligent media planners will include media buyers in the development of media cost estimates. Many agencies and advertisers employ media buying specialists whose sole responsibility is the purchase of media. Such media buyers are in regular contact with the media suppliers with whom they do business on behalf of the agency/client. During the course of the numerous media buyer/seller transactions, the buyer acquires a familiarity with what is occurring in the marketplace. Such familiarity can assist the media planner in forecasting media price changes. Media buyers are expected to maintain good media supplier relations to facilitate this flow of information. Media planners should make it a point to maintain close communications with the media buyers so as to tap this source of media cost information.

3. In many cases, agencies develop an expertise in estimating media cost changes resulting from the total agency's experience. For example, over a period of time, the agency can compile media cost information in various markets, or nationally, by generalizing from their various buying experiences. It is not necessary to breach security within an agency in order to develop this information. Generalized experience is one of the reasons many agencies have gone to market buying as opposed to brand buying so that the individual responsible for buying an individual market or markets is intimately acquainted with the media cost picture in those areas.

Once the media plan has been implemented and the schedules completed, the media planner should examine how closely the media cost estimates compare to actual costs. By conducting such a post-buy analysis, the planner can sharpen the capabilities to forecast costs by reviewing what went into the original estimates. Such trial-and-error devices assist the media professional in developing the personal art of media cost forecasting. Major variations between cost estimate and actual plan delivery cost may uncover flaws in understanding or thinking, or may be the consequence of significant media market-place cost changes that could not have been anticipated. In any event, the media planner, in checking back over the implemented plan, should consider the exercise an important learning experience.

A Discussion of Media Costs

Table 61 shows national media expenditures by major consumer media types for 1973. The chart is helpful because it identifies the media types where national advertisers direct their dollars. Note that television and magazines comprise 35% of national expenditures. The magnitude and complexity of planning and buying these media require close attention to cost implications.

Table 61
National Media Expenditures (1973)

National Media	$ (Millions)	% of Total
Newspapers	1,111	8.0
Magazines		
Total	1,448	10.5
Weeklies	583	4.2
Monthlies	503	3.8
Women's	362	2.5
Television		
Total	3,418	24.7
Network	1,968	14.2
Spot	1,450	10.5
Radio		
Total	450	3.3
Network	70	0.5
Spot	380	2.8
Outdoor	200	1.4
Farm Publications	65	0.5
Direct Mail	3,698	26.7
Business Papers	865	6.2
Miscellaneous	2,590	18.7
Total National	$13,845	110.0%

Note: Local advertising expenditures in 1973 were $11.3 million and thus
    represented a significant volume.
*Source: *Advertising Age,* "Revised Advertising Volume for 1971-1973," *Advertising Age,*
    Aug. 12, 1974, p. 53.

Within these broad media types, there are numerous alternatives available with which the media planner must be acquainted. In addition to requiring an understanding of general media cost relationships, for example, between television and magazines, the professional media planner must be familiar with costs of network versus spot, and the different availabilities within the general broadcast medium as well as the changes over time—a complex and difficult assignment, but a necessary one.

Television Costs

Table 61 shows that television expenditures accounted for 24.7% of total advertising dollars. Most of the television investment was for consumer goods and services. However, there has been a growing use of the medium for industrial and business-related advertisers. In view of the magnitude of the investment in television, a media planning professional must be fully conversant with all phases of the medium. The major characteristic of television, insofar as media costs are concerned relates to the perishability of the inventory. Generally speaking, there is a fixed amount of television time available for sale. Unlike a magazine or newspaper that can expand or contract the number of advertising pages available for sale in any given issue, a commercial minute that is unsold can never be recovered. The sellers of television time must contend with this "perishability" concept in selling the medium.

Although marketplace pricing conditions prevail at any given point of time, these prices are subject to change as advertisers' demand for that time strengthens and weakens. The stronger the demand and the earlier the sale in relationship to the program air date, the more likely that pricing will be higher. Less advertising demand close to air date can create lower pricing, assuming inventory availability. These inter-related conditions of perishability, demand and inventory create a dynamic marketplace. The buyer of television time must, therefore, be alert to these changes by maintaining close contact with the market-place. Within the broad heading of television, there are basically two sub-categories, national network and local spot.

Network Television. There are certain parts of the broadcast day which are programmed by the networks. There are three networks providing such programming, the American Broadcasting Company, the Columbia Broadcasting System and the National Broadcasting Company. Figure 36 illustrates the dayparts when network programming is made available to the affiliates. Network affiliates are the individual stations that comprise a network lineup.

Figure 36
Daypart Programming Available for Network Use

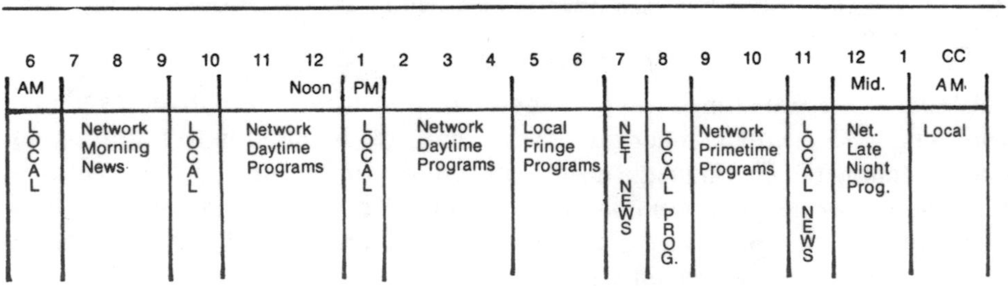

The number of stations serviced by a given network can vary from 150 to 225, depending on the strength of the network programming available. The networks sell commercial time to advertisers to run within specific programs. These programs can appear throughout various parts of the day; for example, daytime network series, prime-time network or late night (post-prime-time) segment.

224

Prime Time (8:00 PM-11:00 PM NYT) because of the high sets-in-use (homes using television), generally provides the highest ratings. This time period tends to reach an all-family audience with high coverage levels of most viewing segments. Media costs for prime-time are generally highest per commercial minute of all the other network time segments available for sale. Cost-per-minute in prime time, as indicated in Table 59, can be in the area of $50,000 to $60,000 or higher for certain programs. Individual program costs will vary depending on rating level and the amount of inventory available for sale. As discussed earlier, the less inventory generally the higher the cost.

Daytime network (10:00 AM to 4:30 PM NYT) is generally the least costly of the other major network dayparts. An average cost-per-minute will be somewhere in the vicinity of $8,700 with an average household rating of approximately 7.0. This results in an extremely efficient cost-per-thousand delivery of homes and women.

Late Night (11:30 PM to Conclusion NYT) network programming tends to vary from network to network and over time. This time period is generally programmed with talk shows and movies. Occasionally, the networks will program different types of entertainment including drama, rock concerts and comedy. Pricing for this time period, since sets-in-use are lower than prime-time, tends to be about $15,300 per minute with an average rating of 6.9. Although the rating levels for late night are comparable to daytime, there is a dual audience (both men and women) included in late night which is not generally the case in daytime. Thus, pricing to that dual audience tends to be somewhat higher than daytime.

Most network programming on weekends (Saturday-Sunday) is in the sports area. Sports programming, for the most part, is the domain of the male-oriented advertiser. Such products as beer, male grooming aids, investment counselling and automobiles are heavily represented on weekend sports programming. In general, there is a limited amount of broad-scale sports programming compared to other network program time. Therefore, pricing tends to be relatively high on a cost-per-thousand basis for the higher interest sporting events. However, the value of identifying with a major high-interest sports event has distinct rub-off effects on brands associated with such programming.

The diversity of programming provided by the networks ranges from the all-family interest generated in prime-time to highly selective shows of interest to perhaps a relatively few households. Such diversity provides the media planner with rich opportunities for reaching broad national markets with programming aimed specifically to target market interests. Costs for such programming will change as market-place demand changes so that the media planner must be ever alert to the buying implications of the programming selected for inclusion in the media plan.

Local station spots. Programming is available for sale in local markets by television stations. These stations can either be affiliated with the network and carry network programming at certain times of the day or they can be independent stations, which means they do not have any network affiliation and thus must program the entire day on their own.

Costs for local spots will vary from market to market based on audience delivered. Generally speaking, the costs for scheduling spots in markets like New York, Los Angeles and Chicago are higher than for smaller markets because of the amount of circulation delivered by these stations. Time is made available for sale, whether network affiliated or independent, across almost the entire daypart. Even within daypart programming by the networks, e.g., prime-time, there are certain segments of time set aside for local sale which means it is possible for a local advertiser, say for example in Chicago, to purchase a 30-second spot (if available) in a network-originated movie.

Since local stations program for the entire day, there are numerous opportunities for the advertiser to select specific dayparts and programming to reach the target audience. In addition to spot, adjacencies next to and, at times, within network programming, commercial time can be selected in what is termed "fringe dayparts." Generally speaking, the fringe dayparts and the programming contained therein are as follows:

(Sample Schedule)

Station	Local Time	Program
A	5:00 PM - 5:30 PM	Local News
	6:00 PM - 6:30 PM	Local News
B	5:00 PM - 5:30 PM	I Dream of Jeannie
	5:30 PM - 6:00 PM	Bewitched
	6:30 PM - 7:00 PM	Andy Griffith
	10:30 PM - CC	Local Movie

Pricing for dayparts and specific programs within dayparts will again vary based on audience delivery and availability of commercial time. It is difficult to generalize pricing relationships between dayparts, stations within market and between markets because of the diversity associated with purchasing spots. However, in general, spot television is a highly cost efficient media vehicle for reaching specialized geographic markets. Such geographic selectivity enables the advertiser to concentrate dollars in markets representing the greatest sales potential.

Print Costs

There are two major print categories, magazines and newspapers. Advertising pricing for print space tends to be somewhat more stable since magazines and newspapers have the capability of adjusting upward or downward the number of pages they print on an issue-to-issue basis. Thus the cost to the publisher of printing is somewhat variable which is in contrast to the fixed commitment of television and its resultant commercial time perishability. Therefore, more newspapers and magazines issue a rate card which covers future costs with a high degree of certainty. A media planner constructing a plan for a year in advance can be relatively assured that the costs will change little, if any.

Magazine Costs

There is diversity within the broad category of magazines. Some of the categories include the following:

General Interest (Dual Audience). Such publications as the *Reader's Digest, TV Guide* and perhaps to some degree *Time* and *Newsweek* are viewed as general interest magazines in view of the diverse audiences they reach. Such publications are generally read by most members of the family. Their editorial content by nature does not exclude any potential reading group. Along with the large circulation delivered by these publications goes a commensurately high cost-per-page as indicated as follows.

	Cost/4-Color Page (Eff. 1974)	Circulation (000)
Reader's Digest	$63,620	18,198
TV Guide	55,000	18,702
Time	41,195	4,672
Newsweek	28,845	2,899
Average	$37,733	8,894

Women's Service Magazines. Editorially more selective publications, such as *Ladies' Home Journal, McCall's, Good Housekeeping, Family Circle* and *Woman's Day* gear their interest primarily to the woman. The woman's role within the family tends to be highly diverse, constituting an occupation in and of itself. The editorial content of these publications is designed to be informative and entertaining. However, male readership is not very high as a percentage of total readership as is the case with the general interest magazines. Following are the sample costs for these selected magazines.

	Cost/4-Color Page (Eff. 1974)	Circulation (000)
Ladies' Home Journal	$35,000	7,082
McCall's	38,625	7,509
Good Housekeeping	27,800	5,704
Family Circle	34,600	8,075
Woman's Day	33,500	8,003
Average	$33,905	7,275

Home Magazines. Other magazines segment their editorial target in a different way, namely environmental considerations like the home. Such magazines as *Better Homes & Gardens* and *American Home* speak to the interests and concerns of home owners. By editorial nature, these magazines tend to be adult and dual audience oriented. Here again, selectivity of editorial content as well as audience permits the advertiser an opportunity for positioning his commercial message in a highly compatible environment. The costs for these magazines are as follows:

	Cost/4-Color Page (Eff. 1974)	Circulation (000)
Better Homes & Gardens	$46,905	7,995
American Home	14,875	3,735
Average	$30,890	5,865

Categorization of these magazines is somewhat arbitrary in that one could argue that *Better Homes & Gardens* could be classified as a general interest publication based on the duality of the readership. In the final analysis, categorization is not nearly as important as the quantity and quality of the readership, compatibility of editorial with the sales message and the cost of running the insertion—all of which must be taken into account by the media planner. However, a cost delivery relationship represents a good starting point in establishing a categorization of magazines from which to select which then can be qualified based on the editorial content within which the message will appear.

Newspaper Costs

There are approximately 1750 daily newspapers in the United States, in addition to 600 weekly newspapers. Such newspapers provide the distinct benefits of flexibility in adjusting effort from market to market, quick closing dates; strong local market coverage and individual market identification. As is the case with the other media discussed, newspapers are also highly diverse in the ways they can be bought and the advertising units available for sale. The major categories include the following:

ROP (Run of Paper). ROP advertising can be purchased in virtually any size unit from full page down to just a few lines in both black and white and color. Generally speaking, two color over black and white costs 20% more and four color relative to black and white is 30% more.

Supplements. Pre-printed newspaper distributed supplements can be purchased either on a syndicated basis (*Parade, Family Weekly, Sunday Metro*) or on an independent basis such as the *Chicago Tribune Magazine Section.* Pre-printed supplements provide all the benefits of newspaper in today's market coverage with four-color magazine-type reproduction when desirable. Costs for independent supplements will vary from market to market. Cost and circulation levels for the syndicated supplements are as follows:

228

	Cost/4-Color Page (Eff. 1974)	Circulation (000)
Parade	$98,475	18,829
Family Weekly	45,990	10,071
Average	$72,233	14,450

In addition to ROP and pre-printed magazine supplements, newspapers provide space for other pre-prints such as Spectacolor, Hi-Fi and hard stock inserts. Costs for these custom-tailored inserts must include production charges since the advertiser provides these preprints directly. Here again, costs must be determined on a newspaper-by-newspaper basis, but it is well for the planner to know of their availability.

Radio Costs

Radio is offered for advertising sale both on a national network and individual local market spot basis.

Network Radio. Network radio programming available for advertiser sale consists primarily of news. There are other types of programming available, including sports and music but, for the most part, the News on the Hour concept dominates network radio programming. Network radio generally provides an extremely large list of affiliated stations. For example, an NBC radio network news program could have 230 stations. Another characteristic of network radio is its relatively low cost. A network radio 60-second occasion could cost an average of $1,450 to $1,525.

It should be kept in mind that, given the nature of network radio programming, individual local market ratings tend to be relatively small. In addition, most of the programming for network radio tends to be adult oriented.

Spot Radio. There are high degrees of variance in spot radio programming formats from market to market. In major markets, such as New York, Los Angeles and Chicago, there are numerous radio formats appealing to a wide variety of listener interest. Programming ranges from talk shows, good music formats and total news. Generally, the multiplicity of radio stations in major markets with attendant diversity and formats provides something for nearly every listener.

As is the case with spot television, it is extremely difficult to generalize costs given the diversity of the medium. However in overall terms, spot radio selectively purchased against designated target audiences can be an exceptionally cost-efficient medium for reaching these selective audiences.

Many station groups have developed and make available computerized reach and frequency programs which help planners measure the effect of different combinations of stations in delivering both gross impressions as well as reach and frequency estimates against selective audience segments.

Media Buying Problems

As indicated earlier, audience delivery and cost estimating represent major considerations in the development of a media plan. Once the plan has been approved, then it becomes necessary to implement the budgeted effort in the most effective manner possible. Knowledge of how media sell their product is vital in connection with both the development of the plan and its ultimate implementation. This next section will touch on some of the timing and buying implications associated with various media. Here again, as in the case with cost estimating, the major distinction rests between broadcast and print.

Network television buying problems. One of the major problems the media planner and buyer of network television time must consider is the topic of timing. Incorrect timing and wrong assessment as to when to buy can lead to severe plan implementation problems. For example, if the network buyer waits too long before committing the designated budget, all of the availabilities could be exhausted, thus leaving nothing to buy. There are basically only three suppliers of such inventory. In general terms, the earlier the network buy is initiated, the more likely it is to obtain desired programming in terms of audience delivery and stability. The later the buyer waits before committing to make a buy for a specified period of time, the less likely it is that the most desirable programming will be available, but with the offsetting consideration of possibly lower pricing.

The planner must indicate to the network buyer exactly what is expected of the buy so as to insure deliverability of the plan. For example, if the plan calls for 50 gross rating points a week during the January-February-March quarter in three or four highly selective daytime network serials, the network buyer would do well to buy sooner rather than wait until just prior to the beginning of the quarter. The need to deliver a specific set of programs and desired weight level dictates earlier purchase rather than later.

Network television time can be purchased on the basis of packages of shows or individual programs. Packages, which mean multiple programs with only a few commercials per program during the course of the schedule, provide maximum programming dispersion and thus tend to generate broader reach for the available budget. In addition, the risk of not delivering the specified weight levels is reduced, since the ultimate outcome of the buy is not based on any one or two individual programs achieving their audience levels. Conversely, networks make individual programs available for sale on a continuity basis. One or two individual shows with regular commercial appearances can be highly effective when the planner can identify specific audience values in those shows that achieve the objectives of the media plan. It might be well if the plan calls for strong male delivery to purchase regular occasions on college or professional football as opposed to distributing the budget over different program types. Here again, the flexibility of the network medium in terms of programming and audience delivery capabilities can serve many purposes.

Networks also have the flexibility to provide both short and long-term time commitments. If time is available, network can be purchased for specific days and time periods, perhaps in support of a very short promotion. Such limited time purchases are generally called short-term buys. The networks also make available for sale yearly buys which are designated long-term purchases. Time that is purchased is not cancellable since there is a contractual obligation between the advertiser and the network for the specific commercial time that is purchased. Therefore, considerable care must be exercised to insure against over-committing for network time.

In some cases, network regional time becomes available. Regional network availabilities can be beneficial to the advertiser in seeking certain types of programming identification. However, regional network time availabilities are very difficult to forecast and are, generally, secured only after considerable planning and discussions with the Network Sales Department.

Spot television. There are approximately 210 Designated Spot Television Markets with around 697 commercial television stations in the United States. The number of stations per market, which directly influences spot inventory, ranges from a high of 12 in Los Angeles to many markets with only one or two stations.

In major markets with multiple stations, there is more spot inventory from which to select. With the multiplicity of spot commercial availabilities in such markets, the buyer has an opportunity to be somewhat selective as far as programming and timing is concerned. Spot schedules are generally purchased two weeks in advance of the start date of the schedule. Spot time can be bought for specified periods of times called "flights" or on a continuing basis until cancelled. Cancellation is generally 2 to 4 weeks prior to the desired end of the schedule. Pricing in spot markets tends to vary widely based on audience, program types and daypart desired.

Magazines. Once the planner has designated which magazines will carry the approved schedule, the plan implementation tends to be relatively mechanical. Most national publications accept space reservations which guarantee that advertising space will be available in the desired issues. Space reservations can be made almost any time in advance of the issue. The final date for contracting to appear in a given issue is called the closing date, that will vary by publication. Closing dates for monthly magazines will generally be 60 to 90 days in advance of issue. Closing dates for weekly publications normally fall about 3 to 7 weeks prior to issue.

National magazines provide regional and test market circulation breakouts for achieving coverage in specified geographic areas. The regional availability can include multiple states or just a limited area like New York only. The remainder of the circulation would either carry another advertiser or editorial material. Magazines also make available test market circulation breakouts which conform closely to television market coverage patterns, thus permitting test translations of national plans into local test areas. Costs and availabilities of such special breakouts must normally be secured from the magazines prior to order since they are subject to change.

Many magazines also make available what is called A & B copy splits. This means two different pieces of copy can appear in alternate copies of the magazine in the same issue. These copy splits provide opportunities for testing alternative copy approaches or can be used by different brands when national coverage is desired and half of the circulation is considered adequate for each brand. Some magazines also make available demographic type circulation. Such demographic breaks might include buying space only in copies going to physicians or businessmen or some other designated type breakout provided by the publication.

The media planner, in the course of his continuing education, should keep abreast of the flexibilities provided by the ever-changing publishing industry.

Newspapers. Space closing for ROP space is only a few days before actual issue. If a special unit is desired, such as two- or four-color half page, then additional time in ordering such space is generally required. However, the advance notice time to the newspapers is still relatively short compared to the longer closing dates of national magazines.

Newspapers have been very aggressive in developing special sections geared to various audiences and issues. For example, for food advertisers, the Best Food Day has been a specific feature offered by many newspapers. Best Food Day in most markets is Wednesday or Thursday, which are the days major food chains schedule their advertising. The advertiser is positioned adjacent to the special sections in which the housewife is reading prior to going to market. Positioning within these sections is generally available at no extra cost.

Other sections that can be advantageous in reaching selective audiences include sports, business and special features on fashion, good grooming and home care. In addition to such regular opportunities for positioning, newspapers offer availabilities for special preprints, such as Spectacolor, Hi-Fi and hard stock inserts. In most cases, the advertiser provides the particular preprint to the newspaper. Such advertising units have to be ordered well in advance to insure space availability.

Network radio. As discussed under the cost section, network radio programming tends to be concentrated in relatively few format types, such as news and sports and some special events. Network radio is purchased in the same way as network television, namely a contractual obligation for a specified number of commercials over a designated period of time.

Spot radio. Spot provides different buying problems in view of the tremendous selectivity and diversity of programming and stations in many major markets. Rating information is available in most markets, but does not provide the total picture in buying radio. The number of men, women and teenagers listening at various times to specific radio stations can be identified. However, the formats, whether it be a contemporary music, country western, stock market reports, music/weather or sports can be an important influencing factor in station selection for a buy. The planner must rely heavily on the buyer's experience in

232

planning a local market radio buy and insuring a close match between the commercial copy, audience and station format.

The primary purpose of this chapter is to impress upon the media planner the essential elements of media costs, accuracy and related problems in implementing the media plan. There is a high degree of art in good media planning in that the audiences of media and the pricing of advertising time/space is in a constant state of change. The professional media planner never stops inquiring and learning. The ability to form sound judgments relative to alternative media values requires intense concentration on the part of the planner. In the final analysis, it is those judgments that distinguish a qualified media professional from a competent numbers manipulator.

QUESTIONS

1. Explain the main underlying bases by which broadcast and print media tend to set their prices.
2. What is the value of analyzing costs *after* a media plan has been implemented?
3. What is meant by the term "perishability of the inventory" in selling television broadcast time?
4. Why do print media costs tend to be more stable and less variable than broadcast media costs?
5. About how much *more* does it cost to print a four-color ad in newspapers than it does a black and white ad? Explain why the extra cost.
6. How does the cost efficiency of radio (in general) compare with other media? Briefly explain why this is so.
7. Why would an advertiser want to buy a magazine that makes available A and B copy splits?
8. What is meant by the term "availabilities" in the sale of spot television time?
9. In planning for pre-prints such as Hi-Fi or Spectacolor, what costs must be considered other than typical space costs?
10. What is the advantage(s) of buying network packages instead of buying a number of different individual programs in which to place commercials?

chapter 13

Setting and
Allocating the Budget

One of the most difficult tasks facing advertising and agency planners is that of determining the optimum amount of money to spend for advertising, a problem that seems to defy solution even though a great deal of time and thought has been given to it. This amount, sometimes called the "appropriation" and other times the "budget," will be called by the latter term in this book. The main difficulty of determining the budget size is that no one knows precisely what effects a given amount of money spent for advertising will have on sales (at all times) or on other marketing goals. The problem was summarized by Herbert D. Maneloveg, a media expert who wrote:

> "Our major problem, I believe, is that we really don't know how much advertising is enough. And we haven't done much about trying to find out. Not until lately. When someone asks about the amount of advertising pressure needed to make a potential consumer aware of the merits of a brand, we fumble and grope. When asked to justify an increase or decrease in advertising budget, we are lost because of an inability to articulate what would happen with the increase or decrease: if sales go up we credit advertising; if sales go down, we blame pricing, distribution and competition. . ."[59]

In other words, there is no simple cause and effect relationship between the amount of money spent, and the sales results that are supposed to occur because of the expenditure. Of course, there are some manufacturers who have been able to learn from experience how much money they should spend to obtain a desired share or sales volume at a given time. But even these manufacturers do not assume that the relationship they use at any one time is constant, and the fact is that, at some other time, they are in the same quandary as most other advertisers.

What further complicates the matter is that each brand usually has a number of competitors whose activities change from time to time so that it is difficult to correctly anticipate what they will do. The dynamic situation in the market-place

---

[59]Maneloveg, Herbert D., "How Much Advertising is Enough?" in *Advertising Age*, June 6, 1966, p. 130

makes the task of budget-setting one of having to estimate probable competitors' activities and allow a portion of money for contingencies, a most difficult task for most advertisers.

Finally, it is well known that advertising isn't the only ingredient that contributes to the sale of a product. Other elements of the marketing mix, such as pricing, sales promotion, personal selling and packaging, also play a role. But who can parse out the precise contribution of advertising from the effects of the other marketing mix elements? Few, if any.

Despite these problems, advertising budgets must be established, and the task is performed on the basis of as much knowledge that is available at the moment. The following discussion deals with some of the major methods and problems of setting budgets.

Traditional Methods of Setting Budgets

There are a number of widely used methods of determing the budget size. Those that are used most often tend to be simple to understand and quick and easy to compute.

The percent of sales method (including modifications). The percent of sales method is essentially one in which last year's (or estimates of next year's) sales are multiplied by a given percentage. The heart of this method is the multiplier, or percentage by which the sales base is multiplied. Sometimes the percentage multiplier is determined on a purely arbitrary basis. At other times someone may check industry standards that are published in the trade press and, using those as a basis, decide on a final multiplier.

Textbooks that discuss the percent of sales method of budgeting often leave the impression, however, that the method is totally inflexible. This is not true. In fact, most often the percent of sales may only be the starting point. After the percent is multiplied by gross sales, the total may be adjusted to compensate for special marketing situations. When there are special marketing needs, extra dollars are added. Some companies, instead of adding to the total, will raise the multiplier when they are introducing a new product or when they are faced with very heavy competition. In some instances, however, the percentage multiplier remains constant year after year no matter how much sales may vary. When this happens the multiplier tends to become a historical figure that is rarely questioned.

Criticisms of this technique center around the seemingly illogical concept that sales cause advertising rather than advertising causing sales. If the trend of sales is rising each year, then the budget will reflect this increase by being larger for the next year. But if sales are declining, then budgets may be reduced at a time it should be increased, so as to help increase sales.

Other criticisms deal with the budget size and its relationship to the profitability of the increase. The percent of sales method tells nothing about the profitability of getting more sales. Perhaps, if more money were spent beyond the total arrived at by this method, profit would increase substantially.

Another criticism of this method is that it seems to work, and probably saves a company money for research to find the relationship between advertising and sales. Alfred A. Kuehn, marketing expert criticized this method as follows:

"Perhaps the best of these rules (methods of setting budgets) for an established brand is "budget a percentage of expected sales equal to the industry average." This rule is of particular interest since it is self-adjusting over time, and appears to be a low risk policy for a firm which does not have a better understanding of the effects of advertising than does its competitors."[60]

On the other hand, if all competitive brands used this method, and employed about the same percent multiplier, advertising budget sizes would be approximately proportional to market share. Therefore, excessive spending for advertising warfare among competitors might be limited.

Competitive spending as a base. This method depends on setting the budget size in relation to the amount of competitive spending. The amount to be spent need not be precisely the same as competitors, though at times it is. At times, a brand that has a smaller share than his competitor may be given an amount equal to or greater than the competitor, as a means of improving the share position.

A major criticism of this approach is that it assumes that competitors know what they are doing; or that competitors' goals are the same as one's own. It also assumes, incorrectly, that a simple increase in advertising expenditures will automatically increase sales and/or share. The products of competitors may be different, or at least be perceived as different by consumers, so that a company's advertising may have to work much harder to make sales than competitor's advertising. Certainly, the marketing goals of one company are not the same as another, and the ability of advertising to create sales also are not the same.

Objective and task method. This method starts with someone setting specific marketing and/or advertising objectives which are then costed out. The total cost represents the budget. Objectives may be sales, share volume levels, revenues expected, income or profit.

There are two main criticisms of this method: (1) It is not always possible to determine how much money it takes to attain any given objective. In fact, most often this cannot be done. (2) It does not consider the value of these objectives and their relationship to the cost of obtaining them. Is it really worth all of the money necessary to achieve any given objective?

Subjective budgeting methods. In this category of budgeting are those that involve decisions made on a subjective basis. Essentially, the executive whose responsibility it is to determine the budget size uses his own experience and judgment as a basis for his decision. This is not to say that these executives would not consider some objective factors as well, such as first determining the minimum job that advertising will be required to do, or perhaps, consider profit

---

[60]Kuehn, Alfred A., "A Model for Budgeting Advertising," in *Mathematical Models and Methods in Marketing*, Irwin Publishing Co., Homewood, Illinois, 1961, pp. 315-316

margins that are available as a basis. After such considerations, the final figure is rather subjectively decided upon.

One subjective budgeting method is known as "All We Can Afford." While at first thought this approach may seem totally illogical or very crude, it may be quite realistic because the subjective decision is accurate. On the other hand, a budget made on such a basis tends to be hard to defend, especially when there is reason to believe that if more money were appropriated, the result would be higher sales and higher profits.

Some Newer Methods of Setting Budgets

Experimental methods. There are a number of individuals in marketing and advertising who feel that the best way to determine the size of a budget is through an experiment where various levels of expenditures are tested to see which will produce the most sales at the lowest total cost. The experimental designs for this purpose may range from a simple before-and-after test in one market to elaborate designs where many markets are tested and compared with control markets.

Although the details of such experiments are usually kept secret, occasionally one is publicized, such as that conducted by the Du Pont Company for Teflon, a product that is used to coat utensils so that foods will not stick to the cooking surfaces.

Marketing executives for Teflon were concerned with the question of how much money should be spent to advertise the new product. It had no direct competition at the time; so an experiment was devised using 12 test markets in which three spending levels were tested against each other in two time periods, Fall and Winter. The variations in number of markets and spending levels are in Table 62.

Table 62
Spending Levels Used in Fall and Winter*

Spending level	No. of Markets
No advertising	1
$500,000	2
$1 million	3
Total	6

The design and results of the experiment appeared as shown in Table 63.

Table 63
Design and Sales Results of Experiment to Test
Various Spending Levels*

			Fall	
	No Advertising		$500,000 level	$1,000,000 level
Winter	No Adv.	2 mkts.	1 mkt.	1 mkt.
	$500,000	1 mkt.	2 mkts.	1 mkt.
	$1,000,000	1 mkt.	1 mkt.	2 mkts.

(SALES RESULTS PER 1000 HOUSEHOLDS)

(For winter only)

		No Advertising	$500,000 level	$1,000,000 level
Winter	No Adv.	25	26	32
	$500,000	29	29	35
	$1,000,000	49	53	70

*Source: McNiven, Malcolm A., "Choosing the Most Profitable Level of Advertising: A Case Study," in *How Much to Spend for Advertising,* Assn. of National Advertisers, Inc., 1969, p. 91.

The results of the experiment were: that there was little difference between the markets where there was no advertising dollars spent and where there were $500,000 levels spent. But there was considerable difference between the $500,000 levels and the $1 million levels, so much so, that Teflon executives concluded that it was "clearly a profitable level." Results are shown in the Table 63.

DuPont conducted other experiments such as one to learn what the optimum expenditure level should be, and which media was most effective in advertising Teflon.

If the experimental method is indeed as good as some individuals assume it to be, why then is it not used more often in determining budget size? There are a number of reasons. George H. Brown, formerly Director of the U.S. Census, and marketing expert, feels that there are two problems that keep this method from being used more. The first is the relatively large cost of conducting the experiment. This involves finding and measuring a fairly large sample. The second is the long calendar time span, perhaps a year or even more, that is required. Brown also pointed out that, while the cost may not be considered too high if the payoff is accurate and valuable, the payoff may not be worth the cost. As for the time required, it may be too long to find an answer because the marketing situation may have changed by the time the final figure is available.

So at present, there are not many companies using the experimental method, although some who have used it are quite content with it. Unfortunately, most of these companies have not revealed the details of their methods so that no evaluation is possible.

The Hendry method of budgeting. The detailed mathematical description of this method is not publicly known, since companies that want to use it must pay the Hendry Corporation for the privilege. However, some of the essential ideas have been made public. Stanley D. Canter, formerly Senior Vice President of Ogilvy & Mather advertising agency has explained some of these ideas in a speech given to the Association of National Advertisers, as follows:[61]

(1) When making a purchase, consumers tend to buy the products and brands they have purchased in the past. But their decision to buy based on past preference is not without a degree of uncertainty. The nature of this uncertainty has not been explained, although it can be estimated that consumers may perceive buying as a risk and wish to minimize such risks. (See Raymond A. Bauer's article titled: "Consumer Behavior as Risk Taking."[62]) The main point is that this uncertainty represents an opportunity for their purchase habits to be changed.

(2) Canter noted: "The degree of uncertainty is a marketing analogy to the properties of entropy in statistical mechanics. In marketing it becomes a measure of brand switching." Therefore, the degree of entropy may be considered the degree of probability that consumers will switch brands.

(3) The relationship between consumers preferences versus their uncertainties can sometimes be shifted one way or another by various marketing strategies, one of them being advertising. However, it should be remembered that other marketing strategies also play a role in influencing buying (price, distribution and personal selling, perhaps).

(4) The additional share of market of a given brand due to advertising is equal to the share of advertising weighted by differences in the effectiveness, multiplied by the entropy of the brand. To illustrate this graphically, see Figure 37.

Figure 37
The Concept of the Hendry Method*

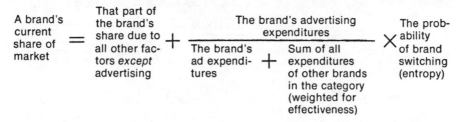

*Source: Canter, Stanley D. "Exposition of the Hendry Advertising Analysis Model," Assn. of National Advertising Workshop on Media Planning, New York, Sept. 30, 1971, p. 2.

[61]Canter, Stanley D., "Exposition of the Hendry Advertising Analysis Model," presented at the Assn. of National Advertising Workshop on Media Planning, New York, Sept. 30, 1971

[62]Bauer, Raymond A., "Consumer Behavior as Risk Taking," in *Dynamic Marketing for a World of Change*, by Robert S. Hancock, American Marketing Assn., Chicago, 1960, pp. 389-398

(5) If the probability of brand switching is zero, then advertising would have no effect on that brand's share of market, and its market share is entirely due to factors other than advertising. "But as the probability of brand switching increases, the opportunity for advertising to work increases, and a greater proportion of a brand's share of market may be attributable to advertising.[63]

(6) As advertising is increased, profits may also increase to a maximum point beyond which profits will decline. Therefore it is important to look at the relationship between advertising, profits and market share simultaneously as shown in Figure 38.

Figure 38
Relationship Between Expenditures, Market Share and Profit*

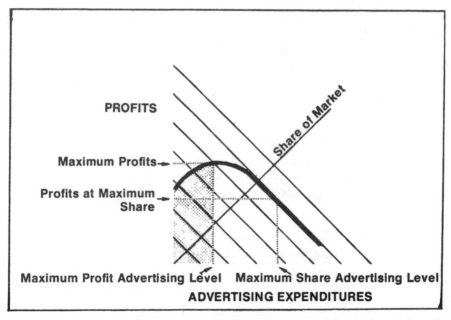

*Source: Kershaw, Andrew, *How to Use Our Media Dollars As A More Effective Marketing Tool*, Assn. of National Advertisers Workshop on Media Planning, Sept. 30, 1971, p. 10

In Figure 38, the advertising expenditures, profits and market share are shown. These are input data that are used for calibration purposes and help position the brand under current marketing conditions on a specific curve, out of a general family of curves describing a generalized relationship between the three variables. That curve is called the profit profile. With the profit profile curve, the marketer can experiment with alternative advertising expenditures to learn his

---

[63]Canter, Stanley D., "Exposition of the Hendry Advertising Analysis Model," presented at the Assn. of National Advertising Workshop on Media Planning, New York, Sept. 30, 1971

240

potential market shares and/or profits. The method of arriving at this curve, however, has not been explained publicly.

When a company comes to Hendry, the first step in determining the advertising budget size is the callibration of the three variables. The third variable may be direct advertising margins (gross sales minus the cost of producing the product.)

Once the calibration has been made, The Hendry company, through its formulas and the use of computer analysis, can then show the relationship between advertising expenditures and market share or profit for that brand. Hendry can also show what share of market and profits would result if the advertising level for a brand were increased or decreased. Allocations by sales territories can be done, as well as learning how much to spend for new product introductions, or what impact advertising expenditures have upon competitor's profits and share of advertising.

It is unfortunate that the details of this method are not known. It is known that some large companies that have used the method have found it successful. For a discussion of the Hendry Method, inasmuch as details are publicly known see: Proceedings of the 19th ARF Conference, 1973, pages 29 to 38.

Some findings of Ogilvy & Mather using Hendry analysis. Andrew Kershaw, president of Ogilvy & Mather has reported some findings using Hendry methods to about 40 different analyses. These findings, to some extent, add to the knowledge about budgeting and its related effects. They are summarized as follows:

"(1) Advertising always makes a measurable contribution to share of market. On the average, one-quarter of market share points of a brand are attributable to advertising." Some brands depend entirely on advertising, but other brands' advertising contribute much less to share.

(2) For every brand there is a point where additional media expenditures do not result in an increase in market share. While some brands have spent more money than needed, others are getting less than 50% of the share they could attain if they spent more for advertising.

(3) "Maximum share of market never results in maximum profits." There is evidence that the advertising expenditures that yield maximum share of market do not maximize profits, so the rule would be to spend less than needed to achieve maximum share.

(4) Many companies choose to advertise at less than maximum profits. Shown on the next page are percentages of brands operating at different levels of profit, Figure 39.

(5) Some product categories spend too much on advertising.

(6) Some market definitions based on consumer usage are too narrow and the brand finds itself with a lower market share. This in turn may require more money to be spent to hold or increase market share.

(7) "It may be far more efficient to adopt a corporate media expenditure policy rather than a brand-oriented one. . . . Thus it is possible to shift media funds from one brand with a lower marginal advertising productivity to another brand with a higher rate of productivity."[65]

Some of these ideas derived from findings using the Hendry method are relatively new, and if valid, may contribute to a change in planning for advertising budgeting.

Theoretical methods of budgeting. There are an increasing number of theoretical budgeting methods that are available and discussions of them have appeared mostly in journals of marketing and/or business. Most are based on rather complex mathematical formuli and none have found continued acceptance in the everyday world of advertising and marketing. This text is not the appropriate place to discuss the alternative theoretical methods, but the reader who wants to know more about them should consult the Selected Readings at the end of this chapter.

Figure 39

Proportion of Brands Advertising Below, At or Above
Level which Results in Profit Maximization*

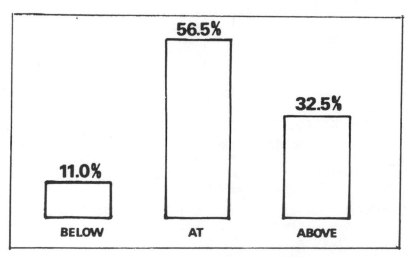

*Source: Kershaw, Andrew, *How to Use Our Media Dollars As a More Effective Marketing Tool,* Assn. of National Advertisers Workshop on Media Planning, Sept. 30, 1971, p. 10

---

[65] Kershaw, Andrew, "How to Use Our Media Dollars as a More Effective Marketing Tool;" speech given to the Assn. of National Advertisers Workshop on Media Planning, New York, Sept. 30, 1971

Factors to Consider in Determining the Size
of an Advertising Budget

While it may not be possible to determine a budget size scientifically, it may be advisable to approach the task by thinking and weighing a number of factors that affect the budget size. Setting a budget in this manner might be called "atomistic" in that one could think about each factor separately (like a collection of atoms) and then assemble these factors, subjectively into a final budget figure.

In weighing each factor some will be found to be more important than others, suggesting that priorities for marketing the brand be determined first. Furthermore, each factor might be considered from the point of view of whether one should spend more, the same as last year, or less. Again this is a subjective decision, but it may help the executive arrive at a final figure more easily.

A brief discussion of these factors follows:

Assessing the task advertising will be assigned to do.   Before deciding on any figure it is reasonable to determine what role advertising is to play. Is it required to do the selling job alone, or will it be in addition to other marketing mix elements such as reduced prices and sales promotion? If advertising must do the selling job alone, the size of the budget may have to be substantial. If it works with other marketing mix elements, the size of the budget may be less.

Very important in this consideration is an understanding of the power of advertising to sell the brand. Some brands are simply not sensitive to advertising, perhaps because they are so much like other brands on the market, or they may not have a unique selling proposition; or it may be difficult to be very creative in presenting the message through printed or broadcast media.

Long and short term goals may affect budget size.   To some extent advertising may have long and short term goals set for it, but when an objective is to build an image, then the budget should be treated as an investment rather than an expense (as one would treat the budget for short-term goals.) If both goals are required at the same time, then more money may be required because advertising has a dual function. The advertising copy for immediate sales may differ markedly from one whose goal is to build an image. In a sense, however, the concept of dividing an advertising budget into an expense for immediate sales, and an investment for long-term image building may be invalid. The reason is, that image-building advertising may not consist of special ads that are designed for that purpose. If the brand image is thought of as a "long-term investment in the reputation of a brand," then every ad that is run, no matter whether it opts for immediate or future image, all contributes to a future image. In summary then, the goals of the company and advertising's relationship with them, affect to some degree the amount of money to be spent. Companies may perceive this relationship somewhat differently, so no general principle can be extracted from the discussion.

Profit margins affect budget size.   There is an assumption in the industry that where there are larger profit margins there will be larger advertising budgets; and the converse is also assumed to be true. Profit margins may be a limiting factor in setting marketing and/or advertising goals. What one would like to do cannot be done simply because there isn't enough money available to do it. It may be ironic that when profit margins must be increased, advertising expenditures also should be increased but there is little or no money available to do the job.

Degree of product usage.   When products are used widely throughout the country it may require more money to advertise them than if the usage were limited to a relatively small geographic area. However, local and regional advertisers may find it necessary to invest heavily in their marketing area due to heavy competitive spending, e.g., fast food firms, automobile dealers.

Difficulty in reaching target markets.   Some markets are so unique that there isn't a single medium that reaches them well, such as the market for expensive yachts. Therefore a number of different media may have to be purchased, requiring more money to be spent. Many times, targets are so spread out geographically that mass media may have to be purchased, resulting in enormous message waste. When this occurs, more money may have to be available to do a reasonable job.

Frequency of purchase.   It is assumed that brands and/or products purchased more frequently will require more money for advertising than those that are purchased infrequently. However, an exception to this factor could be that the advertising goals of infrequently purchased brands may be such that they require more money to be spent than those frequently purchased.

Effect of increased sales volume on production costs.   If there is a danger of demand exceeding supply because of advertising's power, then the consequences could require that a new plant be built. In that situation, the amount of money spent for advertising may have to be limited until a factory is built, or a decision is made to the contrary. The advertiser may want to reduce his advertising expenditures for a while until he can supply the demand.

New product introductions.   It is widely held that new product introductions take a great deal of additional money to break into the market. How much more depends on the size of the market, the degree of competition, and the desirable qualities of the new brand. A rule of thumb that has been used at times is that it takes at least one-and-a-half times as much as established brands to introduce the new brand.

Competitive activity.   In markets where competitors are very active in advertising and sales promotion, it may be necessary to meet their expenditures by as much or more, depending on the marketing goals of the brand in question.

While one may not be able to determine how much to spend for advertising easily through the use of the preceding factors, they do serve as decision-making guidelines.

Allocating the Advertising Budget

Once the size of the advertising budget has been determined, then it must be allocated, or apportioned in some reasonable way. When following the principle of relating advertising to source of sales, advertising budgets are allocated to geographic areas. Many advertisers however, particularly on a national level, allocate their budgets on the basis of media selection with relatively little concern for geographical business skews.

In searching for reasonable ways to allocate the budget, perhaps the one most often used in the industry is to allot at least equal portions to the amount of sales produced by a geographical area. The reasoning behind this method is that one takes a minimal risk in allocating the most dollars to areas where sales are known to have been good. If previous budgets were successful in producing or at least contributing to sales, why would not more money (or an equal amount relative to sales) be the rule? In a sense then, the concept is one of not only keeping the risk low, but optimizing whatever monies are available.

If a geographical area contributed 15% to total sales, then it may be assumed that it would get 15% of the budget. Of course, there may be a problem here. It is possible that it took much more than 15% of the previous year's allocation to produce 15% sales. In such a case, a different method of allocating could be used: one based on the amount of profit produced by the area proportional to total profit for the entire country. So allocating on the basis of profit is simply another method of distributing effort.

Other methods could be based on the market share contributed by each area; the anticipated sales produced by each area; or some index number that is a composite of a number of marketing variables such as population, income, retail sales of the product class plus other related variables.

In practice, formula methods of allocating budgets tend to be only the starting point rather than the end of the allocating procedure. Adjustments usually have to be made to any allocations to take into consideration special marketing problems. One such problem could be that the media in a particular area may cost much more, proportionally, than they do in any other part of the country. So more money may have to be added to the first allocation figure to compensate for this problem. Another problem could be that competitors have started to promote more heavily in areas that have been most profitable for the brand in question. Again special adjustments will have to be made to the original allocation.

Allocating the budget to media in geographical areas. While a budget may be allocated to geographic sales territories, this may not be sufficient to start a marketing/advertising plan in operation—a further allocation may have to be made to media. In fact, one could dispense with allocations to areas and start with allocations to media that reach demographic targets no matter where they are located geographically. To provide an example of how a budget might be allocated to both area and media, the following simulated example is provided:

For purposes of the illustration, it may be assumed that a manufacturer sells his product in five geographic areas of the country. Sales percentages for each of the five areas are shown in Table 64, as is a proportional allocation of the budget to each sales area. Also shown is the percent of network television delivery in each sales area.

Table 64
A Budget Allocated Proportionately to Sales Made by Each Area*

Sales Area	Percent of sales made by each area	Budget Goal	Percent Network Delivery
A	30 %	$1,500,000	25 %
B	15	750,000	15
C	10	500,000	20
D	10	500,000	10
E	35	1,750,000	30
Totals	100	$5,000,000	100

*Source: J. Walter Thompson Company, *Allocating Advertising Weight Geographically*, 1973, p. 9

Table 64 shows that each area received a proportional number of dollars equal to the percent of sales made in the area. However, in studying the relationship of sales and network delivery percents one can find some anomalies. For example, Area A delivered 30% of total sales but has only 25% of total network delivery. As a result, it may be necessary to allocate some of the budget to local television.

A problem arises of how to divide the television budget between network and spot so that each area receives an equitable portion of the budget. One method of doing so involves first finding the relationship of sales to network delivery percents. Index numbers are calculated and the area most out of synchronization becomes a cut-off point. In Table 65, area C with an index of 200 is the cut-off point. Now using the formula below, a figure is calculated that represents the amount to be allocated to network television:

$$\frac{\text{Budget originally allocated to sales area}}{\text{Percent of network delivery in that area}} \times \text{total network budget} \quad \text{or} \quad \frac{\$500,000}{.20} = \begin{array}{l} \$2,500,000 \\ \text{to be allocated} \\ \text{to total network} \\ \text{budget} \end{array}$$

The next step in the allocation process is to multiply each network percent by the newly allocated total network budget. This then indicates how much money should go into each area for network television. Now this amount is subtracted from the original area budget to leave the amount to be spent in spot television in each area. Table 65 shows the process for the original example.

Table 65
Allocation of Budget to Network and Spot TV*

Sales Area	Percent of sales made by each area	Budget Goal	Percent of Total Network Delivery	Index: Network to Sales Delivery	Network Budget	Spot TV (Local) Budget
A	30%	$1,500,000	25%	83	$ 625,000	$ 875,000
B	15	750,000	15	100	375,000	375,000
C	10	500,000	20	200	500,000	—
D	10	500,000	10	100	250,000	250,000
E	35	1,750,000	30	86	750,000	1,000,000
	100%	$5,000,000	100%		$2,500,000	$2,500,000

*Source: J. Walter Thompson Company, *Allocating Advertising Weight Geographically,* 1973, p. 9

Another method of allocating network and local broadcast budgets. A similar concept of allocating dollars, as well as, evaluating markets was proposed by Walter Staab, president of SFM Media Service Corporation in New York. He would first, analyze individual markets on the basis of how difficult it is to create business in various market groups. Since it is usually more difficult to sell products in larger, more competitive markets, the larger markets may get an added bonus that reflects such differences. Table 66 shows how a theoretical brand's potential might look.

Table 66
Market Potential by Groups*

Markets	Percent of U.S.H.H.	Bonus
1-10	34%	+20%
11-20	12	+10
21-30	9	0
31-40	7	-10
41+	38	-20

*Source: *Advertising Age,* "Are You Making Media Plans? Watch for Geographic Skew," March 24, 1975, pp. 39-40

Using the percent of TV homes in U.S. as a base, he would add or subtract percents to groups of markets in order to assess the value of each. For example, New York with 9.29% of TV homes would have an added 1.86% (or + 20%) to give it a potential of 11.15%, market potential.

Figure 40

Geographic Distribution Analysis*

Market	% U.S. TV Homes	(1) Potential	(2) Average Net TV Delivery	Potential ÷ Net TV Del	Ideal Market Expenditure ($000)	(3) Optimum Network TV Expenditure ($000)	Required Spot TV Expenditure ($000)
1. New York	9.29%	11.15%	8.66%	129	$ 1,115	$ 572	$ 543
2. Los Angeles	5.15	6.18	4.84	128	618	319	299
3. Chicago	4.11	4.93	4.05	122	493	267	226
4. Philadelphia	3.34	4.01	3.23	124	401	213	188
5. Boston	2.45	2.94	2.21	133	294	146	148
6. San Francisco	2.34	2.81	1.96	143	281	129	152
7. Detroit	2.29	2.75	2.52	109	275	166	109
8. Cleveland	1.94	2.33	2.18	107	233	144	89
9. Washington, D.,C.	1.84	2.21	1.60	133	221	106	115
10. Pittsburgh	1.63	1.96	1.69	116	196	112	84
Markets 1 - 10	34.38%	41.27%	32.94%	125	$4,127	$2,174	$1,953
11. Dallas	1.54	1.69	1.47	115	169	97	72
12. St. Louis	1.39	1.53	1.33	115	153	88	65
13. Minn./St. Paul	1.29	1.42	1.16	122	142	77	65
14. Houston	1.22	1.34	1.22	110	134	81	53
15. Miami	1.15	1.27	1.09	117	127	72	55
16. Atlanta	1.13	1.24	1.03	120	124	68	56
17. Seattle	1.12	1.23	1.09	113	123	72	51
18. Indianapolis	1.11	1.22	1.07	114	122	71	51
19. Baltimore	1.08	1.19	1.14	104	119	75	44
20. Tampa	1.05	1.16	1.04	112	116	69	47
Markets 11 - 20	12.08%	13.29%	11.64%	114	$1,329	$ 770	$ 559
Markets 1 - 20	46.46%	54.56%	44.58%	122	$5,456	$2,944	$2,512
21. Hartford/New Haven	.93	.93	1.03	90	93	68	25
22. Kansas City	.93	.93	.81	115	93	53	40
23. Cincinnati	.91	.91	.86	106	91	57	34
24. Milwaukee	.90	.90	.89	101	90	59	31
25. Sacramento	.88	.88	.91	97	88	60	28
26. Portland, Oregon	.87	.87	.90	97	87	59	28
27. Providence	.86	.86	.89	97	86	59	27
28. Buffalo	.85	.85	.80	106	85	53	32
29. Denver	.85	.85	.73	116	85	48	37
30. Nashville.	.77	.77	.82	94	77	54	23
Markets 21 - 30	8.75%	8.75%	8.64%	101	$ 875	$ 570	$ 305
Markets 1 - 30	55.21%	63.31%	53.22%	119	$6,331	$3,514	$2,817
31. Columbus, Ohio	.74	.67	.76	88	67	50	17
32. Memphis	.74	.67	.83	81	67	55	12
33. San Diego	.71	.64	.66	97	64	44	20
34. Charlotte	.71	.64	.70	91	64	46	18
35. New Orleans	.68	.61	.73	84	61	48	13
36. Louisville	.66	.59	.66	89	59	44	15
37. Phoenix	.65	.59	.60	98	59	40	19
38. Grand Rapids	.64	.58	.72	81	58	48	10
39. Oklahoma City	.64	.58	.59	98	58	39	19
40. Greenville-Spart	.64	.58	.62	94	58	41	17
Markets 31 - 40	6.81%	6.15%	6.87%	90	$ 615	$ 455	$ 160
Markets 1 - 40	62.02%	69.46%	60.09%	116	$6,946	$3,969	$2,977
41. Dayton	.62	.50	.64	78	50	42	8
42. Albany/Schn/Troy	.61	.49	.70	70	49	46	3
43. Charleston/Hunt	.59	.47	.64	73	47	42	5
44. Wilkes Barre	.59	.46	.70	66	46	46	-
45. Harrisburg	.58	.46	.59	78	46	39	7
46. Norfolk	.57	.45	.65	69	45	43	2
47. Orlando	.56	.45	.58	78	45	38	7
48. Birmingham	.56	.44	.60	73	44	40	4
49. Salt Lake City	.55	.44	.55	80	44	36	8
50. San Antonio	.55	.44	.57	77	44	38	6
Markets 41 - 50	5.78%	4.60%	6.22%	74	$ 460	$ 410	$ 50
Markets 1 - 50	67.80%	74.06%	66.31%	112	$7,406	$4,379	$3,027
Markets 51+	32.20%	25.94%	33.69%	77	$2,594	$2,221	$ 373
Total U. S.	100.00%	100.00%	100.00%	100	$10,000	$6,600	$3,400

Source: ARB Network Program Analysis, May, 1974

Notes: (1) Potential, for this example, is equal to % U. S. TV Homes + 20% (Mkts 1 - 10), + 10% (Mkts 11 - 20), -10% (Mkts 31 - 40), -20% (Mkts 41 - 50), -20% (Mkts 51+
   (2) Average Audience Delivery (%) for all three networks.
   (3) Expenditure Level at which no market or market groups are overspent.

*Source: *Advertising Age,* "Are You Making Media Plans? Watch for Geographic Skew," March 24, 1975, pp. 39-40

Then, the average market potential is divided by average network delivery percent in that market, or in New York, 11.15% ÷ 8.66% = a market index of 129. An index would then be calculated for each market on a list to be used for a given brand.

To determine the total network budget one would find the market with the lowest index number. In Figure 40, that market is Wilkes-Barre with an index of 66. Now multiplying the total budget of $10,000,000 × .66 = a network budget of $6,600,000. The remainder, or $3,400,000, will be the total budget for spot television.

To determine how much of the total network budget should be spent in any market, one simply multiplies the network delivery x total network budget. Thus in New York City the $6,600,000 × 8.66% = $572,000 for network.

Since $1,115,000 was budgeted in New York City, the remainder or $1,115,000 – $572,000 = $543,000 will be spent in spot TV. The analysis of market is shown in Figure 40 on page 248.

Payout Planning

The concept. Another kind of budgeting operation that media planners may be involved with is called payout planning. A payout plan is a budget used in new product introductions where more money than usual is needed to launch a brand. The extra dollars come from sales made by the brand, plus from profits that also are made by the brand, but are used for advertising, for a limited time.

In order to better explain the situation requiring a payout plan the following data may be helpful before studying the formal portions of the plan. A new brand may have the following costs and price:

	Per case
Selling price of brand by factory	$12.00
Costs of manufacturing, overhead and selling the brand	7.00
Amount available for promotion and profit	$ 5.00
Normal amount available for promotion	$2.50
Normal amount available for profit	2.50
Full available for introducing the new brand: promotion + profit	$5.00

So, in new product introductions, the manufacturer may be willing to forego profits for a limited time and invest them in advertising, in addition to the normal amount he would have invested in advertising. This practice of investing both is called "full available."

What is important to understand about this investment is that in the very first months, the brand does not earn enough money to pay for the extra heavy advertising investments that it needs. Therefore, the company, in a sense, invests money (or pays out of its own pocket) to the brand during the early periods of selling. But, as the brand begins to sell more and earn more money, it begins to be in a position to start paying back the investment that the company made. Finally, if everything goes well, the brand will be selling enough of the product to pay back the entire investment, and stand on its own as a profit center. When that happens, the full available is now divided in some manner with a portion going for profits and a portion going for advertising. So in the example above, the full available is invested in advertising plus money the company pays out to the brand.

Explanation of a Payout Plan

The following explanation of the Payout Plan shown in Table 67 is provided. Each paragraph is keyed to the number in parenthesis at the beginning of each row on the plan.

(1) Time periods.   While three time periods were shown on the payout plan, more or less could have been used. Furthermore, these time periods could have varied from one to three years, or one to three six-month periods. The timing, therefore, is a matter of judgment and experience on the part of the planner who must estimate how long it will be necessary to pay back the money necessary to get the brand launched in the market place.

(2) Size of total market in MM Cases.   A market may be described in any way most suitable to the advertiser. Some prefer to use cases. Others use pounds of the product, packages or dollars. The data for the number of cases that will be sold is an estimate, probably based on trend analysis, modified by judgment and experience of the planner. If these estimates are wrong, then the payout plan will have to be adjusted to reality.

(3) Average share for our brand.   As a new product is introduced and begins to be purchased by wholesalers, retailers and consumers, it is obvious that there could be changes in the share of market for each month with considerable variance. So this percent represents the average for the year rather than the total. Either could have been used, but the more modest percentage is probably safer. Again, this is a crucial estimate which, if incorrect, would require the plan to be adjusted immediately.

(4) Year-end total share for our brand.   This figure is shown only as a guide to what the planner hopes to achieve at year end. It is not used in the calculations, though it could be substituted for average share, as previously mentioned.

(5) Cases purchased by pipeline.   When the factory makes its first sales it could be to the pipeline companies such as wholesalers and distributors (depend-

Table 67
A Three Period Payout Plan

(1) Time periods	Period 1	Period 2	Period 3	Total
(2) Size of total market in MM cases	10MM	11MM	12MM	
(3) Average share for our brand	12%	18%	25%	
(4) Year end total share for our brand	15%	25%	25%	
(5) Cases purchased by pipeline	.4MM	.2MM	.1MM	
(6) Cases purchased at consumer level	1.2MM	2.0MM	3.0MM	
(7) Total shipments from factory	1.6MM	2.2MM	3.1MM	
(8) Factory income@ $12 a case	$19.2	026.4	$37.2	
(9) Less cost@ $7 case	11.2	15.4	21.7	
(10) The Budget (Dollars available for promotion and profit)	$ 8.0	$11.0	$15.5	$34.5
(11) Re-allocation of Budget to place heavier weight in first period	$14.9	$11.7	$ 7.9	$34.5
(12) Percent of reallocated budget	(43%)	(34%)	(23%)	(100%)
(13) Allocation of budget to advertising and promotion				
To Advertising (85%)	$12.7	$ 9.9	$ 6.7	$29.3
To Promotion (15%)	2.2	1.8	1.2	5.2
Total	$14.9	$11.7	$ 7.9	$34.5
(14) Profit (or Loss)	($ 6.9)	($ .7)	$7.6	
(15) Cumulative investment	($ 6.9)	($7.6)	0	

ing on how the product is distributed). This group of companies represents a portion of total sales. The amount in the pipeline at any time can be estimated from past experience with similar types of products.

(6) Cases purchased at the consumer level. This figure is calculated by multiplying the average share expected times the number of cases expected to be sold in the total market: (10 MM X 12% = 1.2 MM cases).

(7) Total shipments from factory. Pipeline and consumer purchases are added here: (.4 + 1.2 MM cases = 1.6 MM cases for Period 1)

(8) Factory income @ $12 a case. Since the decision was to price a case at $12 each, then this figure is multiplied by the number of cases expected to be sold for each period (Period 1: 1.6 MM cases × $12 a case = $19,200,000 income)

(9) Less cost of $7 a case. Here $7 was multiplied by the estimated number of cases that will be sold: (Period 1: 1.6 × $7 = $11,200,000 cost)

(10) The budget. Since the budget is composed of dollars allocated both for promotion and for profit (or full available) it is only necessary to subtract the cost of cases sold per period from the selling price to learn what amount of money is available for promotion. The term promotion as used here does not mean sales

promotion, but more broadly, advertising and sales promotion. As a result of the subtraction in each period, there is a given amount of money available in each, when added together, equals $34,500,000.

(11) Reallocation of budget. Although $34,500,000 would be available for advertising and sales promotion, the budget as it is shown in paragraph (10) is allocated incorrectly by time periods. Most of the budget occurs in the third period. On the other hand, most of the money is needed in the first period where extra heavy expenditures usually are needed. So the planner arbitrarily re-allocates the budget total ($34.5 MM) in a manner that is felt to be necessary. As a result, the planner allocated 43% of the $34.5 MM instead of 23.2% that would have been available if the budget were accepted as shown in paragraph (10). ($8.0 ÷ $34.5 = 23.2%)

(13) Allocation of the budget to advertising and sales promotion. This is an arbitrary allocation based on what the planner thinks is needed for each. Some other planner with a different marketing situation and product might think the proportions should be different.

(14) At this point, an investment in the brand must be made. Since the amount of money available for promotion in Period 1 is only $8.0 (paragraph 10) and dollars needed for the same period are $14.9 (paragraph 11) it will be necessary for the company to invest $6.9, which represents a loss for the brand for period 1. The brand now owes the company $6.6 in period one.

In period 2, again the re-allocated budget is more than the brand would earn for that period, $11.7 vs. $11.0. Again the brand loses money; only this time not so much: $0.7. If this .7 is added to the amount already owed to the company from period 1, the cumulative total for Period 2 is now $7.6. This means that the company has to give the brand $7.6 for the extra amount needed above dollars made from sales up to the end of period 2.

However, in period 3, the brand earns enough money $7.6 to pay back the amount given to it by the company. So at this point it has made a profit, paid back the money given to it by the company and presumably will make a profit to keep it going in period 4. When the brand makes a profit, it "pays out" money to the company.

Conclusion. Although media planners have begun to use more scientific tools in budgeting, there are many areas of judgment required. The area of planning that seems to defy solution most is a method of determining the optimum size of an advertising budget. Methods described in this chapter have been used for many years, and are considered relatively crude, but easy and quick to compute. For that reason they have maintained their popularity over many years. Allocation techniques, on the other hand, can be characterized as logical and reasonable. Some involve arbitrary decisions based on estimates of what will happen in the market place, as the payout plan indicates. But in any case, allocation procedures are more advanced than have budget setting. Perhaps the most advances have come in theoretical model building on the relationship between advertising, sales and share of market. None of these have found their way into everyday use, although the Hendry method may be the one most operational at this time. As pointed out earlier, details of this method are still secret; but claims for its success tend to be great.

QUESTIONS

1. What is the difference between setting and allocating a budget?
2. Why is it so difficult to devise an advertising budget using scientific methods?
3. Why is the percent of sales probably the most widely used method of budgeting, considering the fact that it has many limitations?
4. Discuss the question of whether a company that wants larger profit margins should increase or decrease its advertising budget.
5. Often markets are assigned proportions of budgets in direct relation to the amount of sales or share they produce. Under what conditions might this practice not be advisable?
6. While the objective and task method of budgeting is often considered to be one of the best methods, what limitations does it have? Briefly explain.
7. What is the underlying concept of a payout plan?
8. Discuss the question of whether you, as the third-rated brand on the market, ought to consider competitors' budgets before setting your own.
9. Where, in a payout plan, is it possible for making a judgemental error that could affect the outcome of the plan?

SELECTED READINGS

Alderson, Wroe, "The Theory of Advertising Measurement," in *Papers from the 1957 Region Conventions*, American Assn. of Advertising Agencies, pp. 5-16

Canter, Stanley D., *Exposition of the Hendry Advertising Analysis Model*, Speech presented to the Assn. of National Advertisers Workshop on Media Planning, N.Y., Sept. 30, 1971

Dean, Joel, "How Much Should You Spend for Advertising?" in *Advertising Plans: Preparation and Presentation*, Vol. III, 1957, Assn. of National Advertisers, N.Y., pp. 92-107

Friedman, Lawrence, "Game Theory Models in the Allocation of Advertising Expenditures," in *Operations Research*, Operations Research Society of America, 1958, pp. 699-709

Gerhold, Paul, "Measuring the Productivity of Advertising Dollars," in *Papers from the 1957 Region Conventions*, American Assn. of Advertising Agencies, pp. 17-28.

Kelly, Richard S., Ahlgren, Herbert A., Ed., *The Advertising Budget*, Assn. of National Advertisers, Inc., N.Y. 1967, 289 pp.

Kershaw, Andrew, *How to Use Our Media Dollars as a More Effective Marketing Tool*, speech presented to the Assn. of National Advertisers Workshop on Media Planning, Sept. 30, 1971

Kuehn, Alfred A., "A Model for Budgeting Advertising," in *Mathematical Models and Methods in Marketing*, Irwin Publishing Co., Homewood, 1961, pp. 315+

Kropp, H. R., Ehrenberg, A.S.C., Butler, Ben Sr., Gross, I., "Setting Budgets and Allocating Advertising Efforts," (3 Papers from the *19th Annual Advertising Research Foundation Report*), N. Y., 1973, pp.29-38

Little, John D., and Ackoff, Russell L. "How Techniques of Mathematical Analysis Have Been Used to Determine Advertising Budgets and Strategy," in Advertising Research Foundation *Fourth Annual Conference Report*, 1958, pp. 19-24

Mansfield, Frank W., "Budgeting Your Advertising for Profit," in *Advertising Plans: Preparation and Presentation, Vol. III*, Assn. of National Advertisers, Inc. 1957, pp. 108-114

Mason, Kenneth, "How Much Do You Spend on Advertising? Product is the Key," in *Advertising Age*, June 12, 1972, pp. 41-44

McCabe, Thomas B., "How Much to Spend for Advertising," in *Perspectives in Advertising Management*, Assn. of National Advertisers, Inc., N.Y., 1969, pp. 113-123

Newell, Thomas M., "What is the Right Amount to Spend for Advertising?" in *Papers from the 1968 Regional Conventions*, American Assn.

of Advertising Agencies, N.Y.

Parrish T. Kirk, "How Much to Spend for Advertising," in *Journal of Advertising Research,* February, 1974, pp. 9-12

Peckham, James O., "Can We Relate Advertising Dollars to Market Share Objectives?" in Advertising Research Foundation, *12th Annual Conference Report,* 1966, pp. 53-57

Schaffir, Kurt H., and Orr, E. W. Jr., "The Determination of Advertising Budgets for Brands," in *Journal of Advertising Research,* March, 1963, pp. 7-11.

Weinberg, Robert S., "Are We Spending Too Much for Advertising?" in Advertising Research Foundation, *14th Annual Conference Report,* 1968 pp. 29-36

chapter 14

Testing and Experimenting as Aids in Planning

Most of this book deals with the use of statistical data and judgment that can be used by a media planner to help him decide which strategy alternatives are best. The data he uses comes from syndicated research companies whose services are broadly available. This chapter, however, deals with the use of customized research to help the planner do the same thing. *It should be clear to the reader that most such research is not under the direct supervision of a media planner.* But there are some important facts about research that every media planner should know.

Tests and experiments most often used for determining strategy. Most of the research used for evaluating alternative media strategies falls under the general heading of tests and experiments. Briefly defined, a test is a simple field study of some advertising variable. An experiment is a carefully designed study where the researcher controls and manipulates conditions to see how a variable may affect the behavior of his subjects. A more comprehensive explanation of the two kinds of research will be given later.

Why test or experiment? There are a number of reasons why testing or experimenting is necessary. The first and most important reason was explained above: to help the planner make decisions. What often happens is that the planner is faced with equal appearing alternatives or there are differences of opinion between the planner and others (such as account executives or clients) about using a given alternative. A way to resolve these differences would be through customized research.

Another reason for testing or experimenting is related to the consequences of making errors. The rising cost of media time and space, plus the proliferation of many new media alternatives makes it more necessary than ever to avoid costly mistakes. Furthermore, clients of agencies want more and better proof that they are getting their money's worth in media or whether optimum media strategies are being used.

Finally, although media planners use numerical data in making decisions, they often modify the data by their own judgments based on personal experience. But often their experience may not be good enough, or the situation today may be vastly different from what it was in the past so that research is needed to answer the question of which strategy may work best.

Some considerations of tests and experiments. Since both kinds of research are usually field studies they may seem to be alike. But tests are quite different from experiments. These differences are discussed as follows:

A test is a simple piece of research (in advertising or marketing) where one wants to measure a variable (or treatment) introduced into the market to see what effect it has. While advertising can be tested in one market, most often it is tested in two; where each market is given a different treatment. For example, in one market $500,000 could be spent for advertising, while in the other test market $1,000,000 could be spent. The same medium could be used in both markets. Results could be measured on the basis of which produced the greatest sales. When the test is over it might be said that the $1,000,000 produced 10% more sales than did the smaller figure.

Which treatment was best? The answer depends on the decision-maker who, on the basis of experience or judgment, says one expenditure is better than another. But the most important fact about the test was its simplicity and its lack of controls. Although some attempts may have been made to see that the two test markets were alike, the nature of testing is such that it be simple and that not too much trouble be exerted to control extraneous factors that could affect its outcome. Such rough testing became guides to decision-making rather than providing definitive and projectable results.

An experiment, on the other hand, resembles a test, since similar markets are also selected for treatments. But very great care is exerted to make sure that the markets are equivalent in nature. Usually, the same treatments are assigned to two or more test markets, and usually two or more treatments are used. Finally, the treatments must be assigned at random, such as using a table of random numbers, or perhaps, in simple cases, the toss of a coin. Furthermore, in measuring the results that take place because of the different treatments, a random sample must be drawn from each test marketing unit; and two more replications may be made of each advertising treatment.

Once a random sample is drawn from each of the test markets, they are measured through normal survey techniques to determine the effects of the various treatments. Results are analyzed, however, in a much different manner than in tests. In tests, the percent of change from one market to the other is probably the most sophisticated analysis made; in experiments, the data is cast in the form of analysis of variance, or other statistical technique that helps tell the experimenter whether there is a cause and effect relationship between the treatment and the result.

The difference between the test and experiment is that a better basis for decision-making exists in the experiment, as noted by Dr. Seymour Banks, Vice President of the Leo Burnett Co., Chicago, when he wrote:

"The importance of experimental design versus mere testing lies in the fact that the existence of an experimental error permits the use of a whole system of logical inference about the meaning of the data. It may well be the case that a test will produce empirically useful information, but there exists no logically defensible system for evaluating results. A test may come up with the true answer, it may not; nobody really can tell which condition is true."[66]

Which is better: a test or an experiment?   There are advantages and limitations of both testing and experimenting. However, as already noted, the experiment is better where the highest degree of objectivity is needed. In evaluating one versus the other, the following should be considered:

Experiments are better controlled than tests. This means that special efforts usually have been taken to exclude from the study any extraneous variables that could seriously bias the findings. This reason has to rank as most important. But in addition, experiments are designed, or planned, in such a way·as to allow statistical inference to be used in making decisions; whereas tests usually are based on some one person's (or group's) judgment. Therefore the power of statistical inference is usually more valid than judgment. As a consequence, the results of an experiment may be projected to the entire universe; whereas the results of a test may be restricted to the areas where the test occurred.

On the other hand, a test may be less expensive than an experiment. As a result, many a company that could not afford the cost of an experiment would be excluded from learning something about their problems if they did not conduct a test. Furthermore, experiments usually take longer than tests to perform. Many times there just isn't enough time for an experiment, but something needs to be learned that a test can provide. Then too, tests most often can be designed to promise less than an experiment, but what is promised is enough. For example, one may only want some clues, rather than complete logic, for a grand decision. And finally, those who use experiments often make an error by substituting the elegance of their statistics for good, common-sense reasoning. The formulas of statistics are means to an end—not the end. This is not likely to happen in testing because the results are interpreted in the light of experience and judgment.

Yet both experiments and tests may be poor. For example, neither may be able to detect small differences that have occurred. Furthermore, when testing alternative advertising expenditure levels in multi-cities, the total sales of a brand may decline because one market received no advertising for a period of time. Both tests and experiments may also be so visible that competitors not only know they are going on, but they may deliberately foil the research by introducing a national product similar to the one being tested. Sometimes, the sales force of a company can ruin either a test or experiment by working either for it or against it—rather than letting the research commence naturally. They work for it by giving the brand too much or too little attention. When salesmen deviate from their normal handling of a brand the result may be undesirable.

---

[66] Banks, Seymour, "Using Experimental Design to Study Advertising Productivity," in *How Much to Spend for Advertising,* Assn. of National Advertisers, Inc., N.Y., p. 77

One final consideration about both testing and experimenting: neither may produce results that are projectable across the country. As Professor Roy H. Campbell of Arizona State University noted: "Research has shown the projection error from three markets to national market shares ranges from 22% over-projection to 22% under-projection."[67]

But even an experiment may be inadequate because it does not take competitive action (or reaction) into consideration. This concern was expressed by Benjamin Lipstein, Senior Vice President for Research at Sullivan, Stauffer, Colwell & Bayles, as follows:

> "There is serious question as to whether this classical experiment is valid in the social and economic sciences. The experimental design inference process implies that we can draw conclusions from the experiment which will have application in the larger world. If we arrive at some optimum level of advertising expenditures from test marketing situations, these results when applied to the larger environment of the total economy could well lead to serious error since they do not anticipate competitive reaction to our presumed optimum level of expenditures. The experiment in no way makes provision for the independent intellectual life of competition."[68]

Lipstein also noted that, while it may be possible to anticipate competitive reactions to a strategy, statistical theory could give no rules on when and how competitors would really react. His concluding comment on the subject was that competitive reactions would have to be assessed on the basis of judgment, something the experiment was supposed to have eliminated. Lipstein's alternative to classical experiments was a call for non-manipulative experiments in marketing and advertising, where, through mathematical model building, one can estimate what is likely to happen in the real world. These mathematical theories involve the use of non-stationary Markov chains, stability theory, simulation and adaptative control theory.

Introduction to the Use of Test Marketing for Media Planning

What is test marketing? Test marketing is the use of controlled tests, or experiments (depending on how they are done) in one or more geographical areas, to gather certain kinds of information or to gain experience in marketing a brand. In actual practice, however, test marketing may mean different things to different people. Achenbaum pointed out that to research oriented people, test marketing means a precise method for gaining information or experience.[69] But at the other extreme, test marketing can mean to some entrepreneurs: "Let's try

[67]Campbell, Roy H., *Measuring the Sales and Profit Results of Advertising*, Assn. of National Advertising, Inc., N.Y., 1969, p. 54

[68]Lipstein, Benjamin, "Advertising Effectiveness Measurement, Has it Been Going Down a Blind Alley?" in *Papers from the 1969 American Assn. of Advertising Agencies Meetings*, N.Y., 1969, p. 2

[69]Achenbaum, Alvin A., "Market Testing: Using the Marketplace as a Laboratory," in *Handbook of Marketing Research*, Robert Ferber, Ed., McGraw-Hill, N.Y., 1974, pp. 4-32

something out in the marketplace." Between these two extremes exist many other possibilities.

Test marketing is most often done for new brands in existing product categories, or for extensions of a product line. It is important to know that even in new product testing the media portion is usually not the first consideration because it sometimes has to wait for the brand to be developed, packaged and priced, for selling strategies to be determined and even for starting dates to be decided upon. In a sense, then, media planning assumes the same relationship in test marketing that it does in a going-brand strategy: it must wait for marketing considerations to be decided first.

It is important for a media planner to have a good basic understanding of test marketing since he may be involved in it when he translates national media plans to a local level. Although it is beyond the scope of this book to provide all the details of test marketing, the following discussion covers some of the more essential materials for planners.

What the Media Planner Should Know About Test Marketing

Purposes of test marketing. Since most market testing deals with new products, it should be obvious that the risks of making a wrong decision on introducing a new product could be costly to the company. The number of new products that fail each year always is assumed to be high. Essentially then, test marketing is conducted to reduce the risk of failure. It may reduce risk by providing top management with knowledge gained from a limited geographical area on which to base decisions for a larger geographical area. The major objectives of test marketing therefore are to estimate the brand market share that is likely to occur once the brand is introduced nationally; and to evaluate alternative marketing and advertising strategies that also may be used effectively when the brand is introduced nationally.

Specifically, the purpose of test marketing is to help planners work out the mechanics of a market introduction while learning the local share and effect of various strategies. If problems exist, then it is better to learn them ahead of time and solve them before national introduction. By spending a relatively small amount of money, one may have less to lose than if a loss is incurred after national introduction. When top management learns the local brand shares, then it may try to project those findings to the national market, using local shares as a predictive device. At that point, management may decide not to go ahead because there is not enough profit in the brand. In such a case the investment in the test is considerably less than it would have been had the brand been introduced nationally without market testing.

Despite the fact that a brand's share could be learned from local market tests, there is a growing number of marketing experts who feel that the data cannot be projected nationally on the grounds that a few markets simply cannot be truly representative of a national market. Because the number of test markets used tends to be no more than three, the populations found in those markets may not be representative of the national universe. As a consequence, statistical inference usually cannot be used to analyze results. Furthermore, biases of many kinds tend to creep into test marketing operations. For example, in some tests higher distribution levels are present in test markets than could be expected on a national level. Or extra sales efforts were used locally that could not be expected nationally. Sometimes the expenditure of dollars for advertising is excessive at the local level and could not be duplicated nationally. Finally, markets change, people's attitudes change, and the economy may change so that, by the time a test marketing operation has been completed, the national universe, as well as the local universe are too different than they were in the original findings.

One must *not* conclude, however, that test marketing results are always unpredictable of national shares and/or profits. There is still a sizable number of experts who feel that test marketing is here to stay, and believe firmly in the underlying concepts. Their attitudes towards test marketing are based on the following arguments: (1) It is possible to improve the projectibility of local market shares to national shares if better controls are exercised and more than just a few markets are used. (2) Market testing is better than no testing at all. It helps reduce the odds on failure, and it is the best that is available. (3) It has been successful in predicting market shares many times. The track record for some companies using market testing in predicting national share has been excellent. There is some evidence for this in a study made by Market Facts and reported by Verne B. Churchill Jr. He showed that 52% of respondents said their test marketing results were "very predictive;" and in controlled test marketing, the percentage saying it was very predictive was even higher.[70] So it would be incorrect to state that test marketing was totally invalid as a means of predicting national share. Almost all marketing experts agree that there is room for improvement in the degree of control that could be exercised in the use of this kind of research in order to get more meaningful results.

On the other hand, there is less disagreement about the use of market testing for determining alternative strategies. The test market seems to be a laboratory that can help the planner decide which courses of action he should use nationally. However, most of the same limitations that apply to market share prediction should also apply to alternative strategy prediction.

Number of markets to be used in test marketing. Although most marketing men would agree that more rather than less markets should be used in testing, few actually are used. In Churchill's research, 67% (or 36 out of 54) used no more than three markets. Table 68 shows the number used from Churchill's study.

The reason more markets are not used is the prohibitively high cost. Even though management can be shown that the results of an experiment might be considerably enhanced through the use of more markets, there is still a great deal of reluctance to spend the extra money.

---

[70]Churchill, Verne B., Jr., "New Product Test Marketing—An Overview of the Current Scene," an address before the Midwest Conference on Successful New Marketing Research Techniques, March, 1971, p. 4; report published by *Market Facts*, Chicago

Table 68
Number of Markets Used in Testing (From Market Facts Study)*

Number of markets used	Per cent of respondents
1	21%
2	24
3	22
4	15
5	7
6 or more	11
TOTAL	100%

*Source: Churchill, Verne B. Jr., "New Product Test Marketing—and Overview of the Current Scene," Report by Market Facts, Chicago, 1971, p. 4

Using less than three markets could be considered inadequate for predicting national share, but it may have other values. As mentioned earlier, some kinds of information may be learned from two or even one market. But the results usually are not representative of the entire country.

Cost and degree of accuracy are considerations in determining the number of markets that should be used. No simple rules exist for deciding on a number of markets.

Kinds of markets to be included in a test. There are a number of criteria for selecting test markets. The first is that a market should be representative of the universe. Since the markets selected are really samples from the universe, the more like the larger area, the better. This would mean that the markets selected should have the same distribution of population as the country (if the universe is the entire country). One market, Peoria, Illinois, has a population distribution that closely matches the population distribution of the entire country as shown in Table 69.

Because of this similarity, Peoria is often used as a single test market. At times it is used in combination with others. Yet despite this similarity, there should be some question about the life-style of Peoria inhabitants compared to the country as a whole. Other criteria for kinds of markets are: (1) its economy should be independent rather than dependent on a nearby market; (2) competition in the market should be similar to what a brand would expect nationally, and distribution opportunities in the number and kinds of retail outlets should be similar to national; (3) there should be diversification of industry in the community, and the company should not have a strong franchise for other brands.[71]

---

[71]*Advertising Age*, "Anatomy of a Test Market: How it Works in Peoria," No. 1, 1971, p. 147

Table 69
Peoria Compared to the National Population*

POPULATION	METRO PEORIA	TOTAL U.S.A.
Male	49.2%	49.2%
Female	50.8%	50.8%
Children under 18 yrs. of age	35.5%	35.8%
Age Brackets:		
Under 5 years	11.5%	11.3%
5-19 yrs.	26.6%	27.2%
20-34 yrs.	19.1%	18.7%
35-44 yrs.	13.1%	13.4%
45-64 yrs.	20.4%	20.1%
65 & over	9.3%	9.3%
EMPLOYMENT		
Employed Males	53.1%	49.2%
Employed Females	21.8%	23.2%
Unemployed Males	46.9%	50.8%
Unemployed Females	78.2%	76.8%
By occupation:		
Business & Professional	9.6%	11.2%
Salaried & Semi-Professional	7.8%	8.4%
Skilled	63.7%	59.6%
Unskilled	18.9%	20.8%
MEDIAN FAMILY INCOME	$5998	$5660
MEDIAN SCHOOL YEARS		
(males, 25 yrs. & over)	10.2 yrs.	10.6 yrs.
MEDIAN AGE (total population)	29.4 yrs.	30.3 yrs.

*Source: *Advertising Age,* "The Anatomy of a Test Market; How It Works in Peoria," Nov. 1, 1971, p. 147

Achenbaum adds another requirement: that markets should be randomly dispersed so that, in conjunction with large sized markets, the competitors would find it difficult to disrupt the effects of the test.

Market sizes.   There is a difference of opinion about market sizes for test markets. One expert felt that the range should be from 100,000 to 1,000,000 population. Another expert employs a rule-of-thumb that the size should be about 2% to 3% of the national population. Achenbaum felt that the total population involved in test marketing should not be less than 20% of the United States. He felt that anything less would not reduce the amount of statistical sampling variance.[72] Probably the size of each market is not as important as the

[72]Achenbaum, Alvin A., "Market Testing: Using the Marketplace as a Laboratory," in *Handbook of Marketing Research,* Robert Ferber, Ed., McGraw-Hill, N.Y., 1974, pp. 4-46

kinds or numbers of markets used. Where size may be an important consideration is in planning for the cost of the test. Larger markets could be expected to
have relatively high media costs.

What is usually tested. There are a number of marketing variables that could
be tested besides sales volume or share at a profitable level. These could include
testing advertising media weights, varying price levels, store promotion plans,
trial and repeat buying rates, creative approaches, package sizes and assort-
ments, brand names, brand awareness and/or attitude changes and other media
strategies.

Research designs used in test marketing. Research design refers to a plan of
actions to be taken in the testing function. If a careful plan is worked out in such a
way so as to obtain certain kinds of information, that plan could be called the
"design" of the test. Most often research design refers to experimental situations where the test data results will lend themselves to statistical manipulation.

Research design can be very simple, such as observing a market, introducing
an experimental variable, and then observing it again to learn what effects the
variable had on the market. Or, the design can be simple to the extent that two or
more markets, presumably similar in demographic characteristics, are tested at
the same time, with each one getting a different treatment. However, more
complex designs are used in test marketing experiments.

Randomized block design. A randomized block design is one where subjects
to be measured, are first grouped together into a block. Each subject is carefully
chosen so he will be very much like each other subject. The selection process,
however, is done on a random basis so that every person with the same characteristic has an equal chance of being chosen.

Randomized blocks takes into consideration that subjects for experiments
differ so much at times that these differences could mean much more during an
experimental treatment than to the fact that some treatments work better than
others. The matching or grouping of subjects could be on the basis of ages, such
as people 18-34 years old, or people earning $10,000 or more a year, or grocery
stores with less than $500,000 income. Once they are blocked, the experimenter
can compare the results of treatments between blocks. If he does not combine
subjects into blocks, then he may not be able to find significant results of his test
treatments because the differences were too small to be measured. He may
overcome this problem if he uses a very large number of subjects in his experiment. So randomized blocks aid the experimenter in reducing the number of
subjects to be used in an experiment.

Latin square designs. This design technique is more precise than the randomized block because it helps control the problem of two rather than one
source of variation within markets that could not be controlled by careful
selection.

An example of a Latin square used in a marketing experiment was provided by
Lipstein where two variables were being controlled, and three different treatments were being applied. The two variables were geographic variation and

competitive expenditures. It is assumed that in this design each control or treatment is independent of the other and therefore will not affect each other in any way. Table 70 shows how the two variables and the three treatments are applied in a Latin square:

Table 70
A Latin Square Design Applied to a Test Marketing Situation*

Degree of Competitive Spending	Regions of the United States East	Central	West
Low spending levels	A	C	B
Medium spending levels	C	B	A
High spending levels	B	A	C

Treatments: A = high spending level for Brand X
             B = medium spending level for Brand X
             C = low spending level for Brand X

*Source: Lipstein, Benjamin, "The Design of Test Market Experiments," in *Journal of Advertising Research*, Dec., 1965, p. 6

The problem that is shown in Table 70 is: If Brand X should spend varying amounts of money for advertising, (three levels) which would produce the most sales, or brand awareness, or other marketing variable? In order to make the experiment projectable to the entire country, different expenditure levels were tried in different parts of the country, and also where different competitive spending levels took place. By controlling for both variables, the experiment thereby eliminated them as possible reasons for variations in sales that were found through the experiment.

The method of eliminating the effects of both variables would be to add the rows and average out the effect of regions. By adding the columns, it is possible to average out the effects of competitive spending levels. By adding the expenditure levels for Brand X (or treatments) it would be possible to average out the effects of both regions and competitive activity, for a comparison of which Brand X spending level was best.

Factorial design.   A factorial design is one where it is possible to measure the effects of different kinds of treatments, but with the added value of determining whether the factors interact, or whether they are independent of each other. A factor is an independent variable. In conceptual terms, experiments may be designed to determine the influence of two or more independent variables on a dependent variable. Independent variables are those which the experimenter controls, manipulates or varies. Dependent variables are the yield, or the effect variable.

An example of differing treatments in an experiment could be the effects of old packages versus new packages, and an old price for a package versus a new price. The goal is to determine whether price and package changes are related to each other or independent.

Other test marketing designs. Achenbaum suggested that a *checkerboard design* be used as a valid means of obtaining data in test marketing.[73] He described this design as requiring three basic elements: (1) dividing a universe into *groups of markets*. These markets should be randomly selected and be about equal in size. An example might be to select three television market groups from each of Nielsen's ten geographical areas. (2) The use of alternative strategies in groups of three. Perhaps one group would receive 80% of a current spending level while the second group would receive 100% and the third group might receive 120%. He would also use local media such as newspapers, spot television and local magazines as the testing media. Three complete media plans at each spending level would then be produced. (3) Then, through syndicated retail auditing services, he would measure results over a period of a year. The key to the success of this plan is representativeness, good control, and ease of measurement (because it uses Nielsen areas).

Other testing designs are mini-markets, where a test is conducted in a very small area, usually for testing a new product introduction; or in-store tests, used to test marketing variables within a store. Stores may be divided into two groups with each group being given a different treatment. And finally, CATV (Community Antenna Television) tests where two randomly matched groups of homes that have cable television can be experimented with different treatments. At present there are relatively few homes using cable television. But if expectations are correct, the number will be substantially large in the future, allowing for representative national testing.

Media Translations in Test Markets

Role of the media planner in test marketing. Although the media planner may be called upon to work on testing alternative media strategies in various markets, he is more often called upon to aid in determining the market shares locally so that the results may be projected to a national share. The planner's main function is first to create a national media plan and then, through a process called "translation," reduce it to test market levels in building sales, share and profit. While the particular methods employed in this process may differ from agency to agency, there is still a great deal of similarity in them.

---

[73]Achenbaum, Alvin, A., Jr., "Market Testing: Using the Marketplace as a Laboratory," in *Handbook of Marketing Research*, Robert Ferber, Ed., McGraw-Hill, N.Y., 1974, pp. 4, 47, 48

The following concerns the essential principles of media plan translations.

Little U.S.A. versus As Is philosophy. There are at least two varying philosophies of media translations in test marketing. One is called the *Little U.S.A.* concept; the other: *As Is* concept. The *Little U.S.A.* concept describes, in a sense, the idea that some test markets are so much like the country as a whole, that what one finds there could easily be projected to the national market. Therefore, if a media plan calls for the use of one prime time network minute per week with a 20 national rating, the test market translation would be a 20 rating on some local program, or with a number of spot commercials with 20 gross rating points in that market, regardless of the local rating for that network vehicle in the test market. Another way of using the *Little U.S.A.* concept would be to translate it in direct proportion to the weight that would be delivered on a national basis. The measurement could be the average number of impressions to be delivered per household nationally, translated to a proportion the local market should have received.

In the *As Is* concept, the exact media weight planned to be delivered into specific markets is used. For example, the national media plan might call for 200 gross rating points per week to be delivered into the top 20 markets. Therefore, each test market in the top 20 would be allotted 200 gross rating points per week.

The decision to use *Little U.S.A.* vs. *As Is* generally relates to the representativeness of the test area relative to the national plan. If the *As Is* translation method would result in delivering an abnormally high (or low) level of media weight, some adjustment towards the *Little U.S.A.* should be considered.

Number of markets for translations. As discussed previously, the number of markets used in testing should be more than two or three, rather than less. Yet despite consensus that more are needed, such as five, six, or more only one is often used. When a single market is used it is assumed that the "one" is a "Little U.S.A." market. Dangers of projecting from one market are well recognized.

There has been a trend for some time now to test in very large markets such as New York, Los Angeles, or Chicago, on the assumption that these markets are more representative of the United States. However, translations could be carried on in an entire geographic region, such as the west coast, where a number of various sized population centers exist. The regional approach could be much easier to use than a single isolated market because the planner can more easily simulate his national media plan in the area. For example, he could now use regional editions of magazines, whereas in a single market no local editions of a national magazine may exist. The regional test would less likely be affected by local strikes, bad weather or high competitive reactions to the test. Sometimes a region such as the west coast may be relatively inexpensive and flexible to buy in network. But, for most regions, regional network buys may be difficult, if available at all.

Other reasons why regional test markets may be preferred to individual and isolated markets are that it may be easier to obtain distribution in a region and it may be easier to compare market data with media coverage. In local test markets, the media coverage may far exceed market coverage measurements. Finally, in auditing sales, it may be easier and less costly to audit sales in large regions than in isolated markets.

On the other hand, there are three good reasons for not using regional tests: the cost may be prohibitive; there could be a large amount of wasted media impressions because not everyone in the region is being tested, and a regional test is not really a laboratory or sample test, only a small-scale introduction. If the product is not well accepted, the risks of large-scale failure have not been eliminated in the testing procedure.

Translations in radio and television. There are a number of ways of translating a national media plan in radio and television. The cut-in is one way. In a cut-in, a local commercial is inserted in a network or transcribed program by replacing some other commercial originally scheduled in a market for the same advertiser. This is possible when the client already has purchased a commercial on a network, and simply replaces it with the test market commercial by cutting in only in the test market. The remainder of the country would see the national commercial. A cut-in is considered to be an excellent way to translate for broadcast media because it keeps the entertainment or educational environment and it provides the exact national weight in a local market. Its disadvantage is high cost for advertisers who are not in a network program. Furthermore local stations often charge high fees for mechanically inserting substitute commercials.

Finally, the national advertising for some other product may suffer because it was replaced with the cut-in. This could be expensive and difficult to accomplish in the test market.

If a cut-in is not feasible, then the planner will have to substitute local spot announcements for the network commercials. This may be a problem because the spot announcements chosen must provide the same kind of target audience and the same audience sizes that the network program in that market would provide. In order to use spot television, the only times available at a reasonable cost may be fringe times. Since fringe time spots do not produce as high ratings as would prime time network programs, some kind of compensation might be used. Planners add gross rating points to those of the theoretical plan level as a form of compensation. The degree of additional spot weight over the theoretical plan level is usually determined by the research experience of each advertiser. There is no single set of industry standards that applies to such translation methods.

When a prime time spot is used (instead of a prime time network program) then the additional gross rating point compensation may not be as high as the amount of compensation used with fringe spot. In deciding on any compensation, two factors should be considered: compensation for loss of reach and compensation for loss of program environment. Of course, it is assumed that any spots used will be most selective of a target audience.

Compensations will vary in different markets depending on the relationship of audience sizes between prime and fringe times. Daytime spots, on the other hand, may be used in lieu of daytime network programs without compensation since they may be purchased either in or next to the kinds of network programs used in the national media plan.

When a national media plan calls for spot television, no translation may be necessary; spots are simply scheduled in the same number, same number of gross rating points, length, placement, reach and frequency called for in the national plan.

In translating network radio, the method is identical to that used for translating daytime network television. For spot radio, the translation method would be identical to spot television.

Translations in newspapers. Translation of newspapers is direct and simple, because the national media plan would spell out all details for local markets.

Translations in magazines. Magazines may or may not require special translations. If regional, metropolitan or special test market editions of a magazine exist—then there is little difficulty in making a translation.

But if a national magazine has none of the above editions, three alternatives exist for translation; using Sunday supplements adjusted to deliver the same number of impressions in a local market that a national magazine would have delivered; using other magazines that are similar to those in the national plan in a local market, and adjusting differences through compensation; and using ROP color in newspapers with some kind of compensation. The last alternative may be the poorest choice because the reproduction of ROP color in newspaper advertisements is not the same as color printed in most national magazines. But it would be possible to make some kind of compensation for the differences if that were the only viable alternative.

The first alternative, using Sunday supplements in lieu of national magazines may be relatively easy to translate. An example of how this could be done is shown below:

Problem: How many Sunday supplement ads are needed to deliver the same number of national magazine impressions that would be delivered by a national magazine in test market X?

Solution:

    (a) Find the number of target audience members of a national magazine delivered into test market X (either from published data, or by estimate). Suppose the magazine delivers 100,000 readers in Market X.

    (b) Assume that the national media plan called for 20 national ads in that market for a year. Find the total number of impressions in Market X: (100,000 impressions × 20 ads = 2,000,000)

    (c) Find the number of target audience members delivered by one ad in a Sunday supplement in market X. Assume it would be 75,000 readers.

    (d) Calculate the number of Sunday supplement ads that would be needed to deliver 2,000,000 target impressions: 2,000,000 ÷ 75.000 = 27 ads

If the data on target audience delivery is not known in any given market, it could be estimated as follows, working from known data: the number of circulation units delivered into market X can usually be obtained from the publisher. He also can furnish the number of readers per copy for his magazine. Multiply circulation by readers per copy to find the readers in market X. However, these would be total audience readers, not target audience members. The same could be done for Sunday supplement readers or similar magazines, and a translation worked out. At times, the audience data could be further reduced by multiplying it by known recognition scores for a product category and comparing it with the substitute medium's noted score projection.

Translations of Sunday supplements. If a national media plan calls for Sunday supplements in a select group of test markets, then translation is easily done by using the Sunday Metro Group of supplements or test insertions in the nationally syndicated supplements. This magazine group allows purchases to be made in any number of markets. On the other hand, if there is no Sunday metro supplement in a given market, then one could buy a locally edited supplement (if one exists), or use ROP color ads in the local newspaper. In the latter situations, some form of compensation would be required. In some markets, syndicated national supplements make test market breakouts available.

In summary, whenever a direct translation can be made, it is preferable to simulating a national medium in a local market. Almost any simulation will require some kind of compensation based at times on arbitrary rather than empirical means.

Conclusions

Testing and experimenting to find the best media strategy is a reasonable and relatively objective way of finding answers as opposed to simple judgment and experience. Yet there are countervailing forces that work against them. The high cost of research, the pressure of time, the failure to control extraneous factors that could bias the outcomes, all affect the continued use of these methods. But it is likely that as time progresses more companies will pay the cost, take the time and place competent people who understand experimental research in positions of authority so that experiments will be used more for solving problems. At present the number engaged in this kind of research is not large compared to the number of companies for whom media strategies are being devised in a single year.

QUESTIONS

1. Generally, what are the values of testing and experimenting?
2. What are the differences between a test and an experiment?
3. Does an experiment, even if carefully designed and conducted, guarantee an answer that will solve a problem? Briefly explain.
4. Why do some marketing experts feel that the results of test marketing may not be projectable to the entire country?

5. Although Peoria, Illinois may have demographic similarities with demographics of the entire country, why is there still some question that it may not be representative of the country?
6. What is the value of using statistical inference in market testing?
7. What is the main difference between the *Little U.S.A.* and the *As Is* philosophy of media translations?
8. What are the main reasons for not using an entire geographic region such as the west coast, for a media translation?
9. Why may it be important to test in very large metropolitan centers such as New York, Los Angeles or Chicago, apart from other testing?
10. Explain how one can translate a network television program to a local area.

SELECTED READINGS

Achenbaum, Alvin A., "Market Testing: Using the Marketplace as a Laboratory," in *Handbook of Marketing Research*, Robert Ferber, Ed., McGraw Hill, N.Y. 1974, pp. 4-32, 4-47.

Advertising Age, "Test Marketing Full of Inconclusive, Contradictory Evidence, Berdy Says," Nov. 16, 1964, p. 37.

Banks, Seymour, "Using Experimental Design to Study Advertising Productivity" in *How Much to Spend for Advertising*? edited by Malcolm A. McNiven, Assn. of National Advertisers, Inc. New York, 1969, pp. 72-89.

Banks, Seymour, *Experimentation in Marketing*, McGraw-Hill, New York, 1965.

Becknell, James C. Jr., "Use of Experimental Design in the Study of Media Effectiveness," in *Media/Scope*, Aug. 1962, pp. 46-49

Brown, George H., "Measuring the Sales Effectiveness of Alternative Media," in *Advertising Research Foundation 7th Conference Report*, 1961, pp. 43-47.

Campbell, Roy H., *Measuring the Sales and Profit Results of Advertising*, Assn. of National Advertisers, Inc. New York, 1969

Canter, Stanley, "The Evaluation of Media Through Empirical Experiments," in *Advertising Research Foundation, 11th Conference Report*, 1965, pp. 39-44

Casey, Richard F., "Tests for Test Marketing," in *Papers from the 1962 Region Conventions*, American Assn. of Advertising Agencies, Western Region Meeting, Oct. 22, 1962

Edwards, Allen L. *Experimental Design in Psychological Research*, Holt, Rinehart and Winston, N.Y., 1960, 398 pp.

Giges, Nancy, "Advertisers Take Harder Look at Test Market Ways," in *Advertising Age*, Oct. 12, 1972, pp. 3+

Hardin, David K., "A New Approach to Test Marketing," in *Journal of Marketing*, Oct. 1966, pp. 28-31

Honomichl, Jack J., "Market Facts' Success with Controlled Market Tests Attracts Nielsen," in *Advertising Age*, Oct. 8, 1973, p. 3+

Keshin, Mort, "Media Planners' Role in Test Marketing," in *Media/Scope*, December, 1967, p. 14-17

Kroeger, Albert R., Editor, "Test Marketing: The Concept and How It is Changing," Part I., in *Media/Scope*, December, 1966, pp. 63+ Part II, January 1967, pp. 51+

Lasman, L. L., "Determining the Proper Advertising Mix for a Consumer Product," in *NAEA 1964 Summer Meeting Digest*, p. 21-25

Lipstein, Benjamin, "The Design of Test Marketing Experiments," in *Journal of Advertising Research*, December, 1965, pp. 2-7

Lipstein, Benjamin, "Advertising Effectiveness Measurement; Has It Been Going Down a Blind Alley?" in *Papers from the 1969 American Association of Advertising Agencies Annual Meeting*, April 25, 1969, White Sulphur Springs, West Virginia

Marketing Insights, "Test Marketing, The Most Dangerous Game in Marketing." Published by *Advertising Age*, Oct. 9, 1967, pp. 16-17.

Media Decisions, "The Media Testers," in *Media Decisions*, September, 1971, pp. 52+

Orman, Allen, "Which Marketing Alternative Should We Test in the Market?" in *Marketing Insights*. Published by *Advertising Age*, January 22, 1968

Sederberg, Kathryn, "Anatomy of a Test Market: How It Works in Peoria," in *Advertising Age*, Nov. 1, 1971, p. 144+

Sherak, Bud, "Controlled Sales and Marketing Tests," paper delivered to the Advertising Research Foundation Conference, March 15, 1967

"Testing! Anywhere, U.S.A.," in *Sponsor* Magazine, March 8, 1965, pp. 28-34

Zeltner, Herbert, "Guidelines for Media Testing," in *Media/Scope*, September, 1964, p. 12

chapter 15

Use of The Computer in Media Planning

In the early 60's, predictions were made about how computers were going to change the practice of media planning. It was predicted that computers would be able to do complex media data analysis, create improved media schedules, determine which media and strategy were the best and, in general, raise the level of media planning operations. In more than a decade of use, computers have not quite lived up to their predictions, even though large amounts of money, time and effort have been expended on them. Why were predictions mostly incorrect? More important, what is the role of a computer in the future of media planning? The answers to these and other questions about the use of computers comprise part of the purpose of this chapter. The main objective, however, is to place the use of computers into a proper perspective for the media planner so that he can know not only its best potential uses, but some of the continuing problems that need solutions.

What does a computer do? A computer essentially is an electronic calculator that can add, subtract, multiply and divide at lightning-like speeds. But it can also store information in its memory units, and when this is called forth, it can be manipulated arithmetically in many ways. Since the four arithmetic functions are part of many formula needed to solve complex mathematical problems, the computer, if fed the correct data and programmed correctly, can solve the problem quickly.

Specifically in media planning, a computer can do a number of things that, indeed, help the planner as follows: (1) *Constructing media schedules.* Through special programming, the computer can create a schedule showing the names of vehicles, gross number of exposures delivered and the amount of money spent by time period. (2) *Assessing alternative media plans.* A computer can be given alternative media plans that were either created by computer or by hand and evaluate them in terms of reach and frequency, and/or cost-per-thousands. The planner then can either select the best of available alternatives or improve one or more. (3) *Analyzing marketing and-or media data.* The computer can scan a great deal of marketing and/or media data quickly and organize it into a meaningful arrangement. It can compute index numbers of demographic segments of a market and then arrange the data in rank order and calculate reaches and frequencies quickly of any given number of media combinations. It can analyze media expenditures by competitors into percent of dollars spent in various media by various brands in a given market. (4) *Billing and management control.* A computer can be used to tabulate bills and/or payments and analyze other operations within the agency or media department.

Computers and Media Planning

Media planning, therefore, is a special kind of problem that also requires the use of the four arithmetic functions. So theoretically, the computer should be able to devise media strategy and solve media problems if the correct data and program are fed into it. At the heart of the problem, however, is the question of whether it is possible to first create a mathematical model which can solve media strategy problems.

What is a model? A model is a simplified representation of reality, or in the case of media planning, a description of a process. But it is more than a simple description because logical relationships, both quantitative and qualitative, between parts of the process and the whole must be explained. In order to help the model builder better perceive the relationships, models are usually expressed in symbolic or mathematical form. These symbols make it relatively easy to see at a glance the entire spectrum of actions and their relationships.

In media planning, most models are predictive, in the sense that if one is guided by his model, he should be able to achieve certain outcomes. Therefore he can use the model to predict and control the outcomes. Other than simply describing or predicting what happens, a model's value is based on helping one understand a process or reality. This occurs because a good model builder should spell out the relationships, state underlying assumptions on which the model is based, perhaps for the first time, and trace the logic of relationships through parts of the model.

Four Important Terms Helpful in Understanding Media Models

There are many specialized terms that are used in describing a media model for the use of computers in media planning. It is beyond the scope of this book to describe them all. Four of them, however, algorithms, iteration, heuristics and Monte Carlo are so important that it would be helpful to know their meanings for even a general understanding of models and computers. They are explained below:

Algorithms. An algorithm is a procedure (or set of rules) for solving a problem by following a specific number of steps in a certain manner. If the steps are followed carefully, they guarantee a solution. Writing algorithms is an important part of the general procedure of writing computer programs, although they usually precede actual program construction. In order to assist a person in the development of algorithms, and sometimes even to replace them entirely, a flow chart is prepared before a computer program is written. The flow chart, is in reality, a visual-aid to help the programmer see each step in the process and check to see that it is complete. Algorithms (and flow charts) include steps for knowing where to start a process and where to stop. It may even contain a provision for examining every possible output including the ability to recognize erroneous outputs as well as erroneous results. The steps necessary to select media vehicles might be put into algorithmic form if only simple requirements like gross exposures and cost-per-thousands are required. Almost all mathematical formulae can be reproduced in algorithmic form.

Heuristics. The algorithm method of solving problems is direct. If one follows the instructions, an answer is obtained. But sometimes, and especially in the case of media strategy planning, an algorithm cannot be devised because the problem is too complex to understand. Computer experts, therefore, have substituted heuristics for algorithms in such situations. A heuristic is an empirically-based aid or decision rule-of-thumb to follow when the problem cannot be placed in algorithm form. The answers obtained by hueristics may not be a perfect solution to problems, but they are used when there is no other way to solve the problem. An example of a heuristic decision in media planning might be to state that the attention value of any advertisement is the direct function of an advertisement's size. So the computer will give more weight to people who read large ads than those who read small ads. While this heuristic may be true, it isn't always true. For example, it isn't always true that large sized ads always get more attention than smaller sized ads. Yet this heuristic is a simple rule-of-thumb for the computer to follow. Without it the effect of ad sizes on attention might be ignored entirely. On the other hand, a complex set of rules cannot be written very well.

Iteration. Some algorithms execute the same series of instructions to the computer over and over again with slight modifications until an optimum solution is reached. The process could require that the next time an operation is executed, the last estimate could become the next input so a better estimate is obtained each time the computer repeats the instructions. This process is repeated until the best solution is found. An iteration could also be based on a heuristic in the sense that it may require some rules-of-thumb in carrying out its calculations. Iteration includes the repetition of instructions and a set of rules to identify the best solution. In media planning, a set of media data could be fed into the computer showing audience sizes, media costs, ad form weights, and other requirements. Then the computer could examine all vehicles, one at a time, and compare it with the desired solution. The desired solution could be a specified number of unduplicated weighted exposures. If a vehicle does not compare favorably, then the computer could examine it in a different context, such as more weeks of exposure, different ad sizes and with different reaches until it comes closest to the optimum. If it is selected, then the budget may be reduced by the cost of the vehicle and other vehicles cycled through the iteration process until the budget is spent.

The Monte Carlo simulation technique. The Monte Carlo simulation technique is a procedure to obtain approximate evaluations of a solution by using random numbers. The random numbers are applied to empirically observed or measured probability distributions. Like heuristics, the Monte Carlo method may be used when algorithms won't work. An example of Monte Carlo technique applied to media models is the estimation of probabilities that a certain person will watch television or read a magazine. Such probabilities are required in simulation models because there is no other way of estimating viewing or reading. There are no mathematical formulas that can be devised to estimate such behavior, except by direct measurement, and that would be too costly and time consuming. Through Monte Carlo it is possible to estimate media exposure through searching a table of random numbers. Dennis Gensch explained the method applied to the reading-viewing problem as follows:

> ". . . let the probability of a person watching a given show in a given week be 25%. Using this probability value, the computer generates a two-digit random number. If the random number is between 00 and 24, the person is said to have seen the show. If the random number is between 25 and 99, the person is not to have seen the show."

> ". . . The values for the daily shows are generated using the same Monte Carlo approach with a discrete binomial distribution setting the range of the Monte Carlo numbers."[74]

It is important to understand that the 25% figure came from research on viewing habits conducted by one of the syndicated research companies such as Simmons or TGI. The number would change from time to time, so it may have to be updated occasionally. The computer therefore becomes a selector of individuals who are likely to see a given television program or who read a given magazine.

A Brief Description of Two Well-Known Media Models

There are a number of different kinds of media models in existence. For a description of these models see Gensch and Kotler references below.[75] [76] In order to provide an overview of these two models and the roles they play in media planning, the following discussion will cover the two most widely-known models: *linear programming* and *simulation.* Linear programming is known as

---

[74]Gensch, Dennis, H., *Advertising Planning,* Elsevier Scientific Publishing Company, Amsterdam, 1973, pp. 117-118

[75]Gensch, pp. 28, 73.

[76]Kotler, Philip, "Computerized Media Planning: Techniques, Needs, and Prospects," in *Occasional Papers in Advertising,* American Academy of Advertising, Urbana, Ill., 1965

an optimizing model, while simulation is non-optimizing. An optimizing model is created to search for and find an optimum solution to a media schedule. Given the costs of media and other requirements for selection, the model can, through the use of a computer, compile a list of vehicles that meet the constraints. The non-optimizing model, on the other hand, is an assessor of media plans that already have been conceived. Each kind of model has its advantages and limitations.

Linear programming. A linear programming model can be used to deliver a list of media vehicles that represent the best of all alternatives subject to certain requirements or constraints. Typically, the model maximizes the total number of exposures subject to a cost constraint or minimizes costs, subject to an exposure constraint that each vehicle would produce on a recommended list.

The concept of the model is based on a mathematical technique developed by economist Wassily W. Leontief in the 1920s. Further developments were made by George B. Dantzig who is credited with devising the simplex method of linear programming that is used in the media models today. (See Ferguson and Sargent for a discussion of linear programming and the simplex method below.)[77] In essence the model allocates a scarce resource, the budget, to alternative media.

In order to use the model in computer planning, the planner must set up specific constraints that become a criterion function for making selections. For example, this function is a set of weights that are given to each vehicle based on its ability to deliver large numbers of targets. However there are other constraints that usually are added to help the computer decide which media to recommend. One of these is a set of weights that accounts for qualitative differences between vehicles. Some vehicles have a better image, are more believable, or have more authority than others. Still another set of weights is usually applied to different ad forms, such as a half page form versus a 30 second commercial. The sums of the three weights then, are all part of the criterion function called by various names such as Rated Exposure Units (REU) or Rated Exposure Values (REV).

Another important constraint is the advertising budget. Obviously the planner cannot allow a decision that costs more money than is available. Still another constraint could be based on marketing-media objectives, such as reach 70% of all women, plan for year 'round continuity and if daytime TV is used, then use at least two different programs, etc.

The computer output can either be an analysis of alternative media in terms of REU's or a schedule, or a summary of a schedule. Shown in Table 72 is how an analysis of alternatives might look.

A media planner can have a computer print out a summary of his media plan. Then, if he chooses, he can change one or more of the constraints, and have the computer print out alternative schedules on page 274.

---

[77]Ferguson, Robert D., and Sargent, Lauren F., *Linear Programming,* McGraw-Hill, N.Y., 1958, Chapters 1, 4, 5

Table 72
Analysis of Alternative Media Obtained Through Linear Programming*

Vehicle	Ad Unit	Hypo-thetical Cost	REU's delivered	Cost-per-1000 REU's delivered
A: daytime TV show	60 sec.	$2,500	1,499,000	$1.67
B: night network TV	60 sec.	39,000	7,060,000	5.52
	30 sec.	19,500	5,344,000	3.65
C: woman's magazine	4/color page	28,550	4,330,000	6.59
D: general maga-zine	4/color page	40,613	5,098,000	7.97

*Source: Maneloveg, Herbert, "A Year of Linear Programming Media Planning for Clients," (Modified) in *Advertising Research Foundation 8th Annual Conference Report,* Oct. 1962, p. 87

Table 73
A Summary of Three Computerized Schedules*

	Schedule 1 Original output of linear pro-gramming model	Schedule 2 (Change: increase impressions against total women)		Schedule 3 (Change: increase impressions against women 18-34, in 5 member households)	
	(000s ommited)	(000s omitted)	% Chnge.	(000s omitted)	% Chnge.
Total REUs	1,056	912		1,133	
Cost-per-1000 REUs	$2.84	$3.29		$2.64	
Total gross impressions	3,231	5,055	57.3%	4,043	25.8%
Gross against total women	1,699	2,723	60.3	2,107	24.0
Gross against women 18-34	475	921	93.9	674	41.9
Gross against 5+ households	504	912	81.0	649	23.8
Annual % reach against women	86%	94%		93%	

*Source: Maneloveg, Herbert, "A Year of Linear Programming Media Planning for Clients," (Modified) in *Advertising Research Foundation 8th Annual Conference Report,* Oct. 1962, p. 88

Some of the major advantages of linear programming are: (1) it provides for the power of mathematics to be used in making a decision. The formula represents a high degree of precision. (2) It requires the planner to state his assumptions and quantify them, a practice not required in hand planning. Such a practice forces one to establish written relationships. If they are wrong, then they are immediately visible and can be changed. (3) It allows the user to feed audience data into a computer that was obtained from different sources, thus saving time and money. (4) It delivers alternative decisions quickly because it allows the user to examine a number of schedules based on varied constraints. (5) It allows the planner to have thousands of alternatives scanned quickly. For example, if only two monthly magazines were being compared (each with a potential of 12 insertions) it would require the planner to make 169 comparisons. (6) Finally, the computer can find and accumulate many more Rated Exposure Units from among a list of media vehicles than a group of individuals doing the same thing by hand as noted by David Learner of B.D.D.&O. in a discussion on linear programming.[78]

Simulation. A simulation model is based on the concept of reproducing, or simulating, the probable reading or viewing of individuals in the real world to such an extent, that it is possible to predict how they will be exposed to media in the future. The model is quite different from linear programming in that it is non-optimizing, and it contains relatively few, if any, algorithms. With the simulation model, it is necessary to measure the reading or viewing habits of individuals in a sample population. This data is in the form of reading and viewing probabilities.

In addition, the model takes into consideration the value of each individual in the market-place. Obviously some persons are more likely to buy a brand of product than others. Therefore, media vehicles that have large numbers of prospects in their audiences are more heavily weighted than those media with smaller numbers of prospects.

Essentially then, the model, when programmed through a computer, provides the planner with an estimate of exposure delivery of specific media vehicles that have already been chosen and scheduled by time periods. The computer also can rank each vehicle in terms of its ability to deliver target audiences at the lowest unit cost. But the model does not produce a media schedule, nor can it answer the question of how good a media plan is. If a planner devises two or more media plans and uses the model, the computer will print out the reaches and frequencies and cost-per-thousands for each plan. But the ultimate decision on which is better rests on the planner's judgment.

The Monte Carlo method is used in the simulation model to decide which individuals either read or saw a given vehicle. The method was described previously.

---

[78]Learner, D., and Godfrey, M., in Discussion Section of "Mathematical Methods of Media Selection," a report of the Sixth Meeting of the ARF Operations Research Discussion Group, Dec. 18, 1961, p. 10

Elaborate simulation models have been made which do more than simply provide basic reach and frequency data. In some models, the data is modified by impact evaluation variables. One such variable is vehicle appropriateness. It is assumed in this model that some vehicles are more appropriate for carrying advertisements than others. An example might be that television is more appropriate than newspapers to carry dishwasher detergent ads. Television then, might be assigned a weight of 1.10 while newspapers might be assigned a weight of .75. The determination of how much weight to assign each media class is usually decided on by consensus vote of experts since there is little objective data on which to base weights.

Another impact variable may be to weight ad forms differently. A 60-second commercial therefore, would be given a different weight than a 30 second commercial or a full-page black and white ad. The assignment of weights to different ad forms is another area where there is little objective evidence, so decisions on how much weight to give each form is usually done by consensus vote.

Other simulation models take the value of repetition into consideration. Gensch's model required six repeat exposures of an ad in a given vehicle before that ad could have maximum impact. In addition, Gensch's model accounted for memory decay of ad messages.[79] The decision on how to draw a decay curve usually is based on subjective judgment, plus some objective evidence that is available.

The output of a simulation model computer printout may look like the example in Table 74.

Some people believe the simulation model, generally, has a number of advantages over a linear programming model. They feel the former is better because it usually includes fewer simplifying assumptions which, when converted into mathematics, tend to emasculate the media selection problem. As Broadbent noted, the linear programming model may solve a problem, but it may not be the correct problem while simulation models, may come closer to the real problem. Simulation models also are more flexible, theoretically, so that they may be extended into time, if suitable data becomes available.[80]

Simulation models nevertheless, have some disadvantages. Broadbent noted that they "suffer because they are restricted to only one heuristic method of obtaining a solution."[81] To overcome this problem, Gensch recommended that a simulation model assessment of a schedule could be followed by a heuristic program. Since the simulation model may include judgmental weights applied to impact variables, the media planner could use the same data bank to first

[79]Gensch, Dennis H., *Advertising Planning*, Elsevier Scientific Publishing Company, Amsterdam, 1973, pp. 94-95

[80]Broadbent, Simon, "Media Planning and the Computer by 1970," in *Thomson Medals and Awards for Advertising Research, 1965*, Report, The Thomson Organization Ltd., London, p. 68

[81]Gensch, Dennis H., *Advertising Planning*, Elsevier Scientific Publishing Company, Amsterdam, 1973, pp. 144-147

Table 74
Printout of Evaluation Criteria of a Simulation Model*

Page 1 (Media Package selected for week 26)

Media Vehicle No.	Cost	Ad Form
22	$18,040	2
50	17,625	1

Page 2

a. Results of package for week 26
b. Total Cost $35,665
c. Total Number of people reached: 20,238,000
d. Cost per 1000 people reached $1.76
e. Percent of total population reached   39.11%
f. Total number of exposures: 37,535,000
g. Cost per 1000 exposures $0.95
h. Average number of impressions per person: 1
i. Vehicle frequency distribution:

No. of exposures	Frequency	Percent of Population
0	31,506,000	60.89%
1	13,293,000	25.69
2	2,178,000	4.21
3	1,516,000	2.93
4	1,273,000	2.46
5	1,622,000	3.13
6	356,000	.69
7	0	0
8	0	0
9	0	0
10	0	0

j. Ad form adjustment for number of people reached: 17,924,150
k. Cost per 1000: $1.99
l. Ad form percent of population reached: 34.62%
m. Ad form adjustment for total number of exposures: 3,347,150
N. Cost per 1000: $1.07
o. Ad form adjustment of average number of exposures per person: 1
p. Result of package for week 26
q. Ad form frequency distribution:

Number of exposures	frequency	Percent of population
0	32,365,617	62.65%
1	14,919,697	28.88
2	1,606,657	3.11
3	1,162,373	2.25
4	609,600	1.18
5	997,057	1.93
6	0	0
7	0	0
8	0	0
9	0	0
10	0	0

r. Value of media package in impact units: 3,759,373

*Source: Gensch, Dennis, "A Computer Simulation Model for Selecting Advertising Schedules," *Journal of Marketing Research*, May, 1969, p. 213

evaluate a schedule, and then use it through heuristic programming, to find a number of alternative schedules that are better. But the simulation does not find the best schedule, and this is one of its limitations. Finally, many simulation models devised in the past do not have an effectiveness function, although some of the newer ones do.

Other Ways of Using Computers for Media Planning

Automatic Interaction Detection (AID) to find targets. In addition to either building a media schedule, or evaluating schedules, another way of using computers in media planning is to have the computer analyze market segments to find the best prospects. The Automatic Interaction Detector technique is one means of dividing a market into subgroups on the basis of product usage until the best targets appear.

The method starts with a national sample of individuals chosen for their degree of representativeness of the universe, or the entire U.S. Then, through an analysis of purchase rates and demographics, the computer is programmed to determine the average product buying rate for each person, identify the most powerful *demographic* predicter of usage, divide the universe into high and low purchase groups on the basis of the predictor, continue to sub-divide each group until no more meaningful subdivisions can be made.

More precisely, Henry Assael, Professor of Marketing at New York University, explained how the sub-division is done:

> "In operation, the program splits the sample into two subgroups to provide the largest reduction in the unexplained sum of squares of the dependent variable. This is accomplished as follows: group means are determined for each classification of all independent variables, and all dichotomous groupings of each variable are examined. . . . . . The division will take place at the point of greatest discrimination in group means."[82]

The result looks like a decision-tree. Figure 43 shows that the best target market, other things being equal, would be females, living in the north central, who are heavy users of brand X and whose annual income is $12,500 and under. A second group, but much larger in number, would be females in the remainder of the U.S., who are housewives or executives under 55.

Cross-tabulation of demographic market segments. In the past, media planners were handicapped in analyzing marketing data because few cross-tabulations were possible. Probably the most often made cross-tab was one for age and sex. But beyond that, little data was available. The computer, however,

---

[82] Assael, Henry, "Segmenting Markets by Group Purchasing Behavior: An Application of the AID Technique," in *Journal of Marketing Research*, May, 1970, pp. 153-154

Figure 43

Use of "AID" to Find Best Target Markets*

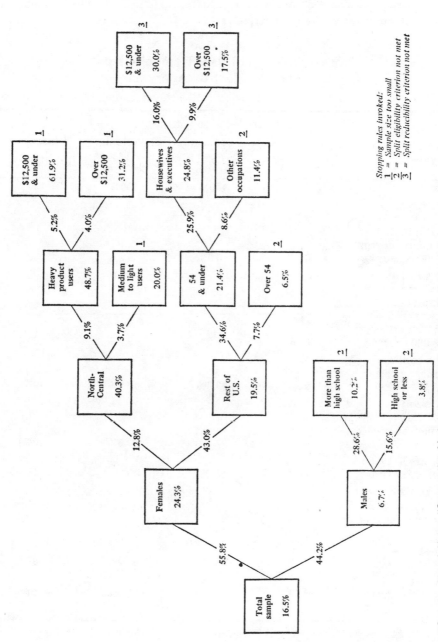

Stopping rules invoked:
1 = Sample size too small
2 = Split eligibility criterion not met
3 = Split reducibility criterion not met

*Source: Assael, Henry, "Segmenting Markets by Group Purchasing Behavior: An Application of the AID Technique," in Journal of Marketing Research, May, 1970, p. 154.

made it possible to provide multiple cross-tabulations to whatever extent the planner would like. The result was that the planner now could look at the relationships of a number of demographic variables at one time. This technique, in addition to AID, provided better opportunities at finding the most precise target market to whom media will be directed. Table 75 shows a sample of cross-tabulation for a product category.

Table 75
Cross-Tabulation of User Demographics*
For a Product Category

| Total U.S. | (Adult Female Usage Patterns) | | | |
	Average No. Times Used Per Week	Percent of women in group	Percent total usages per week	Index of Usage
Total U.S.	4.95	100%	100%	100
H.H. size 1-4; Children 6-17 or none; B, C, D counties; college; $3,000+ income	6.54	6.2%	8.2%	132
H.H. size 1-4; Children 6-17 or none; B, C, D, counties; Grade or high school; $8,000+ income	6.18	7.2%	9.0%	125
Same as above except income $3,000-$7,999	5.30	13.0%	13.9%	107
H.H. size 1-4; Children 6-17 or none; income $3,000+ A counties	5.14	22.0%	22.9%	104
H.H. size 5+; high school or less.	4.83	18.2%	17.8%	98
H.H. size 1-4; children 6-17 or none; income under $3,000	4.58	14.4%	13.4%	93
H.H. size 1-4; children under 6	4.27	13.1%	11.2%	86
H.H. size 5+; some college	3.03	5.9%	3.6%	61

*Reprinted by permission of J. Walter Thompson Company

From Table 75 one can see that the best cross-tabulation for the product market is composed of females in households of 1 to 4 persons, with children from ages 6 to 17, or perhaps none, living in B, C, and D counties, college educated, and income of $3,000 and up.

Miscellaneous marketing and media data analysis. There are many tasks that a computer can do in a fraction of the time it would take a person in the media department to do by hand. These tasks play varying roles in the media planning process, but some are very important. Many times a computer can handle the task at night and have a print-out for the planner to use in the morning.

Most often these miscellaneous jobs are done through the services of an independent computer company that specializes in marketing and media data analysis such as Telmar and IMS (Interactive Market Systems). Media planners can contract for these services directly or can work through an on-line time-sharing system. In the on-line system, the agency would have either a typewriter terminal or a teletype in its office. These machines would be connected with the computer through phone lines. Requests for computer analysis is made through the machines, and the results are printed out on the same machines. Some results can also appear on a cathode ray tube, if the user so desires.

There are many kinds of analyses the computer can provide that can help the media planner do a more efficient job. Listed are a small number of possibilities: (1) Rank media based on criteria such as cost-per-thousands market composition, coverage, GRPs, proportional relationship of demographic or product group to another, (2) Estimate missing pieces of data, adjust old data to reflect changes in audiences or combine related target groups to produce new target information, (3) Perform up to 25 detailed or 400 reach-and-frequency analyses, (4) Eliminate media vehicles that fall outside a budget or that cost too much for the audience delivered, (5) Test alternative combinations of media vehicles through rapid reach-and-frequency analysis of all possible combinations, (6) Get spot TV cumulative reach and frequencies for 1, 2, or 4-week periods and consider seasonal differences in viewing habits, ratings and time periods, (7) Do a local market brand and product sales analysis and provide rankings of sales potentials for each market, and (8) Analyze last year's schedule and show improvements for this year's schedule.

Figures 44 and 45 show samples of how the last two analyses would look after being printed out on a computer:

Test marketing simulations. Another, but very limited, use of computers in media planning has been test market simulations in which media strategy plays a role. The test market simulation model is much like the media simulation model, but the former is more comprehensive. It not only attempts to predict consumer exposure to media, but probable purchase rates, brand-switching rates, attitude changes and, eventually, market share. Since media does play a role in these models, the planner may want to see what responses he could obtain from his advertising in much the same way he would if he had performed a test marketing experiment.

Figure 44
Sample Page from Telmar Computer Print Out
Showing Media Selections for a Given Budget*

```
- - - - -   TELMAR BENCHMARK SYSTEM II    2-MAY-73    06:05 - - - - - -

          BRAND X - MAXIMIZE REACH FOR $500,000 BUDGET


                    MEDIA OBJECTIVES
                    ----------------

              BUDGET GOAL: $  500000

              OPTIMIZATION
                 BASED ON:     REACH

          SELECTION PROCESS VIA MEDIAC MODEL
          ----------------------------------
```

	MEDIA	COST	%REACH	AVG.FREQ	GRP
1	BBB	48000	28.85	1.00	28
1	BBB	96000	36.99	1.56	57
1	AAA	150000	49.68	1.67	83
1	GGG	180000	53.15	1.73	92
1	AAA	234000	58.14	2.02	117
1	FFF	257000	59.79	2.03	121
1	BBB	305000	62.80	2.39	150
1	AAA	359000	65.40	2.68	175
1	BBB	407000	67.17	3.04	204
1	GGG	437000	68.32	3.12	213
1	FFF	460000	69.21	3.13	216

(header: ----- CUME -----)

*** BUDGET GOAL REACHED

--- MARKET SEGMENT SUMMARY ---

BENCHMARK II SUMMARY AND ANALYSIS

USES	MEDIA	COST
3	AAA	162000
4	BBB	192000
2	FFF	46000
2	GGG	60000
11		460000

DEMO NAME	ABCD
POPULATION	50833
GROSS IMPRESSIONS	110282
CPM GROSS IMPRESSIONS	4.17
GROSS RATING POINTS	216
NET REACH	35181
PERCENT NET REACH	69.21
CPM NET REACH	13.08
AVERAGE FREQUENCY	3.13
DEMO WEIGHT	1.00

*Reprinted by permission of Telmar Communication's Corp., (Copyrighted)

Figure 45
Sample Page from Telmar Computer Print Out
of Reach and Frequency Analysis*

```
- - - TELMAR REACH & FREQUENCY: METHERINGHAM - - -

     BASIC REPORT WITH FREQUENCY DISTRIBUTION

              TARGET GROUP A
```

POPULATION: 50,833

MEDIA NAME	# OF USES	UNIT COST	AVERAGE AUDIENCE	CPM	PERCENT COVERAGE
AAA	4	35,000	12,894	2.71	25.37
BBB	3	36,500	14,662	2.49	28.84
CCC	2	16,500	2,580	6.40	5.08
DDD	1	26,000	5,538	4.69	10.89

```
          TOTAL COST           $  308,500
          TOTAL USES                   10

          NET REACH              34,159
          PERCENT NET REACH       67.20
          CPM NET REACH            9.03

          GROSS IMPRESSIONS      106,260
          CPM GROSS IMPRESSIONS     2.90

          AVERAGE FREQUENCY         3.11
```

INSERTION LEVEL	EXPOSED %	EXPOSED (000)	EXPOSED AT LEAST %	EXPOSED AT LEAST (000)
0	32.80	16,673	100.00	50,833
1	19.39	9,854	67.20	34,160
2	13.88	7,054	47.82	24,306
3	10.36	5,266	33.94	17,252
4	7.77	3,952	23.58	11,986
5	5.76	2,927	15.80	8,033
6	4.14	2,103	10.05	5,107
7	2.83	1,437	5.91	3,004
8	1.77	902	3.08	1,567
9	0.95	484	1.31	665
10	0.36	181	0.36	181

*Reprinted by permission of Telmar Communication's Corp., (Copyrighted)

Media billing and accounting.   The last use of computers for media planning is a housekeeping function of billing and accounting. It is obvious that records need to be kept in a fast moving business such as media buying and/or ordering. Computers can perform a great deal of manual labor for the planner so that he can see what he has done quickly and use the information in future planning if the need arises.

The present state of computer-use is still at an evolving level, but one must conclude that, despite the early disappointments, computers have some significant uses today. The following represents an outline of areas where computers can be of most value today.

Helping the planner evaluate alternatives.   One of the principles of media planning widely accepted today is that media vehicles selected should represent the best of all alternatives. But the planner cannot very well examine many alternatives by hand. Through the use of a computer, the planner can expand the number of alternatives at relatively low cost and with minimum effort. The organization of data by a computer also helps the planner study the output with less effort than if he had to do it by hand. Evaluations are made on the basis of reaches, frequencies, cost-per-thousands and frequency distributions both of vehicles and ads in vehicles.

Helping the planner find alternatives to be evaluated.   Through the use of heuristic programming, the computer can develop many alternative schedules quickly. These, then, may be analyzed by the computer through the simulation process.

Saving time and effort in media analysis.   The best use of computers at this time is in the area of media analysis. There are so many computations that must be made that huge quantities of time must be alloted for this task. The computer prints out many kinds of analysis quickly and in convenient order for the media planner. Perhaps one of the major unrealized values in this area is that: if the inputs into the computer are correct, then the output is likely to be free from computational or recording errors.

Computers as a learning tool.   If planners continue to use computers for media planning they will be forced to be more thoughtful about the underlying assumptions under which they operate. While initial outputs of computers may have been wrong, the model builder or planner modifies his assumptions and discards erroneous ones. But through the use of a computer, the planner will have the motivation to change them and learn, as a result.

In conclusion then, the computer is here to stay as an aid to the planner. It can save time, effort and money in helping to provide the kind of accountability for media plans that more sophisticated clients are apt to demand. As the price of media rises, and/or as clients spend more money for media, they will expect more accountability. Furthermore, clients are using computers more for management purposes and they have become acclimated to its outputs. They understand and appreciate the role of computers as an aid to management. It is likely therefore, that they will understand and appreciate the role of computers in media planning, perhaps to the extent of paying for this service if they believe it will better account for the way their money is being spent. The computer has already earned a niche in advertising history as an aid to planners and this role will undoubtedly grow. But it is not likely that they will replace planners entirely, as some individuals originally assumed. They will probably always remain an aid and not become a substitute for individual judgment.

QUESTIONS

1. If you had to build a model of media planning by hand, what elements and relationships would you probably have in the model? Explain.
2. Give two examples of algorithms in common use in media planning without a computer.
3. Give at least three examples of typical constraints that are used in media planning without a computer.
4. What are the advantages and limitations of linear programming for media planning purposes?
5. Can a simulation model produce a media plan through use of a computer? Briefly explain.
6. Explain the value of an automatic interaction detector for media planning purposes.
7. Why can't media planners find a suitable effectiveness criterion (or criteria) by which to objectively judge the value of a media plan before it is implemented?
8. Explain the role of judgment in the use of computers for media planning purposes. Can judgment be eliminated?
9. What are the main differences between a linear programming media model and a simulation media model?
10. Despite the problems associated with the use of computers for media planning, in which areas have computers been helpful for the planner?

SELECTED READINGS

Abelson, Robert P. and Bernstein, Alex, *The Simulation of a Test Market*, from the Simulmatics Corp., N. Y. Aug. 1962

Alpert, Lewis, "Measuring Effects of Simulation," in *Advertising Research Foundation 18th Annual Conference Proceedings*, 1972, pp. 48-50

Assael, Henry, "Segmenting Markets by Group Purchasing Model: An Application of the AID Technique," in *Journal of Marketing Research*, May, 1970, pp. 153-158

Atwater, H. B., Jr., "Mathematical Models to Improve Advertising Decisions," in *Perspectives in Advertising Management*, Assn. of National Advertisers, Inc., April, 1969, pp. 75-88

Bass, Frank M., and Lomsdale, Robert T., "An Exploration of Linear Programming in Media," in *Journal of Marketing Research, May, 1966, pp. 179-188*

Broadbent, Simon, "Media Planning and the Computer by 1970," in *Thomson Medals and Awards for Advertising Research*, London, 1965, pp. 63-86

Broadbent, Simon R., "A Year's Experience of the LPE Media Model," in *Advertising Research Foundation 1965 Conference Proceedings*, pp. 51-56

Brown, Douglas B., and Warshaw, Martin R., "Media Selection by Linear Programming," in *Journal of Marketing Research*, Feb., 1965, pp. 83-88

Brown, Douglas B., "A Practical Procedure for Media Selection," in *Journal of Marketing Research*, Aug. 1967, pp. 262-269

Charnes, A., Cooper, W. W., DeVoe, J. K., Learner, D. B., and Reinceke, W., "A Goal Programming Model for Media Planning," *and* "Note on Goal Programming Model for Media Planning," in *Management Science*, April, 1968, pp. 423-436

Day, Ralph L., "Linear Programming in Media Selection," in *Journal of Advertising Research*, June, 1962, pp. 40-44

Dobbins, Robert and Shiffman, Philip, "What Kind of Mathematical Models if any, are Useful for Day-to-day Activity or Long Range Planning?" in *Media Decisions*, Jan. 1972, p. 52

Ferguson, Robert D., and Sargent, F., *Linear Programming*, McGraw-Hill, N. Y., 1958

Fleck, Robert A. Jr., "How Media Planners Process Information," in *Journal of Advertising Research*, April, 1973, pp. 14-18

Friedman, Lawrence, "Constructing a Media Simulation Model," in *Journal of Advertising Research*, Aug. 1970, pp. 33-39

Gensch, Dennis H. *Advertising Planning*, Elsevier Scientific Research Publishing Co., N.Y. 1973

Gensch, Dennis H., "A Computer Simulation Model for Selecting Advertising Schedules," in *Journal of Marketing Research*, May, 1969, pp. 203-214

Gensch, Dennis H., "Media Factors: A Review Article," in *Journal of Marketing Research*, May, 1970, pp. 216-225

Gensch, Dennis H., "*Computer Models in Advertising Media Selection*," in *Journal of Marketing Research*, Nov. 1968, pp. 414-424

Jones, P.I., "The Future Use of Computers in Media Planning - Research and Planning, A Dichotomy?" in *Thomson Medals and Awards for Advertising Research*, London, 1965, pp. 103-124

Kaplan, R. S. and Shocker, A. D., "Discount Effects on Media Plans," in *Journal of Advertising Research*, June, 1971, pp. 37-43

Kotler, Philip, "Toward an Explicit Model for Media Selection," in *Journal of Advertising Research*, March, 1964, pp. 34-41

Kotler, Philip, "Computerized Media Planning: Techniques, Needs and Prospects," in *Occasional Papers in Advertising*, American Academy of Advertising, Urbana, Ill., 1965

Knowlton, Arch, "Using the Computer to Select and Appraise Media," in *Perspectives in Advertising Management*, Assn. of National Advertisers, Inc., April, 1969, pp. 178-184

Keshin, M., and Lyman, R. F., Ross, K. and St. Georges, J., *Some Important Things I Believe A Young Account Executive Should Know About Electronic Data Processing*, American Assn. of Advertising Agencies, Jan. 1969

Landis, Jack B., "Improving Media Schedules via Computers" in *Computer Operations*, Jan., Feb., 1968, pp. 22-25

Learner, D., and Godfrey M., "Mathematical Methods of Media Selection," A Report of the Sixth Meeting of the ARF Operations Research Discusson Group, N. Y., Dec. 1961

Little, John D., and Lodish, L. M., "A Media Planning Calculus," in *Operations Research*, Feb. 1969, pp. 1-35

Maneloveg, Herbert, "A Year of Linear Programming Media Planning for Clients" in *ARF 8th Annual Conference Report*, N.Y., Oct. 1962

Moran, William T., *Practical Media Models: What Must They Look Like?* Paper presented at the Midwest Conference of the Advertising Research Foundation, Chicago, Nov. 1962

Schreiber, Robert J., "A Practical Procedure for Media Selection: Comments," *Journal of Marketing Research*, May, 1968, pp. 221-224

Schreiber, Robert J., "Instability in Media Exposure Habits," *Journal of Advertising Research*, April, 1974, pp. 13-17

St. Georges, Joseph, "How Practical is the Media Model?" in *Journal of Marketing Research*, July, 1963, pp. 31-33

Stasch, Stanley, "Linear Programming and Media Selection: A Comment," in *Journal of Marketing Research*, May, 1967, pp. 205-207

Stasch, Stanley, "Linear Programming and Space-Time Considerations in Media Selection," *Journal of Advertising Research*, Dec. 1965, pp. 40-46

Teng-Pin-Yu, Tom, "The National Media Simulation Model, " in *Computer Operations*, Sept. Oct., 1967, pp. 11-12

Wilson, C. L. et al, *Mathematical Programming for Better Media Selections*, American Assn. of Advertising Agencies, Papers from the Regional Conventions, 1961.

Zangwill, W. I., "Media Selection by Decision Programming," *Journal of Advertising Research*, Sept., 1965, pp. 30-36

appendix

Sample Media Plan

Introduction. A media plan is presented on the following pages as one example of how the decisions described in this text appear in an organized format. Readers should keep in mind the fact that, although a planner made the decisions on the basis of information that was available at the time, other planners, faced with the same problems and information, could arrive at slightly different solutions.

In studying the plan's details, the reader is urged to focus his attention on certain aspects that may help him see relationships that are so important in media planning:

(1) Note the statement of marketing and creative strategies and to what extent they influence final decisions

(2) Note that the media objectives reflect not only the marketing and creative strategies that were stated, but also marketing objectives that were not stated. Readers can infer what they might have been

(3) Note the manner in which media strategies implement media objectives

(4) Note the manner in which individual local markets were selected to be included in the spot television portion of the plan

(5) Note the rationale for all media decisions

(6) Note the fact that alternative media strategies were presented and rejected for the reasons given

(7) Note the pattern of scheduling and why it was done in the manner recommended

BRAND "X" DOG FOOD

MARKETING STRATEGY

The objectives for next year will be achieved with the following marketing strategy:

(1) National, year-round advertising and promotion, allowing for continuity and trial-stimulating activity.

(2) Exposure of Brand "X" at virtually *all* dog owners regardless of present feeding patterns or habits with special emphasis at those considered to be primary purchasers of dog food.

(3) Communications effectiveness in demonstrating the brand's palatability appeal.

(4) Consumer-oriented promotions on a regular basis, including at least one major promotion backed by intensive sales support.

(5) Flexibility to capitalize on variations in potential based on current commercial market development and support special promotion efforts.

(6) Continued testing designed to provide direction for further business growth.

CREATIVE STRATEGY

Advertising copy for our brand will leave a net impression with dog owners that our brand is new, and that it provides:

(1) Outstanding palatability for dogs.
(2) Mild aroma that will not offend owners.
(3) Complete nutrition.

MEDIA OBJECTIVES

(1) Adult women (18+ years of age) will represent Brand X's primary market segment because of their important role as the "decision maker" in the purchase of dog food. Exposure to other dog owners, however, will be a secondary, yet important, demographic objective.
(2) Media will be used which most satisfactorily provide the best combination of reach and efficiency against adult women since
   (a) reach is of strategic importance in generating meaningful levels of exposure against current and potential dog food purchasers,
   (b) efficiency against adult women will enable Brand X to get increased benefit from its advertising investment.
(3) Brand X will be provided with year-round support at meaningful levels of exposure in order to reach a significant number of established customers on a regular basis.
(4) Increased advertising emphasis will be placed during key periods for the strategic purpose of stimulating new trial among potential customers.
(5) Brand X will be advertised nationally in recognition of its broad distribution and business, but will receive additional geographic spending support in markets of greatest volume and potential.
(6) Media will be used which effectively communicate Brand X's palatability and demonstrate the product's characteristics via "sight, sound and motion."
(7) Flexibility will be maintained to enable Brand X to respond quickly to geographic, seasonal and budgetary considerations.

MEDIA STRATEGY

1. *Use of Television*
   Television will be employed as Brand X's primary medium for the following reasons:
   (a) Television is capable of generating greater reach against the primary demographic of adult women as well as exposure to all dog owners.
   (b) Television is a highly efficient medium for adult women.
   (c) Television most satisfies Brand X's creative requirements of communicating product palatability and taste appeal.
2. *Night Network Television*
   Night network television will be used because it:
   (a) Is a "reach-oriented" daypart, capable of providing broad exposure nationally and at the target audience of adult women as well as other dog owners.
   (b) Can serve to intensify Brand X advertising activity during important sales and promotion periods.
   (c) Offers a more compatible environment for Brand X's selling message because of its greater effectiveness.

3. *Day Network Television*

Day network will be used for Brand X since it:

(a) Is a "frequency-oriented" daypart capable of providing repetitive exposure of Brand X advertising strategy.

(b) Has a high concentration of adult women.

(c) Is highly efficient in reaching adult women.

4. *Spot Television*

Spot television is a highly flexible medium which will enable Brand X to:

(a) Achieve additional advertising pressure in areas where sales volume/market potential is high.

(b) Permit pressure and/or budget adjustments as may be required by changes in market conditions, competitive activity, and/or underdelivery of network schedules in important markets.

5. *Seasonal Spending Patterns*

Day network spending and delivery will be flat throughout the year for continuous advertising pressure against target market segments, who are regularly making decisions to purchase dog food. Additional spending emphasis will take place to recognize the following marketing needs:

(a) Flighted night network levels will be used for additional impact and reach in order to stimulate new consumer trial and broad levels of demographic/geographic exposure.

(b) Additional emphasis via night spot television will be employed to exert meaningful levels of support in important geographic areas during important periods and for extra weight behind major promotions.

6. *Geographic Spending*

Day and night network television will be used for national support of Brand X while spot television will serve to provide additional spending empemphasis in recognition of:

(a) Brand X's brand development or the relation of sales volume to population in each area. High brand development areas will qualify for additional spot support.

(b) Underdelivery of network in certain areas. Markets where Brand X delivery is below desired levels of exposure will receive additional spending support.

PLAN TACTICS

1. *Day Network*

Day network programs to be used by Brand X are Show "A" and Show "B." On the basis of available daytime programming, these programs ranked best according to the following criteria:

(a) Ability to meet desired average rating level.

(b) Coverage.

(c) Cost efficiency.

(d) Ability of these program types to develop optimum daytime "reach."

In addition, it has been agreed that a further opportunity for daytime reach can be developed through the trade of one minute every second week between Show "A" and "Brand Y's" Show "C." The net schedule is unchanged (a total of three commercial minutes each week), and dog food commercials can be scheduled into three different daytime segments. Exhibit 1 summarizes pertinent day network data.

Exhibit I
Continuity Plan — Daytime Network

GOAL:

Weekly Rating Level	25 GRP
Four-week Reach/Frequency	40/2.5

PLAN:

3 Network Minutes/Wk @ 52 Weeks

Show "A" (12:00 N NYT) Alternate Quarter Hours,
    78 minutes/52 weeks

Show "B" (4:00 PM NYT) Alternate Quarter-Hours,
    78 Minutes/52 weeks

PROGRAM PERFORMANCE Based on March, 1971 NTI:

	Average Audience Rating		
	Show "C"	Show "A"	Show "B"
3/11-15/	10.0	8.0	7.9
3/18-22/	9.6	7.8	8.8
3/25-29/	8.3	6.0	6.7
4/1-5/	8.2	6.4	7.0
4-Week Average	9.0	7.1	7.6

	Homes		
	Show "C"	Show "A"	Show "B"
3/11-15/	4,980	3,984	3,934
3/18-22/	4,781	3,884	4,382
3/25-29/	4,133	2,988	3,337
4/1-5/	4,084	3,187	3,486
4-Week Average	4,482	3,535	3,785
Avg. Cost/Minute	$6,400	$4,400	$5,000
Avg. Cost/1000	$1.43	$1.24	$1.32

2. *Night Network*

Brand X dog food's use of corporate nighttime properties includes minute announcements in all three programs: Show "X," Show "Y" and Show "Z." These programs afford Brand X the opportunity to:

(a) Schedule commercials in flights, or waves, at an intensive level at different times during the year.

(b) Provide broad general reach per announcement available only during peak viewing hours of prime nighttime network programming.

(c) Through the above, generate desirable reach and frequency of commercial messages against the average TV home within short periods of time.

(d) Take advantage of in-program commercial placement.

(e) Utilize 60-second announcements against a large audience, a portion of which will be exposed to Brand X dog food's advertising only during these fights.

(f) Communicate at a reasonable cost efficiency level.

Exhibit II summarizes relevant night network data.

Exhibit II
Impact Plan (National) — Night Network

GOAL (During Flights):

Weekly Rating Level	5 GRP (incl. Day Network)
Four-week Reach/Frequency	70/3.2

PLAN:

24 Brand X nighttime show minute announcements
Three flight periods, 5-6 weeks

WAVE I	Week of	9/21	9/28	10/5	10/12	10/19	10/26
	Show "X"	X		X			X
	"Y"				X	X	
	"Z"	X	X	X		X	

WAVE II	Week of	1/12	1/19	1/26	2/2	2/9	2/16
	Show "X"			X		X	
	"Y"		X		X		X
	"Z"	X		X	X	X	

WAVE III	Week of	4/13	4/20	4/27	5/4	5/11
	Show "X"		X		X	
	"Y"	X				
	"Z"	X		X		X

ESTIMATED PERFORMANCE:	# Announcements	Average Audience Rating*
Show "X"	7	25
"Y"	6	20
"Z"	11	18

*Estimated average for Brand X dog food's sponsorship; level required to achieve media goals.

IMPACT PLAN (High Potential Areas)
Night Network Spot

High potential areas are defined as those brand X broker areas in which the market development index (commercial dog food consumption per 1,000 population) is above 110. For purposes of applying extra advertising pressure, these areas have been broken into two groups: those indexed at 160 and above; those indexed from 110 to 159.

GROUP A BROKERS

GOAL (During Night Network Flights):

Weekly Rating Level .... 100 GRP
(Includes Day & Night Network)

Four-week Reach/Frequency 85/4.7

PLAN:

1. Night Spot TV—to achieve 45 GRP weekly—fringe and prime announcements—24 markets in eight broker areas accounting for 15% U. S. population, 29% U.S. dog food, 27% brand X food's estimated sales.

GROUP B BROKERS
GOAL (During Night Network Flights):
Weekly Rating Level .... 85 GRP
(Including Day & Night Network)
Four-week Reach/Frequency 83/4.0
PLAN:
1. Night spot TV to achieve estimated 30 GRP weekly— fringe and prime announcements — 23 markets in nine broker areas accounting for 12% U.S. population, 15.5% U. S. dog food, 15.6% Brand X dog food's estimated sales.
2. Three five-week flights, one six-week flight. Three flights, or waves, will run concurrently with night network.

Exhibit III
Next Year's Media Plan & Estimated Cost

(Cost: $000)

Television

Day Network—3 Anncts/Wk x 52 Wks	$ 711.9
Night Network—24 Anncts. (3 flights)	1,009.2
Night Spot—17 Broker Areas; 27% U.S. Population; 44% Dog Food Sales; 42% Brand X dog food (4 flights) - 21 Wks	298.2
Network Replacement,* Special Activity, Rate Increase Reserve	130.7
TOTAL TV	$2,150.0

Print

Grocery Trade, 3 Publications - 2/Yr	$ 6.0
Professional Dog Magazines	5.9
Promotion Support—Midwinter Promotion	110.0
TOTAL PRINT	$121.9

Total Media $2,271.9
*Spot Television Reserve for those markets not clearing network programs

---

ALTERNATE USES OF TELEVISION
Several alternative media plans relying primarily on television have been examined and rejected.

100% Night Network
Use of only night network television was considered but rejected because of. . .
(1) The reduction in number of commercials and annual ratings versus the approved plan.

	Approved Plan	All Night Network
Annual		
Announcements	205	52
GRP	2,010	1,067

Exhibit IV
Next Year's Approved Advertising & Promotion Budget
($000)

Advertising

Television	$2,150.0
Print (including promotion support)	121.9
Production & Reserves	118.5
Total Advertising	$2,390.4

Promotion

Booklet Offer	$ 70.0
Mid-Year Promotion	141.0
Other Consumer & Trade	59.0
Package Changes, Coupons	27.6
Total Promotion..	$297.6

Other

Research	$ 51.0
Publicity, etc.	193.0
Total..	$244.0
Total Budget...	$2,932.0

---

(2) The lack of flexibility in:
   (a) budget
   (b) added support for high-potential areas.

(3) The possibility of program non-clearance or poor performance in important markets.

100% Spot (National Basis)
Use of an all-spot plan was considered but rejected primarily because of
(1) The lack of ability to reach large audiences (prime time) with 60-second messages.
(2) The cost of developing a comparable national continuity plan which would be greater with day spot than with the use of day network.
(3) The inability to place commercial messages within programs.

Combination Spot (National Basis) & Network
There has been limited agreement that the media strategy could be served by a plan calling for day network to provide continuity and night spot for impact. Rejection of such a plan was based primarily on these factors:
(1) Limited use of 60's against large audiences
(2) The assumption that in-program 60's could offset the somewhat greater frequency that would be generated by night spot relying heavily on 30's between programs.
Utilizing the spot dollars provided in the approved budget, the possibility of using spots on top of the night network waves was considered and rejected.

Exhibit V
Recommended Media Plan - Next Year
Estimated Monthly Cost

Television	Oct.	Nov.	Dec.	Jan.	Feb.	Mar.	Apr.	May	June	July	Aug.	Sept.	Total
	($)	($)	($)	($)	($)	($)	($)	($)	($)	($)	($)	($)	($)
Day Network	73,000	59,200	63,600	70,600	59,200	68,600	60,800	56,400	48,640	53,120	48,640	50,100	711,900
Night Network	336,400	42,050		168,200	210,250		168,200	84,100					1,009,200
Night Spot	35,500	35,500		35,500	42,600	42,600		42,600	28,400	35.500	35,500		298,200
Network Replacement Rate Increase & Reserve	10,890	10,890	10,890	10,890	10,890	10,890	10,890	10,890	10,890	10,890	10,890	10,890	130,700
Print													
Grocery		1,000	2,000					1,000	2,000				6,000
Professional			625		625		600	1,100	625		1,700	625	5,900
Promotion				55,000	55,000								110,000
Total	455,790	148,640	77,125	347,300	378,565	79,490	283,090	181,890	97,655	99,510	61,230	61,615	2,271,900

NOTE: Day network costs for October-March include Show "C" trade-off costs.

Network Cost per Minute by Program:

Day	Winter	Summer
Show "A"	$4,400	$3,520
"B"	$5,000	$4,000
"C"	$6,400	$3,520

Night	Original	Repeat	Replacement
Show "X"	$43,770	$32,220	$24,154
"Y"	$50,815	$36,790	$30,401
"Z"	$38,494	$20,093	—

Exhibit VI
Alternate Spot TV Plan
(Next Year's)

Night Network Performance

WAVE I Night Objective = 45 GRP's/Wk. - 5 Weeks
6 Weeks - GRP Objective = 225
Night Network Schedule

Wk. Of	9/21	9/28	10/5	10/12	10/19	10/26	
Prog. X			X	X		X	Est. Rtg. = 25 = 75
Prog. Y				X	X		Est. Rtg. = 20 = 40
Prog. Z	X	X	X			X	Est. Rtg. = 18 = 72
							187

Estimated total spot GRP's necessary to meet
objective of 225 = 38 − 40 GRP's

WAVE II Night Objective = 45 GRP's/Wk. - 6 Weeks (1/13-2/23) = 270
Night Network Schedule

Wk. Of	1/12	1/19	1/26	2/2	2/9	2/16	
Prog. X			X		X		Est. Rtg. = 25 = 50
Prog. Y		X		X		X	Est. Rtg. = 20 = 60
Prog. Z	X		X	X	X		Est. Rtg. = 18 = 72
							182

Estimated total spot GRP's necessary to meet
objective of 270 = 88 - 90 GRP's

WAVE III Night Objective = 45 GRP's/Wk. - 5 Weeks = 225

Wk. Of	4/13	4/20	4/27	5/4	5/11	
Prog. X		X		X		Est. Rtg. = 25 = 50
Prog. Y	X					Est. Rtg. = 20 = 20
Prog. Z	X		X		X	Est. Rtg. = 18 = 54
						124

Estimated total spot GRP's necessary to meet
objective of 225 = 120 - 121 GRP's

The primary reasons for this decision were:

(1) The high potential areas would not develop the net reach available under the approved plan, and would have three flights instead of four.

(2) An analysis of estimated advertising costs/ton by broker areas grouped according to potential showed a strong balance in favor of the approved plan and against an even distribution of spot funds, in that advertising cost/ton was brought more nearly in line.

For comparison purposes, exhibits VI through X show the relationship between the approved plan and the alternate discussed earlier.

Exhibit VII
Alternate Spot TV Plan
(Next Year)

National Level

WAVE I - No spot TV
WAVE II - 15 GRP's /Wk. - 6 Wks. = $120,000
WAVE III - 20 GRP's   - 5 Wks. = 127,500

TOTAL SPOT TV = $249,500

High Potential Area - Additional Weight
Group I Markets - (Mkt. Index of 160 or More)

Total TV H.H. = 7,976.2

WAVE I - No spot TV
WAVE II - 30 GRP's/Wk. - 5 Wks. = $30,512
WAVE III - 30 GRP's/Wk. - 6 Wks. = 36,615

TOTAL GROUP I = $ 67,127

Group II Markets - (Mkt. Index of 110-159) + Louisville & Milwaukee*)

Total TV H.H. = 6,110.3
WAVE I - No spot TV
WAVE II - 15 GRP's/Wk. - 5 Wks. = $11,685
WAVE III - 15 GRP's/Wk. - 6 Wks. = 14,022

TOTAL GROUP II = $ 25,707

*Test Markets

Total National Spot TV	$247,500
Total High Potential Mkts. Spot TV	92,834
Reserve for Special Markets	12,466
TOTAL SPOT TV	$352,800

Exhibit VIII
Alternate Spot TV Plan
(Next Year)

		Reach And Frequency Estimates - All TV				
National Spot - TV	# Weeks	Wkly. GRP Day Ntw.	Wkly. GRP Night Ntw.	Wkly. GRP Night Spot	Total Wkly. GRP	4 Week Reach/Freq.
Wave I	5	25	30	–	55	69/3.3
Wave II	6	25	30	15	70	78/3.6
Wave III	5	25	25	20	70	78/3.6
High Potential Markets Group A						
Wave I	5	25	30	–	55	69/3.3
Wave II	6	25	30	45	100	85/4.7
Wave III	5	25	25	50	100	85/4.7
High Potential Markets Group B						
Wave I	5	25	30	–	55	69/3.3
Wave II	6	25	30	30	85	83/4.0
Wave III	5	25	25	35	85	83/4.0

Exhibit IX
(Next Year)
Comparison - Recommended - Alternate Plans
(See Alternate Media Plan)

Broker Territory	Anti-cipated Next Year Volume	Mkt. Dev. Index	Brand Dev. Index	Estimated Expenditures Recom-mended Plan	Alter-nate Plan	Est. Cost/Ton Recom-mended Plan	Alter-nate Plan	Cost/Ton Index Recom-mended Plan	Alter-nate Plan	Annual GRP's Recom-mended Plan	Alter-nate Plan
	(Tons)			($)	($)	($)	($)	(%)	(%)		
GROUP A											
A	691.7	221	252	47,746	37,044	69.03	53.56	66.7	51.8	2,738	2,213
B	571.9	212	242	41,714	32,693	72.94	57.17	70.5	55.2	"	"
C	476.3	195	177	35,615	25,363	74.77	53.25	72.3	51.5	"	"
D	1,520.0	188	122	157,045	28,148	103.32	84.31	99.8	81.5	"	"
E	629.1	177	160	75,838	57,263	120.55	91.02	116.5	88.0	"	"
F	1,641.9	175	198	111,396	99,130	67.85	60.37	65.6	58.3	"	"
G	59.1	165	332	8,180	5,117	138.41	86.58	133.8	83.7	"	"
H	99.5	160	320	14,620	9,656	146.93	97.05	142.0	93.8	"	"
	5,689.5			492,154	394,414	86.50	69.32	83.6	67.0		
GROUP B											
I	697.3	152	127	2,905	45,649	76.26	65.47	73.7	63.3	2,423	2,058
J	366.3	146	147	28,299	23,464	77.26	64.06	74.7	61.9	"	"
K	608.6	132	134	90,206	74,671	148.22	124.34	143.2	120.2	"	"
L	140.3	119	85	28,018	23,304	199.70	166.10	193.0	160.5	"	"
M	267.2	114	160	17,457	14,633	65.33	54.76	63.1	52.9	"	"
N	95.8	113	117	15,598	11,597	162.82	121.05	157.3	117.0	"	"
O	695.8	113	117	70,484	57,419	101.30	82.52	97.9	79.7	"	"
P	212.5	103	123	9,673	5,597	45.52	26.34	44.0	25.5	"	"
Q	118.8	102	143	21,296	15,547	179.26	130.87	173.2	126.5	"	"
	3,202.6			333,936	272,881	104.27	85.21	100.8	82.3		
ALL OTHERS											
R	336.8	165	331	9,270	10,544	27.52	31.31	26.6	30.3	1,793	1,983
S	1,068.1	104	102	76,761	94,829	71.87	88.78	69.5	85.8	"	"
T	203.1	103	97	27,809	30,331	136.92	149.34	132.3	144.3	"	"
U	421.6	100	120	38,339	44,084	90.94	104.56	87.9	101.0	"	"
V	511.6	100	95	52,933	56,235	103.47	109.92	100.0	106.2	"	"
W	178.7	99	71	20,322	23,416	113.72	131.04	109.9	126.6	"	"
X	85.8	97	100	10,874	12,304	126.74	143.40	122.5	138.6	"	"
Y	243.3	94	87	22,283	25,221	91.59	103.66	88.5	100.2	"	"

300

Exhibit X
Media Schedule

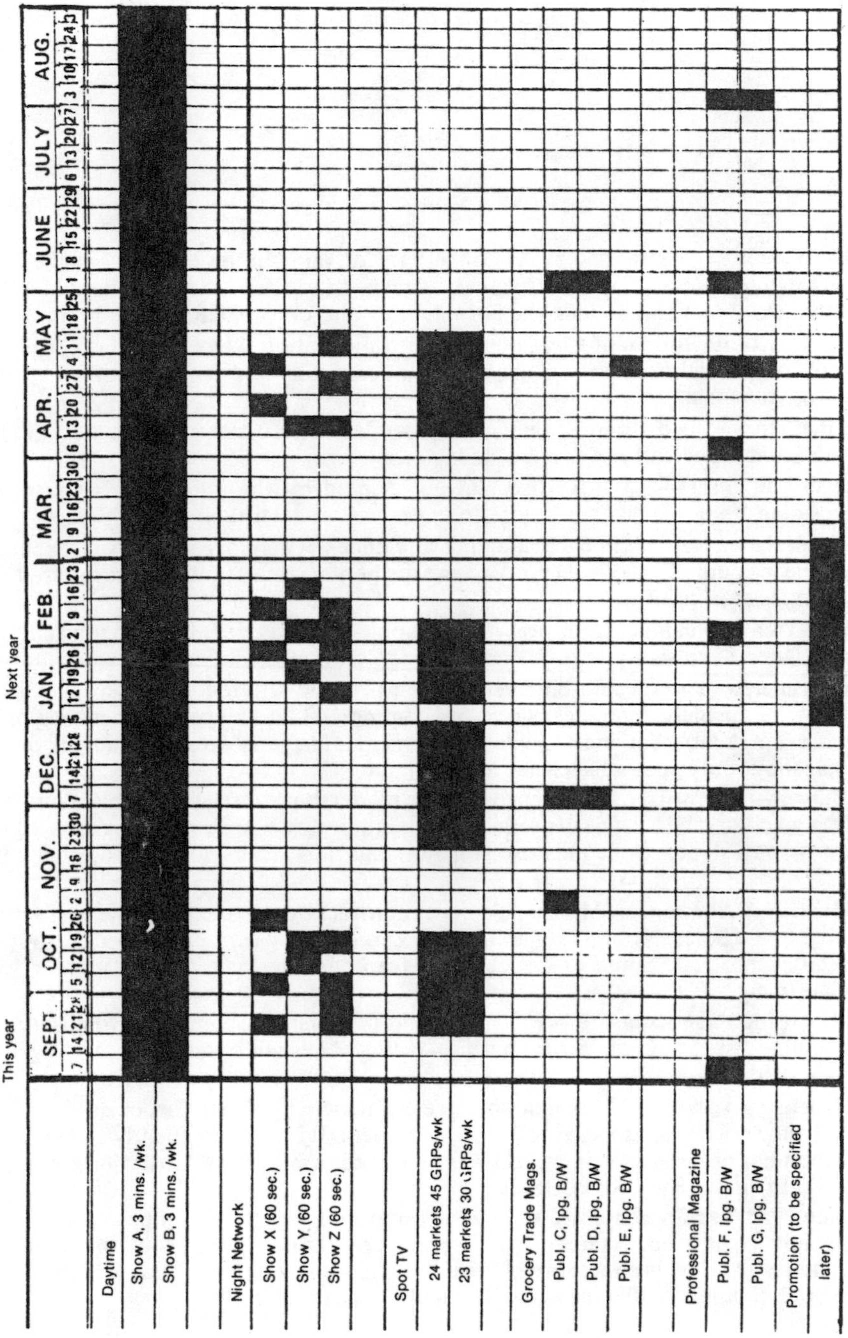

glossary

a

"A" Counties—As defined by A. C. Nielsen Co., all counties belonging to the 25 largest metropolitan areas. These metro areas correspond to the SMSA (Standard Metropolitan Statistical Area) and include the largest cities and consolidated areas in the U. S.

A.B.C. (Audit Bureau of Circulation)—An organization which provides certified statements of net paid circulation of magazines and newspapers, supported jointly by advertisers, agencies and media.

A.B.P. (Associated Business Publication)—A trade association of business (industrial, trade, and technical) paper publications.

Accordion Insert—An Advertisement not printed by the publisher, but inserted in a magazine, folded in such a way as to appear as an accordion fold.

Accumulation—A method of counting audiences wherein each person exposed to a vehicle is counted once, either in a given time period such as four weeks for broadcast, or for an issue in print.

ADI (Area of Dominant Influence)—Geographical market definition wherein each county is assigned exclusively to only one television market as defined by Arbitron.

Adjacencies—The specific time periods that precede and follow regular television programming, usually 2 minutes. These are commercial break positions between programs that are available for local or spot advertisers. There is no such thing as a network adjacency; only spot adjacencies are available.

Adnorm—A term used by Starch to indicate readership averages by publication, by space size and color, and by type of product for ads studied by Starch in a two-year period. Used to provide a standard of comparison for individual ads against averages of similar types of ads.

Advertising Allowance—Money paid under contract by the manufacturer or his representative to a wholesaler or a retailer for the express purpose of being spent, to advertise a specified product, brand or line. Usually for consumer advertising. See: Cooperative Advertising.

Advertising Page Exposure—A measurement of physical opportunity to observe a print ad; defined as the act of opening a pair of facing pages wide enough to permit glancing at any advertising.

Advertising Weight—The amount of advertising being planned for, or used by, a brand. While it is not limited to a particular measurement, it is most frequently stated in terms of the number of messages or impressions delivered or broadcasts/insertions placed over a period of time. (Syn. SUPPORT).

Agate Line (usually simplified to Line)—A unit of space by which newspaper and other print advertising space is sold. One agate line represents a space 1 column wide and 1/14 of an inch high. This is a measure of area, not shape—a 210 line ad can be 1 column x 210 (15''), 2 columns x 105 lines (7½'') or 3 columns x 70 (5'').

Aided recall—a measurement technique in which respondents are helped to remember portions or all of ads by having an interviewer provide clues.

Alternate Week Sponsor—An advertiser who purchases full or participating sponsorship every other week of a network program for a full 52-week broadcast year. Each sponsor will receive billboard commercial time on his week of sponsorship.

AM (Amplitude Modulation)—AM is the standard broadcast transmission system used by the majority of licensed radio stations and radio listeners. The term is commonly used to differentiate between AM and FM radio.

ARB (American Research Bureau, Inc. now called ARBITRON)—A television and radio rating service using a daily diary technique to measure viewing/listening audiences. Arbitron publishes both a monthly radio network rating report and TV and radio reports for selected individual markets (no network TV).

Arbitron—A device producing instantaneous electronic TV program ratings. Also name of an audience rating service.

Audience—The number of people or households who are exposed to a medium. Exposure measurements indicate nothing about whether audiences saw, heard or read either advertisements or editorial contents of the medium.

Audience Composition—The demographic makeup of people represented in an audience with respect to income group, age, sex, geography, etc.

Audience Duplication—In broadcast, a measurement of the number of listeners or viewers who are reached by two or more programs sponsored by the same advertiser. In print, the measurement of the overlap of potential exposure between different issues of the same magazine or among issues of different magazines.

Audience Flow—Changes in audience of broadcast programs. May be reported on a minute-by-minute basis, by five-minute intervals, or from show to show.

Audience Holding Index—A measurement of the retentive power or audience loyalty of a given program. A. C. Nielsen, for 30 minute programs, uses an index based on the percent of homes tuning to the same program 25 minutes later. It is a simple measure of the ratio of average audience rating to total audience rating of a given program.

Audience, Potential—In broadcasting, the number of sets in use in the time period to be studied, or the number of set owners. In print, the total audience of an issue in which an advertisement studied appears.

Audience, Primary—In a study of audience accumulation, the noncumulative potential audience of an advertising message. In print, the number of individuals or homes to which the issue was originally circulated. May be called primary readership or the people to whom the editorial content is specifically directed.

Audience Profile—The characteristics of the people who make up the audience of a magazine, TV show, newspaper, radio show, etc. in terms of age, family size, location, education, income and other factors.

Audience Turnover—The process of change or "turnover" in audience during the broadcast of a specific program or series of programs.

Audilog—The diary which members of Nielsen's local rating panels fill out to show what they are viewing on television.

Audimeter—An electronic device developed by the A. C. Nielsen Company that records set usage and tuning on a continuous basis. These data are recorded automatically on film. Nielsen has a national sample of approximately 1,200 audimeter homes which are used to measure television usage and program audiences.

Audit Report (White Audit)—Official document issued by the ABC detailing its findings as a result of an audit. (Printed on white paper to differentiate it from semi-annual publishers statements which are printed on colored paper). Audit Reports are issued annually covering the 12 month period of the two previous publisher's statements. (See Publisher's Statement.) If the auditor's findings differ from the information in the publisher's statements, the discrepancies are reported and explained in the Audit Report.

Availability—A specific period of commercial time offered for sale by a station or network for sponsorship.

Average Audience (AA)—In broadcasting, this rating measures the number of homes tuned in to a TV program for an average minute (a Nielsen network TV measurement).

Average Frequency—The number of times the average home (or person) reached by a media schedule is exposed to the schedule. This is measured over a specific period of time, e.g., four weeks in broadcast media.

Average Net Paid—Average circulation per issue arrived at by dividing the sum total paid circulation for all the issues of the audit period by the total number of issues.

b

Back-to-Back Scheduling—Two or more commercials which are run one immediately following the other.

BAR (Broadcast Advertising Reports)—An organization that monitors network TV activity and spending by brand as well as non-network activity in selected markets and reports to subscribers the position, length, and advertised brand of all announcements broadcast during a given week. Also reports network radio.

Barter—Acquisition by an advertiser of sizable quantities of spot time or free mentions at rates lower than card rates from broadcast stations in exchange for operating capital or merchandise. While direct negotiation between the advertiser and station is possible, it is more common for barter to be arranged through a middleman, a barter agency or a film producer or distributor, who may have procured the time through an exchange of film or taped shows.

"B" Counties—All counties not included under "A" that are either over 150,000 population or in a metro area over 150,000 population according to the 1970 census.

Billboard—An identifying announcement of sponsorship at the beginning, end or breaks of radio sponsored programs and television programming. Billboards are not sold, but usually are a bonus, based on the advertiser's volume or commitment with the program or the broadcaster. Usually 5-10 seconds in length. Also an outdoor poster.

Black & White (B&W, B/W)—Printing with black ink on white paper (or vice versa); no color. Also known as monotone.

Blanket Coverage—Total coverage by television and radio of a given geographic area.

Bleed—An advertisement in which part or all of the illustration or copy runs past the usual margins out to the edge of a page. Bleed insertions are generally sold at a premium price, usually 15% over the basic rate.

Brand Development—The number of cases, units or dollar volume of a brand sold per one thousand population; often indexed on an area-by-area basis to the national level for a Brand Development Index, or BDI. Also called Category Development.

Broadside—A promotion piece consisting of one large sheet of paper, generally printed on one side only.

Brochure—An elaborate booklet, usually bound with a special cover.

Bulk Circulation—These are sales in quantity lots of an issue of a magazine or newspaper. The purchases are made by individuals or concerns and the copies are usually directed to lists of names supplied by the purchasers. In the A.B.C. report, bulk circulation is listed separately from single-copy sales.

Bulk Sales—Sales of copies of a publication in quantity to one purchaser to be given free by him. Many advertisers do not consider Bulk Sales to be a valuable part of a publication's circulation. (See Circulation).

Bulldog Edition—An edition which is issued and on sale earlier than regular editions. Usually applies to morning newspapers. There are also Bulldog Sunday editions which go on sale Saturday night.

Business Building Test—Tests run by specific brands designed to determine if a marketing or advertising plan change will produce enough additional business for the brand to pay the required costs of the change.

Business Paper—A publication directed to a particular industry, trade, profession or vocation. A horizontal business paper is designed to reach all groups in a broad trade or industry regardless of locations or occupational titles. A vertical publication is for a specific profession, trade or occupational level within or across various industries.

C

Cancellation Date—The last date on which it is possible to cancel advertising. Such dates occur for print, outdoor, and broadcasting.

Car Card—A standard 11" high siderack card, generally with poster-like design, placed in buses, street cars and subways. Common sizes are 11" x 28", 11" x 42", 11" x 56".

Card Rate—The cost of time and space quoted on a rate card.

Case Allowance—An allowance or discount which a manufacturer or wholesaler gives to a retailer on each case of product he purchases in return for which the retailer is to use the money to advertise the product.

Cash Discount—A deduction allowed by print media (usually 2% of the net) for prompt payment (e.g., within 15 to 30 days), generally passed along by the agency to the advertiser to encourage collections.

Cash Refund Offer—A type of mail-in offer used by a brand, or group of brands, which offers cash to the consumer if she provides proof of purchase.

Category Development Index (CDI)—Means the same as a Market Development Index. Essentially, the percent of total U.S. sales of a product category related to population percent in a geographical market.

C.A.T.V.—Community Antenna (or cable) TV services that deliver high quality TV signals to homes via coaxial cable. Also called cable television.

C.C.A. (Controlled Circulation Audit)—An organization which audits the circulation statements of publications which are sent free to selected lists.

"C" Counties—All counties not included under "A" or "B" that are either over 35,000 population or in a metro area over 35,000 population according to the 1970 census.

Center Spread—An advertisement appearing on the two facing center pages of a publication.

Chainbreak—A 15-to 20-second announcement between network TV programs, generally in Prime Time. In radio, it is normally 30 seconds.

Checking Copy—A copy of a publication sent to an advertiser and his agency as proof that the advertisement appeared as ordered.

Circulation—In print, the number of copies of a vehicle distributed based on an average of a number of issues. In broadcast: the number of television or radio households that tune in to a station a minimum number of times within a broad time period (once a month, or once a week). In outdoor, total number of people who have an opportunity to see a given showing of billboards within a specified time, such as an 18-hour period.

City Zone—A geographic area which includes the corporate limits of the central city of the market plus any contiguous areas which have substantially the same built-up characteristics of the central city. This provides a method of reporting newspaper circulation according to ABC standards.

Class A, B, C Rates—Rates for the most desirable and costly television time usually between 6 p.m. and 11 p.m., are called Class A rates; the next most costly is Class B, and so on. Each station sets its own time classifications.

Class Magazines—The term loosely used to describe publications that reach select high-income readers in contrast to magazines of larger circulations, generally referred to as mass magazines. There is a growing trend at present to classify the readers of these magazines by their interests rather than income.

Clear Time—Process used by an advertiser to reserve time or a time period with a local station and by a network to check with its affiliates on the availability of a time period.

Clearance—To obtain a time period for a program or commercial on a station or to obtain approval to use advertising from clients, legal and/or medical counsel or network continuity departments.

Closing Date—The final date to contractually commit for the purchase of advertising space. Generally, cancellations are not accepted after the closing date, although some publications have a separate cancellation date which may fall before the closing date. Also used in connection with supplying ad material to the publication.

Coaxial Cable—Usually abbreviated to "cable." The mechanical facility used by networks for the transmission of a "live" program from city to city. The cable is actually owned by A.T.&T. and, in turn, is rented to the networks by them. Sometimes, microwave broadcasting operations are utilized instead of these cables. More generally, coaxial cable is any electrical cable capable of carrying large information loads with minimal distortion (cf. CATV).

Combination Rate—A discounted rate offered to encourage use of two or more stations, newspapers, magazines, etc., having common ownership. Occasionally, an advertiser has no choice but to buy the combination as space/time may not be sold separately.

Commercial Audience—The audience to a specific commercial as determined by a survey which elicits information of what program viewers were doing just before, during and just after the commercial. The commercial audience is operationally defined as those people who were physically present in the room with the TV set at the time the commercial was on.

Commercial Break—In broadcasting, an interruption of programming in which commercials are broadcast.

Commercial Delivery—That part of the audience actually exposed to a particular commercial.

Commercial Minutes Per 100 TV Homes—These data are the product of the average rating of a program or spot by the number of commercial minutes delivered.

Commercials Per 100 TV Homes—Measure of the gross weight of a broadcast effort. The data are developed by mutiplying the average rating of a program or spot by the number of commercials delivered.

Confirmation—Broadcast media statement that a requested time slot is available to a prospective client.

Consecutive Weeks Discount—A discount which is granted to an advertiser who uses from 26 to 52 weeks of advertising on a station or network without interruption.

Consumer Magazine—A magazine whose editorial content appeals to the general public, or a specific segment or layer of the public without regard to occupation. As differentiated from trade magazines.

Contiguity Rates—In network broadcasting, reduced rates offered to an advertiser who sponsors two or more programs in adjacent time periods. Such rates may be applied to non-contiguous time periods when an advertiser contracts for a minimum time allotment during one day (vertical contiguity) or during one week (horizontal contiguity).

Continuity—A method of scheduling advertising so that audiences have an opportunity of seeing ads at regular intervals. There are many patterns that could be used from advertising once each day of the year to once a month.

Controlled Circulation Publications—Publications that confine or restrict their distribution to special groups on a free basis. Some controlled circulation is solicited, while most is non-solicited.

Cooperative Advertising—Advertising run by a local advertiser in conjunction with a national advertiser. The national advertiser usually provides the copy and/or plates and also shares the cost with the local retailer. In return, the national advertiser receives local promotion for his product. The name of the local advertiser and his address appear in the ad.

Co-Sponsorship—The participation of two or more sponsors in a single program where each advertiser pays a proportionate share of the cost.

Cost Efficiency—The effectiveness of media as measured by a comparison of audience, either potential or actual, with cost and expressed as a cost-per-thousand units of audience.

Cost Per Thousand (CPM)—A figure used in comparing or evaluating the cost efficiency of publications or broadcast schedules. For publications, it is determined by dividing the rate or specific advertisement cost by the circulation or number of readers or number of ad noters. For broadcast media, it is determined by dividing the commercial rate or specific program cost by the number of homes or people tuned in. In determining the CPM homes or people reached per commercial minute by a program or spot, the average audience is used. Simply, the advertising cost to reach 1,000 units of audience.

Cost Ratio—Term used by Starch. The cost ratio is an adjustment made to the score obtained on each readership measure. The score is translated into "Per $" terms (based on the magazine's reported *primary* circulation and the cost of the ad in terms of size, color, etc.) and then stated as a percentage of the average "Per $" scores of *all* ads studied in the same issue. (See Noted, Per $, Starch).

Coupon Insert—An IBM-type coupon attached to a carrier unit which is bound into the subscription copies of a magazine much like a normal page is inserted. Several configurations are available depending on the size of magazine, the manner in which it is bound, and the number of coupons to be carried. (See Back-up Page, Tip-ins)

Couponing—Distribution of coupons by a manufacturer through the mail or by household calls offering a price reduction at the store on a product.

Coverage—A term used to define a medium's geographical potential. In newspapers, the number of circulation units of a paper divided by the number of households in the metro area. In magazines, the percent of a demographic market reached by a magazine. In radio-television, the percent of television households that can tune-in to a station (or stations) because they are in the signal area. In outdoor, the percent of adults who pass a given showing and are exposed in a 30-day period. In previous years, coverage meant the same as reach. Today, the meaning will depend on which medium is being discussed.

Cross-Plug—An advertiser who purchases a network TV program on an alternate week basis frequently wants to receive exposure on the show every week. Therefore, he trades off a commercial, usually a minute with another alternate week sponsor of the show.

Cume—A term used in broadcast which is Nielsen's shorthand for net cumulative audience of a program or of a spot schedule (radio or TV) in 4 week's time. Based on total number of unduplicated TV homes or people reached.

Cumulative Audience—The net unduplicated audience of a campaign, either in one medium or a combination of media. Sometimes called "reach."

Cut-Ins—In a specific market or region, different copy or another advertisement is used to replace an originating commerical in a network program. This is frequently used in testing products.

Cycle—An interval within a contract year at the end of which, upon proper notice, an advertiser may cancel network stations and/or facilities. Weekly and multi-weekly program cycles usually are 13 weeks in length while co-sponsored program cycles usually encompass 13 major broadcasts. Also refers to the 13-week periods used as a base for talent and use fee payments.

d

"D" Counties—Essentially rural counties in the Nielsen classification system of A, B, C, D counties.

Daypart—A broadcast day is divided into parts for analytical purposes. Usually morning, afternoon, early fringe, prime time and late fringe.

Direct Mail Advertising—Letters, folders, reprints or other material sent through the mails directly to prospective purchasers.

Direct Response Advertising—Advertising material reproduced in quantity and distributed directly to prospects, either by mail, house-to-house delivery, bag stuffers, etc.

Directory-Type Advertising—Advertising in a directory and popularly used to signify any advertising which consumers may deliberately consult, i.e., department store or food advertisements.

Discounts—A reduction from regular rates when an advertiser contracts to use quantities of advertising. Discounts in print may consider amount of space bought and frequency of insertion. Discounts in network broadcasting may be based upon number of dayparts used, frequency or weight and length of contract; in local broadcasting, discounts will consider number of spots per week, length of contract or purchase of plans or packages.

DMA (Designated Market Area)—A Nielsen term for those counties in which the home stations have a plurality of the counties's share of television viewing or the largest average quarter-hour audience.

Downscale—A general description of a medium's audience of lower socio-economic class members.

Drive time—The times of day (both morning and afternoon) when most people drive to or from work (about 7 to 9 a.m. and 4 to 6:30 p.m.).

Duplication—The number or percent of people in one vehicle's audience who also are exposed to another vehicle.

e

Earned Rate—The rate which an advertiser has earned based on volume or frequency of space or time used to obtain a discount.

Efficiency—Ratio of cost to audience used to compare print media. The cost of advertising to reach a particular audience, generally expressed in terms of cost-per-thousand circulation, cost-per-thousand readers, etc. Newspaper efficiency is expressed in terms of milline rates. (See: Milline)

Episodes (Programs) Per 100 TV Homes—This figure, like Gross Rating Points, is a measure of the gross weight of a television or radio effort. It can be figured as the product of the Total Audience rating and the number of programs delivered during a 4-week period. Commercial Minutes Per 100 TV Homes are a product of the Average Audience rating and number of commercial minutes delivered.

Ethnic Media—A catch-all term for those newspapers, magazines, radio and television stations which direct their editorial and/or language to specific ethnic groups.

Expansion Plan—An outline of the media to be used and timing thereof for a brand which plans to apply a theoretical national plan to portions of the country subsequent to testing and prior to actual national application. The *Expansion Areas* are the geographical units in which the product is to be sold.

Exposure—Open eyes facing a medium. Practically, however, measurements are based on respondents who either say with assurance that they have looked into a given magazine, or that, after looking at a list of magazines, respondents say that he looked into those he checked on the list. In broadcast, those who are sitting in the room while a television or radio program is being broadcast.

Exposure, Depth of—The value credited to an increased number of broadcast program commercials or multi-page spreads in the form of heightened consciousness of an advertisement. While the audience for such media usage generally does not increase proportionally with the amount of additional investment made, the depth of exposure tends to provide adequate compensation.

Exposure, Opportunity of—The degree to which an audience may reasonably be expected to see or hear an advertising message.

f

Facing—Used in outdoor advertising to refer to the number of billboards used in one display. A single facing is one billboard. A double facing is two billboards either joined or with less than 25 feet between them. A triple facing is three billboards, etc.

Farm Publication—A publication devoted to general agricultural topics edited for farm families or farmers.

Field Intensity Map—A broadcast coverage map showing the quality of reception possible on the basis of its signal strength. Sometimes called a Contour Map.

Field Intensity Measurement—The measurement of a signal delivered at a point of reception by a radio transmitter in units of voltage per meter of effective antenna height, usually in terms of microvolts or millivolts per meter.

15 and 2—The usual terms on which advertising media is ordered by advertising agencies for their clients, i.e., 15% commission is allowed by the media on the gross cost, plus 2% discount on the net amount for prompt payment.

Fifty-Fifty Plan—In cooperative advertising, the equal sharing by a manufacturer and a dealer of the cost of a manufacturer's advertisement which appears over a dealer's name.

Flat rate—An advertising rate that does not include any discounts.

Flighting—A method of scheduling advertising for periods of time after which no advertising is done, followed by a resumption of an in-and-out pattern.

FM (Frequency Modulation)—FM is a radio broadcast band in the broadcast spectrum different from that used by AM stations. There is no static in FM radio reception.

Forced Combination—Morning and evening newspapers owned by the same publisher which are sold to national advertisers only in combination. Some forced combinations are morning and evening editions of the same newspaper.

Four-Color (4/C)—Black and three colors (blue, yellow, red). Standard color combinations used by practically all publications offering color advertising.

Fractional Showing—In outdoor, a showing less than No. 25, offered in certain areas.

Franchise Position—A specified position in a publication (e.g., Back Cover, frontispiece) for which an advertiser is granted a permanent franchise (or right to use) as long as he continues to use it. Franchise positions are sometimes specific locations such as "opposite punched hole recipe page" in Better Homes & Gardens. Some positions are negotiated for specific issues, while others may be granted by frequency of use (i.e., six out of twelve issues.) If a given position is not used one year, it usually must be renegotiated to regain it.

Free Publication—A publication sent without cost to a selected list of readers. Circulation may or may not be audited by CCA, but cannot qualify for ABC audit unless at least 70% of circulation is paid.

Frequency—The average number of times an audience unit is exposed to a vehicle. Usually referred to as Average Frequency.

Frequency Discount—A discount given for running a certain number of insertions irrespective of size of advertisement within a contract year. Similar discounts are available in broadcasting, but may be of two types: frequency per week as well as total number of announcements in a contract year.

Frequency Distribution—A breakdown of the relative frequency of occurrence of various types of results in a collection of data. A frequency distribution can be presented either in a table or graphically as bar charts, pie charts, other symbols or ideographs, or as curves.

Fringe Time—Time periods preceding and following peak set-usage periods and adjacent network programming blocks. Usually represents for television, Class B or C time—4:30-7:30 p.m., or after 11 p.m..

Full Position—Preferred position for a newspaper advertisement, generally following and next to reading matter, or top of column next to reading matter. When specifically ordered, it costs more than a run-of-paper (ROP) position.

Full-Program Sponsorship—A regular program sponsored by only one advertiser.

Full Showing—In car card advertising, usually denotes one card in each car of a line in which space is bought. In the New York subways, a full showing consists of 2 cards in each car; ½ showing, 2 cards in every other car. In outdoor poster advertising, a full or "100-intensity" showing indicates use of a specified number of panels in a particular market.

g

Gatefold—A special space unit in magazines, usually consisting of one full page plus an additional page or part of a page which is an extension of the outer edge of the original page and folds outward from the center of the book as a gate.

General Editorial Magazines—A consumer magazine not classified as to a specific audience.

Geographic Split-Runs—A split-run where one ad is placed in all of the circulation which falls within specified geographic area and another ad is placed in other geographic areas or the balance of the country.

Grid Card—A rate card in which a station's spots are priced individually, with charges related to the audience delivered.

Gross—The published rate for space or time quoted by an advertising medium, including agency commission, cash discount and any other discounts.

Gross Audience—The combined audience of a combination of media or a compaign in a single medium. For example, if Medium A and Medium B have audiences 7 and 6 million, respectively, their gross audience is 13 million, To go from gross audience to net audience, one must subtract all duplicate audiences.

Gross Impressions—The sum of gross audiences of all vehicles used in a media plan. This number represents the message weight of a media plan. The number is sometimes called the "tonnage" of the plan, because it is so large.

GRP (Gross Rating Points)—A measure of the total gross weight delivered by a TV or radio program or a spot schedule. It is the sum of the ratings for the individual spots or programs. A rating point means an audience of 1% of the coverage base. Hence 150 gross ratings points means 1.5 messages per average home. Gross rating points are not a measure of net audience, but the sum of ratings for all elements in a broadcast advertising schedule. (See Chapter 5 for additional uses).

Gutter—The inside margins of facing pages; the point at which the publication is bound.

h

Half-Page Spread—An advertisement composed of two halp-pages facing each other in a publication.

Half Run—In transportation advertising, a car card placed in every other car of the transit system used. Also called a half service.

Half Showing—One half of a full showing of car cards; a 50-intensity showing of outdoor posters or panels.

Hiatus—A period of time, usually during the summer (commonly of eight to thirteen weeks) when a sponsored program is discontinued due to the seasonal change in audience habits. The word indicates that the advertiser will return at a later date.

Hi-Fi Preprinted Insert—A full page, four-color rotogravure advertisement printed by a supplier on coated newsprint and furnished to a newspaper in roll form for insertion in lieu of a page of standard newsprint. As the roll is red into the newspaper, the newspaper prints normal editorial/advertising matter on the reverse side and, in some cases, a column of type of the advertisement itself. The advertiser pays the supplier for producing the ad and the newspaper for distributing the ads as part of the newspaper (usually B&W space rates plus an insert on charge). Generally, the cost efficiency is twice as expensive as ROP color. Because there is no accurate cut-off on Hi-Fi pages, the copy and illustration has a repeating "wallpaper" design in order to insure full ad exposure.

Hitchhike—An isolated commercial for a sponsor's secondary product (not advertised in the main body of the show) which is given a free ride following the end of the program.

Holding Power—The degree to which a program retains its audience throughout a broadcast. It is expressed in a percentage determined by dividing the average audience by the total audience.

Holdover Audience—The audience a program acquires from listeners or viewers who tuned to the preceding program on the station and remained with the station.

Home Service Book—A publication with editorial content keyed to the home and home-living. Examples of this are *Better Homes & Gardens* and *House Beautiful*.

Horizontal Cume—The cumulative audience rating for two programs in the same time period on different days.

Horizontal Discount—Broadcast media discount earned by company to advertise over an extended time period, usually a year.

Horizontal Half-Page—A half-page of advertisement running from the left hand to the right hand or right hand to left hand side of a page.

Horizontal Trade Publications—A business publication editorially designed to be of interest to a variety of businesses or business functions.

H.U.T.—A term used by Nielsen and referring to the total number of TV households using their television sets during a given time period. Can be used for the total U.S. or a local market.

i

ID—An 8-10 second announcement between TV programs. Usually station identifications are superimposed on the commercial. In that case, there are eight seconds of video for the advertiser and 10 seconds of audio.

Impact—The extent and degree of consumer awareness of an advertisement within a specific medium, and the degree to which a medium affects its audience.

Impression Studies—Starch provides studies of print ads and TV commercials; called, respectively, "Starch Reader Impression Studies" and "Starch Viewer Impression Studies," which try to evaluate the *kind* of impression made by the ad.

Imprints—Used in cooperative poster advertising programs. Sometimes the local dealer pays a portion of the cost of the poster space and the parent company pays the remaining portion. The dealer's name is placed on the bottom portion of the poster design (about 1/5 of the total copy area) so that his store is listed as the place to buy the product advertised.

Index—An Index score is a ratio in percentage terms of a number of some stated base or average which has been converted to a score of 100. Starch scores are put in "Index" terms when stated as a percentage of the appropriate Starch Adnorm for ads of the same size and color-use for the same product class in the same magazine among the same sex. Also, regional per capita sales can be put on an index basis relative to the U.S. average.

Industrial Advertising—Advertising of capital goods, supplies and services directed mainly to industrial or professional firms which require them in the course of manufacture.

Inherited Audience—The carry-over from one program to another on the same station of a portion of the preceding program's audience.

In-home—Refers to that portion of media exposure (reading, listening or viewing) done in the home.

Insert—A special page printed on superior or different paper stock by the advertiser and forwarded to the publisher for binding in the publication or to be inserted loose. Usually used for fine color work.

Insertion—An advertisement in a print medium.

Insertion Order—Authorization from advertiser or agency to publisher to print an advertisement of specified size on a given date or dates at a definite rate. Copy instructions, cuts or complete plates may accompany the order or be sent later.

Issue-Life—The time during which a publication accrues most of its total readership. For a weekly, this is generally five weeks. For a monthly, three months.

Instantaneous Rating—The size of a broadcast audience at a given instant (or point in time) expressed as a percentage of some base.

Intensity—In outdoor advertising, the strength of combinations of poster locations throughout a city in terms of coverage or repetition opportunities. A 100 showing has a 100 intensity. A 100 showing (therefore, a 100 intensity) varies from city to city.

Interim Statement—Sworn circulation statement of a publisher made quarterly to the ABC at the publisher's option and issued unaudited but subject to audit. A situation that might call for an interim statement would occur when a community served by more than one newspaper loses one of them through consolidation or discontinuance and its circulation is absorbed by the other newspaper. (See Publishers' Statement.)

Island Position—Newspaper and magazine advertisement entirely surrounded by reading matter or margin. This position is not generally sold. Also, the placement of a commercial away from any other commercial; i.e., with program content on both sides.

Isolated 30—A straight 30-second commercial (rather than one in piggyback).

j

Junior Page—In print, a page size which permits an advertiser to use the same engraving plates for small and large page publications. The ad is prepared as a full-page unit in the smaller publication, appears in the larger publication as a "junior page" with some editorial on two or more sides.

Junior Panel—A small-scale version of the 24-sheet poster displayed in suburban shopping areas and neighborhood store walls. Also called Six-sheet Poster.

Junior Unit—In print, a page size which permits an advertiser to use the same engraving plates for small and large-page publications. The advertisement is prepared as a full-page unit in the smaller publication (such as Holiday) as a "junior unit" with some editorial matter on two or more sides.

k

Keying an Advertisement—Identification within an advertisement or coupon which permits inquiries or requests to be traced to a specific advertisement.

l

Lead-In—Words spoken by announcer or narrator at the beginning of some shows to perform a scene-setting or recapitualation function. Also a broadcast program positioned before another program.

Lead-Out—In relation to audience flow, the program following an advertiser's program on the same station.

Life—Of an advertisement, the length of time responses are received from an advertisement designed to elicit inquiries or other reactions. Of a publication, length of time responses to a specific advertisement are received.

Line—Agate line, the basic unit of publication space for measuring depth of space. In physical dimension, a line is one column wide and $1/_{14}$-inch deep. A newspaper ad that is 1500 lines in size would be, say 6 columns wide by 250 lines deep. Newspaper space is usually bought in terms of lines.

Lineage—A newspaper term denoting the number of (agate) lines in an ad or an ad schedule. Also, amount of total space run by a publication in certain categories, i.e., retail grocery lineage.

List Broker—In direct-mail advertising, an agent who rents prospect lists, compiled by one advertiser, and sold by the agent to another advertiser. He receives a commission for his services.

List House—In direct-mail advertising, an agent who sells prospect lists compiled by his organization to an advertiser.

Listener Diary—Method of TV or radio research whereby audience keeps continuing record of viewing or listening in a diary.

Listening Area—The geographic area covered by a station's signal, usually divided into primary and secondary areas.

Little America (or Little U.S.A.)—A test market translation method which equalizes the media weight in the test area with the weighted average (per capita) of the media weight which will be delivered by the national plan in all areas of the country.

Live Time—The time that the actual performance of a program is transmitted by interconnected facilities directly to the receiving stations at the moment of performance.

Live Time Delay—A delay which coincides with the local live time. Usually occurs when the station is non-interconected and thus unable to take a live feed.

Lloyd Hall Editorial Analysis—A study of the number of editorial pages a magazine devotes to various categories of product interest over a period of time. For example, the number of pages a magazine devotes to articles on food, home furnishings, fiction, news. This information is frequently used in analyzing the editorial content of a magazine before advertising is placed in it.

LNA-BAR (Leading National Advertiser-Broadcast Advertiser Reports)—A monthly analysis of television commercial allocations and gross time billing by brand, station line-ups, and program production talent estimates. A second volume reports network radio stations' line-ups by programs and advertisers.

Local Advertising—Newspaper advertising by local retailers, usually at a lower rate than that charged national advertisers.

Local Channel Station—A radio station that is allowed just enough power to be heard near its point of transmission and is assigned a channel on the air wave set aside for local channel stations (usually 250 watts.).

Local Media—Media whose coverage and circulation are confined to or concentrated in their market of origin. Usually, they offer two sets of rates: to the national advertiser and the local advertiser.

Local Rate—Rate charged by a medium to the local retail trade.

Local Time—Availabilities or times of broadcasting quoted in terms of local time rather than New York Time.

Locally Edited Supplements—Sunday magazine supplements similar in character to syndicated magazine supplements but which are owned and edited by the newspapers distributing them. These supplements are available in most of the larger cities throughout the country. Certain of them have banded together into groups for purposes of more efficient soliciting of national advertising and they offer group rates to advertisers who buy all the papers.

Loyalty Index—Frequency of listenership to a particular station.

m

Magazine Supplement—A magazine section of a Sunday or daily newspaper either distributed locally or nationally.

Mail-In Premium—A premium offered at the point-of-sale in a retail store to be obtained by the consumer by mailing a box top, coin or label to the manufacturer.

Mail Order Advertising—Type of advertising in which the complete sales transaction is handled through advertising and by mail.

Mail Survey Map—A broadcast coverage map prepared by tabulating cumulative, unsolicited mail received during a certain period or by tabulating listener response to a special order or contest run during a certain period.

Makegood—The rebroadcast of a program or announcement by a station free of charge when the original scheduled time is not available due to special events or when the orginal program or announcement was faultily transmitted. Also, the re-run of a print advertisement due to similar circumstances.

Market-by Market Allocation (MBM)—The MBM system of media/marketing planning that allocates a brand's total available advertising dollars against current and/or potential business on an individual TV market basis. MBM spends all advertising dollars (national and local) available in each market in proportion to current and/or anticipated business in the market. The result of MBM planning is to spend more accurately against anticipated sales and thereby generate greater business for a brand.

Market Index—The factor chosen to measure relative sales opportunities in different geographic or territorial units. Any quantitative information which makes it possible to estimate this might be used as a market index. A General Market Index is a factor developed which influences the purchase of a specific product or groups of related products. Sometimes called Market Development Index (See Category Development Index).

Market Outline—The measurement of the share on total purchases of a particular brand or groups of similar brands within a product category during a specific time period.

Market Pattern—The pattern of a product in terms of the relation between the volume and concentration of ither by total market or by individual market. A Thick Market Pattern one in which a high portion of all people are prospects for a product. A Thin Market Pattern is one in which a low portion of all people are prospects for a product.

Market Potential—That portion of a market that a company can hope to capture for its own product.

Market Profile—A demographic description of the people or the households or a product's market. It may also include economic and retailing information about a territory.

Market Share—A company's share of an industry's volume.

"Marriage" Splits—Occurs when more than one advertiser buys the total circulation of a magazine and each of the advertisers runs his ad in only a portion of that circulation. For example, an advertiser which has distribution in the western U.S. and one with distribution in the eastern U.S. may split an ad in a magazine which permits this. In this case, the advertiser with distribution in the west would use only that part of the magazine's circulation which reaches the west and the other advertiser would use the remainder.

Masked Identificaton Tests—A method of assessing an ad's effectiveness by finding the percentage of respondents who can identify the advertiser or brand when all identifying marks are concealed by paint or strips of tape.

Mass Magazines—Magazines of a general nature which appeal to all types of people in all localities. Such magazines are not selective in the types of audience they appeal to.

Maximal Rate—This represents the maximum cost of one line of advertising per million circulation at the open or flat rate.

Maximil-Minimil—Milline rates for newspapers offering sliding scale discounts. The maximil is the milline computed on the maximum line rate. The minimil is computed on the lowest line rate available.

Media Records—A quarterly detailed report of advertising volume in selected daily and Sunday newspapers in selected cities.

Media Strategy Statement—Prepared by an agency, outlining the specific media which they believe best accomplish the brand's marketing objectives (as outlined in the Market Strategy Statement) within the funds available. The Company media section is responsible for approving or suggesting appropriate changes.

Media Translation—The process of reducing a national advertising campaign to local level in order to test a product or campaign locally. It also can mean the expansion of a local advertising campaign to a national level.

Media Weight—The total impact of an advertising campaign in terms of number of commercials, insertions, reach and frequency, advertising dollars, etc.

Medium—Any vehicle used to convey an advertising message to the public such as newspapers, magazines, direct mail, radio, television, billboards, etc. Also called a medium class to distinguish it from individual vehicles. A magazine is a member of a medium class. *Newsweek* is a vehicle.

Message Weight—Refers to the gross number of advertising messages delivered by a vehicle or group of vehicles in a schedule.

Metro Area—A well-defined county or group of counties which comprise the central core of a market (usually based on governmental lines).

Middle Break—Station identification at about the half-way point of a show.

Milline Rate—A means of comparing rates of newspapers. It is the cost of 1 agate line per million circulation. The Milline Rate is computed by multiplying the line rate by 1 million and then dividing by the circulation. The factor of 1 million is used merely to provide an answer in the convenient terms of dollars and cents rather than in fractions of a cent.

Mills Shepard—A researcher whose New York-based firm studies readership of advertising in publications for various special industries.

Miniline—The milline rate for a newspaper at its minimum rate. See Maxiline

Minimil Rate—This represents the minimum cost of one line of advertising per million circulation at the lowest rate available after deducting all space or frequency discounts. (See Maximal-Minimal)

Minimum Depth—Most newspapers have minimum depth requirements for advertising. In general, an ad must be at least one inch high for every column it is wide. For example, if an advertiser wants an ad to run that is 8 columns wide, it must be at least 8 inches high.

Minimum Frequency—The minimum number of insertions which the company believes to be necessary in order to insure adequate continuity in a sustaining print compaign. For monthly magazines it is eight insertions in a year; for weekly magazines and Sunday magazine supplements the minimum adequate frequency is thirteen insertions yearly.

Minute-by-Minute Profile—Nielsen minute-by-minute program audience data. Used to study audience gains and losses during specific minutes of the program and to aid in placing commercials at times in which they receive maximum audiences.

Monitor—To check timing, program and commercial content of individual broadcasts of radio and/or television shows.

Multi-Network Area Rating—This rating, which is tabulated by Nielsen, measures a program's performance in 70 cities with 3 or more TV stations. West coast stations are not included in the MNA.

Multistation Lineups—The policy of buying more than one station in a market.

n

National Advertising Rates—Rates for newspaper space which a national advertiser must pay as distinguished from local rates applying to local retailers. National advertising rates are higher than local rates.

National Plan—The tactics in advertising campaigns of trying to get all the business that can be secured all over the country at one time. When correctly used, it is the outgrowth of numerous local plans.

National Rating—A rating of all households or individuals tuned in to a program on a national base. Sometimes the base is all televison or radio households in the country. Other times, the base is only those households that can tune in to the program because they are in the signal area of a station carrying the program.

NCH (Nielsen Clearing House)—Handles the administration work associated with processing coupons.

NCS (Nielsen Coverage Service)—This provides station coverage and circulation information rather than program audience measurements. The data are reported for each station in terms of total daytime and total evening audiences over the span of the day, week and the month, on a county-by-county basis.

National Media—Media which are national in scope, and have only one rate base, a "national" rate.

Net Paid Circulation—A term used by ABC audit reports and Publisher's Statements referring to circulation which has been paid for at not less than 50% of the basic newsstand or subscription price.

Net Plus—The net cost of a print ad, commercial or program with an earned discount added on.

Net Unduplicated Audience—The combined cumulative audience for a single issue of a group of magazines or broadcasts.

Net Weekly Audience—In broadcast research, the number of families tuned in at least once to a program aired more than once a week.

Network—Two or more stations contractually united to broadcast programs, i.e., Network Programs.

Network Affiliate—A broadcast station which is part of a network and therefore offers network programs.

Network Franchise—A brand's right to retain the sponsorship of a program at the sponsoring brand's discretion. This right is acquired by agreeing to sponsor a program on a continuing basis.

Network Identification—Acknowledgment of a network affiliation at the end of a network broadcast.

Network Option Time—Time on network affiliates for which the network has selling priority. Also called Network Time.

Newspaper Syndicate—A business concern which sells to the press special material (columns, photographs, comic strips) for simultaneous publication in a number of newspapers.

N.I.A.A. (National Industrial Advertisers Association)—An organization of advertisers, agencies and media, formed to promote the effective use of industrial advertising and marketing.

Nielsen—The A. C. Nielsen Company is the world's largest research company with world-wide operations. It operates a wide variety of syndicated services: NTI—a national television rating service using audimeters to collect set-tuning data: Food & Drug

Index—a service collecting information on retail sales movement by means of store audits: NMS—a service collecting audience data by personal interview and diaries to television programs, publicatons (magazines and newspapers): NSI—a local television rating service.

Nielsen Market Section Rating—A. C. Nielsen reports television ratings by zone breakdowns as well as nationally. These rating breakdowns are: Territory; County-Size Groups; Age of Housewife; Age of Household Head; Size of Family; Time Zone.

Nielsen Rating—TV program rating which uses set-tuning data from audimeters. The Nielsen rating is used to refer to households who have viewed a program six or more minutes. This audience definition is also referred to as the "total" audience as opposed to the "average" audience which is the audience to the average minute of a program.

90-Day Cancellation—All poster advertising is cancellable on 90 days' notice to the plant. This means that the advertiser or his agency must notify the poster plant owner 90 days prior to the contract posting date.

N.O.A.B. (National Outdoor Advertising Bureau)—A sales representative organization which services outdoor advertising for member advertising agencies and their clients.

Noted—The basic measure of the Starch method for testing print ads. The *Noted Score* represents the percentage of respondents (claimed readers of the issue) who say they saw the ad when they first read or looked into that magazine issue: i.e., claim recognition of the ad.

NSI (Nielsen Station Index)—A service that measures local TV station ratings.

NTI—Nielsen Television Index. A report on network televison viewing.

O

O.A.A.A. (The Outdoor Advertising Association of America, Inc.)—An organization composed of standard poster advertising and painted display advertising plant operations.

O & O Station—A station owned and operated by a network.

Obtained Score—This is a Gallup and Robinson term for the actual percentage of respondents who prove recall of a print ad *before the score is adjusted* for color and size or converted to an index score. It is the basis for the final score.

Off Card—The use of a special rate not covered by a rate card.

Offensive Spending—Advertising activity intended to secure new business.

One-Time Rate—The highest rate charged by a medium not subject to discounts. Sometimes called "open" or "transient" rate.

Open End—A broadcast that leaves the commercial spots blank to be filled in locally.

Open End Transcription— A recorded program usually sold on a syndicated basis in various cities and produced so that local commercial announcements may be inserted at various points throughout the show.

Open Rate—In print, the highest rate charged to an advertiser on which all discounts are placed. Also called base rate.

Option Time—Network Option Time is that time reserved by the networks in contract with their affiliates and for which the network has prior call under certain conditions for sponsored network programs. Station Option Time is that time reserved by the local stations for local and national spot shows.

Orbit—A scheduling method used by stations which consists of rotating an advertiser's commercial among different programs and/or time periods. Usually sold along with a spot package.

O.T.O.—One-time-only, a spot that runs only once; bought outright or a makegood.

Outdoor Advertising—Display-type advertising (billboards, posters, signs, etc.) placed out-of-doors, along highways and railroads, or on walls and roofs of buildings.

Outdoor Advertising Plant—An organization which builds and maintains outdoor displays consisting of painted bulletins and/or poster panels.

Overlapping Circulation—Duplication of circulation when advertising is placed in two or more media reaching the same prospects. Sometimes desirable to give additional impact to advertising.

p

P.A.A.A.—Premium Advertising Association of America, Inc.

P4C—Abbreviation for Page Four Color. Other abbreviations are P2C (Page Two Color), PB&W (Page Black and White), 3/5P4C (3/5 Page Four Color), 2C (second cover), BC (back cover), etc.

Package—A special show or series of shows bought by an advertiser (usually for a lump sum), which includes all components ready to telecast. Also, a program property in which all elements from script to finished production are owned and controlled by an individual or organization, commonly known as a "packager." A combination of programs or commercials offered by a network for sponsorship as an entity at one price. Also spot TV is sometimes sold as a package.

Packaged Goods—Mostly food, soap, and household products that are marketed in the manufacturer's package, wrapper or container.

Package Inclosure—A premium inclosed in a package.

Package Inserts—Separate advertising material included in packaged goods.

Package Plan—A plan by which an advertiser purchases a certain number of TV or radio spots per week, in return for which he receives a lower rate per announcement from the station. The advertiser agrees to run the specific number of spots each week and cannot split them up over a period of time.

Package Plan Discount—In spot television, a discount based upon frequency within a week; e.g., "5-plan," "10-plan."

Packager—An individual or company that produces a broadcast program or series of programs which are sold as complete units.

Painted Bulletin—This structure is approximately 50' long by 15' high and has a molding around the outer edges similar to a poster panel, but the copy message is painted on the face of this steel structure as contrasted to the poster panel.

Painted Display—In outdoor, a display painted on a bulletin structure or wall, which may be illuminated, and sold as an individual unit. The three standard structures are The Deluxe Urban Bulletin, The Standard Highway Bulletin, and The Standard Streamliner Bulletin. In addition to these are the Semispectacular (embellished painted bulletin) and the Painted Wall.

Painted Wall—An outdoor advertising unit, purchased individually, usually situated on a high-traffic artery or in a neighborhood shopping area.

Panel—A fixed sample of respondents or stores selected to participate in a research project and who report periodically on their knowledge, attitudes, activities. This is in contrast to the technique of using fresh samples each time. Also a master TV or radio control board, usually in a master control room. (See Consumer Panel and Store Panels.)

Panels—Regular & Illuminated units of outdoor advertising. A "regular panel" is a billboard which is not lighted at night. An "illuminated panel" is a billboard which is lighted from dusk until midnight.

Pantry Audit—Consumer research. A survey to tabulate brands, items, varieties of grocery store products in the home.

Parallel Location—An outdoor advertising location in which the poster panel is parallel to the road.

Participation Program—A commercial program co-sponsored by a number of "participating" advertisers. A program in which the audience participates; e.g., quiz show.

Participations—A station or network may program a segment of time to carry "participation announcements" which are sold to various advertisers for commercial use. The announcements are usually :30 to :60, but may be longer. Participations are announcements inside the context of programs as opposed to chain or station-breaks which are placed between programs.

Pass-along Audience—That part of the audience of a publication over and beyond those in the household of the original subscribers or purchasers.

Pass-along Reader—A person who reads a publication that he or a member of his family did not purchase. These readers must be taken into account in determining the total numbers of readers of a particular issue or a particular publication. (See Secondary Audience)

Pay TV—A television system providing programs which are available only to subscribing homes. Signals are generally transmitted via coaxial cables or telephone lines, and the subscriber is usually charged on a sliding scale for the number of programs actually tuned in.

Penalty Costs—In test market and expansion operation this refers to the premium which local replacement media cost over the national media that the brand would be using under their national plan.

Penetration—The percentage of total homes in a specified area owning at least one TV set.

Penetration Study—The study of the effectiveness of advertising on the public.

Percent composition—The percent of a demographic segment that use a given product within a given time period (or those exposed to a given medium). Example: if there are 7,672,000 female household heads who are aged 18-24 and 868,000 of them used a product within a given time period, then that represents 11.3% composition. The base is the 7 million female household heads.

Percent coverage—The percent of *all* users (not just a segment as in percent composition) who used a product within a given time period (or who were exposed to a medium). Example: if the 868,000 women, aged 18-34 years old used a product within a given time period, what percent of all users does that represent? (All users represent 9,349,000 users). Answer: 9.3%. Percent coverage for a demographic segment when added together equal 100%.

Per Inquiry Advertising (P.I. Advertising)—An agreement between a media owner and an advertiser in which the owner agrees to accept payment for his facilities on the basis of the number of inquiries or completed sales resulting from advertising, soliciting inquiries or direct sales.

Persons using radio (PUR)—The percent of an area's population (over 12) listening to a radio at any given time.

PIB (Publisher's Information Bureau, Inc.)—PIB Service is a monthly analysis of both advertising space and revenue in General Magazines, National Farm Magazines and Newspaper Sections. It is designed to give convenient summaries of national advertising expenditures by advertisers and by media.

Piggyback—The back-to-back scheduling of two or more brand commercials of one advertiser in network or spot positions.

Piggybacking—This is the integration of either positive or negative film prints. A piggyback film print contains two *different* commercials (e.g., :30/:30 or :40/:20) integrated so that two separate products of a company can be broadcast in the time normally allotted for one, while the expense remains the same.

Pilot (Pilot Film)—A sample of a proposed TV series used for demonstration.

Plan Rates—The rate paid by an advertiser who purchases a TV or radio package plan. The rates are lower than if the spots were purchased otherwise since the advertiser agreed to run a specific number of spots each week. (See 12-Plan)

Plant Operator—This term is applied to the company that owns and maintains poster panels in any given market. The "plant operator" rents space on his poster panels to advertisers in 30-day units. He leases or owns the land on which the poster panel is erected.

Pony Spread or Junior Spread—An advertisement appearing on two facing pages of a publication with the advertisement occupying only part of each page. This contrasts with a full-page spread advertisement which occupies the complete facing pages.

Pony Unit—A smaller-size version of a standard advertising unit. These are developed when a large page-size publication allows the use of plates from small or page-size publications. (See Junior unit.)

Position—An advertisement's place on a page and the location of the page in the publication. A Preferred Position is an especially desirable position obtained by paying an extra charge, or granted to an advertiser who has placed a heavy schedule in a publication, occasionally rotated among advertisers who have contracted for space above a specified minimum. In broadcast, programs or time spots considered most desirable by advertisers.

Post-Test—Study of actual, finished advertising *after* it has been published and telecast in actual media. Post-tests rely on the normal patterns of behavior to expose respondents to advertising.

Poster—A product sign intended to be displayed on a store window, or on an inside wall, large enough to be legible at a reasonable distance.

Poster Frames—In point-of-purchase advertising, frames for blowups of advertisements or posters. Layers of advertisements may be mounted on one frame, and the top one torn off to reveal a new one.

Poster Panel—A standard surface on which outdoor advertisements are mounted. The poster panel is the most widely used form of outdoor advertising. The standard panel measures 12' x 25' long, is usually made of steel with a wood, fiberglass, or metal molding around the outer edges. The 24-sheet poster is actually posted on this structure.

Poster Plant—The organization which builds and services poster panels and hangs poster sheets on them displaying illustration and/or message of advertiser.

Poster, Regular—A non-illuminated poster.

Poster Showing—Poster advertising is sold in packages called "showings." It is possible to buy #25, #50, #75, #100 and #200 showings. Basically, the #50 showing gives the advertiser adequate general coverage of traffic circulation in the market. The #100 showing is designed to provide more intense coverage of practically all major streets in a market. The #200 showing is one designed for maximum impact. Each poster plant owner decides how many panels will constitute a #50 showing or a #100 showing in his city.

Pre-emption—Recapture by the station or network of an advertiser's time in order to substitute a special program of universal value. For example, when the President speaks, he pre-empts the show regularly scheduled at that time.

Preferred Position—A position in a magazine or newspaper which is regarded as very excellent in terms of its ability to generate a large readership. Preferred position is usually located next to editorial material which has a high interest rate among the magazine readers.

Preprint—A reproduction of an advertisement before it appears in a publication.

Pre-Test—Study of advertisements prior to distribution via regular media channels. Advertising may be studies in rough or finished form; pretesting relies on some special means of exposing respondents to the advertisement other than the regular media planned—portfolios, dummy magazines, techistoscopes, etc.

Primary Audience—Members of an original family subscribing to or buying a publication who have at least opened and glanced through the publication in question.

Primary Circulation—The residents of households who get a publication (in contrast to pass-along circulation).

Primary Households—Households into which a publication has been introduced by purchase, either at the newsstand or by subscription, rather than by pass-along.

Primary Readers—The readers of a publication who reside in primary households.

Primary Service Area—In AM, or standard, broadcasting, the area in which a station signal is strongest and steadiest. Defined by Federal Communications Commission rules as the area in which the ground wave (the primary wave for broadcast transmission) is not subject to objectionable interference or objectionable fading. No similar term is officially used in TV broadcasting, although television engineering standards recognize three zones of signal service, existing in concentric rings from the transmitting tower: City Grade Service, A Contour, B Contour.

Prime Time—Time periods covering peak broadcast set-usage and highest ratings. Also is used as synonym for highest rate-classification time periods—Class A or better. For network television, usually considered to 8:00-11:00 p.m. CNYT.

Product Protection—Protection that an advertiser wants and sometimes gets against adjacency in a medium to advertising of a competitive product. Has special interest in television advertising.

Program Basis—A Nielsen cost estimate of a television show which takes into consideration the length-of-commitment discount as determined by whether the program is normally telecast every week, less-than-weekly, more-than-weekly or one-time-only. This discount is determined by the number of telecasts of the show and not the number used by a specific advertiser. Also, this basis disregards other programs sponsored by an advertiser which affect his discount structure.

Program Coverage—The number (or percent) of television households that can receive a program over one or more stations, because they are in the signal area of some station carrying the program.

Program Delivery (Rating)—Percentage of sample contacted tuned to a particular station at a particular time.

Program Station Basis (PSB)—A rating expressed in terms of a program's household coverage area rather than as a percent of total U.S.

Program Station Rating—A rating based on the television homes located in the area in which a program was telecast which permits an unbiased comparison of different programs regardless of variation in the number of homes capable of receiving the two programs.

322

Programming, Counter—A technique used by the networks to regulate audience flow by offering a program of a different type from that broadcast by a strong competitor in the same time period.

Promotion Allowance—Money received by a wholesaler or a retailer from a manufacturer or his representative for sales promotion other than advertising. (See Advertising Allowance.)

Psychographic—A term that describes consumers or audience members on the basis of some psychological trait or characteristic of behavior.

Publishers Information Bureau (PIB)—Supplies comprehensive monthly reports on advertising expenditures for national magazines.

Publisher's Statement—A notarized statement made by the publisher of his total circulation, geographic distribution, methods of securing subscriptions, etc. These are often used to fill in the time between audited statements.

Pulse (The Pulse, Inc.)—A research company generally concentrating on local TV and radio audience, but also offering other market research facilities. Use recall to collect listening/viewing data, often using rosters to facilitate the process.

Pure program ratings—A measurement of audience size in which estimates are made excluding program pre-emptions that have occurred during the survey period.

q

Qualified Issue Readers—Respondents who "qualify" for interview on the advertisements therein on the basis of having read the study issue of a magazine. Requirements for such qualification vary: for Starch interviews, readers have merely to claim they looked into the issue when shown the cover; for Gallup and Robinson studies, respondents most prove reading by correctly describing some article when shown the cover and Table of Contents.

Qualified Viewer—Respondent who has demonstrated viewing of a Tv program (on the basis of recall of at least one part of th episode), thus making him eligible or qualified for interview about commercials aired on that show.

Quantity Discount—A graduated discount on quantity purchases scaled to the number of cases in a single order; or, a periodic refund based upon the value of purchases over a period of time.

Quintile—The division of any sample of respondents into five equal-size groups ranging from the heaviest to the lightest amount of exposure to the medium. Samples may also be divided into quartiles or deciles in the same manner.

Quota—A pre-determine media goal in a market. Goals can be established in dollars spent, number of spots to be purchased, or GRP's to be achieved. Used as a target for the agency time buyer in implementing a media plan.

r

R.A.B. (Radio Advertising Bureau)—The promotion organization for the radio industry.

Radio Rating Point—One percent of the homes in the measured area whose sets are tuned to a station, used for making comparisons of spot stations.

Rate Card—A listing put out by a medium containing advertising costs, mechanical requirements, issue dates, closing dates, cancellation dates and circulation data. Rate cards are issued by both print and broadcast media annually or more often.

Rate Class—In broadcast media, the time charge in effect at a specified time.

Rate Differential—Among newspapers, the difference between the national and the local rates.

Rate-Holder—A minimum-sized advertisement placed in a publication during a contract period to hold a time or quantity discount rate. Also, an ID spot bought by the advertiser for the same reason.

Rate Protection—An advertiser who has contracted for advertising with a medium and generally is guaranteed that the advertiser's current rate under the old rate card will be protected for a period, usually from 3 to 6 months, should a new rate be used.

Reach—The number of different persons or homes exposed to a specific media vehicle or schedule at least once. Usually measured over a specific period of time, e.g., four weeks. (Also known as cume, cumulative, unduplicated or net audience.)

Reach, Cumulative—The total number of homes reached by a medium during a specific time period.

Reader Impression Studies—Studies carried out by Starch over and above their regular Readership Study to find out something of what the advertisement *meant* to respondents who "noted" the ad.

Reader Interest—Expression of interest by readers in advertisements they have read. Sometimes evaluated by unsolicited mail. Sometimes evaluated by the numbers of people who can remember having read material with interest. Also, an evaluation of the relative level of general interest in different types of products.

Reader Traffic—The movement from page to page by readers of a publication.

Readers—People who purchase a particular publication are called primary readers. Secondary readership (See Pass-Along Readers) must also be taken into account in determining the total numbers of average readers of a particular publication.

Readership—The degree of extent of reading advertisements by members of the publication who make up its potential audience. (See: Starch, Gallup and Robinson.)

Readership or Audience—The total average number of people who read a publication as distinguished from the circulation or number of copies distributed.

Readex—Research firm (located in St. Paul, Minnesota) which measures readers' claimed *interest* in the editorial matter and advertising in a number of specialized publications. The survey is handled by mail and is self-administered.

Read Most—Starch ad readership measurement term referring to magazines or newspaper readers who read 50% or more of the copy of a specific advertisement.

Rebate—A refund which reduces the contract price for merchandise. A term frequently used for advertising allowances. (See Floor Stock Protection.) Also given to advertisers by a certain media as a result of an advertiser's exceeding the contract minimum and earning a greater discount.

Recognition—The technique used to determine whether a person saw or heard a given print advertisement or broadcast commercial by actually shoeing him the ad or commercial (or playing it for him and inquiring whether or not he saw or heard it at a previous date in a specific medium. This technique was pioneered and is still being used by Starch.

Recordimeter—An electro-mechanical device utilized by the A. C. Nielsen Company in conjunction with the Audilog. It measures the amount of time that a radio or TV set is turned on during the day, but cannot distinguish among stations as does the audimeter.

Regional Edition—A geographical section of a national magazine's circulation which can be purchased by an advertiser without his having to purchase the rest of the magazine's circulation (as is required in a split run). A higher circulation CPM is usually paid for regional edtions, and Demographic Edtions.

Regional Network—A network of stations serving a limited area.

Remnant Space—Magazine space sold at reduced price to help fill out regional editions.

Remote—A broadcast originating outside the regular studio. Also called Nemo Broadcasts or Remote Pickups.

Remote Control—The operation of broadcasting a program from a point removed from the regular studios of the station.

Renewals—These are extra posters over and above the quantity actually needed to post the exact number of panels in a showing. They are shipped to the plant operator and, if one of the posters on display is damaged the poster plant operator has a complete poster design on hand to immediately replace the damaged poster. In print, this refers to magazine or newspaper subscriptions which people extend past their expiration dates.

Rep—Publisher's representative or station representative.

Replacement Media—Local media which are being used to replace national media in a test market or expanison area, i.e., local Rotogravure supplements, comic sections, black and white daily newspapers.

Response function—An effect of an ad in a medium, sometimes called "impact." These effects may be attitude change, degrees of brand awareness, or sales.

Retail Trading Zone—The area beyond the city zone whose residents regularly trade to an important degree with retail merchants in the city zone. These are defined by the Audit Bureau of Circulation.

Returns Per Thousand Circulation—A gauge of the effectiveness of media used in support of promotions computed by dividing the total number of returns by the circulation of the publication to which the returns are attributable. (See Keyed Advertisements)

Roll-out—A marketing strategy technique in which a brand is introduced in a limited geographical area. If it succeeds in that area, it is then introduced in adjacent areas and, if successful, in other adjacent areas until the entire country is covered.

R.O.P. (Run of Press)—A newspaper advertisement for which a definite position is not specified is inserted as run-of-press (or run-of-book), but usually in the general news sections. The term is also used in connection with color newspaper advertising to distinguish color advertising in the main portion of the paper from that placed in the magazine section (Sunday supplement).

R.O.P. Color—Color advertising in daily newspapers which may be placed anywhere in the newspaper at the discretion of the publisher. This term has generally come to mean any color advertising placed in the body of the daily newspapers (without regard to positioning) to differentiate it from comics or Sunday supplement color ads.

R.O.S. (Run-of-Schedule)—A broadcast commercial for which a definite time is not specified. For example, if it is nighttime commercial during prime time, it may be run at any time during this period. Also, times of a spot may vary from week to week, depending upon other requirements.

Roster Recall—Method of research in which a list of radio or TV programs is submitted to respondents for recall.

Rotating Painted Bulletins—Moving the advertiser's copy from one painted bulletin to another, usually every 30 days. This service is available in a limited number of cities. Offers advertiser an opportunity to cover a large area or a given market (over a long period of time) with a limited number of painted bulletins.

Rotation—The practice in store management of moving the older stock forward when restocking shelves or cases. The practice, in retail advertising, of scheduling a branded product or group of products to be featured at intervals throughout the year to maintain a desired stock balance. Also, the process of continuing a series of advertisements over and over again in a regular order.

Rotogravure (Roto)—Printing process where an impression is produced by sunken or deep etched letters or pictures in copper or zinc plate. The ink is held in indentation in the plates, not on the surface as in offset, or on the tops of dots or letters as in letterpress.

Runs—In television film syndication, the number of times a film has been telecast in a given area. The number of times a film may be run according to an advertiser's lease. A rerun among television film syndicators is an available program previously telecast in an area.

S

Sales Promotion—Those sales activities that supplement both personal selling and marketing, co-ordinate the two, and help to make them effective; for example, displays.

Satellite Station—A station which relays TV signals to areas which are beyond the usual coverage area of the parent TV station.

Saturation—A level of advertising weight several times above normal coverage and frequency levels standard for the market or product involved. Saturation implies simultaneous achievement of wide coverage and high frequency designed to achieve maximum impact coverage or both.

Saturation Showing—In outdoor, a showing of maximum intensity, designed to surpass complete coverage (the 100 showing) with repeat impressions. Often a 200 showing.

Scatter Plan—The use of announcements in a number of prime, nighttime network programs.

Schedule—A list of media to be used during an advertising campaign. A list of a product's advertising to be included in a medium's vehicle during a specific time. The chronological list of programs broadcast by a station.

Secondary Audience—Pass-along Readers who read a publication that they did not purchase. These readers must be taken into account in determining the total number of readers of a particular publication.

Secondary Service Area—The distant area in which a broadcast station's signal is subject to interference or fading, but can still be received.

Sectional Magazine—A magazine which is distributed only sectionally and not nationally (like Sunset, which is confined to the western states).

Selectivity index—Percent of total viewers or readers in a demographic or user group as divided by percent of population.

Selective Magazines—Magazines which, because of their nature and editorial content, appeal only to a certain type of audience.

Self-Liquidating Point-of-Purchase Unit—One for which the retailer wholly or partially pays.

Self-Liquidating Premium—A premium whose total cost is recoverable in the basic sales transaction.

Self-Mailer—A folder, booklet or other direct mail piece which provides space for addressing, postage and sealing, and therefore requires no envelope for mailing.

Semi-Liquidators—Premiums offered to the consumer whose cost is partially recovered by the manufacturer or merchant offering the inducement.

Sets-in-Use—The total number of sets tuned in to some program at a given time of day and day of week. At one time sets-in-use was equivalent to H.U.T., but today, its meaning is limited to sets, not households.

Share or Share-of-Audience—The audience to a program as a percent of all households using the medium at the time of the program's broadcast.

Share Identification (ID)—8 to 12-second spot announcement accompanying station identification.

Share of Market—The percentage of the total sales of a specified class of products which is held by or attributed to a particular brand at a given time.

Share of Mind—The percentages of the relevant population (or a sample of that population) who indicate awareness of, or preference for, the various brands within a product group. Specific meaning varies considerably with the method of measurement. It may be a test of salience or a test of total recall, aided or unaided. Usually refers to consumer awareness of brands in comparison with like measures of awareness for competing brands.

Shelter Magazines—Magazines dealing editorially with the home such as decorating, maintenance, gardening, etc. Additionally, these magazines carry a considerable amount of food editorial matter. Examples are *Better Homes & Gardens, American Home*.

Shopping Newspaper—A Newspaper published in a local community and containing mainly local news, shopping hints and suggestions, and advertisements. Often called a "shopper."

Short Rate—The additional charge incurred when an advertiser fails to use enough media time or space to earn a contract discount envisaged at the time of the original order.

Showing—In outdoor advertising, the number of posters offered as a unit in terms of 100 intensity and variations thereof. In transit advertising, the number of cards included in a unit of sale.

SIC (Standard Industrial Classification)—A classification system defined by the bureau of the budget for business establishments by type of activity. Used to facilitate analysis of business paper markets.

Simmon's Data—Print and broadcast media audience exposure and product-usage data reported by the W. R. Simmons and Associates Research Company.

Sliding Rate—A space or time rate in a medium which decreases as the amount of space or time used by an advertiser increases over a period of time.

Space Position Value—In outdoor, an estimate of the effectiveness of a particular poster location. The factors considered are the length of approach, the speed of travel, the angle of the panel to its circulation and the relation of the panel to adjacent panels.

Space Schedule—A schedule sent to the advertiser by his agency, showing the media to be used, the dates on which advertising is to appear, size of advertisements and cost of space.

Special—An elaborate one-time TV show employing known talent and running an hour or longer. Also, "spectacular."

Spill-in (or spill out)—The degree to which programming is viewed in adjacent ADI (or DMA) areas. Depending on the perspective, this is either spill-in or spill-out. Milwaukee television programming spills out of the Milwaukee DMA and spills into the Madison, Wisconsin area.

Split-in-Coverage—Coverage by a medium in a market which originates outside of that market. For example, circulation of a Chicago newspaper in Milwaukee.

Split-Run—A split-run consists of running two or more versions of an ad in alternate copies of the same magazine or newspaper. There are also split-runs in which one version of the ad appears in newsstand copies and one in mail subscription copies. Splits may also occur geographically.

Split-Run Tests—Research designed to test the effectiveness of various copy elements, prices, or types of offers by placing them in alternate copies of an issue. The various forms of the advertisement are evaluated by means of coupon or inquiry returns, or by orders placed for trial offers.

Sponsor Identification (SI)—The extent of identification of a program's sponsor or knowledge of his product or service. The percentage of listeners or viewers who correctly associate a program with the sponsor or his product is Sponsor Identification Index (SPI).

Sponsor's Rating—A rating determined by applying the sponsor identification index to the total audience rating.

Sponsor Relief—An advertiser who has a regular television program may wish to suspend activities for an off-season period; and makes the time available to another advertiser.

Spot—A time period filled entirely be a commercial or public service message and sold separately from the adjacent time periods. To buy time (programs and/or announcements) on a market-by-market basis from stations through their representatives. Also a time period.

Spot Announcement—Commercial placed upon individual stations, radio and TV often referred to merely as "spots."

Spot Programming—The process by which an advertiser secures the rights to a television program and places it on stations in selected markets without regard to network affiliation. The advertiser may own the television program outright, have rights to the program for a specific length of time or have the rights to the program in only a certain part of the country.

Spot Radio—The use of stations in selected markets without regard to network affiliation. May involve spot announcements or complete programs.

Spot Schedule—(1) A local spot announcement buy or a standard form which the agencies submit showing specific times, adjacencies, etc. of a brand's current spot announcements in a market.

Spot Television—The use of stations in selected markets without regard to network affiliation. May involve spot announcements or complete local programs.

Spread—An advertisement appearing on any two facing pages of a publication. Also, gross profit. The markup over cost expressed in cash or percentage terms. (See Gross Profit, Markup)

SRDS (Standard Rate & Data Service, Inc.)—A service which publishes the rates and discount structures of all major media. They also publish market research studies, often on media or market areas.

Staggered Schedule—Several advertisements scheduled in two or more publications, arranged so that the dates of insertion are alternated or rotated

Standard Metropolitan Statistical Area—An area which consists of one or more entire counties meeting specified criteria pertaining to population, metropolitan character, and economic and social integration between outlying counties and the central county determined by the Bureau of the Budget with the advice of the Federal Committee on Standard Metropolitan Areas composed of representatives of the major Federal government statistical agencies.

Standby Space—Some magazines will accept an order to run an advertisement whenever and wherever it wishes, at an extra discount. Advertiser forwards plate with order. Helps magazine fill odd pages or spaces.

Starch Method—A term which refers to the recognition method used by Daniel Starch and Staff in their studies of advertising readership.

Station Break—A time period between two programs when a station announces the call letters, channel number, etc. and also broadcasts commercials.

Station Log—The official, chronological listing of a radio or television station's programming and commercial announcements throughout the day.

Station Rep.—A sales organization or person representing individual stations to national advertisers. Short for Station Representative.

Store Check—An in-the-field personal review of merchandise conducted in retail outlets by non-sales personnel.

Store Distributed Magazines—Any one of several magazines (*Family Circle, Woman's Day*) whose primary channels of distribution are retail grocery stores.

Store Panel—A selected sample of stores used repeatedly for market research to collect data on retail sales movement, e.g., A. C. Nielsen Company's food store Panel. (See Consumer Panel)

Sunday Newspaper Supplements—Any printed matter which is inserted in a Sunday edition of a newspaper on a continuing basis and is not part of the newspaper itself. Two main publications fitting into this category are magazine supplements and comic sections.

Supplements—Sunday Magazine or Comic sections of newspapers. A supplement may be either syndicated nationally or edited locally.

Sustaining Program—A program, either local or network, which is not sponsored, i.e., a program produced and paid for not by an advertiser, but by the network or local station.

Sweeps—Both ARB and Nielsen survey all television local markets three times yearly (November, March and May). These are called "sweep months."

Syndicated Program—The packaging of a TV program or programs for sales to advertisers or stations for local market participating spots.

Syndicated Sunday Magazine Supplements—A magazine supplement which is distributed through a group of newspapers and is owned by a single publisher. The distributing newspapers pay the publishers for the privilege of distributing the supplement which in turn helps to build circulation for the distributing newspapers.

T.A.B. Traffic Audit Bureau.—An organization supported by advertisers, agencies and outdoor media which audits traffic exposure of outdoor advertising.

Target Audience—The desired or intended audience for advertising as described or determined by the advertiser. Usually defined in terms of specific demographic (age, sex, income, etc.) purchase or ownership characteristics.

TGI (Target Group Index)—Print and broadcast exposure and product-usage data reported by the Axiom Market Research Bureau, Inc.

Tear Sheets—Actual pages of advertising as they appeared in an issue of any publication. Tear sheets are used to serve as proofs of insertion.

Telecast—A broadcast, program or show on television.

Telephone Coincidental Survey—In research, the interview method in which telephone calls are made while a particular activity, usually a broadcast program, is in progress.

Test Market—A given marketing area, usually a metropolitan census region in which a market test is conducted. Sometimes used as a verb to refer to introduction of a new product.

Test Market Translation—The use of local media that are available in a specific market to replace the national media included in a brand's national plan. The theoretical national plan must be reproduced as carefully and as accurately as possible in the test market since sales results will be used by company management to determine whether or not the product should be expanded to national distribution.

30-Sheet and Bleed Posters—The 30-sheet poster offers advertisers 25% more billboard space than the 24-sheet poster. Bleed posters are the entire metal face of the billboard and are difficult to handle, as the posters quite often have to be trimmed to fit the billboard after they are put up.

3-Sheet Posters—These are approximately 84″ high by 43″ wide and are used primarily in areas where there is not enough room to build a standard 24-sheet poster panel. Usually, a 24-sheet poster company does not handle 3-sheet posters. 3-sheet poster advertising accounts for a very small part of the national billing in outdoor advertising.

Through the Book—A technique of determining a print medium's audience size by having respondents go through a stripped-down issue with an interviewer to learn which articles are most interesting. After this preliminary examination, respondents are asked whether they are sure they looked into the magazine. Only those who answer positively are counted as readers.

Tie-Ins—Advertisements run by retail outlets in a newspaper referring to or associating with an ad in the same newspaper. Tie-ins are paid for by the retail outlets running them.

Total Audience—Audience viewing all or any part of a program in excess of five minutes. For programs of less than ten minutes duration, households viewing one minute or more are included. Also total number of unduplicated readers of a magazine.

Total Audience Impression—The sum of all exposures to several issues of the same publication of several issues of different publication.

Total Net Paid—Total of all classes of a publication's circulation for which the ultimate purchasers have paid in accordance with the standards set by the Audit Bureau of Circulation's rules. Includes single copy sales, mail subscriptions and specials.

TPT (Total Prime Time)—A television research project of Gallup and Robinson evaluating all paid commercials aired during the evening period when national network programming is shown; i.e., both program commercials and station breaks. Offers data both on percentage of commercial audience able to recall the commercial, plus an estimate of actual audience in station coverage. At date of report, such operations were confined to Philadelphia Metro Area.

Traceable Expenditures—Published reports on advertising expenditures by media for different advertisers. Currently, traceable expenditures are available for consumer

330

magazines, farm publications, supplements, newspapers, spot TV, network TV (gross time only) and outdoor.

Trade Advertising—Advertisements of consumer items directed to "the trade" wholesalers and retailers in the distribution channel.

Trade Magazines—Magazines edited specifically to reach members of occupational groups or businessmen in general

Trade Paper—The chief function of the trade paper is to cover the commercial activities of wholesale and retail outlets, but many of them reach the sales departments of manufacturers. Trade papers include all publications that offer an advertiser the opportunity to reach those who will sell the product for him, either from the standpoint of the retail or wholesale level.

Trading Area—The area surrounding a city set up by the Audit Bureau of Circulations whose residents would normally be expected to use the city as their trading center.

Traffic Audit Bureau (T.A.B.)—An organization designed to investigate how many people pass and may see a specific outdoor sign to establish a method of evaluating traffic and measuring a market.

Traffic Count—The evaluation of outdoor poster circulation by an actual count of traffic passing the poster.

Traffic Flow Map (Outdoor)—An outline map of a market's streets scaled to indicate the relative densities of traffic.

Traffic, in-the-market—In outdoor advertising, all the people who live in a city who are found in the traffic flow within that city, or traffic within a county, or within a limited section of a larger city. Other traffic is called Out-of-market Traffic.

Traffic Pattern—Comparisons of customer count to establish averages. How customers act similarly as to shopping time, hour of day, day of week, frequency.

Transient Rate—Same as one-time rate in buying space.

Transit Advertising—Advertising on tnsportation vehicles such as buses, subways, street cars, etc. Uses poster-type ads.

Transit Radio—The broadcasting of radio programs and commercials in buses.

Translater—An independent TV station that picks up programs from a given station and rebroadcasts them to another area on the upper 13 UHF channels (chs. 70-83). Translators serve from several hundred to, in several instances, up to 50,000 TV homes.

Truline Rate—A rate concept sometimes used at the local level. It is computed by multiplying the agate-line rate by 1 million circulation and dividing it by the retail trading zone circulation.

Turnover—The ratio of a weekly rating to a four week reach. This ratio serves as an indication of the relative frequency with which the audience of a program changes. The greater the turnover in the audience, the higher the ratio.

TVAR (TV Advertisers Report)—A bi-monthly report from Trendex which gives indexes of TV audience characteristics in 3 categories: Audience composition, program selection and sponsor identification.

TVB (Television Bureau of Advertising)—The promotion arm of the television industry.

24-Sheet Poster—An outdoor poster that is 8'-6" high and 19'-6" long. In the early days of advertising the poster consisted of 24 individual panels pasted together to form an advertisement. Today about 10 to 12 panels are used, depending on the type of artwork and copy used.

U

UHF (Ultra High Frequency)—Television channels 14-74.

Unaided Recall—The process of determining whether a person saw or heard a given ad or commercial sometime after exposure with only minimal cueing such as mention of product class (not brand). Note: Such recall seldom, if ever, occurs completely spontaneously: some degree of cueing or aiding of response is almost inevitable. Thus, the term "unaided recall" is a relative term.

Upscale—A very general description of a medium's audience indicating upper socio-economic class membership.

V

Vehicle—A particular advertising medium, e.g., a particular magazine or station.

Vertical Cume—In broadcast research, a cumulative rating for two or more programs broadcast on the same day.

Vertical Discount—Broadcast media discount earned through maintenance of specified frequency during given time period, e.g., six spots per week.

Vertical Half-Page—A half page where the long dimension of the ad is vertical.

Vertical Publication—A business publication which appeals to a specific trade, industry, business, or profession.

VHF (Very High Frequency)—Television channels 2-13. Generally, VHF stations have the greatest range of coverage, whereas UHF stations cover a much smaller area.

Viewer Impression Studies—A service of Daniel Starch and Staff which provides qualitative data about TV commercials. It is based on interviews with respondents who have seen a commercial in the context of normal at-home viewing. Viewers are asked probing questions about the communication of the commercial and its meanings.

Viewers Per Set (VPS)—The average number of persons watching or listening to a program in each home.

Volume Discount—A discount given for running a certain volume of space in a publication. An advertiser might use many small insertions to make up the required number ot pages.

W

Waste Circulation—The audience members of a magazine or newspaper who are not prospects for a particular advertised product. Circulation in an area where an advertiser does not have distribution of his product.

Women's Service Book—A publication with editorial content keyed to women's activities and her home.

Women's Service Magazines—Magazines appealing directly to women, (house-wives specifically) and whose editorial contents are designed to further their knowledge as home makers.

index

a

A counties 32, 302 (see county-size classifications)
ABC, 129-132, 302
Achenbaum, Alvin A., Jr., 258, 262, 264
ABP, 302
Accordion inserts, 302
Accountability, media, 2
ADI, 22, 302
Adjacencies, 302
Adnorms, 302
Advertisements, recall of, 135
Advertising
  allowances, 302
  page exposures, 206, 302
  weights, 171-180, 302
Advertising Age, 68
Agate line; 302 (see Line, 314)
AID, 280-281
Algorithms, 272
Appel, Valentine, 204
Arbitron, 108, 110, 303
Area of dominant influence (ADI), 22, 302
  Chicago ADI map, 25
"As Is" translation concept, 266
Assael, Henry, 280-281
Audience
  accumulation, 14, 91-92, 94
  classifications of, 17-21
  composition, 88-92, 303
  duplication, 98, 303
  measurements
    actual or potential sizes, 90
    computer produced data, 14, 271-287
    concepts of, 89
    problems in, 12-14
  potential, 90, 303
  ratings, radio and television, 111, 114-116, 303
  target, 26, 78, 329

total
  concept of, 91, 133, 303
  primary, 133, 304
  secondary, 133, 136, 326
turnover, 125, 303
viewing habits, 106-107
wasted, 101
Audience Concepts Committee of ARF, 204-209
Audits and Surveys Company, 66
Audit Bureau of Circulation (ABC), 129, 304
  audit report, 303
  Publisher's Statement, 130-132
Automatic Interaction Detection, (AID), 280-281
Availabilities in television
  programs, 14, 224, 230, 304
  spot times, 226, 231
Ayer, N.W. applies media weights, 172-173
Axiom Market Research Bureau, 66

b

B counties 32, 304 (see county-size classifications)
Banks, Seymour, 5, 121
BAR, 48, 58-61, 304
Barter, 304
Black targets, reaching, 190
Blair, William S., 102
Blum, Milton L., 204
Bogart, Leo, 46

supplements, 228-229
Cost per gross rating point, 100
Cost per rating point, 100-101
Cost per thousand, 99, 307
  based on gross impressions or net reach, 220
  importance of, 168
  related to audience sizes, 98
County-size classifications, 32, 302, 304, 305, 308
Coverage, 307
  broadcast, 105-107
  circulation related to, 96
  concept of, 92
  levels needed, 93, 168
  magazines, 93-94
  meanings of, 14, 97
  media planning, in, 93-94
  newspapers, 93
  outdoor, 96
  supplements, 192
  television and radio, 94-95
Creative strategy in planning, 6, 10, 76-77, 154
Cross-tabulations of data, 103, 280-282
Cumulative audiences (see Audience accumulation)
  cumes, 92, 308
  meanings, 14, 91-92
Cut-ins, 266, 308

frequency, 310
horizontal, 311
quantity, 323
vertical, 332
volume, 332
DMA, 24, 308
Drive time, 194, 308
Duplication, 97-98 ,139, 308

e

Editor & Publisher Market Guide, 68
Estimates of audience sizes, 90
Ethnic media, 190
Expenditures, competitive, 46-65, 83-84, 223
Experiments in media, 253-255 (see Testing)
Exposure, media, 4-5, 205-206

f

Factorial research designs, 262
Flexform ads, 141
Flexibility, 166, 189, 192-194, 198
Flighting, 165 (see Wave Strategy)
Frequency
  average, 121, 304
  broadcast media, in, 118
  distribution of, 118
  effective range of, 162-164
  level needed, 164
  outdoor media, in, 197
  print media in, 137
  programs that develop, 120
  quintile analysis, 122
  relationship with reach, 119-120
  transit media, in, 198
  unbalanced, 121
  wearout, 163
  weighting, 210-211

d

D counties, 32, 308 (see county-size classifications)
Data analysis bases, 26
Dealers and distributors, 82
Defining Advertising Goals for Measured Advertising Results, 85
Designated Market Areas (DMA), 24, 308
Direct Mail, 308
  limitations of, 196
  reasons for using, 195-196
Direct response advertising, 308
Discounts, media, 181
  cash, 305
  consecutive week, 306

g

Gallup-Robinson tests, 135
Gensch, Dennis, 171-172, 274, 278-279
Geographical weighting, 86
　concentration form, 178
　guidelines to, 176
Geographic split runs, 310
Gross rating points, 311
　concept of, 97
　cost per, 100
　media, for, 97-98
Gross impressions, 311 (see Impressions)

h

Heuristics, 273
Heavy-up weighting, 182
Hi-Fi inserts, 141, 189, 311
　cost of, 229
Horizontal trade publications, 312
Households using television (HUT),
　106-107
H.U.T., 106-107

i

Impact, 78, 147, 312
Impressions
　gross, 310
　meaning of, 126-127
　studies, 312
Index numbers, 26, 312
　calculation methods, 26-28
　cautions in using, 28
Industrial media, 3
In-home reading, 133
Intermedia comparisons, 8, 89
　cautions in making, 188

broadcast vs. print, 188
non-measured media for, 199
problems in making, 187
Intramedia comparisons, 8
Investment, return on, strategy, 174
IQ of vehicle audiences, 43
Iteration, 273

j

Joyce, Timothy, 172

k

Krugman, Herbert, 213-214

l

Latin Square design, 263-264
Leading National Advertisers (LNA)
　class/brand $, 48, 52-53
　company/brand $, 48, 54-55
　outdoor, 48, 56-57
　Publishers Information Bureau (PIB),
　　49, 61-62
Learner, David, 277
Life style research, 43 (see
　Psychographics)
Linear programming models, 274-277
Lipstein, Benjamin, 258, 263-264
"Little USA" translations, 265
Local markets
　definition of, 22
　lists, 168
　map of Chicago, 25
　planners perception of, 22
　weighting guidelines, 86, 176

LNA, 48-49, 52-57 (see Leading National Advertisers)
Lucas, Darrell B., 204

m

Magazines
  ads in, how perceived, 3
  audiences, when reached, 140
  buying problems in, 231
  class, 306
  costs, 227
  coverage, 93-94
  demographic editions, 140
  limitations of using, 191
  opportunities in, 139
  position of ads in, 185
  reading, how measured, 13
  reasons for using, 190-191
  translations, 268
Markets
  allocations in market by market (MBM), 245-249, 315
  cut-off points on lists, 181
  demographic analysis of, 37
  geographic selection, 78-80
  local, how planners define, 22-25
  media, matching, 88-89
  meanings, different, 14
  problems in matching with media, 101-103
  selection principles, 79-80, 180
  targets, consumers, 78
Marketing
  budgets, 76
  channels and sales data, 34
  data classifications, 17-22
  data sources
    Advertising Age, 68
    Associations, 69
    Audits and Surveys, 66
    Axiom Marketing Research Bureau, 66
    Census data, 68
    Consumer Bulletin, 69
    Consumer Reports, 69
    Editor & Publisher Market Guide, 68

    Marketing Research Corporation of America (MRCA), 66
    Nielsen, A. C., 66
    Sales Management Survey of Buying Power, 67
    Selling Areas—Marketing (SAMI), 66
    Simmons, W. R., 66
    Standard Rate & Data Service (SRDS), 67
  media alternatives, related to, 6
  objectives, 6, 76
  situation analysis, 6
Marketing analysis, 6, 17-22
  buying power indices in, 34-36
  distribution analysis in, 29
  heavy-users, 32-33
  market-by-market, 33-34, 315
  profile chart, 39
  targets identified, 38
  where to advertise, 29-31
Marketing Strategy
  competitive strategies and, 83
  dealers and distributors, and, 82
  media plan, and, 6
  plan, 6, 71-74, 85-86
Marketing Research Corporation of America, (MRCA), 66
Marshak, Seymour, 135
Mass media, 2
Matthews, Leonard, 7
Matthews, William E., 13
Mediac media model, 212
Media
  alternatives, search for, 10
  audiences, wasted, 101
  audience composition, 88-92, 303
  authority and prestige of, 166
  business paper, 3
  buyers role, 222
  buying, 152, 220, 230-232
  buying service, 100
  cost estimating, 219
  dramatic use of in planning, 166
  effectiveness, year around, 166
  industrial, 3
  professional, 3
  objectives
    related to marketing plans, 151
    samples of, 158-159
  specialized, 3
  vehicles, defined, 2
  wasted, 101

q

r

t

s